Investing in Your College Education

Learning Strategies with Readings

Thomas Stewart

Kutztown University

Kathleen Hartman

Kutztown University

Houghton Mifflin Company　　Boston　New York

Publisher, Humanities: Patricia A. Coryell
Senior Sponsoring Editor: Mary Finch
Development Editor: Shani B. Fisher
Editorial Associate: Andrew Sylvester
Senior Project Editor: Fred Burns
Editorial Assistant: Brett Pasinella
Manufacturing Coordinator: Carrie Wagner
Senior Art and Design Coordinator: Jill Haber
Senior Composition Buyer: Sarah Ambrose
Marketing Manager: Elinor Gregory
Marketing Assistant: Evelyn Yang

Photo Credits
Page 2: Yellow Dog Productions/Getty Images; page 8: © Tim Kiusalaas/Masterfile; page 33: PhotodiscBlue/Getty Images; page 47: © Robert A. Flischel/Mira; page 66: © Tom Stewart/ Corbis; page 73: © John Henley/Corbis; page 99: Chris Shinn/Mira; page 105: © Dex Images/ Corbis; page 119: Bryce Duffy/Getty Images; page 123: © James Marshall/The Image Works; page 126: APF photo by Cesar Rangel/Getty Images; page 157: White Packert/Getty Images; Mira; page 164: Mira; page 182: © Bob Daemmrich Photography; page 193: © Bob Daemmrich Photography; page 199: Scala/Art Resource, NY; page 199: Erich Lessing/Art Resource, NY; page 200: From *The Formation of Islamic Art*, by Oleg Grabar, copyright © 1973, Yale University Press. Reprinted with permission; page 200: Bildarchiv Preussisher Kulturbesitz/Art Resource, NY; page 201: Werner Forman/Art Resource, NY; page 202: Luis Castaneda, Inc./Getty Images; page 202: SEF/Art Resource, NY; page 204: *A Woman Seated Beside a Vase of Flowers (Madame Paul Valpincon?)*, 1865, Hilaire-Germain-Edgar Degas (French 1834–1917). Oil on canvas: 29 × 36½ in. (73.7 x 92.7 cm.). H.O. Havemeyer Collection, Bequest of Mrs. H.O. Havemeyer, 1929 (29.200.128). The Metropolitan Museum of Art, New York; page 205: The Ballet Class, Edgar Degas, c. 1880, oil on canvas, W1937-2-1, Philadelphia Museum of Art. Purchased with the W.P. Wilstach Fund; page 206: © Bettman/Corbis; page 215: © Bob Daemmrich Photography; page 222: Photodisc Blue/Getty Images; page 247: Taxi/Getty Images; page 253: Photodisc Red/Getty Images; page 278: © Masterfile; page 283: © Bob Daemmrich Photography; page 292: © Image 100/Royalty-Free/Corbis; page 297: Photodisc Green/Getty Images.

Cover Credit: Copyright Shirlee Simon-Glazeas

Printed in the U.S.A.

Library of Congress Control Number: 2004114146

ISBN: 0-618-38223-2

2 3 4 5 6 7 8 9—CW—08 07 06 05

Contents

Chapter 5   Critical Thinking Strategies for the Academic Investor   118

Chapter 8   Banking on Your Health   212

Chapter 9   The Bottom Line: Managing Your Money in College   242

Chapter 10   The Payoff: Your Career and Your Future   273

Preface

When you hear the word *investing,* one word you may initially associate it with is money. Certainly, you've heard a lot of clichés about money: "Money makes the world go 'round." "Money can't buy happiness." "Money is the root of all evil." "Money talks." Although going to college isn't all about money, it certainly does cost a lot of money, and most students are aware that having a college degree is one way to improve one's income down the road. But the college degree itself isn't what allows you to earn more. It is the knowledge you gain—the way you learn how to think—that can ultimately increase your quality of life, not just because you are able to earn more but also because you can gain a greater appreciation of the world around you. This knowledge is in itself the return on your investment. In effect, it is the knowledge itself that becomes a form of currency, an opening not only into a world in which you can make more money, but also into a world enriched by new experiences and a deeper understanding of the world around you. This book's title, *Investing in Your College Education: Learning Strategies with Readings,* reflects the fact that while you have already made an initial investment in deciding to come to college, now that you're in college you have to continue to invest. The investments you make in this first year of college will reap rewards both in your college career and beyond.

Perhaps one reason that you are going to college is to increase your earning potential. Perhaps you hope you will be able to enter a particular field of work or to get that dream job that will provide you a great salary and all the trappings that go with it. Maybe you want to pursue your interest in art or history or science—you name it. You might want to become an expert in a particular field. Or perhaps you need a college degree to have the life you've always wanted. But getting a degree is probably at least four years away. In the meantime, you are literally investing in the future of your dreams—financially, emotionally, and with a lot of hard work. Right now, you need something more important than money, but which is just as practical: ways to succeed.

Thematically, *Investing in Your College Education: Learning Strategies with Readings* is based on the idea that *you are making an enormous investment* by going to college—an intellectual investment, a financial investment, and an investment of time. Yet before you make these investments, you need to learn how to manage them effectively: How will I choose a major? How much time should I be studying? How can I balance my social life and my academic life? How can I handle all of this reading? How do I stay healthy? How do I best study for tests? Should I invest my time in a job, service learning project, or campus activities? How do I keep within my budget? This book will provide answers to these questions and will show you ways to make these investments to the best of your ability. In this text, you will be exposed to new learning strategies, skills, and ideas, and you will gain knowledge. All of these can add to your success over the next four years. And beyond college, you will need these strategies to grow and advance in graduate school, in a career, in life. This book is designed to get you there. With this book, you will make an initial investment, during your first year, to yield the dividends of success in years to come.

Your college career is your investment portfolio, and you're putting stock in many different areas. By maintaining a proper balance in all areas of your life—academics, social life, athletics, nutrition, exercise, family, and so on—you will be able to succeed in the process. This book is structured thematically in a way that helps you identify quickly and clearly all the different elements you must balance. You are then presented with the tools you need to maintain that important balance.

There are ten chapters in this textbook, and each chapter focuses on a particular theme. Each theme covers an area for you to invest in during your first year of college. These important areas of investment range from knowing what is expected of you as a college student in the classroom, to keeping healthy, to being involved in opportunities beyond the classroom.

Each chapter has the following unique features:

▶ **What Worked for Me** Stories of students who have applied strategies highlighted in the chapter and have been successful.

▶ **The Hard Way** Stories from students who did not do well initially but learned from their mistakes and went on to realize success in college.

▶ **Get Involved!** Suggestions on how students can become active on campus and in their careers. The stories of real students will serve as examples.

▶ **Think About It** Questions interspersed throughout the book that encourage active thinking about what you are reading.

▶ **Team Activities** Group activities that encourage you to work together with other students in your class.

▶ **Time Out Tips** Quick tips on the application of learning strategies.

▶ **DIY-Do-It-Yourself Activity** Suggestions for short activities to help you make connections to the chapter topic.

▶ **Lifelines** Reminders of resources on campus—counseling, tutoring, health center—that can help you if you find yourself in a pinch.

These features will stand out from the regular text. Investing some time in these features as you read along will help you better understand and begin to apply what you've been learning in the chapter.

What is particularly unique about this textbook, however, is that it contains *both learning strategies and readings to which you can immediately apply some of the strategies*. In college, you're going to be required to do a *lot* of reading, certainly much more than you were used to doing before. In addition to reflecting the chapter's theme and a particular discipline that you will be exposed to in college, the readings at the end of each chapter reflect the different types and the different levels of reading with which you will be confronted:

▶ **A TEXTBOOK CASE** As the title suggests, at the end of each chapter, you will find a selection from an actual textbook. These excerpts are from textbooks used in content courses you will most likely take in college, usually in your first two years. You will find selections from education, business, physical science, psychology, communications, literature, history, art history, math, and technology. The textbooks in every discipline have their own unique features and require specific strategies to help you understand the content. These features and strategies are provided for you before you begin the readings in the *"Unique Features and Comprehension Strategies"* sections.

▶ **LIFE AFTER COLLEGE** These readings will give you the opportunity to explore possible careers within the disciplines featured in *a textbook case*. Taken from prominent magazines, newspapers, and journals in the various disciplines, the articles will show you some of the possibilities available, including some careers about which you may never have thought. Since one of the reasons you are investing time in college is to enter a career field that requires a college degree, the sooner you expose yourself to what's out there, the better you are positioning yourself as an investor.

▶ **CURRENT ISSUES** These readings are related to the theme of each chapter and provide you with an opportunity to read about and discuss issues that matter to you now and could impact the future of your careers. These articles take the subject matter out of a strict academic context and allow you to see the importance of the issue beyond the classroom.

Prior to the readings at the end of each chapter, you will find a rationale for the placement of each of the readings in that particular chapter. The readings that have been selected are quite diverse with selections from literature and computer science textbooks, for example. You will have a chance to read about the careers of teachers, writers, and people in business, to name just a few. You will read about current issues ranging from the use of language to ethics in the business world. What should you be getting out of all of this? Part of the answer to this depends on what your instructor asks you to get out of it, whether that means an assignment or a quiz or just being prepared for a class discussion. Beyond just doing the assignment, though, you have an opportunity to learn more about the world in general and about what role you want to play in that world, in terms of your major and your career.

Finally, you will find questions to answer before you read to help you assess your prior knowledge and to prepare you to focus on the topic. After you have completed each reading, you will have questions to answer to enable you to assess your comprehension and to think about and discuss the topic as it relates to your own life experience and work in college.

The diverse readings in this textbook are meant to be a steppingstone for your own explorations. Reading about the gender issues in the use of language may lead you into a study of gender roles in society and even a class in sociology. Learning about one man's work to preserve his Native American heritage could lead you to a major in history. At this point in your career, you don't know—you can't know—but you should allow yourself to be open to the possibilities.

If you are really interested in a particular subject or issue highlighted in a chapter, or if your instructor requests that you research a topic further, you will find a list of more articles and books you may wish to read in the section entitled "Compounding Your Interest." Beyond this list, you can find an infinite number of resources within your grasp with an Internet search. Some resources are better than others, of course, and learning to distinguish them is a form of critical thinking we discuss in the book (Chapter 6). The point is that, if you find something that piques your interest, you should follow up on it. There's no telling where that search might take you.

As you can see, *Investing in Your College Education: Learning Strategies with Readings* is designed to help you make the right investment choices now that you are a college student. As you take your first steps as a college student, use this textbook as a guide. And remember that this is just one part of a support system that includes your family, friends, professors, roommates, coaches, advisors, counselors, and the many others who wish you as much success as you wish for yourself. Good luck in your journey and invest wisely!

To the Instructor

When creating *Investing in Your College Education: Learning Strategies with Readings,* we felt it was important to use the same pedagogical approach we use for our own FYE classes: *holistic, hands-on, and interactive with a sense of usability and humor.* We aim to challenge students with our holistic approach. Activities in the text are structured in such a way that *students are encouraged to be active learners;* readings *invite critical thinking* on the part of the students. Activities emphasize *hands-on involvement* and *teamwork* in the form of group assignments.

The three categories of readings at the end of each chapter—*a textbook case, life after college,* and *current issues*—are connected to each other and to the overall theme of each chapter. They will allow you to show the students how to apply the strategies in the chapter right away with readings that are engaging and enlightening and that allow for extended discussion. They also help to further connect their college experience to other areas of their lives. Best of all, there is no need for you to search for related readings. Not only are three readings included, but, in the "Compounding Your Interest" section, you will find related readings that can serve as resources if you want your students to go further in their research or discussion.

As instructors of first-year seminars ourselves, we have always wanted to find a diverse group of readings for students. We ended up searching for them from a variety of sources because we could never find everything we needed in one place, especially since we also wanted to teach learning strategies. In this textbook, we have put everything in one place—diverse readings and learning strategies—in order to allow you, as an instructor, to concentrate on other elements of teaching your class.

The readings we chose have been selected to cover both a broad range of topics and a broad range of styles and purposes. In every case, we have aimed to connect the readings in some way to the theme of the chapter. For example, "Chapter 7: Keeping a Balance," which discusses health-related issues, features a selection from a history textbook. What's the connection? The connection is made in the "Current Issues" reading, which features a newspaper article documenting the spread of SARS in China. This article illustrates the relation between health and global events. It serves as a piece of current history, an artifact that can be used by future historians to understand something happening at the beginning of the twenty-first century. These connections are made explicit to students in the introduction to the readings.

As an instructor, it is naturally your decision which if any of the readings you would assign to your students. The text is written in such a way that you could assign all of the readings from a chapter, one or two of them, or even none at all. While everything is integrated, the book is written in a modular manner that allows you to assign as many or as few of the readings as you want.

For example, if your course is primarily focused on choosing a major or career, you could focus specifically on the "Life After College" readings. Reading about different careers—and the paths people took to get them—can give students ideas about where their own interests might take them. A course focusing primarily on reading could lean toward "A Textbook Case" readings. These readings are taken from actual textbooks in fields as diverse as math and history. Rather than having to go out and find a selection of textbook readings, you have all the readings and related activities at your fingertips. Alternatively, in a class focusing more on a critical examination of current events, you could emphasize the "Current Issues" readings. These readings give students a chance to examine everything from cloning to the growing use of text messaging and its effects on the written language.

These readings can also serve as a springboard to further research, whether that means investigating more details of various careers or finding out more about a recent issue in the news. As the instructor, you may also want to bring in more related resources or have students find more related resources on their own. With the Internet making subject searches so simple, you can quickly come up with additional information to bolster what is already in the text. By getting the students to find information, you can help them learn more about the process of researching a topic.

In addition to the material contained within *Investing in Your College Education: Learning Strategies with Readings,* there are additional resources available for you as an instructor:

▶ **Instructor's Resource Manual**: For each chapter, you will find summaries, lecture suggestions, and explanations of textbook exercises, as well as additional activities, suggestions for using the readings, and chapter tests. You will also find a detailed explanation of the text's overall themes, suggestions for using the text for a variety of course types and student populations, sample course syllabi, and suggested grading systems. The IRM is located on the Class Prep CD and instructor's website.

▶ **HM Class Prep CD:** In addition to providing a printable version of the IRM, the instructor's Class Prep CD contains mid- and end-of-term tests, tips on choosing your own course readings, reproducible masters, PowerPoint slides, and information on additional resources to use in your course.

▶ **Web Site (*http://studentsuccess.college.hmco.com/students* and *http://studentsuccess.college.hmco.com/instructors*)**: A student website for this text contains additional quizzes, including comprehensive quizzes for the readings, current events and career-related web search activities, additional case studies, a reading inventory for students to take when they begin and finish the course, and other exercises and resources. An instructor's site also provides additional resources for you to use.

These resources are designed to help you incorporate this book into your first-year courses as effectively as possible as you help your students at the beginning of their journey through college.

Acknowledgments

We would like to thank the wonderful staff at Houghton Mifflin with whom we have been privileged to work, especially Mary Finch, Shani Fisher, and Andrew Sylvester. They made our experience of writing this textbook a rewarding one with their energy, encouragement, and expertise.

We would like to acknowledge our colleagues at Kutztown University who shared their time and expertise: Bill Bateman, Patricia Derr, Ken Ehrensal, Mary Gutekunst, Tom Pirnot, Bruce Rowell, Chris Sacchi, Jack Schellenberg, Larry Sechney, Carole Wells, and Brian Wlazelek. We would also like to acknowledge the contributions of Donene Holland, Mary Campbell Stewart, and Ed Warzala, who each shared their unique talents. We would also like to thank our students.

From Kathy: I would especially like to thank my husband and best friend Damian, who was there every step of the way, who always believed in me, and who proofread every page. As he is in my life, he is very much a part of this book. I would also like to thank my children, Ian and Brett, who are my inspiration, and the rest of my loving family. Finally, I would like to thank my world class 2004 Odyssey of the Mind team and co-coach Jan Rigge. They taught me that a dream and an investment of time and energy can make great things happen.

From Tom: I would like to thank my wife, Joanne, my family, the Hartman family, and all of the others who contributed to this project.

We would also like to thank those instructors who contributed valuable ideas to strengthen the effectiveness of this text:

Theresa Ammirati, Connecticut College
James H. Berry, St. Clair County Community College, MI
Kelly Deasy, SUNY—Cortland
John W. Dickson, DeSales University, PA
Beth Glass, Appalachian State University, NC
Sharon L. Gorman, University of the Ozarks, AR
Mary Groom Hall, The University of Montana
Reginald Jean, Boston University, MA
Laura Scappaticci, Kutztown University, PA
Dawn Leonard, Charleston Southern University, SC
Linda L. Long, University of Wisconsin—Whitewater
Matthew W. Mayo, Santa Clara University, CA
Lee Rademacher, Purdue University—Calumet Campus, IN
Mary Todd, Concordia University, IL

Karen E. Tompson-Wolfe, Westminster College, MO
Mary Walz-Chojnacki, University of Wisconsin-Milwaukee
Jodi E. Webb, Bowling Green State University, OH
Cindy Martinez Wedig, The University of Texas—Pan American

Tom Stewart and Kathy Hartman

Chapter 1

Making the Initial Investment

L et's get right to the point here . . . you're in college for a reason. Or maybe for a lot of reasons. You always expected to get a college education. Your parents wanted you to go. Your dream job requires a college degree. Your friends were all going, so you thought you had to go. You're a good student. You had nothing better to do. The best initial investment you can make to reap the benefits of success in college is to decide why you are here. Then you can decide what you need to do to succeed. Tough questions, but answering them will yield great dividends for you over the coming years. This chapter is designed to walk you through these questions and to help you understand what college is about, what it means to be a student, what professors expect and what you can expect of them, and how you can use all the resources available to you to get the most out of your investment. It's all up to you.

First Things First

Getting into college is a lot of work. In fact, you may have been so focused on getting to college that you have spent little time actually thinking about what to do once you get there. Now that you are here, though, it's time to refocus. This can be a difficult adjustment for many students. It may be your first time away from home. You may have none of your old friends at the new school. Your first day of classes might be intimidating as you realize what your workload is going to be. At times, you may question the wisdom of your decision to attend college. Sometimes you may even feel like dropping out. It is important to realize that the first few weeks can be the hardest and that hanging in there through this period is part of the process. You must keep your goals in mind and even begin thinking ahead to where your career as a college student will lead you. But the first thing you need to do is get used to your new role as a college student.

Think About It

Answer the following questions in the space provided.

Why am I in college right now? _____

_____

_____

What would I be doing if I were not in college? _____

_____

_____

Understanding What It Means to Be a College Student

College, you will soon discover, is much different from high school. First of all, the workload is considerably different. On the surface, it may seem like you have less work. After all, the typical college student is in class only about 15 hours a week, half of the time a typical high school student spends in the classroom. This, however, means that you have to learn to manage your time better, because more of the responsibility of ensuring that you learn all the material falls on your own shoulders. Furthermore, many students enroll in colleges that are much bigger than their high schools.

Now that you are in college, you may not have your parents to make sure you get out of bed in the morning. You may not get an extra day to turn in an assignment. You may not be told exactly what to do on a paper. You may have to read five chapters in one night . . . and the list goes on. College, you will find, is going to demand that you be an independent learner.

That, luckily, is not as hard as it may seem. Being an independent learner, after all, doesn't mean that you have to do everything on your own. There are lots of resources on campus that will help you. What it *does* mean is that you will sometimes have to take the lead in seeking out help, looking for opportunities, and making the most of them.

The Hard Way

"I thought I knew it all when I first got to college. I went to the local state university, where my brother and sister also went a few years before. I had visited many times, and I knew where all the good parties were and the best place to live. What I didn't know, I later found out, was how to be a good student." Jake recalls with some regret the time he lost after leaving college at the end of his freshman year. He is now back, a senior ready to graduate with a degree in business, six years after he began. "It turns out I didn't really try to understand why I was in college. I went because my brother and sister went. It was just expected of me. I started out as a psychology major, with little idea of why I chose that. But what I really majored in was partying. After my freshman year, I had a 1.2 GPA. I hardly ever made it to class. I never talked to my professors or asked questions about what was expected of me. I flunked test after test but never went for help. I never asked myself what I should be majoring in or what I wanted to do when I got out of college. Then I realized, after my freshman year, that I needed to take time out. My parents said so too. So for the next two years I went to work at a small construction company. I did some pretty hard labor, since I did not have a degree, but soon the boss was letting me come with him to seek clients and close deals. I knew I had what it took to do that, to be my own boss. I knew I wouldn't get anywhere without finishing school. So I returned to the same university and majored in business. And this time, I talked to my professors, got involved in campus activities, and sought out tutors when the going got tough. I will soon graduate with a 3.0. I hope to own my own company some day."

What to Expect of Your Professors *and* What They Expect of You

You will soon discover that your professors have some pretty high expectations of you, the new college student. They expect you to attend class. They expect that you will contact them when you miss a class. They expect that you will arrange to get the information and assignments that you missed. They expect that you will ask questions and seek help during their office hours or from a tutor. They expect that you will put time into the course and take pride in your work. In short, they expect you to care.

In turn, you can expect them to provide you with a syllabus; their office hours, phone number, and e-mail address; and plenty of work. They will also provide you with assistance in completing that work. Be sure to take advantage of posted office hours; most professors are more than happy to meet with you and appreciate the extra effort on your part. This is a good way to get to know your professors and to begin the networking that is an important part of success in college. If you make an appointment during a professor's office hours, be prepared. Have a plan. You want to come across as a well-organized student. If you're visiting because you don't understand the material, you should have questions written down for your visit. Some professors, particularly those who teach large classes, have TAs (Teaching Assistants)

who are assigned to help. These are typically graduate students who are becoming experts in the field and may even be preparing to become professors themselves.

Even though professors have high expectations of you, they will treat you a lot differently than teachers did in high school. In high school, if you skipped class, your teacher would know right away, and you would probably get detention. In college, you're certainly not going to get detention. Many of your college professors (though not all) will say little or nothing if you miss class. In a large lecture class, they probably won't even notice. But that doesn't mean that you should attend class only when you please. One of the main reasons why students fail in college is that they don't go to class. And don't be fooled by students who seem to be having a great time and not going to any classes. Unfortunately, many of those students won't be around to enjoy themselves the next semester. Don't be one of them.

Personal Responsibilities

What are all of the personal responsibilities of a college student? If you're entering college right out of high school, this is really the first time in your life that you have been totally responsible for yourself. Let's take a look at some of the major responsibilities of a first-year college student:

- ▶ Getting out of bed in the morning on your own.
- ▶ Going to class—every day, even if it starts at 8:00 a.m., and even if you have a slight headache or minor sore throat.
- ▶ Eating a healthy diet and getting enough rest.
- ▶ Managing your time.
- ▶ Managing your money.
- ▶ Balancing work and school.
- ▶ Getting exercise.
- ▶ Doing your laundry.
- ▶ Cleaning your room.
- ▶ Studying—going to class is not enough.
- ▶ Turning in projects and papers on time.
- ▶ Knowing what's on the syllabus and following it.
- ▶ Getting the notes and assignments from a fellow student when you miss class and not expecting your professor to give them to you.
- ▶ Taking responsibility for your own decisions.
- ▶ Drinking responsibly—or not drinking at all.
- ▶ Learning to deal appropriately with conflict (roommate problems, disagreements with a professor, and the like).
- ▶ Maintaining healthy relationships.
- ▶ Meeting college deadlines that govern registering for classes, paying bills, withdrawing from courses, applying for financial aid, signing up for campus housing, and so on.
- ▶ Getting help when you need it, whether it be academic, personal, or financial help. Knowing whom to ask is an important part of this.

That's a lot of stuff. Although many of the items on this list may be new to you, help is always available. Usually an advisor, counselor, faculty member, or more experienced student can at least point you in the right direction.

But you can begin on your own right now. Simple steps such as putting your alarm clock on the other side of the room instead of right next to your bed can make a big difference. If it's right next to your bed, it's all too easy just to hit the snooze or shut it off and go right back to sleep. And don't set your clock radio to your favorite station. Getting up in the morning isn't about listening to your favorite songs. If you like rock music but hate country, set your radio alarm to a country station. That makes it more likely that you will get up to shut it off.

For finances, keep an active eye on your budget. In Chapter 9, we will talk more about specific ways of managing your money. Watch out for the easy lure of credit cards. Set up a schedule of when your assignments are due—and when you are going to work on them. When you go to do your laundry, don't go empty-handed. Take some notes, or, better yet, go with a friend who is in the same class and turn it into an impromptu study session.

Get to know your college catalogue; it will list dates for such activities as registering for class, add-drop, and course withdrawals. Try to recognize potential conflicts before they get out of hand. If you are unhappy with your roommate because he listens to loud music late at night, try talking to him, and if that doesn't work, the two of you should sit down with your RA (resident assistant) or hall director and work things out. Be prepared to learn the importance of compromise. In real life, a "my way or the highway" philosophy isn't going to get you very far. It's no secret that a lot of students run into problems in college for reasons that have nothing to do with their ability to handle the academics. They get into trouble because they aren't prepared for the numerous responsibilities that have suddenly been thrust upon them.

Getting Critical: Switching to College-Level Thinking

It may be obvious, but it's nevertheless worth repeating here: College is not high school. At this level, the expectations of you as a student are much different. How? First of all, you must start becoming a critical thinker. It's not just memorization any more, although you certainly have some of that, too. You probably had some practice in critical thinking in high school, but now it's the rule rather than the exception. Your opinion matters. How well others respond to your opinion will be tied to how well you can learn to express your opinion, to frame an argument, and to convince others. What that means is that the rule will no longer be "Here's what you need to study for the test" and then you simply recite that information. Professors will question you more in class about your attitudes toward issues. Of course, we all have a right to an opinion, but getting other people to understand why we feel the way we do—and even swaying others' opinions—is what you'll be doing in college.

Along with this freedom to express your opinion comes the responsibility for taking your learning into your own hands. You will have to locate a lot of infor-

What Worked for Me

"I was the first person in my family to go to college." Ashley, a senior education major, looks back with amazement at how far she has come. "My parents never went to college, and I am the oldest child in my family. Everything was new. I also chose a college that none of my friends from high school attended — four hours away from home. I knew when I first got here that it was sink or swim. I came to college undeclared, because I had no sense of direction. My parents own a restaurant and I knew I did not want to do that for the rest of my life. I always thought I would make a good elementary school teacher, but I didn't know any teachers, and I didn't know if I had what it would take."

Ashley now credits a campus scavenger hunt project with helping find key people and resources that helped her become a successful education major. "During my first-year seminar, my professor gave us a scavenger hunt project. During this project, I located the Advising Center. In the Advising Center, I met a great professor who walked me through the process of declaring a major and reviewing the courses I would need to take. I went to see her every week. She was a former high school teacher and became the role model I never had. She helped calm my fears and show me I had what it takes. By the end of my first semester, I had a 3.0 GPA and was accepted into the Elementary Education program. I never looked back."

Ashley is currently student teaching in a first grade classroom and knows she made the right decision. Her advice for freshmen is to find an advocate, a professor or staff member who can answer the questions that may overwhelm them. "It may have been easy to quit, but instead, I found a person who believed in me. She told me what classes to take, where to get a tutor when I was failing math my first semester and what to do to declare a major. One person really can make a difference. I hope I can do the same when I am a teacher."

mation on your own. You will have to find your own way around the library, for instance, and your college library may be extremely intimidating when you first arrive. In any given course, you could be expected to take responsibility for locating materials that will supplement information presented in your textbook and in the lectures. A critical thinker does not wait for information to be provided. A critical thinker seeks out information independently. If you do not have enough information about a subject, you can't really think critically about it. The responsibility for equipping yourself with enough information lies in your own hands.

Learning to be a critical thinker doesn't end in the classroom. As you move through life, you will be held responsible for your own actions. You will need to make critical decisions every day when you are in college. This can be as simple as deciding to eat healthy foods or something as complex as trying to decide how to help a friend who has mentioned suicide. Learning how to deal with these issues is not easy, but it is part of becoming an educated person. The relatively simple issue of deciding when and whether to renew your housing contract is an example. You could end up missing important deadlines if you do not take it upon yourself to seek out information you may not have been given. You may not even realize how many housing opportunities you have unless you gather information, think critically about your options, and make an informed decision.

For most students, the biggest difference between high school and college is not the work itself but the need to navigate through the decision making necessitated by the independence that college brings.

Finding Your Place on Campus: Diversity and New Experiences in College

Your first few days or even weeks on campus can be an overwhelming experience. You may have a roommate who comes from a totally different environment. You may see people dressing differently from what you encountered at your high school. You may be surprised at the number of religious organizations represented on campus. Racial, ethnic, and socioeconomic diversity will also play a role in your college experience. From the very beginning, you may find that the students in your classes and in your residence hall are from much more diverse backgrounds than you were used to in high school. You may realize that you're no longer the best athlete in the school or that you're suddenly surrounded by students of all different ages. The faculty members may act very differently from your high school teachers, and they will probably have very different expectations of you. You may come to ask yourself, after the first few days or weeks, "Where do I fit in?" That is a good question, and sooner or later, everyone finds the answer.

Finding your place on campus and coming to enjoy and benefit from the diversity of a college campus is your responsibility, as much as becoming the critical thinker and independent learner you are expected to be. This is not to say, however, that you will not get any help. Help is all around you. Here are some things you can do early in your college experience to find your way:

▶ Try to get to know your roommate, if you don't know each other already. Even if you seem to have only differences, you can learn from those differences.

▶ Talk to your resident assistant or floor supervisor if you live on campus. In the beginning, residence halls often have socials that can help you get to know people right away so that you don't feel like an outsider.

▶ Try to get to know at least one person in each of your classes. Not only will this help you avoid feeling alone in the class, but it will also give you someone you can turn to if you have a question, if you need study help, or if you miss some of the notes.

▶ If you get to know your professors outside of class, they may not seem as intimidating or as different from the teachers you have learned from in the past.

▶ Try to join at least one extracurricular activity as soon as possible. Whether you like politics, chess, art, or music, there's probably a club for you. And if there isn't, consider taking the lead and forming one. These clubs give you a chance to socialize and share your interests with others.

▶ Go to a cultural event on campus that you would not normally see. For example, you could go to a ballet, a symphony, a drum circle, or a gallery opening. This sort of exploration could lead to a whole new area of interest.

▶ If you think your schedule will permit, consider working on campus, even for a few hours a week. This will make you feel more connected, and it will also help you to meet new people.

▶ If you're a commuter, your campus may have a commuter lounge or group where you can share lunch and meet others who have a similar experience.

▶ If you're a nontraditional student, remember that most campuses have a nontraditional student group that may be very supportive and helpful. It may also be especially important for nontraditional students with families to think about striking an effective balance so that they maintain a healthy family life while being a student. One suggestion is to get your family involved in your college experiences. Many campuses have family days, festivals, or cultural activities that spouses, children, and other family members can attend. Such opportunities can help them feel more familiar with what you're doing in college.

▶ Sports are a good way to get to know others. You don't have to be a state champion to get involved. Most colleges have intramural sport leagues. And any trip to the campus gym should give you an opportunity to play pick-up basketball, racquetball, or tennis.

▶ Fraternities and sororities have long been a tradition at many college campuses. They can be a great way to get to know other students. Often, members end up living together in the "house." The best of these organizations not only support strong academic performance but also actively encourage it.

▶ College parties are also a long-standing tradition. And, of course, they can be a good way to meet and get to know others. As with anything else, moderation is the key. Save the parties for the weekend and don't overdo it.

The best time to try to find your place on campus is from the very beginning. Remember that all the other new students are trying to do the same thing. If you wait too long, you may miss out on some opportunities. Also, a few weeks could go by, and you could start to feel very isolated from the campus community. Trying to find your place right away will prevent this isolation and help you feel more connected.

College students traditionally think of their courses as the main sources of learning. This is partly true—you do learn in your courses—but it is also true that you will learn as much, if not more, from the experiences that you have outside the classroom. In other words, if you simply go to classes and then go home and study, you're not going to have all that much to say for yourself when you graduate. Most employers and graduate schools are looking for a well-rounded person —for someone who, in addition to having made good grades, can show that he or she has been involved in activities that go beyond the classroom.

 DIY: Do-It-Yourself Activity

Find and arrange to meet a professor in the field you are interested in pursuing. You can find a professor in a particular field by checking the campus directory or your school's website, which would identify professors and their respective departments. When you meet with the professor, ask him or her the following questions:

1. How did you get into your field?
2. What level of education do you recommend?
3. Am I in the right major?
4. What can I do now to prepare for this career?

You may find some of the answers surprising, and you just might be laying the foundation for a mentoring relationship—and a letter of recommendation when you graduate!

Finding and Using Campus Resources

Campus resources are there for you. Only you can decide what you can get out of them by investing your time and effort. Campus resources may include

Career Services Office Houses information about specific jobs, job outlooks, job qualifications, résumé writing and interviewing, and graduate schools. But don't wait until you're a senior to take advantage of Career Services. These offices also can help you find summer jobs and internships in areas related to your major. This will be an enormous help to you down the road.

Student Activities Office Provides information on clubs and activities that students can participate in both on and off campus. Everything from the outdoor club, which might take canoeing trips, to the finance club for future entrepreneurs. You can start networking today.

Residence Life Office If you're living on campus, you're going to need to know this office, which is the place to go for everything from changing roommates to getting a job as a resident assistant (RA).

Tutoring Center Provides tutors to students in various subjects and general study skills. This is also a good source of employment on campus. If you're good in math, for example, why not get paid to help somebody else learn it while building your résumé at the same time?

Greek Life Office If you're on a campus with fraternities and sororities, the Greek Life Office will be the focal point for coordinating activities and housing.

Financial Aid Office Don't stay in the dark about student loans, grants, and scholarships. Much more may be out there than you know about, and the Financial Aid Office is a veritable warehouse of valuable information that can help you stay in school. Also, the Financial Aid Office can often provide information about work study jobs (which are tied to financial need).

Bursar's Office Pay your bills here!

Registrar's Office This office is responsible for helping you register for classes, drop and add classes, and withdraw from classes and for maintaining academic records. Also, if you need a transcript for a job or graduate school, this is where you will go.

Advising Office Many campuses provide full-time academic advisors to help you develop an appropriate academic plan. Take advantage of this service so you can avoid staying in school longer than you need to.

Counseling Center College can be a stressful and difficult time emotionally and psychologically. If at any time you feel that you're getting overly stressed, you don't have to bear the burden alone. Trained counselors are there to help you, and that help can often very quickly get you back on track.

Volunteer Center Besides being a nice thing to do, volunteering is another great way to build your résumé. It also can give you a taste of a job that interests you, and you can help people along the way. Many colleges work with both local organizations such as soup kitchens and national organizations such as Habitat for Humanity and the Red Cross. Feel good about yourself while learning more about careers and meeting other students.

Teamwork Activity

For this assignment, work in a group. Each member of the group will find out about a specific service or office on your campus that will help you achieve academic success. You are being given no clues. It's up to you to find such resources and complete your assignment. Good luck!

Oral Portion: All group members will present their findings orally. Include helpful handouts and visuals.

Written Portion: Each group member should write down the answers.

Answer the following questions individually.
1. Who is your advisor?
2. Where is his or her office?
3. What single most important piece of advice did she or he provide to help you achieve academic success in your first year of college?

Answer the following questions in groups.
1: What is tutoring? Who is in charge of this service here on campus? How can you take advantage of it? How might it benefit you? How will you be able to use this information in the future for your academic success?

2: Where is the Career Services Office? What services does it provide for students? How can you utilize it as a first-year student?

3: What does the Counseling Center provide for students on campus? Where is it located? Who is the contact person for this office? Besides the other services that this office provides, how does the staff in this office help students achieve academic success?

4: Where can you go to become a volunteer? What do you need to do to get involved? What are some of the volunteering opportunities that are available? How can these be of value to you as a first-year student?

5: What is the Student Activities Office? Where is it located? What are some of the activities on campus? How can becoming involved in student activities enrich your first year on campus?

Finding a Mentor

Another thing to consider early in your college career is finding the people who can help you through the many twists and turns of college life. A mentor is one such person, and finding one promptly can be one of the best things you can do for yourself. In *The Odyssey,* Mentor was a close friend of Odysseus. Athena, the goddess of wisdom, disguised herself as Mentor in order to serve as a guide for Telemachus in the search for his father. From Homer's classic tale, the term *mentor* has come to mean a guide or an advisor to someone less experienced. How does this work in today's world? A rookie pitcher in baseball may be guided by a veteran. A new account executive at an advertising agency, showing some potential, may be taken under the wing of a senior executive. In college, a professor of biology may show a promising undergraduate the ropes. Or a senior may help a new student learn her way around campus and pick the best professors. Mentoring can mean many different things, and it has advantages for both parties. The mentor gets to share his or her knowledge. The person being mentored gets to learn from someone who has already done what he or she is about to do. Mentoring relationships take time to cultivate, however, and the best time to find a mentor is now, in your first year.

How do you find a mentor? You can begin by going to class. Of course, going to class is no guarantee that you will find a mentor. But it opens up the possibility that you might find a mentor in the person of one of your professors. You're even more likely to cultivate a mentoring relationship by visiting your professors outside of the classroom. Where? Professors usually have posted office hours. They might serve as advisors to different student groups, such as honor societies, volunteer groups, and the student branches of various professional organizations. Another way to get to know professors in a way that might lead to a mentoring relationship is through campus employment. Interested in psychology? See whether any jobs are available in the department office. Or perhaps you could become a tutor in the subject.

Professors are not the only potential mentors, however. People working in your future field can also be valuable mentors. How do you meet them? One of the best ways is through summer employment, starting with the summer immediately following your first year of college. Let's say you want to be an accountant with a major accounting firm. You're not going to be working as an accountant during your first year out of college (you might not even have taken an accounting class yet), but you could certainly get a job in the company in another position (such as the legendary mailroom). In these jobs, take advantage of opportunities to talk with people who have the kinds of jobs you are seeking. You might find someone who is interested in helping you get ahead in that field. The one summer you spend in the mailroom could lead to a job the next summer that is closer to your desired position.

Finally, you may not have to do all the work yourself. Many campuses have organized peer mentoring programs in place. They can be set up by majors, honor societies, residence halls, and athletics programs. Don't be afraid to give these a try. You may find after a year or two that you've gone from mentee to mentor and are sharing *your* knowledge with a new student.

A Major Decision: Thinking Early and Often About Majors and Careers

"So, what's your major?" If you haven't heard this line already, you will soon enough. To the world at large, you're identified by which college you attend: "I go to --- College." Within your college, though, along with your fraternity/sorority, sports team, residence hall, clubs, or even hometown, your major is one of the key identifiers that tells your peers about you. You might feel a little frustration if your answer to that question right now is "Undeclared" or "Biology, but I am switching to something else," but you don't need to worry just yet. Studies show that the average college student switches majors three to four times. Yet even though you may need this year to get your feet wet in college, now is still as good a time as any to start *thinking* about your major. You should do it now—and do it often. There are plenty of opportunities to get started on this important process:

▶ **Reflect on the classes you are taking.** Usually, in your first year in college, you have a number of general education classes in everything from speech and composition to psychology and mathematics. What courses do you enjoy the most? How are you doing in these courses? You might find you are fascinated by something you never even considered when you were in high school.

▶ **If there's a course you like and in which you are doing well, talk to the professor.** He or she may have some insights to share with you about how the course is related to particular majors or career choices you could pursue.

▶ **Join a special-interest club.** You might find more information about a particular major or career and also meet people with similar interests—not only students but also professors and other professionals in the field.

▶ **Talk to your advisor.** Your advisor is trained to give you advice not only on what courses to take but also on what courses fit into what degree programs. He or she can help you decide whether a change in major is appropriate. If you are undeclared, speaking with your advisor is especially important as you sharpen your focus.

▶ **Visit the career office on campus.** In addition to providing information about careers, this office gives students an opportunity to take self-assessments that will help them zero in on a major or possible career. It's a good idea to take these self-assessments early, especially if you did not do so in high school. You

Lifeline

If you think you might need a tutor for a course, sign up early in the semester. Studies show that tutoring works best with repeated visits. If you wait until the last minute, it is not likely to help much. Besides, at most campuses, tutors are assigned on a first-come, first-served basis, so if you wait too long, a tutor may not be available.

may be surprised by the results. Remember that these services are helpful only if you take advantage of them.

A Quick Overview of Which Majors Lead to Which Careers

Getting a bachelor's degree is like becoming a member of an exclusive club; having the degree can open many doors for you, regardless of what your major is. In other words, even if you have a degree in English, you may be able to get a job in business. If you have a degree in psychology, you may find yourself with an opportunity to break into sales. Except in very technical fields—such as nursing, accounting, and chemical engineering, where you would be required to have a specialized degree—a bachelor's degree in almost any subject will be enough to get your foot in the door. What happens after that, of course, is up to you. Even so, your choice of major will provide direction for the types of opportunities you pursue. There are plenty of majors that really do provide you with a very straight path to particular job opportunities if that's the way you choose to go:

Major	Typical Jobs*	Other Possibilities*
Education	Elementary Teacher	Corporate Trainer
	High School Teacher	Tour or Museum Guide
	Day Care Provider	Public Relations Trainee
Business	Accountant	Restaurateur
	Manager	Sports Agent
	Financial Planner	Computer Consultant
Physical Science	Chemist	Sales Representative
	Flavorist	Teacher
	Quality Control Inspector	Chef
Psychology	Counselor	Sales Representative
	Social Service Position	Web Designer
	Psychologist	Manager
Mass Media	Radio/TV Personality	Sales Representative
	Public Relations Staffer	Corporate Trainer
	Radio/TV Producer	Web Designer
English	Editor	Sales Representative
	Writer	Corporate Trainer
	Public Relations Staffer	Teacher
History	Teacher	Journalist
	Researcher	Antiques Dealer
	Museum Curator	Art or Furniture Restorer
Visual and Performing Arts	Artist	Teacher
	Dancer	Architect
	Actor	Interior or Set Designer

(continued)

Major	Typical Jobs*	Other Possibilities*
Math	Actuary	Sales Representative
	Mathematician	Claims Adjuster
	Computer Programmer	Teacher
Technology	Programmer	Technical Writer
	Network Administrator	Technology Reporter
	Web Page Designer	Computer Sales Person

*Some fields may require further education or training.
For more information on job possibilities related to different majors, go to the website at
http://studentsuccess.college.hmco.com/students.

You will notice that some fields, such as sales, are open to people from just about any major. The point of a chart like this is to suggest the possibilities and also to illustrate the lack of limitations. There are many examples of English majors who became business executives and business majors who decided to become teachers. Don't be limited by the stereotypes, but do research the possibilities. The time to start is now.

Now that you have a good idea of what is expected of you and how you can begin to meet those expectations, it's a good time to reflect on what you have learned about what lies ahead. Ask yourself: **What do I need to do to be a successful college student?**

Get Involved!

"Plain and simple—I was lost." Pedro, now a senior communications major, looks back on his first year in college with a laugh. "My senior class in high school had 45 students in it. Then I came here, and there were four thousand freshmen on campus. I didn't know what to do. I went from knowing everybody in my whole school—teachers and students—to knowing, out of all five classes, exactly one other student."

"I had gone to a college in another state because I didn't want to go where all my friends were going. But I had no idea how big a challenge I was facing. Everything was new, I didn't know anybody, and after a little while, I started to feel like I was invisible." Pedro says he spent a couple of weeks hanging out alone in his room. "My roommate and I didn't have much in common, and he was never there anyway, so I just kind of hid out. But I realized I couldn't do that forever. If I didn't find something soon, I'd be heading home." A sign in the student union one afternoon captured his attention. "The student newspaper was looking for some people for the layout staff. I didn't think of myself as much of a writer, and I didn't know anything about newspapers, but I had a little experience with some of the computer programs they mentioned, so I thought I'd give it a try. Turns out they had all the people they needed for layout, but they took my name and number, along with those of about 20 other people." Pedro left the meeting thinking that was the end of that. "I was shocked when the sports editor called the next morning and asked me to cover the football game that day. Nobody else could do it. I asked her if she had the right number, but she said they were desperate. The regular reporter was sick, and she was tied up at the office. They would set me up in the press box. I just had to take notes, and she would help me write it up if I needed it. I actually did very well on my own and gained the confidence to write more."

Increasing Your Yield

Readings for Practical Application

This chapter has provided a general overview of what you need to know to get a head start on a successful college career. There is no doubt that this is a lot to think about. That's why it's good to start thinking about it all early in your college career. As you navigate your way through your college experiences, keep applying what you are learning to the big picture: How is this experience helping me figure out what I want to study, where I want to be, and who I am? You're learning how to be a student, and these same strategies apply to helping others become better students. This is one of the many things an educator does. As you begin to look at possible careers, we begin by exposing you to the career of teaching as one of your many options. What you do in college in terms of being a student can be readily applied to the day-to-day life of a teacher.

In this chapter, you have read about the first steps in your college education. The readings in this chapter focus on education as both a career and a subject. The "Textbook Case" reading is from a college text used in education classes. One of the greatest challenges that new teachers face is not content mastery but classroom discipline. This excerpt from *Teaching Strategies: A Guide to Better Instruction* discusses the issue of how to manage a classroom.

In the "Life After College" section, the reading focuses on the reflections of a veteran teacher. With "Why I Entered, Why I Stay," Judith Shively reflects on her early career through the lens of decades of experience. In particular, she reveals how what seemed like minor events—the kinds of things you may be going through right now—turned out to be life-changing moments.

Finally, in the "Current Issues" article, "Parents in a Haze?" Katy Kelly takes a look at hazing among high school students and at parents' reactions to it. She takes a close look at what parents think the consequences of their children's actions should be and how parents' opinions often differ from the opinions of school officials.

Reading and Study Tips: Education

Unique Features and Comprehension Strategies

These textbooks emphasize putting theory into practice. They present pedagogy (theories of learning) and then explain how to apply this theory to everyday life in the classroom. Good teaching is grounded in a solid grasp of theory. The challenge for a new teacher is putting that theory into practice. Education textbooks help students to make this leap by providing real-life examples. Be aware of these examples not only to understand better the theory presented by texts in your education courses, but also to use this information effectively when you are in the classroom. **Develop your own real-life examples. As you read education textbooks, be sure to study the examples provided, which apply the theory and will help you understand you can do the same. The best way to determine whether you truly understand a concept or theory, however, is to see if you can apply it to a new situation not spelled out in the textbook. As you do with definitions and terms, make note cards for each theory or concept. As you work your way through them, try to come up with examples of your own from class discussions and** from what you have experienced yourself. You will also remember better what you explain in your own words. What is yours will stick with you.

These texts contain much of the jargon (specialized vocabulary) of the field—frequently in boldface type followed by definitions. Education, like most professional fields, has its own language. To the outsider, the terms that educators use may seem totally unfamiliar, but it is essential that anyone trying to enter the field learn this new language. Education textbooks often highlight important terms by printing them in boldface type. This emphasizes their importance and alerts readers to the necessity of learning and understanding them. In "A Textbook Case," the textbook reading that follows, the term *norm* appears in boldface type. This is an important term in the field. It is defined as "a behavioral rule or pattern accepted to some degree by most members of a group." This definition is provided, and examples follow to help the reader make sense of the term. **Internalize vocabulary. As you have been told, education has its own language, made up of definitions and terms that are unique to the field and that educators need to know to become successful practitioners in the field. How do you remember these terms and definitions? You can best do so by making them your own. First, make a note card for each word or term. Use them in sentences and apply them to situations you can remember from your own experience as a student. Also, think of how they may be applied when you are a teacher. Use the words when you write papers and when you talk in class. Keep the note cards to refer to as you go through all your education courses in college. These cards will become your own customized dictionary.**

Sections are introduced by headings printed in boldface type, and this makes the sections easier to outline. When reading an education text, a student can get a sense of where the chapter is going, as well as of the important ideas, by reading all the boldface section headings that appear in the chapter. Doing so helps the readers organize the ideas better and facilitates the comprehension and application of material. **Outline the chapters. Before you begin to read a chapter in an education textbook, preview it and jot down the major boldface headings. These will be the major points in an outline that you can subsequently fill in with supporting details when you read the chapter. Outlining the text will keep you focused and will reinforce your recall of the major ideas presented in each chapter. You can also use this outline later when studying for a test.**

Other content areas, such as psychology, sociology, and political science, play a role in education textbooks. Education, like psychology and sociology, is a social science. As such, it draws on other social sciences for much of its theory. Be aware of the contribution that these related content areas make to education texts. In "A Textbook Case," the textbook reading that follows, you will see references to psychological terms, such as *norm*, and to legal decisions, such as *Davis v. Monroe County School Board*, that would be easier to understand if you had a background in political science. **Make connections with the other social sciences. As an education student, you will be likely to take courses in psychology and other social sciences. Don't think of these courses in isolation. Always try to make connections, even if your professors don't. Also, think about taking your general education**

courses, such as psychology, before your education courses so that you can apply this background knowledge to your education textbooks.

Charts and diagrams are used to illustrate theory and practice. In the reading "Changing Definitions of Discipline," a chart is provided to illustrate the key areas of knowledge that new teachers need to master in order to help their students learn most effectively. Although this information could be provided in text form, the chart format helps readers immediately see what area is most important—in this case, classroom management. **Pay attention to charts and graphs, and learn how to read them. Charts and graphs often play an important role in education textbooks. They are excellent tools for quick review of major concepts, as well as an alternative way to understand theory and examples. They can offer historical perspective or statistical information. They can provide definitions and make comparisons between theories or legal cases. How you use charts and graphs can make a difference in how well you understand and remember information for tests and for its later application in an actual teaching situation. Table 2 in "Changing Definitions of Discipline" lists, by race (black or white) and by year (1993 or 1997), the percentage of high school seniors who reported being victimized. You first need to see that there are five columns in the chart and that each column has a major heading. Then you can read down and across to see readily how the percentages of victims compare across both races and years. You can then make note of the most striking differences, for example. (That would be a good test question.)**

Education textbooks are informed by historical developments. Much of current educational practice is informed by historical events in the field. You will note that the history of education plays a key role in your education textbooks. **Apply what you will learn in Chapter 8 about reading history textbooks to reading and understanding the history of education. Education has its own "stories" that you will need to learn so that you can apply their lessons to your understanding and your practice.**

Reading 1: A Textbook Case

The following textbook chapter excerpt is included here because of the connection between being a good student and helping other students learn how to learn. As a new college student, you are beginning the process of deciding what you want to do after you graduate. At the same time, you are learning what it takes for you to be a successful student. This reading will both expose you to the world of teaching and show you what it takes to have a well-managed classroom. Of course, effective classroom management is but one of the many aspects of being a successful educator. This textbook excerpt also clearly illustrates some of the unique features of an education textbook. Pay attention to them as you read, and apply the strategies suggested above. Remember as you read the following passage that it is written for teachers and potential teachers. If you are not an education major, however, this reading is still important. Think about the other general electives you are taking or will be taking in the future. The classroom is no different from other communities within the larger society. How do rules apply in other situations and places? How does sociology or psychology play a role in what you will read here? Finally, you are now a student and have spent a great deal of time as a student. What have your experiences been with classroom discipline? Think about them as you read this textbook passage.

BEFORE YOU READ

1. How were discipline problems handled in schools that you have attended?
2. What seemed to work the best? What didn't work?
3. Why is understanding discipline important for a future educator?
4. Preview the following reading selection. Write down the boldface headings and terms, and formulate questions from them. How can these questions form a guide for you as you read?

Changing Definitions of Discipline

D. C. Orlich, R. J. Harder, R. C. Callahan, and H. W. Gibson

Why are classroom management issues of such concern? Two events in the late 1990s might illustrate the increased concern. The *Davis v. Monroe County School Board* decision and the fatal shootings at Columbine High School in Colorado may or may not be familiar events to you. However, these two events shook the pillars of education throughout the country. In *Davis v. Monroe County*, the U.S. Supreme Court ruled that educators who are deliberately indifferent to student-to-student sexual harassment might be liable under a federal anti-bias law (Greenberger 1999). If you, as a teacher, overlook some "children just being children" behavior that others deem harassment, you may be liable.

The Columbine High School shootings displayed the gross inadequacies of educational institutions to address planned violence. The U.S. Department of Education's National Center for Educational Statistics showed that in the 1996–1997 school year, metal detectors were permanently installed in 1 percent of schools, 4 percent used handheld metal detectors, 19 percent had drug sweeps, 24 percent controlled access to the grounds, 53 percent controlled access to the building, 80 percent had closed lunch (prohibiting students from leaving campus for lunch), and 96 percent required visitors to sign in. Yet Education Department statistics showed that the overall crime rate in schools was 128 crimes per 1,000 students in 1996 (Henry 1999).

Your essential tools to prevent and mitigate such events are observation and preparation. Know what to look for and what to do when you identify potential problems.

Discipline is usually defined as the preservation of order and the maintenance of control—the two traditional outcomes of classroom management techniques. However, this view of discipline is far too narrow. Teachers must make on-the-spot, split-second decisions and must react spontaneously when using classroom management techniques to solve problems that arise in the classroom. Classroom management techniques are determined by *teacher-student-situation* factors. The at-

Table 1

Seven of Thirty Selected Categories for Emergent Knowledge Base for School Learning

Category	(Indicates Ranking)
Classroom management	1
Student and teacher social interactions	5
Social and behavioral	6
School culture	10
Classroom climate	11
Student and teacher academic interactions	14
Teacher/administrator decision making	18

SOURCE: Wang, Haertel, and Walberg, 1993, Table 4.
Note: This Table 1 is a truncated list. Our purpose is to illustrate the importance given to management criteria as components for classroom teachers' knowledge base.

titudes students develop in formal classroom settings are influenced by the teacher's classroom management skills. Your ideas about what a classroom should look like and how it should function will determine your classroom's atmosphere.

The classroom management elements listed in Table 1 were found to be essential ingredients to effective student learning outcomes and teacher preparation.

Principles of Democratic Discipline

➤ As the adult member of the class, the teacher must add the rational dimension to the rule-making capacities of the group.

➤ Rules administered by the teacher should reflect the wisdom and fairness of a judge who participates in a trial as an impartial observer and arbiter.

Initially, the major emphasis of teacher preparation programs was classroom control. Accepted ideas about "mental discipline," physical punishment, order, and obedience provided educators with a consistent frame of reference. Later, school administrators began to shift more of the burden for establishing classroom climate and managing student conduct to the individual teacher. While this shift in responsibility was occurring, the results of relevant studies of discipline by social and behavioral scientists began to be applied in schools. The shift to individual responsibility, combined with social and behavioral research, set the stage for **"democratic discipline"** (see the box above).

Classrooms began to change even more dramatically during the 1970s and 1980s. Four changes have had a distinct effect on classroom management. First, families have become very mobile. It is not uncommon for even rather stable schools to show a 25 percent annual student turnover. Such a high degree of turnover impacts both the learning environment and the expected patterns of student behavior and classroom systems. Thus today's classrooms tend to be relatively unstable social systems.

The second phenomenon is the so-called breakup of the nuclear family. More students now live with single parents than at any other time in history, and this number is increasing. Only about 6 percent of all families now resemble the classic two-parent model: father as breadwinner, mother at home, and two children at school (Dwyer 1999).

Third, an ethos has developed among many students that views school as a place to "get through." Social promotion (promoting failing students with their age group) has firmly taken hold; as a result, students feel entitled to advancement. How can teachers motivate students if there is little threat of failure and little reward for achievement?

Fourth, urban schools developed a distinct set of problems (gangs, violence, high dropout rates, poverty) that are quite different from the problems facing sub-urban and rural schools. One can no longer compile a singular list of rules and expect it to apply to all schools.

Core Management Concepts

Our approach to classroom management is based on a **humanistic orientation** to-ward the classroom environment that views students as diverse individuals seek-ing acceptance and fulfillment. Teachers must be mindful of the fact that young minds and attitudes are shaped by overt and covert teacher behaviors. Thus in this section we discuss three concepts that are both central to the principles of class-room management and an important influence on student development norms, power, and awareness.

A **norm** is usually defined as a behavioral rule or pattern accepted to some de-gree by most members of a group. For example, raising one's hand before speaking is a norm in many classrooms. All group members feel some obligation to adhere to the behavioral rule, so it introduces a high degree of regularity and predictabil-ity into their social interaction (see the box below).

Norms

▶ Are valuable to social relationships
▶ Reduce necessity for direct, informal, and personal influence
▶ Adherence provides for the control of individual and group behavior with-out anyone overtly exerting power

---

Norms are not recorded, like the laws of a country. However, there exists in the minds of group members an ideal standard directing how each member ought to behave under specific conditions. Norms are part of the culture and are tacitly un-derstood by all members. An observed deviation from the norm usually results in a negative response.

By virtue of your role and position in the classroom, you as teacher have influence, or **power.** Unrestrained use of that power creates insecurities and resis-tance among students, adversely affecting their learning. Students can retaliate against the teacher (and other students) by forming cliques, creating irritating dis-turbances, and making threats (see Table 2). To be an effective manager, you must learn to exercise the least amount of power necessary to accomplish the desired re-sult (see Leriche 1992).

We use the term **awareness** to refer to a teacher's attention to and insight about the classroom environment. A class constantly gives its teacher verbal and nonverbal cues. Children's behaviors also offer insights regarding student-to-student interactions (Power 1992). Furthermore, communication occurs both be-tween the teacher and individual students and between the teacher and the class as a whole. The master teacher understands how to handle this mix of communi-cation. Knowing which communications to ignore and which to quickly attend to separates the pros from the rookies.

Initially, a teacher must determine how his or her class presents cues. The teacher who simply complains that "my class was particularly lousy today" has not

Table 2

Change in Percentage of High School Students Who Reported Being Victimized (Nationally), by Race, 1993 vs. 1997

Offense Reported	Black		White	
	1993	1997	1993	1997
Experienced stolen property	46.0	42.8	41.6	37.6
Experienced property deliberately damaged	26.3	18.8	25.8	25.5
Injured with a weapon	6.4	7.1	4.3	4.3
Threatened with a weapon	23.5	13.7	13.8	9.6
Injured without a weapon	11.5	11.1	11.0	12.0
Threatened without a weapon	22.3	19.3	23.8	22.4

SOURCE: U.S. Department of Education 1999, *The Condition of Education 1999,* Supplemental Table 26-1.

adequately analyzed the information provided by the class. This teacher must define with some precision what is meant by *lousy.* What behaviors did the class exhibit that led to the inference that the class was lousy? Did students recite inappropriately, not pay attention, or not accomplish the work requested? The teacher must be able to specify what behaviors are being alluded to when the class is identified as "lousy" and how students can model the appropriate behaviors (Evertson 1995).

Teacher Strategies for Discipline Versus Classroom Management

Discipline

▶ Giving in-school suspensions
▶ Sending misbehaving students to the office
▶ Contacting parents
▶ Using a check or demerit system
▶ Lowering grades
▶ Taking away privileges

Classroom Management

▶ Emphasizing rules at the start of the school year
▶ Planning for smooth transitions; leaving minimal time between activities
▶ Paying attention to the entire class; continuously scanning the group
▶ Pacing activities effectively
▶ Giving clear and concise instructions
▶ Carefully designing the classroom environment
▶ Organizing activities in advance

SOURCE: Based on information from Rita Seedorf. Used with permission.

We use the terms *discipline* and *classroom management* throughout this chapter. The Instructional Strategies box describes how the two concepts differ operationally.

The list for discipline may be summarized as showing reactive teacher behaviors. The classroom management behaviors illustrate proactive teacher actions. This comparison shows how much management differs from discipline. Being proactive reduces the need to be reactive.

AFTER YOU READ

1. Take a closer look at Table 2. What does this table tell us about the prevalence of violence in school? What does it tell us about the difference between black and white students in terms of their experience with violence?

2. Imagine you are a ninth-grade teacher. One of your students, "Alex," is not paying attention and has his head down on the desk. When you confront him, he starts to yell at you and throws his chair. What do you do?

3. How is what you learned in this reading related to your field of study and to the other courses you are now taking?

4. Think about your favorite teachers from grade school and high school. What made them your favorites? On the basis of what you have just read, do you think those teachers used a "discipline" approach or a "classroom management" approach? How did that affect what you thought of them? What did other students seem to think of them?

5. Choose one of the terms in boldface type. Define it in your own words, and then come up with examples from you own life to help explain the term.

6. Develop a classroom management plan for your class. What behaviors should be expected? How do you think everyone should be treated and treat others in the class? How should these expectations be related to course grades?

Reading 2: Life After College

Because you are thinking about professions, now is a good time to learn what professionals in different fields think about their careers. In Chapter 10, we write specifically about how important it is to connect with people in different fields. Find out what they think about their work, what they like and don't like, and what they do on a day-to-day basis. The selection that follows is one teacher's reflection on her career choice: how she decided to become a teacher and the realities of the job that keep her going in the profession. As you read this article, think about the comprehension strategy noted above, which emphasizes application of theory to everyday life. How has this writer done that?

BEFORE YOU READ

1. What do you think some of the positives of being a teacher are? Some of the negatives?

2. The author of the following article writes about a career in which she has spent her entire professional life. Are there any careers you can envision pursuing for your whole life? Statistically, most people have several careers—they reinvent themselves. Some celebrities are famous for doing this: the singer turned actor, the athlete turned announcer. What are some well-known cases of this? Do you know any individuals in your personal life who have reinvented themselves successfully?

Why I Entered Teaching, Why I Stay

J. Shively

Questions that probe my heart are hard to answer. Not because I don't have an answer, but because I'm not sure I have the right words. I'd rather not say anything than be misunderstood. Such a question came to me recently: Why did I enter teaching?

I've thought of it often. Why did I become a teacher? It was a gift. A gift from my high school principal. During my senior year, he asked about my plans for college; I explained I had none but wished I did. He felt I would qualify for a scholarship and offered to take me for an interview at George Peabody College. He and the superintendent were going to Nashville the following week and would take me along if my parents agreed. I was thrilled. I was scared.

Very early one morning in March 1957, we left for Nashville. Me in the backseat, my principal driving, and the superintendent up front. I prayed I wouldn't get carsick. They talked and talked, and I sat quietly in the backseat wondering what was to come and hoping I wouldn't embarrass myself. Hoping I'd be good enough. It turned out to be the most important car ride of my life.

I survived the interview and the exams. Made it through lunch and the fried seafood platter, recommended by my friends. I'd never eaten fried seafood in my life. I would have chosen the hamburger platter. Maybe they felt it was the beginning of my education.

A few weeks later, I received a letter announcing that I was awarded a scholarship. I was thrilled, my parents were proud, and college was to be a part of my life. George Peabody College was and is dedicated to educating teachers. Therefore, I was on my way to my career as a teacher. Not because of a drive on my part to be a teacher but because of a desire to go to college, to make my world bigger than my hometown, and to "do better." I was on my way because one man believed I could, and his believing it helped me believe it, too.

So, why did I enter teaching? It was the best I could do.

The better question may be, "Why do I stay?" This profession has many critics. Teachers themselves seldom feel satisfied with their abilities. We participate in workshops, attend conferences, go to summer school. We struggle to validate our philosophies as educators and find better ways to teach. Our days interacting with active young people are stressful and demanding. Hours of at-home planning, kids to agonize over, little credit. Who needs it?

I do.

I love my job, although I know many people who, truthfully, can't make that statement. Each year, as school begins, I am nervous. That first day of school never gets easier. I awake early, my stomach feels tight, and I reexperience the feelings of my childhood. Will I be good enough? Can I do it? I am again in the backseat of the car.

And it happens again: "Hello, Mrs. Shively," spoken with the warm smile and sparkling eyes of a child. A gift. It is those first smiles, those greetings, those hugs and clasped hands from peers and children that magically make me a believer in myself and what I'm about. We have a secret. We know that we are involved in serious business.

Diversity and Sameness

The year unfolds with the diversity and sameness that life gives to all things. I read stories to students; they in turn read to me. We write together, share our pieces, struggle to make them better. We read and discuss novels, tell stories, learn about authors, work on research projects, laugh, argue, and create the magic of learning together.

After sharing some rainbow stories one week

in first grade, Matthew, a boy who seldom spoke and looked at me from behind half-closed eyes, ran into my office shouting, "Mrs. Shively, there's a rainbow out front, come see! " We arrived in time to hold hands and watch it melt from the sky.

This year, Rachel and Becky approached me with big smiles and books in their arms. "We like to check out the same library book now. We decide which pages to read so we can discuss the story as we go along. It's fun." Not an unusual story except that Rachel is in the talented and gifted program; Becky is labeled "slow learner." The girls have become friends because Becky is no longer pulled out of the classroom. Friendship has made Rachel into a peer tutor. She reads challenging material on her own, but on this day the book selected was one that Becky could read, too. How rewarding to know that your example of shared book experience has led third-graders to discover this specialness about reading.

The gifts continue to come. Three years ago, I began a presentation to kindergarten teachers by saying, "The first responsibility we have in kindergarten is to help kids believe in themselves as readers and writers." Their gasps, quickly followed by folded arms, told me these teachers disagreed. "These kids can't read or write. We have a readiness program," they told me. "Can we talk about this?" I asked. That old backseat feeling hit me again. Teachers become comfortable with what they are doing and don't readily welcome questions or suggestions.

But Lucretia, a fine teacher, began to question what was happening in her classroom. After much exploration and study, she, too, has embraced the whole-language/natural-learning philosophy. Our interpretations aren't always the same, fortunately, but we now share a common vision. She has become excited about a job that had become routine. She says, "I'm a new person."

When Nick read his dinosaur story to me, it was a celebration of the growth and development of Nick and Lucretia. "Nick, tell how you wrote this story." "Okay," Nick replied. "It's about a dinosaur coming to dinner. I told what we did before dinner, what we ate, and what we did after dinner. You know what I did to spell my dinosaur's name?

I went to my dinosaur book and looked for the word under the picture and wrote it the same way." "Wonderful," I responded. "That's just the way adults spell long words correctly. They check them out in a book."

Perhaps more important is Tommy. He was in an eighth-grade remedial reading class with 11 boys and 3 girls. School had never been fun for any of them. The first day we met, Tommy announced, "Ain't nobody made me read books and you won't neither." At 15, he stood taller already than my five feet, five inches. I smiled and said, "Welcome to room 208. Find a seat you'd like."

We made an agreement. I believe a student has the right to choose to fail if that's what he wants, and I explained this to Tommy. He liked the idea. For a while.

We began reading and discussing our readings. Tommy listened and attempted to join in. I quietly gave him a brief "shh" sign to remind him of our agreement. After a few weeks of boredom, a request: "Give me one of them notebooks. Maybe I'll read this book."

Each class began with 15 minutes of sustained silent reading. And there was Tommy with long hair, blue jeans, blue-jean jacket, heavy work boots, stretched out reading. Suddenly, he turned toward me and blurted out, "Is this dog going to die? I don't want this dog to die."

"Shh," again from me. "Just read on, Tommy." I glanced at the clock. Reading time was almost up. My pulse raced. Would the kids notice? I couldn't ruin this moment for Tommy. His lips were occasionally moving as he read, but his body was rigid. I knew he was reaching the climax of the story and the dog was going to die. Kids often cry at this point in the book because it is so powerful. What would he do?

I peeked at the class while pretending to read, hoping the restless ones wouldn't announce "Time's up." I couldn't read a word. Ten more minutes passed. Slowly Tommy closed the book and sat staring down at his lap. I could hardly breathe: Tommy wasn't big on sensitivity. His dialogue mostly expressed how tough he was: "I could do that." "I could live on my own." "Nobody tells me what to do." But this book had made him quiet.

Books started closing. Kids coughed. Pencils dropped. Yet, I continued to read. Tommy needed a gift of time. He stood up. Still, I read. He sauntered toward my reading chair, stopped at my desk, and dropped the book there. I looked up. "I want another book just like that one."

Why did I enter teaching? It was a gift from my high school principal. Why do I stay? Because of the magic, the joy, and the celebrations. Because the growth and development of the kids is the growth and development of me. It is my way to make the world more beautiful.

AFTER YOU READ

1. What daily rewards do you hope to get from your job after college? Provide some specific examples.
2. What daily rewards do you hope to get now, during your time in college? Provide some specific examples. (Why do you stay in college?)
3. How does reading an article like this help a college student decide whether to choose education as a major?
4. One of the comprehension strategies we learned about in this chapter is the use of real-life examples to present information. How does the author use examples from her own experience to help the reader understand the day-to-day life of a teacher?
5. When you graduated from high school, you ended a dozen years in the school system. What did you feel when you graduated? What do you think your teachers felt? Has your perspective changed since then, whether it was a few months or several years ago? How well do you think your high school experience prepared you for college?

Reading 3: **Current Issues**

Katy Kelly's article "Parents in a Haze?" takes a look at hazing among high school students and at parents' reactions to it. As a student and as a possible future educator or parent, you may have witnessed hazing. Think about what your reaction was or might be. Think about what happened to the students involved in the incident reported in this article in light of the textbook article you read on discipline. Was the punishment just? Was the parents' reaction warranted? Remember the comprehension strategies for education texts highlighted earlier in this chapter. One way to understand educational issues better is to connect them to other academic areas. To employ this strategy, consider the following questions: How would you discuss this incident from a psychological perspective? From a sociological perspective? What is the historical background of hazing? How might hazing affect students' ability to function as students?

BEFORE YOU READ

1. Should hazing be handled by school administrators, parents, or law enforcement? Why?
2. Have you ever been a victim of hazing? Have you ever heard about or witnessed hazing? If so, what happened? How did you feel about it? If you never experienced or heard about any specific hazing incidents, what do you know about hazing?
3. Come up with a definition of hazing. Take a poll. Determine the opinions of the students about the seriousness of hazing. Develop questions, and then tally the results on the board. What do the results of the survey say about the attitudes and values of the class? Are there differences between males' and females' responses? Between the responses of students with different majors?

Parents in a Haze?

K. Kelly

Sure, the girls may have been brutal and sadistic. But should that keep them out of Harvard?

On the first Sunday in May, in the affluent Chicago suburb of Northbrook, junior and senior girls from Glenbrook North High School met at a park for the annual "powder puff" football game. Nobody really cared about the game. Indeed, some say no one even brought a ball. The gathering was actually a hazing ritual in which the seniors initiate their junior classmates.

One junior expected to be doused with ketchup. Instead—and this was videotaped—the juniors were punched and slapped, covered with urine, paint, fish guts, and trash, wrapped with pig intestines, and smeared with feces. One girl needed stitches; another suffered a broken ankle. Alcohol was available and may have fueled the sadism.

As brutal and appalling as the teenagers' behavior was, many were equally shocked by the parents' reaction. When principal Michael Riggle suspended 28 girls and four boys for 10 days—the maximum punishment allowed—Craig Yudell, father of an 18-year-old who was allegedly involved in the hazing asked the school board to reconsider: "They made one mistake, and you're punishing them for the rest of their lives," the Chicago Tribune quoted him as saying. "This may affect college." Three families sought legal orders to rescind the suspensions, claiming that missing school would cause the students irreparable damage. Marnie Holz's complaint noted that the suspension meant she would not be able to attend her prom.

Marnie's mother, Leslie Holz, defends the suit. "I understand people think, 'Take your punishment,' but that isn't even the issue. . . . We were asking [that the suspension be overturned] on the grounds that [the incident] didn't occur during school hours or at a school-sponsored event." The family also objects to Riggle's recommendation that the students be expelled. "Expulsion [carries] a stigma in terms of jobs, resumes, and college," says Leslie Holz. She insists that Marnie was not among the violent offenders.

Well, what does warrant stigma? While the Illinois hazing incident is an extreme example, doing the wrong thing is becoming more common nationally. The 2002 Ethics of American Youth survey found that 3 of 4 high school students admitted to cheating on at least one test during the previous year. Some 38 percent acknowledged stealing something from a store, and 37 percent said they would lie in order to get a good job.

Also on the increase are the number of parents asking that infractions be overlooked or punishments watered down. "Love is a powerful emotion, and it taints the process sometimes," says Michele Rhule, a principal in Mercer, Pa. Most parents support school rules, she says, but there is a national trend to take complaints to the top. "People don't like to have their children punished."

Wrongs and rights. In 2002, a Kansas City, Kan., teacher found that 28 students had plagiarized on their botany projects. After parents protested, the school board ordered the teacher to lower the weight of the project in the final grading. And this year in Bethesda, Md., the family of a boy who was kicked out of school for helping another student cheat on the SAT exam filed a suit. The family is asking for $1.1 million to compensate for the "loss of invaluable childhood friendships . . . and loss to his reputation."

Protecting children from the consequences of their actions is a temptation as old as parenthood. Most parents agree in theory that wrong choices should have consequences, but many back down, fearing the resulting blemish on the school record will bump the child off the team or keep him out of an elite college.

But the consequences of no consequences can be much bigger than that, says Michele Borba, author of *No More Misbehavin'*. "To raise the trophy kid, [the focus is often on] the grades, the SATs, the Ivies" rather than moral development. The trade-off: "No conscience, no sense of remorse, accountability, or empathy."

For a dozen girls and three boys accused of participating in the hazing, serious consequences arrived Friday when they were charged as adults with misdemeanor battery. Marnie Holz was not charged. At Glenbrook North High School, "the mood is somber," says spokesperson Diane Freeman. The 2,000 students who did not participate "are as horrified as anybody else."

AFTER YOU READ

1. Compare the hazing reported in this article to the cheating that was also discussed. How would you compare these actions? Are they equally serious? Is one behavior worse than another?
2. Do you think cheating is becoming more commonplace? Explain your answer.
3. What do you think should happen to the students involved in this incident? Explain your reasons.

Compounding Your Interest: Further Readings

Covey, S. (1989). *Seven Habits of Highly Effective People*. New York: Simon and Schuster.

Fitzgerald, F. S. (1995). *The Great Gatsby*. New York: Scribners.

Grabe, M., & Grabe, C. (2001). *Integrating Technology for Meaningful Learning*. Boston: Houghton Mifflin.

Keen, S. (1991). "The Price of Success." *Fire in the Belly*. New York: Bantam.

Morning, M. (February 2001). "This Is Not Your High School English Class." *Campus Life*.

Wilmes, R. (August 2002). "Compromise Is the Key to Roommate Harmony." *USA Today Magazine*.

Chapter 2

Motivations and Expectations for Your Investment

Now that you have an idea of what to expect and what is expected of you in college, you may be wondering what your motivations are for doing well and what expectations you can have for reaping rewards from your investment. The first thing to keep in mind is that you need to make the investment early in college. The earlier you get started, the greater the reward will be. This chapter will help you do that by creating an investment plan: a plan to manage your time, to study the way that works best for you (a time saver in itself!), to figure out what your GPA is (and how to get it where you want it to be), to think about your major early and often. Like any good investor, you, as a college student, will do well to research the market before investing, to "pay yourself first," to consult with others who have more information than you, to invest on a regular basis, to adhere to the "law" to avoid trouble, to know the true cost of investing, and to diversify your investments across different areas. A smart college student knows that nothing will be gained in the end if investments aren't made in the beginning. It is as simple as that. This chapter will show you how to make those early investments—and why. It will all be worth it in the end.

First Things First

Let's face it; being a college student takes a lot of your time. Or it should. The irony is that it often seems as though you have more time in college than you did in high school: Classes don't meet every day; you have a 10 a.m. class and don't have another one until 2 p.m.; you might not even have class on Tuesdays and Thursdays. This kind of schedule can fool you into thinking you have more time than you actually do. That is why drawing up a good time management

Think About It

Answer the following questions in the space provided.

What one investment (i.e., a time management plan, thinking about careers, etc.) do you think is best to make first? Why? _____

_____

_____

_____

_____

plan is the best first investment you can make. In fact, it is the investment on which all others depend. Making a time management plan may itself take a little time, but it will save you time in the long run. Keeping a time management plan isn't just about keeping a calendar, however; it is also about how best to use the time you have. You use your time wisely when you really get to know who you are and how you work best. Keeping a calendar is just the beginning.

Managing Your Time

Question: How many hours should you spend studying outside of class? The answer: You should study about two hours outside of class for every hour you spend in class. If you are a typical first-year college student, you are taking a 15-credit load. Multiply that by 2 and you have 30. Thirty hours should be spent studying outside of class. If that sounds like a full-time job in itself, it is. Being a college student is now your full-time job.

How much time do you actually have? That is a good question. To begin, fill out the following weekly calendar. First, fill in all the things you have to do: classes, work, sports, clubs, exercising, even eating and sleeping. Estimate as best you can.

	Sunday	Monday	Tuesday	Wednesday	Thursday	Friday	Saturday
7:00 a.m.							
8:00 a.m.							
9:00 a.m.							
10:00 a.m.							
11:00 a.m.							
12:00 p.m.							
1:00 p.m.							
2:00 p.m.							
3:00 p.m.							
4:00 p.m.							
5:00 p.m.							
6:00 p.m.							
7:00 p.m.							
8:00 p.m.							
9:00 p.m.							
10:00 p.m.							
11:00 p.m.							

Monitor your activity for a week after making this schedule, and then make adjustments to your schedule as needed. Now that you know how much time you need for all the things you must do, you have a better idea of how much "free" time you have to devote to your job as college student. Now take a highlighter and fill in each space that is not already filled. These highlighted spaces show you how much time you have left to study. And you *do* need to schedule your study time. If you don't, your studying simply will not get done. Procrastinators and last-minute "crammers" learn the hard way that planning one's study time all along actually creates more time for relaxation. You may wonder how to fill in the blank spaces or when to do which type of activity. Here are some tips:

▶ *Are you a morning person or a night person?* Don't plan to wake up at 5 a.m. to read your sociology textbook when you normally don't go to bed until 2 a.m. Likewise, if you can't keep your eyes open past midnight, don't even bother trying to fight it. Go to bed and get up before your first class. An hour in the morning when you are fresh is worth at least twice as much as an hour when you are tired and have to read everything three times.

▶ *Take a closer look at those wasted hours*—those hours between classes that you normally might spend hanging out with friends, watching TV, or taking yet another nap. If you are still on high school time, you need to rethink when you do your work. Many students think of studying (homework) as night work—or at least as after-school work. But now that you're in college, you probably have free time in the middle of the day that often goes to waste. Take the two hours between your 8 a.m. and 11 a.m. classes, and schedule an appointment with yourself. Every Monday for those two hours, you can read your biology text . . . you get the picture.

▶ *Use those wasted minutes as well.* Not only can you get some studying in during a brief ten-minute wait before a class starts or a few minutes in line for lunch, but this type of studying is actually some of the best you can do! What can you do in brief ten- to fifteen-minute blocks of time? You can preview a chapter you have to read later, you can brainstorm ideas for a paper, you can go over your notes, you can review some flashcards, or you can quiz a friend. Short, frequent study sessions help you remember better than one long cramming session right before a test. Think of how many of these short periods of time you have wasted because you thought you couldn't get anything done. These short sessions really add up and keep information fresh in your mind. Also, think about getting to the room ten minutes before class to review your notes from the previous lecture. This strategy can help you get in gear and stay focused in class.

▶ *Plan to study each subject soon after the class and before the next one.* You will learn later in this book about the importance of reviewing material soon after you first encounter it. If you do so, it is less likely that you will have to review the information over again—it will stay in your memory. This in itself will save you a lot of time. Look at your schedule. Plan to review what you have learned and complete any reading in each subject soon after the class and before the next one. You will stay one step ahead of the game.

▶ *Work harder for shorter periods of time.* Many students will block off a long period of time to study one subject but are unrealistic about what this really means. For instance, just saving five hours for studying calculus isn't helpful if you can't really concentrate for five hours on calculus. You'd be better off blocking off an hour at a time with a scheduled break in between study blocks. Just promise yourself that you will really *work* for that full hour.

▶ *Reward yourself later*—defer gratification until you've earned it. Students frequently make the mistake of having fun before they study. All too often, they have so much fun that they never get around to studying. Or when they do, it's not at a time that is conducive to true concentration. The best way is to be disciplined enough to get your studying finished (or at least started) before going on to other activities. Remember the tip you've just learned about using your daytime hours, because if you get your work done during the day, you'll have more evening hours to socialize, play basketball, listen to music, or watch TV.

▶ *Understand priorities.* Figuring out what's most important before the fact is a key to success. It's not going to be very helpful if you realize only after the final that you should have studied more. Or that you should have prepared for your presentation by practicing longer. Successful students (not to mention successful business executives, accountants, lawyers, computer programmers, and so on) are those who are very good at prioritizing the items on their busy schedules.

Time Out Tip

For tomorrow, try using a to-do list. Either before you go to bed or first thing in the morning, sit down and make a list of the things you'd like to accomplish that day.

A Sample To-Do List

Before you make a to-do list, first consider your priorities. If you have a test the next day, studying for that test should take on higher importance than working on a paper that's due in two weeks or rearranging your furniture in your dorm room. Keep this list realistic; it should contain items that you really can accomplish in one day. If you've managed to cross everything off, it will give you a feeling of satisfaction, whereas if you don't (and sometimes you won't), you will know what needs to be a top priority tomorrow. Many successful people are known for keeping lists.

DAY 1 (MONDAY)
Final draft of essay (DUE TOMORROW!!!)
Read and annotate chapter 7 for psychology.
2:00 PM - Dr. Jamison to go over test.
Study group 7 PM - library
LAUNDRY!!!
Movie - 9 PM

DAY 2 (TUESDAY)
Study for Psych test next Monday
LAUNDRY!!! Seriously...
Study group 7 PM - library
Buy new printer cartridge

As you can see, items that are not finished one day can move to the next day on the list. Always remember to prioritize the items on your list, making your number-one item most important. Items that are low on the list are also of low priority. Don't procrastinate by doing only the easiest things.

Long-Term To-Do Lists

Of course, you also want to plan for the long term. At the beginning of a semester, it may seem that you have a lot of time, but time can go very quickly. Furthermore, you never know what activities or responsibilities may come up along the way to make getting a particular assignment done more difficult. Think about keeping a calendar for the whole semester.

DIY: Do-It-Yourself Activity

1. Go out and purchase a semester calendar.
2. Gather the syllabi from all of your classes.
3. With syllabi in hand, write on the calendar the due dates of every paper or project and the scheduled dates of every test and exam.
4. Then go back a week before each due date to remind yourself that the deadline is approaching.
5. Post this calendar in a conspicuous place where you will be sure to see it every day.

Avoiding the Costly Art of Procrastination

It's Saturday. You have a test on Tuesday. You promised yourself you would spend this afternoon studying for it. Do you suddenly find yourself drawn to such otherwise mundane tasks as straightening your room, emptying your trash, sharpening all of your pencils, and clipping your toenails? Has it suddenly occurred to you that the wilted plant in your window that you haven't noticed for a month needs to be watered? Do you feel an urgent need to call an old high school friend—whom you haven't seen since graduation? If you find yourself in this position, you're practicing something that many students have refined into an art form: procrastination. It's a natural instinct to want to put off things that seem unpleasant. Studying for a test can be hard work. But there is a cost to such a delay, a price to be paid. If you don't study on Saturday, you're going to feel guilty on Sunday. If you put it off again on Sunday—guess what? It's now Monday night. You feel completely unprepared. What typically happens next is often that venerable—but mostly ineffective—college tradition: the all-nighter (see Chapter 4 for reasons to avoid this).

Here are a few tips for avoiding procrastination:

Make a schedule—and stick to it. If you don't have a schedule, you may be tempted to do the easier tasks first, or just to do what your friends are doing. Having your own list will help you keep track of your own deadlines. Also, writing down what you need to do helps you *remember* what you need to do. Your deadlines are there in black and white.

Reward **yourself when you stick to it**—but only after you've completed the task! If you study as planned on Saturday afternoon, go out and have pizza with friends that night—guilt-free!

Start working in small chunks. Don't say, "I'm going to chain myself to the desk for five hours." Try, "I'll sit here for fifteen minutes and see what I get done." What you'll often find is that once you break the ice and get started, your work will gain some momentum of its own. Fifteen minutes will turn into an hour.

Recognize when you are procrastinating. Learn to recognize the signs. If you suddenly have an urgent need to do something trivial that hasn't been done for months, you're probably procrastinating. (If the distracting mundane task happens to be doing the laundry that has been piling up or cleaning up your room, move to another study location so that you can focus. Also, you can add these items to your to-do list so that you can get them off your mind and get back to the important task at hand.)

Recognize the price you will pay for procrastinating. Just because you have put something off now doesn't mean you're never going to have to do it. What it means is that you will have even less time to do it and be more rushed.

It's only natural to feel some aversion to things that are, or at least seem, unpleasant. That impulse to avoid must itself be avoided. Remember that very often, the task isn't so bad once you get started; it's just getting started that is the problem.

And that pizza you have with your friends is going to taste a lot better if you did your studying first. Ultimately, successful students learn to overcome the urge to procrastinate—a temptation that we all experience—and start doing what they need to do on time.

Knowing Yourself as a Learner

Now that you understand what kind of time commitment being a college student will demand of you, you also probably realize that you don't have much time to waste. That said, the best thing you can do to make the most of your time is to know yourself as a learner. What does that mean? It means to understand how you learn best, what it takes for you to remember something, and what times and environments are best for you to study. It is not complicated, but it does require a little reflection.

Remember the earlier questions: Are you a morning person or a night person? Can you wake up early and be ready to go? Do you prefer to sleep in and really come alive at around 11 p.m.? Likewise, do you do better studying in your dorm room alone, or do you prefer studying with a friend at the student union? Do you need someone to expect you somewhere at a specific time in order to get motivated to

What Worked for Me

"I was always a good student," Carlos said to his economics professor one day when he went to see her during office hours. "I just don't know why I am flunking this class." His professor asked him what he did to prepare for the last exam. "I studied for hours!" Carlos said, exasperated. When his professor asked him how he studied, Carlos replied that he looked over his notes. His instructor explained that although this approach may have worked in high school or for other classes, Carlos might not be studying in the best way for his learning style. Carlos didn't even know then what a learning style was. But he went to the tutoring center on campus and took a learning styles inventory. It turned out that Carlos is a visual learner. "I was amazed to find this out," Carlos said. But he didn't just learn this about himself. He actually applied this knowledge to his study techniques with the help of a tutor. Now he always makes index cards. He creates charts and graphs whenever he can. He even makes silly pictures and diagrams to help him learn the information. "I was just wasting a lot of time before I applied my learning style to my studying. Putting in time does not guarantee a grade. Studying the right way does." Carlos, by the way, pulled his economics grade up to a B.

study? If you think back on your own behavior and experiences, these are not hard questions to answer. The harder question may be how to adjust your time and habits once you become aware of what you really should be doing.

Knowing Your Learning Style—and Putting That Knowledge to Use

One of the most helpful things you can know about yourself as a learner is your style of learning. Think back to something you were learning for the first time. Did you learn it best by actually doing it—practicing and failing until you got it right? Or did you learn best when someone explained it all to you first? Or did you examine diagrams or view a video and then go right out and try it? Imagine that you're taking a human anatomy class (maybe you don't even have to imagine it!). Memorizing the parts of the human body can be difficult. How would you approach it? Would you sit there with a diagram or would you draw it over and over again? Would you look at the list of terms and try to associate them with their definitions? Or would you talk about the terms with someone else in your class? Many students combine more than one approach. The key is knowing which technique is most effective for you, because many students make the mistake of using one that does not make the most of their natural inclinations.

You just learned about time management. Learning about your learning style is a time management issue. If you don't take the time to figure out what your style is, you may be wasting many hours learning in an ineffective way. For example, if all you did in high school was look over your notes, that may have worked—then. But if you really are the kind of learner who needs to learn complex information by writing it down or talking it over, you're going to need to learn some new approaches. Otherwise, you will end up with a low return on your investment of time.

Basically, out of many different ways to learn, there are three main learning styles:

▶ **Visual.**
▶ **Auditory.**
▶ **Kinesthetic.**

It's important to have a general idea of your own personal learning style. One way to find out where your strengths lie is to take a look at your own style. There are many tests that will help you do this, and some of them are probably available in your campus tutoring center or online. To get a general sense, look at the following student profiles and see which one most closely resembles you.

Antonio prefers to get his daily news from the radio rather than from the newspaper. When he bought a new cell phone, he learned to program it by asking a couple of friends who had bought the same model. When Antonio has trouble with a math problem, he speaks the numbers out loud to work through it. He studies for tests primarily by talking to his friends in study groups. Sometimes, he records lectures so that he can listen to them again later.

Shanelle doodles all the time in her classes and when she's talking on the phone. When she bought her new cell phone, she spent an hour looking at the diagrams in the manual that came with it. She keeps up with what's going on in the world by checking the Internet or the daily paper. When Shanelle gives directions to a friend, she mentions all the visual landmarks. She can't do math in her head or out loud; she has to write everything down on scratch paper. She likes to sit quietly and read her notes alone to study for tests. She finds index cards especially helpful.

Ian likes to walk around when he studies. Sometimes, he even juggles bean bags while he's memorizing information. He likes math puzzles and projects. Ian tends to press down heavily with his pencil when he writes and often retraces words and diagrams on his paper.

Who are you most like? If you are like Antonio, you are an auditory learner. If you are more like Shanelle, your strengths are visual. And, finally, Ian is a kinesthetic learner. Of course, you could have some combination of these characteristics. You can learn from all of them. Depending on your predominant style, use the following suggestions to help you determine how to study optimally.

Style	Definition	Adaptations
Visual	Visual learners learn through spatial relationships and associations.	To take full advantage of your visual learning strength, be sure to make outlines, charts, or concept maps of the information you must learn. Draw silly pictures or stick figures to represent terms or concepts. Put your information on note cards that you can look at over and over again. Try to take classes with professors who present information in forms other than a

(continued)

Style	Definition	Adaptations
		lecture: PowerPoint, charts, slides, videos. Learn to take information from an auditory format, if that is all you have, and turn it into visual information. The more you do this, the easier it will become. And it will take less time for you to learn, understand, and remember the information. It just makes sense.
Auditory	Auditory learners learn through listening. They associate ideas and instructions with procedural steps and with the physical location or situation they were in when they first heard the idea.	Tape record lectures (with the professor's permission, of course) and then listen to each lecture again later. Tape record yourself reading your notes. Work with a study partner and discuss the material. When taking a test, try to recall where you were sitting when you first heard the information. Often, you will "hear" the material again as you recall it. It's a nice technique that not enough auditory learners use. Most people have heard of visualizing. Let's just call this "auditorializing."
Kinesthetic	Kinesthetic learners learn through their actions and through the physical movements their body makes, whether it be movements of the hands, the feet or the body as a whole.	When studying, write down material, walk around while memorizing material, and, if necessary, study in bursts of ten or fifteen minutes divided by two- to three-minute activity breaks (walk around the room, do calisthenics).This will enable you to dissipate any nervous energy and to focus effectively on the study task at hand.

Active versus Passive Learning

What words would you use to describe an active person? How about energetic, on-the-go, dynamic, bustling, animated, industrious, engaged, quick, lively, practical, eager, earnest, enterprising. The list goes on. How about passive? Inert, phlegmatic, apathetic, placid, resigned, out of it, motionless, listless. You get the picture. Many students are able to get through high school as passive learners, but college is a different story. College is not a TV show where you just sit back and let the action unfold in front of you. It's more like a play, but you're not in the audience now, you're on the stage. How would you feel if you were on stage and had no idea what your lines were because you hadn't prepared? That's how you're going to feel in college if you continue to be a passive learner.

Active Learner	**Passive Learner**
Asks questions in class	Sits quietly in class
Seeks help from professors and/or tutors	Stays confused
Forms study groups	Studies alone (or not at all)
Finds outside supplemental material	Uses only the course textbook
Studies according to learning style	Studies the same old way

Being an active learner is important in college. There's no way around that. Why? The amount of information you need to process is greater. The amount of time you need to learn it in is often shorter. The complexity of the information is considerable. Moreover, in many courses, professors don't want you just to recite information back to them. Rather, they want you to interact with the material, as we will discuss later in the chapter on critical thinking. For now, though, think about what you can do to be an active learner.

Is it possible to go from being a passive learner to being an active learner? Of course, although it's not always an easy transition. First, you need to recognize passive traits in your own study habits and replace them with active ones. Here are some techniques to get you started.

▶ **Force yourself to ask questions in class.** Don't wait for others to speak up because they may not, and you'll be left without the answer you seek. Set a goal for yourself. Ask at least one question a week for starters. Sometimes you just need to break the ice internally, and over time, you'll become more comfortable with it (and you'll start to see the benefits).

▶ **Answer questions in class.** The more engaged you are in the discussion, the better you will remember the material. If you know it, show it. Too many students wait for someone else to answer, even when they know the answer.

▶ **Visit your professors during their office hours.** Plan to see each one at least once during the semester, preferably early in the semester. For one thing, it helps them know who you are, and it will help you feel more comfortable speaking up in class.

▶ **Form a study group.** Find others in your class who seem interested and prepared for class. See whether they want to meet up once or twice a week to discuss and review material. One caveat: Make sure that your group is really studying. Sometimes, study groups can disintegrate into a social hour, which doesn't really help. The more opportunities you have to talk about the information, the more likely it is that you'll remember it. Sometimes the best way to learn is to teach. Also, if you missed something or didn't quite understand it, this is a good way to clear up the confusion.

▶ **Get extra material.** Most classes have a textbook and notes. But you can rest assured that your professor didn't get all the materials for her lectures from the textbook alone. Professors use lots of supplemental materials. So should you. Do your own research at the library or on the Internet. Sometimes, reading about the material from another person's viewpoint will shed more light on it.

▶ **Know your learning style.** And study accordingly.

Teamwork Activity

 Be active! The object of this activity is to create your own *active* learning activity. Gather three or four students from your class and form a "creative team." Pick a topic and create an activity for the rest of the class to do that would require active learning on their part. For example, let's say you wanted to teach the students three new words in another language. What might you do to get them actively involved? What if you wanted them to learn a few important facts about another country? What would you do that would keep them from being passive learners? What if you wanted the students to understand a new math concept? Find your topic. Form your lesson plan. Then try it out on the rest of the class. See how active they are and how much being active affects their ability to learn and remember the information. You will be convinced!

The Ins and (Mostly) the Outs of Cheating

Cheating. No matter what, there are probably always going to be some people who cheat in college. After all, college is really no different from any other aspect of society. In recent years, just as there have been some major scandals at some large companies, there have been major cheating scandals at some of the nation's top colleges. But remember, you are making a major investment in coming to college. It pays to learn the rules up front so that you don't cheat *yourself* out of your returns. College has many rules, and not cheating is one of them.

It's easy enough to say that you shouldn't cheat because it's wrong. For many people, the fact that cheating is intrinsically wrong is enough of a reason not to do it. For those looking for external reasons, your college's handbook of policies and procedures should give plenty of reasons not to cheat. Penalties for cheating range from getting a failing grade on an assignment to getting an F in the class and, in some cases, dismissal from the institution. Your reputation is at stake. You don't want to damage your integrity in the future by taking an unethical shortcut now.

Types of cheating vary, but they range from bringing in cheat sheets to "previewing" tests—getting a copy of the test in advance and memorizing the answers. Some students have even gone high tech, using cell phones and mobile pagers to "share" answers on tests.

One of the most pervasive forms of cheating is plagiarism. Plagiarism is the act of representing someone else's words as one's own. It can take many forms. The student who purchases a paper off the Internet and puts her name on it is practicing an extreme form of plagiarism. But you're also plagiarizing if you borrow a paragraph or two from a book or article and fail to cite that source accurately in your paper. In the past few years, some very high-profile scholars—Stephen Ambrose and Doris Kearns Goodwin, for example—have had their reputations tarnished by accusations of plagiarism. One rule to remember: **If in doubt, cite it!** Some students are anxious about citations because they're not comfortable with the rules. Sometimes students are afraid to cite too often. First of all, most professors would rather you made a mistake or two with your formatting than cheated. And it's hard to imagine a situation in which a professor would penalize you for having *too many* citations. On the contrary, most professors would be pleased to see that you did so much research. When you read scholarly articles for your research, you'll notice that those articles have dozens and dozens of citations, often more than one per sentence. In your college writing class, you will learn more about plagiarism and how to cite work. Typically, you will learn to use the MLA (Modern Language Association) guidelines or the APA (American Psychological Association) guidelines. Whichever system you use, don't expect to understand it all up front. You will become more familiar with it as you use it—you're learning. And even experienced scholars typically keep a guidebook next to their desk as they write. As for cheating by buying papers from other sources, such as the Internet, be aware that many universities subscribe to services that help them track down cheaters. They simply submit your paper to the service, and it will let them know whether it is original material.

Honesty in scholarship is important. Would you want a doctor who had cheated her way through medical school? Or an engineer who had "previewed" the answers to her licensing test? How would you feel about being represented at trial by a lawyer who had someone else write his papers in law school? Probably not so good. What you're learning now matters more than the grade. If you have to cheat to get the grade, then you're not really learning the material. And you're going to be developing a habit that will catch up to you sooner or later.

Cheating Hall of Shame

Basically, cheating is always a dumb move. But the following students did things that were dumber than most. Names have been changed to protect the not-so-innocent.

Cheating Hall of Shame

What the student did	What happened next	The end result
Roxanne paid her cousin to write her paper for her.	Roxanne's cousin took the money and then, without telling her, simply copied an article from the Internet.	The professor recognized that it wasn't Roxanne's writing; she received an F on the paper and dropped the class with a WF (Withdrawal-Fail); it's unknown whether Roxanne got her money back.
Not prepared for his chemistry test, Harrison wrote a cheat sheet with some of the main formulas.	Harrison had written it on yellow legal paper. When he put the paper under the white test paper, it was clearly visible.	The professor immediately saw it, and Harrison received an F on the test and for the course.
In a basic writing class, Giselle had trouble writing a paper, so she copied an article she found at the library.	The article she copied was from the *Journal of the American Medical Association*. Not surprisingly, the professor realized it wasn't Giselle's writing.	Giselle strongly denied she had cheated—until the professor dug up the article. Giselle failed the course.
Rob turned in a paper for an online course that contained a "hot-link" Internet source.	The professor clicked on the link to check the source.	The professor was surprised to find that the link took him to Rob's paper, which happened to be an article on the Internet written by another author.
Dylan, hearing from other students that his professor didn't read the entire paper, decided to find out. He wrote the first and last pages of the paper and then filled the middle pages with the words "[expletive deleted] you" over and over again.	The professor read the entire paper.	The professor wrote " 'F' you, too!" and Dylan failed the course.
In the middle of taking attendance, the professor	Several students mentioned the incident to	Janine was charged with academic dishonesty, received an

(*continued*)

What the student did	What happened next	The end result
was called out of class. Janine walked up to the open grade book, changed an F she had received for a test into a B, and sat back down.	the professor privately. In addition, the professor could clearly see the change, and she had already transferred all of the grades—including Janine's F—to an "Excel" spreadsheet anyway.	F for the course, and was dismissed from the university.
For a math quiz, Sarah received the answers from a friend who had the same class and professor earlier in the day. She wrote the answers on the inside of the label for her water bottle.	The water distorted the answers, making them much bigger. The professor spotted them immediately as he monitored the room.	Sarah received an F for the quiz and the course. For added irony, the answers weren't right anyway. The professor had used a different version of the quiz.
Chas had run out of time to write a book review for his political science class, so he asked his fraternity brothers for some help. They dug up a review from their "files," and he handed it in on time.	Upon reading it, his professor was initially surprised at the quality of Chas's writing. He was even more surprised when he recognized a certain familiarity in the writing. He had written the review himself three years earlier and had published it in a leading scholarly journal.	The professor initially complimented Chas on the quality of his writing. As soon as Chas took the bait, the professor brought out the original journal where it had been published. Chas received an F on the paper and in the course.

Your Choice of Major

One of the biggest decisions for college students, and often one of the most difficult, is deciding on a major. Many students see so many alternatives and have so many interests that they find it hard to narrow the choice down. Others can't seem to find any area that jumps out at them; a student in this category may feel that "I can't find anything I want to do for the rest of my life." The main thing is not to panic. First of all, the average college student changes majors three or four times. As a first-year student, you have plenty of time to make up your mind and explore different areas, because many of the general education classes are the same regardless of your major. And as for worrying that your major might confine you to doing one thing for the rest of your life—don't. Your major will naturally point you in one direction or another, but it's not a contract that you have to fulfill. There are plenty of English majors who work on Wall Street, history majors working in sales, geography majors working in insurance, and pre-med students who decide to become teachers. The list goes on and on. The important thing is to get a college degree; this will be the key that will open all kinds of doors for you.

That having been said, it is still naturally in your best interests to find a major that's appropriate for you and your skills. If you struggled in math all through high

The Hard Way

"When I was in high school," says Ray, a freshman and member of the football team, "I wrote all my papers at the last minute—or had someone do it for me. I always got away with it. I also let people borrow my papers and notes. We were all in it together." But Ray learned that things weren't the same in college. First of all, he couldn't write papers at the last minute. And his friends were always having the same problem. Last semester, in his freshman composition class, he actually finished a paper ahead of time because the topic came easy to him and his coach made the team go to study hall three nights a week to get work done. "I was feeling like I had things under control." Then his friend Aaron asked him for help on the same English paper. Instead of saying he didn't have the time, Ray let him see his essay. The next day, Ray turned in his paper and was expecting an A. "Needless to say, I was shocked when the professor called me and Aaron into his office a few days later." It turns out that Aaron and Ray turned in exactly the same composition. Aaron denied knowing anything about it. And Ray, of course, said he wrote his own paper. The professor failed them both. "I was angry," said Ray, "I deserved an A on that paper." Ray knows, however, that he *could* have failed the whole course. Aaron finally admitted he took Ray's paper. It was a tough lesson for both of them. "Even friends can mess up sometimes. And professors do read your papers and do flunk you. I will be sure never again to turn in something that is not my own or let someone else take something of mine. There is just too much at stake."

school, maybe engineering isn't the best field for you. If you hate to write, maybe you don't want to become an English major. If you are still unsure of your major, one thing you can do to help you choose a major is research the different majors on your campus. Even if you have picked a major, you can learn about some other possibilities through this kind of research. Many colleges have dozens and dozens of majors. Often, a single department has two, three, or more twists on the major (English writing and English literature, for example). You can research the requirements of the different majors by using the college catalogue or the Internet. A major in psychology might sound appealing, but through your research, you would discover that if you want to be a psychologist, you will need to go to graduate school to get a Ph.D. And to be a psychiatrist? Medical school. Thus, in those fields, a four-year degree is only going to be the beginning. In your research, you can find out what you can do with a bachelor's degree in your major of choice. Some majors, anthropology and philosophy, for example, are generally a stepping stone to graduate school, whereas others, such as elementary education, are themselves the main prerequisite to launching a career as a teacher.

How, then, do you know what majors and careers your skills and interests are suited for? Most colleges and universities have a career center, and this is one of the best resources on campus for finding out this information. Typically, the career center will have resources such as the Major-Minor Finder, the Focus online assessment, and numerous others. In addition, the career center is likely to be a good source of information about salaries in various careers, projections of demand for specialists in different areas, and information about graduate and professional

Get Involved!

Jaleel spent his whole first semester doing little but studying. He was the first in his family to go to college, and he didn't want to disappoint anyone. His father worked at a construction company his whole life, and although Jaleel knew his father was happy, he also knew he wanted to do something different. He just wasn't exactly sure what that something was. He was taking general education courses and getting all A's, but he knew he needed direction. At the beginning of his second semester, his roommate Sam told him he had to do something other than study. Soon Sam had Jaleel coming along with him to the basketball games that he was covering for the campus newspaper. One day when Sam was unable to make a game, he asked Jaleel to stand in for him. It turned out that Jaleel had a great time, and he discovered he was very good at sports writing. After taking a class or two, he joined the newspaper staff and declared journalism as his major. He is hoping to work for a major city newspaper some day. "The opposite of not taking your classes seriously is taking them so seriously that you never take the time to see what else is out there," Jaleel said of his learning experience. "If I hadn't taken some time off, I might never have found what I really enjoyed. My education began outside the classroom."

schools. Even as a first-year student, it's not too early to begin looking through this information.

Even though there's no rush, in the beginning of your college career, to declare a major immediately, you don't want to wait longer than necessary. Why? Because at a certain point you need to start taking courses in the major in order to progress in a timely way toward graduation. In fact, at most colleges you must declare a major at about the halfway point (around 60 credits). If you wait too long, you may end up taking courses that you don't need and adding to the total number of credits (not to mention time) you will accumulate by graduation. Also, some departments won't allow you to take courses in their majors unless you've declared that major.

Being Undeclared

If you truly cannot find a major, then there is always the possibility of being an undeclared major (also called undecided). One of the advantages of this status is that if you are unsure, it gives you the option of exploring a number of majors before picking one. Some students are admitted to college as undeclared students whereas others revert to that status after starting with one major and realizing it is not working out for them. Other students choose undeclared upon admission because they find the program they want is full, and they feel that they can come in as an undeclared and then transfer into the program they want. This can work, but be aware that sometimes the program that's full upon first admission will remain full (or at least very competitive) all the way through. If switching to such a popular major is your plan, be sure you have a Plan B that you can fall back on. There is nothing wrong with being an undeclared student, but if you are undeclared, you should take it upon yourself—make it your mission—to research actively all of the opportunities you have available.

Declaring and Changing Your Major: What You Need to Know

We earlier noted that the typical student declares and changes majors several times. This is part of the process of being a college student and exploring the possibilities for your future. In fact, it's quite a luxury. In many countries, students essentially choose their majors before college—sometimes even before what we would call high school—and then focus all of their studies on one particular area. Most U.S. colleges not only allow but even encourage students to shop around. The general education curriculum enables you to explore many different courses and areas before you start to narrow your focus to one area.

But what do you need to know before you declare or change your major? First of all, you need to be sure that the major fits your interests and abilities. Is it going to get you where you want to go as a student? Where you want to go professionally? After all, why would you be an accounting major if what you really want to do is become a high school principal? Next, you need to know whether you meet the requirements of the major you are considering. Does it require a certain number of credits, a minimum QPA, or a portfolio? Is being admitted a competitive process where many potential students are applying, or do you simply fill out a form in the department? Once you've determined the basic application procedures, you need to look at the curriculum. What courses are required? Which of them have you already taken?

This process is even more important when you are changing your major than when you are declaring a major for the first time. Why? Because if you're changing majors, you need to know how the courses you've taken already fit into the new curriculum requirements. This is especially important if you're well into your academic career. If you decide to change from a marketing major to a speech communications major, and you already have 90 credits, you are almost certainly going to end up adding credits to the total number you're going to need to graduate. The bottom line: If you change majors late in your career, it's probably going to delay your graduation. Early in your career, it's probably not going to be such a big problem, but in either case, it is highly recommended that you seek out your advisor before making such a decision. Again, as with all of your decisions as a college student, you want a decision of this magnitude to be a well-informed one.

Figuring Out Your QPA

Your QPA, or quality point average (sometimes also called a GPA, or grade point average), is the barometer by which your achievement as a college student is measured. It's only a number, true, but rest assured that this number, for better or worse, is going to be the single piece of data that represents to most people how well you did as a student. When you graduate, many employers will want to know what your QPA is. Naturally, a student with a higher QPA will have more of an initial appeal. You may know how great a personality you have, how well rounded you are, and the like, but if your QPA is below sea level, chances are you're never going to get to the interview to share those traits with anyone. And don't believe what you might hear about having *too high* a QPA and intimidating prospective employers. Although you may be very impressed by the 3.5 QPA you graduated with (and you should be—well done!), the person interviewing you might have graduated with a 4.0. It's a competitive world. If you're planning to go to graduate school, law school, medical school, or some other professional school, your QPA will be one of the main factors used in determining whether to admit you (the others are standardized test scores, references, your application essay, and so on). While you are a student, your QPA will determine whether you're eligible for the Dean's List, honor societies, and scholarships, and it may even be used to determine whether you can be admitted to a certain major. If you're not doing so well, a low QPA can lead to placement on academic probation, loss of financial aid or athletic eligibility, or dismissal from the college. Needless to say, your parents and friends won't be too impressed, either.

For QPAs, most (though not all) colleges use a 4-point system. An A represents 4.0, a B represents 3.0, a C represents 2.0, a D represents 1.0, and, of course, the lowly F represents 0.0. Sounds simple enough. Let's complicate it a little by considering the fact that some colleges have a plus-and-minus system. A B+ might represent 3.33. Or it might represent 3.5. It depends on your college. This information is available in your college's catalogue. The other complicating factor is that the number of quality points you receive for a class depends on the number of credits the class is worth. For example, an A in a 4-credit science class with a lab will earn you more than a 1-credit seminar. Are you confused yet? Let's look at it a little bit differently by examining a sample fall semester grade report for Tran Ly, a first-year student.

Name Tran Ly	Grade	Quality Points	Number of Credits	Total Quality Points Earned	Quality Point Average
English 1	C	2.00	3	6.00	
Biology 100	A	4.00	4	16.00	
College Math	B	3.00	3	9.00	
Psychology 10	B	3.00	3	9.00	
Speech 1	C	2.00	3	6.00	
TOTALS			16	46.00	2.875

As you can see, the QPA is the sum of the total quality points earned (in this case, 46) divided by the total number of credits (16). The Biology 100 course in which Tran received an A helped her average because it was worth 4 credits. That extra credit boosted her quality points by 4.

Now, let's assume Tran is taking 15 credits in the spring semester. Tran needs to have a 3.0 QPA to get into her desired major of biochemistry next fall. How can she figure out what she needs to earn next semester to get that average? First she needs a few pieces of information:

1. Grade point average she is trying to achieve.
2. Credits attempted (including during spring, the current semester).
3. Quality points already earned.

We already know this information. First, she is trying to get a QPA of 3.0. Second, she will have attempted 31 credits by the end of the spring semester. And she has already earned 46 quality points. Now, we plug that information into the following formula:

Credits attempted $\times$ QPA desired $-$ quality points earned = number of quality points needed to earn desired QPA

Let's try it and see how it works using data from Tran's grade report.

31 (credits attempted) $\times$ 3.0 (QPA desired) = 93
93 $-$ 46 (quality points earned) = 47 (number of quality points needed)

In other words, she needs at least 47 quality points to get a QPA of 3.0 for the fall. With 15 credits, if she achieved all A's, or a 4.0 QPA for the semester, that would give her 60 quality points for that semester, raising her overall QPA to 3.42.

Will Tran need any A's in order to get her desired QPA? Yes. At the minimum, she will need four B's (which will give her 36 quality points) and one A (12 more) for a total of 48.

Try this a few times on your own to see what you need to do in order to get the QPA you want. Remember, this formula works for a first-semester first-year student as well as for a junior who is graduating in two semesters. As long as you know the total credits attempted and the quality points earned, you can figure it out. Naturally, the more credits and quality points you have, the more it's going to take to change your QPA significantly. For example, Melanie has a QPA of 3.44 and 265 quality points earned so far, with 77 credits completed. Including the current semester with 15 credits, she will have attempted 92 credits. She wants to get into a professional honor society that requires a cumulative QPA of 3.5. Let's try the formula:

92 (credits attempted) $\times$ 3.5 (QPA desired) = 322
322 $-$ 265 (quality points earned) = 57 (number of quality points needed)

Melanie needs 57 quality points to achieve a 3.5 QPA in one semester. If you remember that an A in a 3-credit class is worth 12 quality points, then you can see that Melanie has to have a very good semester in order to achieve her goal. She will need to get at least four A's and one B—or a 3.8—in order to gain entry into that honor society. She can obviously make it, but you can see the difference the weight of all those credits makes.

When using this formula, just keep in mind a couple of rules:

1. If you repeat a class in which you've gotten an F, you subtract the number of credits of the class from the number of credits attempted.

2. If you repeat a class in which you've gotten a D (or, in some colleges, you can repeat C's), you must subtract the quality points earned from that class from the quality points earned, as well as subtracting the number of credits earned.

Repeating F's (and in some cases higher grades—check with your advisor) is one of the best ways to improve your QPA. Having an F is like having an anchor on your QPA.

Let's look at Rose Swanson's first-semester transcript. She took exactly the same first-semester schedule as Tran Ly. Rose, however, struggled with the adjustment to college. Problems at home affected her grades, as seen below, and she is now in danger of ending up on academic probation:

Name Rose Swanson	Grade	Quality Points	Number of Credits	Total Quality Points Earned	Quality Point Average
English 1	C	2.00	3	6.00	
Biology 100	C	2.00	4	8.00	
College Math	F	0.00	3	0.00	
Psychology 10	F	0.00	3	0.00	
Speech 1	D	1.00	3	3.00	
TOTALS			16	17.00	1.06

Now, with a 1.06, Rose has a long way to go to a 2.0 QPA if she takes 15 new credits.

31 (credits attempted) × 2.0 (QPA desired) = 61
61 − 17 (quality points earned) = 44 (number of quality points needed)

Using our formula, Rose would find she needs 44 quality points, basically all B's (a 3.0 QPA) just to get back to a 2.0 QPA. That's a lot to ask of a student who is just coming off a 1.06.

If, however, Rose decided to retake the two F's, the formula would look like the following (remember that the two F's don't count as new credits, so we've subtracted 6 from the credits attempted):

25 (credits attempted) × 2.0 (QPA desired) = 50
50 − 17 (quality points earned) = 33 (number of quality points needed)

That puts her in much closer range—four C's and one B will equal 33 quality points in a 15-credit schedule. What if she retook the D as well? She might do this in certain circumstances, such as if the class were in her prospective major and required a minimum of C. We'll run the formula again, removing the 3 credits from credits attempted. Remember, we will also have to subtract the 3 quality points she earned for the D.

$$22 \text{ (credits attempted)} \times 2.0 \text{ (QPA desired)} = 44$$
$$44 - 14 \text{ (quality points earned)} = 30 \text{ (number of quality points needed)}$$

Now Rose just needs to get all C's, and she will be back in good academic standing. Before you repeat any course, talk to your advisor, because doing so can have implications for financial aid and other areas. The truth of the matter is, however, that repeating F's (the class, not the grade!) is one of the fastest ways of getting back in good academic standing. Better still, you should avoid ever getting an F in a course if at all possible. One way to do that is through withdrawal.

Withdrawing from a Course: When and Why

Withdrawal policies vary widely from college to college. Some colleges have very liberal policies, allowing you to withdraw from as many courses as you want until very late in the semester. Others are very restrictive, allowing you to withdraw from only a limited number of courses in your career. Most limit the number of weeks into the semester that you can go before withdrawing. Whatever the case, there are two things you need to know about course withdrawal. First, you must clearly understand your college's policy. You don't want to wait too long and find you've missed the deadline. Or discover too late that you've used up all your allotted withdrawals. Second, you need to know that you obviously don't get credit for a class from which you've withdrawn. Also, at most colleges, a withdrawal will appear as a W grade on your transcript. A final transcript that is peppered with W's might raise questions among potential employers or graduate schools.

Under what circumstances should you withdraw from a course? The only courses you should consider withdrawing from are courses in which you are getting a D or an F. Before you actually go about withdrawing from a course, there are three things you should do:

1. **Do a self-assessment.** Are you failing the course? Is there anything you can do to improve your performance? Is it a course you will have to take again with the same professor?
2. **Discuss your thinking with the professor.** Find out what your grade really is. Some students think they are failing but don't realize that the professor is counting participation heavily or that the professor grades harder at the beginning than at the end of the course. Ask the professor what your chances are of achieving the desired grade.
3. **Discuss your decision with your advisor.** How will a withdrawal affect your academic progress, financial aid, and so on? What are the policies and procedures governing withdrawal?

Withdrawing from a course is a big decision and shouldn't be taken lightly. It means that you will receive no credit for all the work you've already done in the course. Don't give up on a class too quickly if there's still a chance that you can pass it. If you do your research, though, you can at least be sure that you are making a well-informed decision about a withdrawal.

Incompletes—When to Take Them, What to Do Later

Sometimes, for reasons beyond your control, you may find that you are unable to complete the work in a class. Maybe you have a major illness during the last two weeks of the semester and are unable to complete the work for a course. Perhaps there's a death in the family that requires you to be out of town for the final. Most colleges have a provision for that known as an Incomplete or I grade. Normally, if you didn't take a final, you would get an F for the course. But because of certain extenuating circumstances, the professor will give you an I grade instead.

There are a couple of things you need to know about I grades. First, they are given only in exceptional circumstances. If you simply sleep through your 8 o'clock final, your professor is more likely to give you an F than an I. Second, a professor has to *know* what's going on with you. If you simply don't show up for the last two weeks, the professor might think you've just dropped the class. If you have an illness or family problem, the best thing to do is to call or e-mail the professor. In a major crisis, you can let the dean of students or the equivalent officer at your college know. At most colleges, that person will inform all of your professors. Finally, getting an I is only the first step. You still have to complete the work in a certain amount of time—usually by a specified time during the next semester. Your college's handbook will tell you exactly how long you have. At most colleges, the I turns into an F automatically if the work is not completed in time. Many professors strongly recommend that, if at all possible, you finish your work during the original semester without taking an I. Why? Because they have seen too many students not finish the work and end up getting an F.

Increasing Your Yield:

Readings for Practical Application

This chapter has covered what is expected of you in college and how you can stay motivated to do your best. You have learned how to manage your time and avoid procrastination. As a time-saving strategy, you have also learned to apply knowledge of your learning style to your own unique study habits. In light of the importance of studying well, this chapter has also discussed avoiding an age-old shortcut: cheating. Learning to learn to the best of your ability, however, is of value only if you can apply it to a field in which you are interested and capable. That is why this chapter also covered choosing or changing your major. Finally, this chapter looked at charting your progress through understanding your GPA and explained how to use the system to your advantage by withdrawing from courses when necessary or taking incompletes so that you have more time to work on the course when you are best able.

In college, it is important for you to keep track of your own performance. In the workplace, the same is true: It is important for you to be able to manage your time to get the job done. Ethical issues in the workplace are another key consideration. The idea of picking your major and knowing your learning style is akin to knowing what career is best for you. If you know you want to be in business, for example, there are many different avenues to pursue in the field: accounting, finance, entrepreneurship, management, and so on. That is why the readings in this chapter focus on the world of business.

The "A Textbook Case" reading, "Gender Differences in Leadership Style" comes from a business textbook. See how understanding your learning style applies to understanding leadership style as discussed in this chapter.

The "Life After College" reading, "How to Design the Perfect Product," gives you an opportunity to think about one of the many options a business major might have in the world of work. If you have never thought about the world of product design, this will be a real eye-opener. It also gives you a glimpse into the differences between engineers and designers and into the roles they play in product development. Think about where you fit into this picture.

Finally, the "Current Issues" selection, "School Lies," looks at the effects of dishonesty in the corporate world. How is dishonesty in the corporate world related to cheating in college? Are there similar consequences? What are the ramifications?

Reading and Study Tips: Business

Unique Features and Comprehension Strategies

Business textbooks are more practical than theoretical. Although theory is introduced in many business textbooks, the emphasis is on how to apply this theory in practice. Examples are often provided to explain this application to the reader. **Try to apply the information to what you know in your "real life." (Work in groups to do this so that you can get ideas from other students.) If you keep up with your reading, applying real-life examples will be much easier. When you take tests or write papers in business courses, professors will be assessing your ability to make real-life applications. Practicing this before tests and papers will give you an edge. Take advantage of this very practical strategy.**

Business textbooks stress real-world (global, national, local) applications. Business textbooks often feature case studies to explain important concepts. The example typically provides the reader with realistic scenarios that include an individual, couple, or small group. Reading through the case study requires the ability to recognize either the mistakes or the effective decisions that the characters made—or, in some cases, failed to make. Often, the case study is drawn from real-world events, and absolute right or wrong decisions are not evident. By reading through the preceding text and then thinking about what factors are or can be applied to the characters in the case study, you will enhance your understanding of real-world applications of the presented material. **Keep up with current business news and trends. Doing so will help you understand what you read and help you make better applications of the concepts you learn in the text. To do this, try to read the newspaper on a regular basis. Whether you read the business section of a local paper or the** *Wall Street Journal,* **you will be better informed about what is going on in the world of business, and you can apply this background information to what you are reading in your textbooks. Not only that, but you will better be able to make informed decisions when it comes to choosing a business major and career, if that is where your interest lies.**

Visual literacy (ability to read charts and graphs) is emphasized. Because a great deal of information can be conveyed through a visual representation of data, charts and graphs are commonly used. Many examples are time-based and, as such, can be better represented through a graph than through words. A typical scenario is compound interest: *The x-axis displays the number of years that an investment is held at an average yearly rate of interest while the y-axis shows the cumulative value of the investment assuming that no money is withdrawn. The value line of the graph would start near the origin of the graph, gradually increase in height relative to the x-axis as the line moves to the right, representing the passage of time, and then increase rapidly along the y-axis relative to the progress along the x-axis as the value of the investment grows.* Now that's not very clear; however, a graph would convey the same information in a much more concise and understandable way. **"Read" the visual information as well. Do not read the charts and graphs first, however. Read the text first, and then use the visual aids to increase your comprehension of the material. Preview the visual aid first by reading the title of the graph or chart; next read the heading and subheadings. Look for any keys available to help you understand the visual display better. Make connections between the visual presentation and what you just read in the text. Try to apply the ideas presented in the visual aid to examples of your own. If you do not understand a visual aid, be sure to ask about it in class, especially if the professor does not review it. Just because something is not reviewed does not mean it will not be on the test.**

Business textbooks emphasize accuracy and ethics. Business textbooks stress the bottom line. The business world is driven by the need to make a profit; therefore, much of the information and many of the examples given revolve around company balance sheets and other financial statements. **Often, the text refers to these accounting tools and forms, and the reader is required to analyze them while**

working through the text. Problems sometimes demonstrate the detrimental effects that intentional abuses and inadvertently unethical practices have on a business's growth and good will as a means of stressing the importance of good judgment and proper business behavior. Pay attention to the ethical concerns as you read through these examples.

Business texts can be very "programmed." Understand the organizational plan of your textbook. Take the time to preview your textbook chapters to get a feel for the author's plan in setting up each chapter. You will then start to see a pattern in the texts and will know when to expect the author to use graphs, charts, or case studies, for instance, to emphasize and explain important information. **Focus on and understand terms, definitions, and concepts highlighted in boldface and italics. Take the time to make note cards (flash cards) for each important term, definition, and concept. Write the information in your own words so that you can remember it better. Also, try to come up with at least one example of your own for each new idea—to help you practice applying information. Such applications could appear on tests—and most likely will!**

Note what the professor is emphasizing in the lecture, and then review those concepts in the text. Professors often lecture from the textbook, emphasizing only the most important information the book contains. **Take advantage of the information that such lectures provide you as the reader. If you are pressed for time, or if you feel overwhelmed with the material presented in your business textbooks, start with the information your professor reviews in the class. This is a good clue to what will be on the tests. Make sure you take extra time to make study cards and notes on this information, and compare these notes to the notes you took in class. If you still have questions, ask in the next class.**

Reading 1: A Textbook Case

The following textbook chapter is included here because of the connection between leadership styles, the topic of this excerpt, and learning styles, which you learned about in this chapter. A good leader recognizes his or her own style of learning, working, and communicating with others, just as a good learner understands his or her own best way to learn. Finding out about yourself in college is one of the best ways to prepare for the world of work, just as is gaining experience in leadership roles through campus activities and organizations. Another interesting subject in this chapter is the difference in leadership styles between males and females. As you read this chapter, think about what type of leader you are and how you could best use your strengths as you participate in campus activities and think about a career.

BEFORE YOU READ

1. Identify ways in which men and women are different. Write your answers in your journal, and then discuss how these differences affect interactions in classes, participation in campus organizations and activities, and possible careers.
2. Think about one male leader and one female leader you know. How do they lead differently?

Gender Differences in Leadership Style
A. J. Dubrin

Controversy over whether men and women have different leadership styles continues. Several researchers and observers argue that women have certain acquired traits and behaviors that suit them for relations-oriented leadership. Consequently, women leaders frequently exhibit a cooperative, empowering style that includes nurturing team members. According to this same perspective, men are inclined toward a command and control, militaristic leadership style. Women find participative management more natural than do men because they feel more comfortable interacting with people. Furthermore, it is argued that women's natural sensitivity to people gives them an edge over men in encouraging group members to participate in decision making.

Here we look briefly at some of the evidence and reasoning that shows that gender differences do and do not exist between the leadership styles of today's organizational leaders. We emphasize the present because many more women hold formal leadership positions today than in previous decades. Also, sex roles are less rigid today.

A significant side issue here is that the terms *sex* and *gender* arouse controversy for both scientific and political reasons. As the term is used by many researchers, *gender* refers to perceptions about the differences among males and females. An example would be believing that women managers tend to be better listeners than their male peers. Sex differences, however, refer to actual (objective and quantitative) differences, such as the fact that the mean height of men exceeds that of women. Despite these observations, the terms *gender* and *sex* are still used interchangeably in general usage and to some extent in scholarly writings. In this era of celebrating diversity, we hope no reader will be offended by either term.

The Argument for Male-Female Differences in Leadership Style
In an article that stimulated considerable debate, Judy Rosener concluded that men and women do tend toward opposite styles. Based on self-reports, she found that men tended toward a command-and-control style. In contrast, women tended toward a transformational style, relying heavily on interpersonal skills.[15] Reporting from Britain, Cary Cooper contends that men tend to manage by punishment and women by rewards. He observes that women are socialized to manage people and relationships in the home, and have taken their skills from the home and transformed them to the workplace.[16]

Bernard M. Bass has found some specific male-female differences in leadership style. Data collected from subordinates suggest that women are less likely to practice management-by-exception (intervening only when something goes wrong).

SOURCE: A. J. Dubrin, "Gender Differences in Leadership Style." In *Leadership: Research Findings, Practice, and Skills,* 3rd ed. (Boston: Houghton Mifflin, 2001), pp. 136–138. Copyright © 2001 by Houghton Mifflin Company. Reprinted with permission.

[15] Judy Rosener, "Ways Women Lead," *Harvard Business Review,* November–December 1990, pp. 119–125.

[16] Quoted in Roz Morris, "Management: Why Women Are Leading the Way," in Michael Syrett and Clare Hogg (eds.), *Frontiers of Leadership* (Oxford, England: Blackwell Publishers, 1992), p. 271.

Yet women and men appear to use contingent recognition with equal frequency. Even when the women leaders studied do practice management-by-exception, they typically temper criticism with positive feedback. Bass also found that women leaders are slightly more likely to be described as charismatic. In a survey of sixty-nine world-class leaders (nine women included), women scored higher on the transformation factor than did men.[17]

Another perspective on gender differences is that women entrepreneurs are more likely than their male counterparts to perceive their business as a family. (Remember Pat Moran of JM Family Enterprises?) As corporate managers, women tend to place greater emphasis on forming caring, nurturing relationships with employees. Women are also more likely than men to praise group members. And when an employee falls short of expectations, women are more likely to buffer criticism by finding something praiseworthy.[18]

A study conducted by Brooke R. Envick uncovered differences in managerial behavior between men and women entrepreneurs. Her most surprising finding was that controlling behavior, previously considered a typically male trait, was actually more prevalent among women entrepreneurs. Envick believes that women entrepreneurs are motivated by the desire to be in control, so it makes sense that control is exhibited at work. The study also found that women entrepreneurs are more likely than men to engage in internal communication and human resource management.[19]

Fundamental differences in the biological and psychological makeup of men and women have also been used as evidence that the two sexes are likely to manifest different leadership styles. One such set of differences has been uncovered by brain researchers Raquel Gur and Ruben Gur.[20] They found that women may be far more sensitive to emotional cues and verbal nuances than men. Women leaders would therefore be more suited to responding to the feelings of group members and understanding what they really mean by certain statements. Gender differences in communication also are reflected in leadership style. Above all, women are more likely to use spoken communication for relationship building and giving emotional support than are men.[21] Men focus more on disseminating information and demonstrating competence. Women are therefore more likely to choose a relationship-oriented leadership style.

The Argument Against Gender Differences in Leadership Style

Based on a literature review, Jan Grant concluded that there are apparently few, if any, personality or behavioral differences between men and women managers. Also, as women move up the corporate ladder, their identification with the male

---

[17] Cited in "Debate: Ways Men and Women Lead," *Harvard Business Review,* January–February 1991, p. 151.

[18] Debra Phillips, "The Gender Gap," *Entrepreneur,* May 1995, pp. 110, 111.

[19] Brook R. Envick, "Behaviors of Entrepreneurs: A Gender Comparison," *Journal of Business and Entrepreneurship,* March 1998, pp. 106–115.

[20] Research reported in Michael Schrage, "Why Can't a Woman Be More Like a Man?" *Fortune,* August 16, 1999, p. 184.

[21] Much of the research on this topic is summarized in Mary Crawford, *Talking Difference: On Gender and Language* (London: Sage Publications, 1995).

model of managerial success becomes important; they consequently reject even the few managerial feminine traits they may have earlier endorsed.[22] Studies reviewed by Bass (other than his own research) indicate no consistent pattern of male-female differences in leadership style.[23]

To what extent these stereotypes of men and women leaders are true is difficult to judge. Even if male and female differences in leadership style do exist, they must be placed in proper perspective. Both men and women leaders differ among themselves in leadership style. Plenty of male leaders are relations-oriented, and plenty of women practice command and control (the extreme task orientation). Many women believe that women managers can be more hostile and vindictive than men managers.

A more important issue is how to capitalize on both male and female leadership tendencies. Connie Glaser believes that the best approach to leadership takes advantage of the positive traits of both men and women. She sees a new management style that blends the male and female sides:

> While the female may impart that sense of nurturing, the sensitivity to individual and family needs, that's offset by certain traits that the male brings to the table. The ability to make decisions quickly, the sense of humor, the risk-taking—those are qualities that traditionally have been associated with the male style of management.[24]

AFTER YOU READ

1. Do you think more evidence exists for gender differences in leadership style or for no gender difference? Provide specific examples.
2. Note the researchers who identify the more nurturing, communicative style of women. What is the basis for this style, according to the researchers?
3. Create a Venn diagram showing the difference between male and female leadership style, according to the chapter.
4. Create a table with the different learning styles as headers for the columns and with the different leadership styles as headers for the roles. In the appropriate spaces, identify where a learning style and a leadership style would blend well. Explain why.
5. Think about a leader or boss you know. Do the characteristics described here fit that person? Why or why not?
6. Do you agree with the statement that the ideal leader would be a blend of male and female styles? Why or why not? Provide an example.
7. What type of leader do you think you are? How will this knowledge help you in college and as you decide on your future career? Be as specific as possible.

---

[22] Jan Grant, "Women as Managers: What Can They Offer Organizations?" *Organizational Dynamics,* Winter 1988.

[23] Bernard M. Bass, *Bass & Stodgill's Handbook of Leadership: Theory, Research, & Managerial Applications,* 3rd ed. (New York: The Free Press, 1990), p. 725.

[24] Quoted in Phillips, "The Gender Gap," p. 112.

Reading 2: Life After College

This reading is included to invite you to ponder the many opportunities in the world of business. Have you ever wondered how a successful product came to be available in the stores? Have you given any thought to the process, time, creativity, and business decisions behind a product you buy? This article offers a glimpse into this world. It also provides an interesting follow-up to our discussions of learning style and time management, as well as to the textbook reading on differences in leadership styles. When it comes to product development, engineers and designers think differently. When you have finished reading this article, ask yourself whether you see yourself as more of an engineer or a designer. Your answer could be very helpful as you begin to explore majors, another topic that we considered in this chapter.

BEFORE YOU READ

1. What would your "perfect product" be? Why?
2. Think about a new product that you have used or purchased. How do you think this product came to market? Why?

How to Design the Perfect Product

K. Hammonds

A visit to Craig Vogel's cluttered office at Carnegie Mellon University is a journey to the intersection of creative destruction and American consumerism. His shelves are a graveyard; a loving anthology; and a shrine to the good, the great, and the truly idiotic. Here's that indestructible metal toaster you used when you were a kid. A few black rotary telephones—the kind that Ma Bell used to make. There are radios, coffeemakers, blenders. And there are potato peelers—lots of potato peelers. More on those later.

Vogel is a professor of design. With Jonathan Cagan, a mechanical-engineering professor at the university, he teaches a course in product development. The two academics research and consult on the subject of new product design for such companies as Ford Motor, Motorola, and Whirlpool. This is what they've learned so far: Companies don't do a very good job of developing new products.

The issue: Engineers are from Mars, designers are from Venus. Engineers tend to obsess over the details of getting products to work—but they're uncomfortable with the critical questions that have to be answered before a new product ever gets to manufacturing. Who will buy it? What value will it add? Designers revel in those sloppier issues, but they tend to cower when confronted with problems related to craftsmanship, durability, and reliability. That results in product after product that fails on one dimension or the other—or worse yet, both.

In their book *Creating Breakthrough Products: Innovation from Product Planning to Program Approval* (Prentice-Hall, 2002), Vogel and Cagan advocate an integrated approach to product design. Innovative new products, the authors argue, come from mastering the "fuzzy front end." They happen when a company delivers on both style and technology in a way that can provide some measure of fantasy.

Surrounded by Coke cans from eras past, toasters, and the occasional potato peeler, Vogel and Cagan spoke with Fast Company about inventing and delivering successful new products.

SOURCE: K. Hammonds, "How to Design the Perfect Product." Reprinted from *Fast Company,* July 2002, 122.

Managing the Fuzzy Front End

Design problem: Merge style with technology. The 1935 Sears Coldspot, developed with designer Raymond Loewy, was a bold leap forward for the lowly refrigerator. Loewy gave the clunky cold box a clean new look, wrapping the cooling unit with sheet metal. He made it easy for owners to open the door, even when their arms were filled with groceries. And he replaced the metal shelves inside with aluminum to prevent rusting. This was an early example of the integration of style and technology—and sales soared.

CAGAN: The "fuzzy front end" is a term we heard used a lot in the industry. It's a very early stage of product development, when you're really not sure what you're designing yet. You're trying to figure out what your opportunity is—and to assess the whole context for that opportunity.

VOGEL: Many people, especially engineers, are uncomfortable with the fuzzy front end. They see getting through it as something you do on the way to a place where you can measure things more effectively. But our message is, you absolutely have to treat that part of the process well. The Coldspot was a very early example of what happens when a company spends enough time on the front end—and the result was effective. Sears and Loewy answered the question, How do you bring this monster machine from the back porch into the kitchen? They saw the opportunity.

CAGAN: A lot of companies just worry about getting the product out. They figure, Let's not worry about this early stuff. We'll focus on manufacturing, and we'll get it to work at the end. So they either create beautifully made products that no one wants, or they miss all of their deadlines because they're trying to catch up at the end. We found that by investing time in the fuzzy front end, you can accelerate the development process.

Form and Function Fulfill . . . Fantasy!

Design problem: Make an impersonal machine into a personal tool. The Wave, from Crown Equipment Corp., isn't your father's forklift. After reviewing industry trends and witnessing the difficulties that warehouse employees had when using rolling ladders to get parts, Crown developed an entirely different product.

The Wave extended Crown's core technical capabilities with less scale and weight. It was safer, quicker, and easier to control.

VOGEL: The traditional definition of value has been to produce the most number of units for the lowest price while getting them into the hands of the most people. But what people value and the way that they interact with a product goes beyond price. The visual form, the way that they handle it, and how it makes them feel are all part of the value statement.

CAGAN: We have tried to create a way for companies to understand their target markets by identifying value opportunities. By really thinking about where the market is at and where you want to go, you can understand the opportunities—and then you create product goals. That's how you help define product.

VOGEL: We've gone from the concept of mass value, where you can have a huge, well-defined market, to a world where value is subdivided and defined in more discrete ways. People still have shared values at one level. But they also bring very discrete values that they want from a product. So a consumer who wants a Subaru Outback is much different from one who wants a Mercedes SUV—even though they both want an all-weather, four-wheel-drive vehicle.

CAGAN: Value is all about fulfilling fantasy. For engineers, their driving statement traditionally has been the concept that form follows function. For designers, it's usually the opposite. But you need both. Your goal is to create a great experience—the fantasy— for the customer.

Fantasy doesn't have to be exotic. You could be working in a warehouse in a parts-pick job. You're running around in sneakers on a rolling ladder and you're mad at the world and it's a terrible job. Wouldn't it be great if you had more control and more power? The Crown Wave is a great example of fulfilling that fantasy. It's small and fun to use. It empowers people. Although it's more expensive than a rolling ladder, workers become more efficient, and they stay in their jobs longer because they're happier.

Scaling the "Sheer Cliff of Value"

Design problem: Find the beauty in a potato peeler. Sam Farber, already a successful entrepreneur, sensed an opportunity in the housewares industry after watching his wife, an arthritis sufferer, struggle with existing kitchen tools. Farber's insight introduced utensils that weren't just comfortable to use, but that also set a new aesthetic standard.

VOGEL: Here's a generic potato peeler, the same one people have used for a century. You have sheet metal wrapped around a form to give it a basic shape, with a center line running through it that both locks the handle together and integrates the blade into the handle. This is about the cheapest way to deliver on a form that has both a blade and a handle. It's dictated more by manufacturing than by the function of its use.

Now look at Farber's version, OXO's Good Grips Swivel Peeler. There's a broad Santoprene handle that makes it easy to grip. The flexible fins make the handle appear lighter and add comfort. And the curved blade shield echoes the shape of the handle. This potato peeler was built from the customer backward rather than from the manufacturer forward. Part of the fantasy here is, I have arthritis and I can't use a standard peeler, but I have an alternative with OXO's version.

CAGAN: It also elevates potato peeling to an aesthetic statement of who we are. Now everyone can own a contemporary product that looks beautiful and has a sort of richness. It takes a mundane task and makes it more enjoyable. You can even hang it up. The upshot is, there's value in that fantasy. The OXO potato peeler costs about $7, which is five times the price of the generic version, but it doesn't cost that much more to make.

VOGEL: We think of product design in terms of a two-by-two matrix: One axis is style, and the other is technology. The generic potato peeler falls into the lower left of the map. It's functional, but it has very little style or defining technology. Great, value-driven products such as the OXO peeler move into the upper right.

CAGAN: You can't just throw an engineer and a designer together and say, Create something in the upper right. There has to be a commitment to do the proper research, and you have to understand the needs and desires of your target market. You have to understand what the opportunity gap is by scanning the social and technology factors and then understand what that gap means—so that when you create a new product, you're bridging that gap. You have to do something significant to get into the upper right. That's why we call it the "sheer cliff of value."

VOGEL: To scale that cliff, you also have to commit yourself to a comprehensive way of working. In the fuzzy front end, there is a lot of trial and error, and you have to be ready for the fact that there are going to be a lot of misses. You need to have people thinking across disciplines and thinking about innovation. What we've seen is that it takes a different sort of commitment to do that.

Now let's look at the Rotato Potato Peeler, which falls into the lower-right quadrant. It is a technically driven peeler, the latest incarnation of the frightening 19th-century mechanical peelers with exposed blades.

CAGAN: As seen on TV!

VOGEL: Companies often try to improve on the generic product simply by adding new technology. Add more gadgets, and make it spin, electrify it, or hand-power it. The Rotato supposedly reduces the amount of labor—but it also takes off at least an eighth of the vegetable.

CAGAN: Plus, the Rotato is cumbersome to use. And it's ugly. You don't really get very much lifestyle impact.

VOGEL: But the American ethic says, If you add more technology, it's always better. If you add a power train or a turbo boost, you've automatically improved it.

CAGAN: The Rotato has an electric arm!

VOGEL: Applying technology to everything isn't always the best solution. And that's what's proven. If you see the Rotato, you might be captivated. My daughter loves it. She wants one of these. But it doesn't create lasting value.

CAGAN: That's not to say you can't have a high-tech product in the upper right—but the technology should match up with the application. The

Apple iMac is a good example. While most personal computers come with lots of features and aren't that easy to use, the iMac has taken an alternative approach, which is virtually the opposite. It comes with a Zen philosophy: Let's be minimalist and give people what they need—and only that.

Staying in the Upper Right

Design problem: Create new value from an old standard. A Black & Decker engineer happened upon the opportunity in his own workshop. He needed a hands-free rechargeable task light that was flexible and could wrap around objects. The SnakeLight debuted in 1994, supported by heavy TV advertising. At the time, Black & Decker projected sales of 200,000 units in the first year. It sold over 600,000. In fact, it took 18 months to catch up with demand.

CAGAN: To stay in the upper right, you have to keep injecting useful, usable, and desirable features. Take the latest OXO peeler. It still has a good grip, but this updated version integrates brushed steel, which is a more contemporary look.

VOGEL: In certain markets, the upper-right quadrant has been less sustainable than others. But the OXO Swivel Peeler has been remarkably sustainable.

Consider Motorola's Talkabout two-way radio. This was a great upper-right product, but it was instantly challenged by companies that were in the walkie-talkie industry and that were wired to compete. They started producing cheaper knockoffs. Motorola had been making huge profits as a result of the Talkabout, and it had to lower prices very quickly to stay competitive.

CAGAN: Here's another example: Look at the SnakeLight. Black & Decker did a great job with patents, but it didn't continue to inject useful, usable, and desirable changes into the product. It dominated the market for four years—but eventually, it lost market share.

VOGEL: It wasn't that the competition was so great. Here's one knockoff: the Pretzl Lite, which is so bad, it's not even in the upper left. It doesn't work well; it looks terrible. But it managed to disguise its problems. When you see the Pretzl Lite in its package, you don't realize all that. The Pretzl Lite successfully drafted off of the SnakeLight's success. So even though the knockoffs were sued successfully, they created a lower-end market segment where people decided that they didn't have to pay as much. As a result, when the knockoffs didn't work, it hurt the credibility of the SnakeLight. And then Black & Decker didn't add any features. After four years, everyone who wanted one already had one.

Keith H. Hammonds (khammonds@fastcompany. com) is a Fast Company senior editor based in New York.

AFTER YOU READ

1. How does the interview approach used in the previous article affect your understanding of the article? Do you think this is a good approach for the topic? Why or why not? What are some potential drawbacks?

2. How are engineers and designers different? How are they the same? Make a chart to illustrate these differences. What do Vogel and Cagan argue that both professionals need? How is being an engineer or a designer also related to different learning styles? What learning style would an engineer tend to have? What learning style would a designer tend to have? Why?

3. Think again about the product you identified in your reflective writing before you read this article. Do you now think differently about how the product came to be? Why?

4. Vogel and Cagan argue that subdivided and discrete values have replaced mass values. Provide your own example that suggests this is true.

5. Do you see yourself as more of an engineer or more of a designer? Why?

6. Discuss as a group what Vogel and Cagan mean by the "fuzzy front end" of product design. Choose a current product that you use and identify what you think was the "fuzzy front end" of its creation. Would this product be in Vogel and Cagan's "upper right"? Why or why not? Create a visual aid and present your product and discussion to the class as a whole.

Reading 3: Current Issues

This chapter focused on the important topic of cheating—why it should be avoided and how to avoid it. You have had the opportunity to reflect on why cheating in school could have serious consequences. The following article will give you an opportunity to think about the negative consequences of cheating in the corporate world—specifically, lying about one's own credentials. Think about how important a college degree is to you. Are you willing to exert the effort required to achieve your goal? What if someone who never attended your college or university claimed he graduated from the institution? How would that make you feel? Also, how important do you think credentials are? Are they more important than experience? Is falsifying your credentials wrong or not? Consider how you feel about these issues as you read this article.

BEFORE YOU READ

1. Which do you think is more valued in American business, honesty or success? Explain your answer.
2. How important is honesty at work? Why?

School Lies

D. Gross

The past few weeks have seen a spate of mini-controversies about top executives fudging their educational credentials. On Oct. 18, TheStreet.com's indefatigable Herb Greenberg revealed that Bausch & Lomb CEO Ronald Zarrella falsely claimed an MBA from New York University's Stern School of Business. While he attended the program from 1972–76, he never obtained the sheepskin.

On Oct. 4, the résumé of Kenneth Lonchar, the CFO of Veritas Software, was found deficient in *veritas*. Lonchar said he earned an accounting degree from Arizona State University and an MBA from Stanford. But all he actually has is an undergraduate degree from Idaho State University.

And in late September, Ram Kumar, director of research at Institutional Shareholder Services, the influential firm that advises shareholders on whether takeovers are good deals, was cashiered when it was discovered that he didn't have a law degree from the University of Southern California, as he had claimed. (He was a few credits short.)

Does it matter if executives overstate their educational credentials? After all, every corporation has an apparatus—it's called a corporate communications department—that churns out occasionally misleading data aimed at burnishing the image of the company and its executives. It's easy to see how an eager flack could enshrine a casual exaggeration into a permanent feature of an executive biography.

SOURCE: D. Gross, "School Lies: Why Do So Many Executives Lie About Their Education?" *Slate,* October 22, 2002. Retrieved December 21, 2003, from http://slate.msn.com/?id=2072961. Reprinted by permission of United Media Enterprises.

In this era of scandal, résumé-padding is being portrayed as a kind of gateway crime on the way to Enron-style fraud. The implication is that executives who fudge their résumés may be more likely than other bosses to play games with their numbers. Now-disgraced Salomon Smith Barney analyst Jack Grubman, for example, said he attended Massachusetts Institute of Technology, when he in fact studied at nearby Boston University. Merrill Lynch analyst Scott Phillips downgraded Veritas after the Lonchar disclosure. "Our first concern is that the CFO's falsification of his educational credentials could suggest the financials are suspect."

If analysts followed Phillips' logic and cut ratings based on executive fibs—casual and not-so-casual—the street would be hit by a slew of downgrades. What precisely constitutes an episode of downgradable dishonesty? Cheating on your wife? Writing a 7 instead of the 8 you really shot on the 13th hole at Pebble Beach?

There's no evidence that exaggerating academic prowess is a contraindicator for competence. The financials of Veritas, which sports a $6 billion market cap, are comparatively sound. Ram Kumar's ISS work was sufficiently esteemed that many feel his report tipped the balance in favor of the Hewlett-Packard Compaq deal.

What's more, some of the most egregious recent episodes of financial chicanery were perpetrated by people who told the truth about their education. Jeffrey Skilling surely never lied about having attended Harvard Business School. However, his congressional testimony calls to mind Mary McCarthy's famous dis of Lillian Hellman: "Every word she says is a lie, including 'and' and 'the.'"

Still, it's mystifying why a mature, successful executive would lie about a degree he may or may not have obtained 20 or 30 years ago. Sure, an MBA from Stanford or Harvard might gain its holder entrée into a prestigious firm. But at the top of the profession, experience and track records tend to matter far more than credentials. No 50-year-old executive gets hired for a top job simply because he has the right degree. And the absence of an MBA is no barrier to raising capital or rising in a corporation. (Or to being regarded as a management genius: Neither Jack Welch nor Bill Gates has an MBA. Gates never even finished college.)

Company boards rarely discuss the university educations of their candidates for top executive positions. When Bausch & Lomb's board hired Zarrella as CEO a year ago, it knew all it needed to know about him firsthand. Zarrella had spent nearly a decade at the company and rose to president and chief operating officer before leaving in 1994 for a senior post at General Motors. And if a board member were to hear a rumor that a sitting CEO had trouble spots on his résumé, it's doubtful he would raise a stink. To a large degree, the top echelons of corporate America are a private club in which members simply don't ask impolite questions about other members.

In fact, some large corporations today probably conduct more exhaustive background checks on entry-level security guards than they do on CEOs. For even a cursory probe would uncover educational fibs quickly. Companies like Kroll Associates provide a background check for a mere $5,000. A free-lance fact-checker will divine the necessary data for $15 per hour. Given the fact that the unearthing of a suspect educational credential can be costly—Veritas' stock lost nearly $1.14 billion on the news of Lonchar's resignation—it's certainly a worthwhile investment.

But those who falsely claim the most cherished diplomas rarely escape being found out. Graduates of credential mills like Harvard and Stanford are inordinately jealous of their diplomas and have developed exceptional abilities to ferret out posers. That's why Lonchar's presumption of a Stanford degree was so brazen. Silicon Valley is rotten with Stanford MBAs, and it's a place where discussing school ties is a way for people to break the ice and establish connections. Falsely claiming a Stanford degree on Sand Hill Road is a little like walking around Park Slope, Brooklyn, and trying to pass as a book editor—within a few minutes you'll run into somebody who, with a well-aimed "Do you know?" or "I just had lunch with," can unmask your falsehood.

Self-created entrepreneurs have frequently found it necessary to invent the educational credentials that those in the circles to which they aspire possess effortlessly. Take last century's greatest self-made entrepreneur. Jay Gatsby claimed he was "educated at Oxford, because all my ancestors have been educated there for many years." In his pocket he carried a "souvenir of Oxford days," a photo of himself holding a cricket bat with, among others, the Earl of Dorcaster.

Gatsby's claim to an Oxford education—he may have spent a few months there but certainly didn't have a degree—impressed the book's most significant financier. Meyer Wolfsheim took a shine to Gatsby in part because, as an "Oggsford" man, he was presumed to have important "gonnegtions."

It took a jealous Yalie, Tom Buchanan, who made a "small investigation of his past," to lay bare Gatsby's lie:

> *"An Oxford man!" He was incredulous. "Like hell he is! He wears a pink suit. . . . Oxford, New Mexico," snorted Tom contemptuously, "or something like that."*

AFTER YOU READ

1. From what novel is the quotation at the end of this article? What is the significance of comparing current dishonest CEOs to Jay Gatsby? If you are unfamiliar with the novel from which this quotation is taken, how effective do you think it is to use an excerpt from a novel as an analogy?

2. What confuses the author about a 50-year-old executive lying about where he graduated from college? Do you find it confusing or not? Why?

3. What do you think the author believes is more important—from what college one graduates or what experience one gains over the years? Why? What do you think?

4. This chapter discussed the unique features of business textbooks and how you could better comprehend them by applying specific comprehension strategies. One such feature is the case study. Business textbooks tend to use case studies to help readers understand important concepts. What case studies were provided in this article? How do they help the reader understand the content of the article? As a group, research a particular case study of corporate cheating not mentioned in this article (the example could involve any form or cheating or dishonesty in the workplace). Present your case study to the class, including the details of the wrongdoing and the results.

Compounding Your Interest: Further Readings

Bassidy, L., & Charan, R. (2002). *Execution: The Discipline of Getting Things Done.* New York: Crown.

Covey, S. (1989). *Seven Habits of Highly Effective People.* New York: Simon and Schuster.

Fitzgerald, F. S. (1995). *The Great Gatsby.* New York: Scribners.

Keen, S. (1991). "The Price of Success." *Fire in the Belly.* New York: Bantam.

Morgenstern, J. (2000). *Time Management from the Inside Out.* New York: Henry Holt.

Velasquez, M. G. (2001). *Business Ethics: Concepts and Cases*, 5th ed. New York: Prentice-Hall.

Chapter 3

Earning the Grade by Reading and Note Taking at the College Level

If this is not your first day at college and you have been to a few classes, you have already become aware of another important fact about college: You have to read and take notes. A lot. There is no escaping this reality. In fact, you will do it extensively in most of the classes you take in college.

The sheer amount of reading assigned at the college level can be overwhelming. In fact, you may regularly be expected to read as many as three chapters between one class meeting on, say, Monday and the next on Wednesday. If you carry at least fifteen credits, you could have five professors asking you to do the same amount of work. And this doesn't even take into account the fact that much of this reading consists of difficult material about which you have very little prior knowledge. You are not alone. Whether you love or hate a subject, whether you had it in high school or not, whether the text is boring or exciting, the sheer amount of words and the content you need to grasp and remember may never seem greater than when you first come to college. You need to learn some "tricks of the trade."

As far as notes are concerned, many of your classes will be primarily lecture. Some professors, in fact, rely more on their lecture notes than on the textbook when it comes to exams. Even if you are an efficient reader, you cannot let your note-taking abilities slide. Reading and note taking go hand in hand. Needless to say, then, going to class is a very good idea. So is being prepared to take good notes while still paying attention. Finding a balance is the key.

Now that you recognize the importance of reading and note-taking at the college level, you have certain options in how you approach it: Don't do it; avoid it until the last minute and get very little out of your effort; set out with no

---

Think About It

Answer the following questions in the space provided.

What approach do you take now when you read a chapter in a textbook? Is it an effective strategy? Why or why not? _____

_____

_____

_____

plans or strategies and let it consume all of your time; or build a reserve of tips and strategies to get the job done well, efficiently, and with time to spare. This chapter will help you choose and use the last one.

First Things First

Before embarking on a reading and note-taking journey, you need to know a few things. First, what are you supposed to be reading? What are you supposed to be taking notes on? What will the tests cover? Are there supplemental materials you need to read in order to be prepared for tests? All these questions should be answered on your professor's syllabus. If they are not, ask! All your effort will be a waste of time if you are reading or taking notes on the wrong content. Second, know what kind of time you have to read and how much time you will have to review your notes before each exam. Managing your reading and note review time is a very important part of the learning process. A little planning goes a long way to avoid last-minute panic.

Previewing Your Textbooks

Think about this for a moment: Would you rent a movie without reading the back of the tape or DVD? Chances are you read the preview on the back either to remember what the story was about from when you saw it in the movie theater, or to decide whether you will enjoy it. Likewise, the preview on the back tells you something about the main characters, the plot, and the setting. If you have ever turned on a movie without knowing anything about it, chances are you had a lot of questions or were at least a bit confused. Plunging right into reading a textbook chapter without previewing it is a lot like this. And who wants to get about five pages into a difficult chapter due the next day, only to have to go back and reread it? Previewing works.

Here's how to preview a textbook chapter:

1. Read the **title** and **introduction** to the chapter.
2. Read all the **headings** printed in boldface type.
3. Look at all the **graphs**, **charts**, **illustrations**, and **photos.** This will let you know what the textbook author(s) considered important enough to enhance with graphics. Moreover, graphics are often easier to understand than text at first glance.
4. Read the **conclusion** or chapter summary. (This is not like a novel. When you study, you don't want to be surprised at the end!)
5. Read the **review questions** at the end of the chapter and skim the **vocabulary words** that may appear at the end. These are the terms you want to watch out for while you are reading the chapter.
6. You are almost ready to begin reading—after you write some guide questions.

Using Guide Questions

Guide questions give you something to *look for* as you are reading. Furthermore, writing your own guide questions and reading to find the answers is an active learning activity. Reading alone can be very passive, but the more active we make it, the better our comprehension and memory of what we have read. This technique, then, also becomes a time saver. Far too many students who don't read actively end up having to read all over again before the test. And that just doesn't make any sense.

When you set up questions and read to find the answers, you have a better chance of remaining focused on the task at hand. Also, you actually see whether you are making progress and comprehending what you are reading. Can you answer the questions? If so, you are on the right track. The key, however, is to answer the questions *in your own words*. Simply writing down the exact words from the textbook is just another passive activity. And transferring them from the text to your notebook doesn't mean you understand them. Explaining in your own words does.

Here are some tips for writing guide questions:

▶ Turn the boldface, or bold, chapter headings into questions.
▶ Turn the bold terms that appear throughout the chapter into questions.
▶ Create "main idea" questions about the whole chapter.
▶ Take a shortcut and use the study questions at the end of the chapter. Read them, write them down, and then read the text to find the answers as you go along.
▶ For readings without headings, take a cue from the title. What do you think the reading will be about? Read the introductory paragraph. From the title and introductory paragraph, develop some questions you hope the rest of the reading will answer.

Below you will find a brief excerpt from a chapter in the textbook *An Introduction to Chemistry* by Mark Bishop. Skim the passage, but do not read it. Next, note the guide questions that follow the passage. With the guide questions in mind, go back and read the passage. Then try to answer the questions.

Accuracy and Precision

Precision describes how closely a series of measurements of the same object resemble each other. The closer the measurements are to each other, the more precise they are. The precision of a measurement is not necessarily equal to its accuracy. **Accuracy** describes how closely a measured value approaches the true value of the property.

To get a better understanding of these terms, let's imagine a penny that has a true mass of 2.525 g. If the penny is weighed by five different students, each using the same balance, the masses they report are likely to be slightly different. For example, the reported masses might be 2.680 g, 2.681 g, 2.680 g, 2.679 g, and 2.680 g. Because the range of values is $+/-0.001$ g, of 2.680 g, the precision of the balance used to weigh them is said to be $+/-0.001$ g, but notice that none of the measured values is very accurate. Although the precision of our measurement is $+/-0.001$ g, our measurement is inaccurate by 0.155 g (2.680 − 2.525 = 0.155). Scientists recognize that even very precise measurements are not necessarily accurate.

Guide Questions

1. What is precision?
2. What is accuracy?
3. What is the difference between the two?
4. What is an example of each?

M. Bishop, "Accuracy and Precision." In *An Introduction to Chemistry* (San Francisco: Benjamin Cummings, 2002), p. 20. Reprinted by permission of Mark Bishop.

When you encounter a textbook section like the one above, skim the text and then try to form guide questions like the ones created above. These questions will focus your reading and help you know what information to gather. Also, being able to answer them will determine whether you understand what you have read.

To Highlight or Not to Highlight

That is a good question. And one with a clear answer—most of the time. Sometimes nothing is more inviting than a shiny new yellow highlighter waiting to be slid across a pristine white page. Doing so can even convince you that you are really reading something. But you may be deceived. Most of the time, the answer to the question of whether or not to highlight is *don't*. Think about it. What do you do when you highlight? What are you really doing when you take that nice thick marker to the crisp new page of your textbook? You are simply changing the color of your text from black to yellow or green or blue. Have you really done anything else? Sure, you have decided something looks important enough to highlight. That in itself is a good step. But all too often, many things look important, and pretty soon the whole page is yellow. Then you are back to where you started. If your ratio of yellow text to black text is very high, you haven't accomplished the aim of highlighters in the first place. That is why, in most cases, using them is just not a

The Hard Way

"When I was in high school, I always did fine by listening in class and studying at the last minute. I didn't bother taking textbooks home," lamented Lea as she looked back on her habits coming into college last semester. "I actually always got good grades and never thought anything of it. College, however, was a different story." Lea was able to be philosophical about it later: "My first semester, I took a few difficult courses—biology, psychology, and economics. I had textbooks, but thought I could get by just going to class and taking good notes." Lea realized later how wrong she was. "I got very involved during my first semester—cheerleading, pledging a sorority, going to parties. . . . I didn't think I had the time to read the books. After my first psychology test (I got a 42), I knew I needed to read the book and read it well. So I read every chapter assigned for the next test. I was ready. When I got the test back, however, I only got a 64. What I was doing wrong was not reading right. I didn't take notes or look for the important information while I read. I was forgetting everything, so I went to the Academic Skills Center on our campus and sat down with a graduate student. She showed me how to annotate my texts. The next test, I got an 80. I was on the way up!" Best of all, Lea realized that she did have time to read. Annotating allowed her to read in small chunks and check her comprehension as she went along. Then she just studied her notes when it came time for the test. "Annotating may seem like extra work, but it was actually a great time saver."

good idea. Highlighters are meant to separate information out from a sea of text—to help us focus on main ideas, important terms, and so on. Yet all too often, plain and simple, too much gets highlighted. And this highlighting, then, also becomes a passive activity. How active does your brain have to be to run a yellow marker over some black type? Instead, get out the same pen you used to write some guide questions and start thinking about having a conversation with your text. Force yourself to write something in your own words (see **Annotating Your Textbooks** below). Then, when you have done that, you may want to go back and use the highlighter—sparingly—when you know what really is important. You can also highlight key words when you are trying to formulate your guide questions. It works.

Annotating Your Textbooks

There is very little mystery to reading for understanding and long-term memory. In order to accomplish these things, you must make your reading an active pursuit. It has to be more than opening the book to the assigned pages, moving your eyes across the text, and putting in the time until you get to the end of the chapter. One of the best ways to turn reading at the college level into an active pursuit is to learn how to annotate your textbook. If you give annotation a try, you may never go back to other ways of reading your texts. It is highly efficient and pretty painless once you get used to it.

Some students may cringe at the thought of having to take notes while reading, which is exactly what annotating is. However, those same students may be the ones who don't remember what they have read and always have to go back and do it over again. Annotating enables you to read something once and read it well. This is because you have a conversation with your text. You read short sections of information at a time, decide what information is most important from that short section, express it in your own words, and write those words right in the margin of the text, thus reducing the text to what is most important. Think of it as "clearing the clutter." While you are doing this, you may even underline or circle important words or terms with the same pen you are writing with—no highlighter required.

Five Easy Annotation Steps

1. Throw away the highlighters and pick up a paper and pen or pencil instead.
2. Preview what you are about to read.
3. Begin reading in "chunks." That is, take the information in small sections or paragraphs. When you have finished reading a small section or paragraph, go back and underline the most important points.
4. Then summarize the information in your own brief words and phrases—not sentences (that takes too long and defeats the purpose!). This will help you check your understanding of that section and distill the text down to what is most important. Do not tell yourself you will do it all after you finish reading the chapter; chances are you won't, and you won't remember each paragraph anyway. Take the time to write summaries after each section. Have an ongoing conversation with yourself. Talk out loud if it helps, asking yourself, "What did I learn here?" or "What is the gist of this section?" Then use abbreviations or numbers to speed the process along.
5. Repeat step 4 until you have finished the reading assignment.

Two Bonus Steps (for even better results)

6. Go back and transfer your marginal notes to **index cards**, again rewording and reducing to get one point or idea on each card. These cards can be set up as question and answer cards as well.
7. Finally, *live with the cards*. Cards don't help the night before a test. Create some after each reading assignment and review a few of them daily, in your spare moments (and you can find plenty of those if you try). Also, carrying a few cards beats carrying a few heavy textbooks, which you probably won't do. You can take index cards anywhere. If you live with and review the cards, you will be amazed at how much you remember at test time and how little rereading you will have to do. Your memory works best when given time, and you will always remember best what you say in your own words. A little review over a long period of time goes a long way! You will never again waste time when reading for a test.

Remember: It may seem to take more time to get reading done when you first use this strategy, but stick with it. Always abbreviate and summarize concisely in

Classification of Matter

Before getting started on your chemistry homework, you go into the kitchen to make some pasta for your six-year-old nephew. You run water into a pan, adding a few shakes of salt, and while you're waiting for it to boil, you pour a cup of coffee. Then you add some sugar to your coffee.

Compound: Contains 2 or more elements. Atoms in elements combine in same # ratio

Pure water, the sucrose in white sugar, and the sodium chloride in table salt are all examples of chemical compounds. A **compound** is a substance that contains two or more elements, the atoms of those elements always combining in the same whole-number ratio. There are relatively few chemical elements, but there are millions of chemical compounds. The compounds in our food fuel our bodies, and the compounds in gasoline fuel our cars. They can alter our moods and cure our diseases.

Water = H_2O
Sugar = $C_{12}H_{22}O_{11}$

Water is composed of molecules that contain 2 atoms of hydrogen and 1 atom of oxygen. We describe the composition of water with the chemical formula H_2O. White sugar is a highly purified form of sucrose, whose chemical formula is $C_{12}H_{22}O_{11}$. Its molecules are composed of 12 carbon atoms, 22 hydrogen atoms, and 11 oxygen atoms. Sodium and chlorine atoms combine in a $1:1$ ratio to form sodium chloride, $NaCl$, which is the primary ingredient of table salt.

Chemical Formula = parts of compound Elements in symbol # of atoms in subscripts

Note that a **chemical formula** is a concise written description of the components of a chemical compound. It identifies the elements in the compound by their symbols and indicates the relative number of atoms of each element with subscripts. If an element symbol in a formula is not accompanied by a subscript, the relative number of atoms of that element is assumed to be 1.

Pure substance = constant composition Mixtures = or more pure substances (composition variable)

Pure water, sodium chloride, and sucrose always have the composition described in their chemical formulas. In other words, their composition is constant. Elements, too, have a constant composition described by a chemical formula. (We have seen that the formula for hydrogen is H_2.) When a substance has a constant composition—when it can be described by a chemical formula—it must by definition be either an element or a compound, and it is considered a **pure substance**. For example, the symbol Na refers to pure sodium. The formula Na_2CO_3 refers to pure sodium carbonate and tells us that this compound is always composed of sodium, carbon, and oxygen in a constant atom ratio of $2:1:3$.

Bishop, *An Introduction to Chemistry*, "Classification of Matter," pp. 96–97. (San Francisco: Bejamin Cummings, 2002). Reprinted with permission of Mark Bishop.

your own words. And realize that you will be making up the time on the other end—when it matters most—right before tests and finals. You will come to like this strategy, and the more you use it, the easier it will get. You will never pick up a highlighter again.

Above you will find another passage from Bishop's textbook *An Introduction to Chemistry*. Read the passage and see how the reader annotated it.

Try it yourself: Read the following passage, and then annotate using the steps given above.

How do your marginal notes look?

Equal and Unequal Sharing of Electrons

Let's first consider the compound hydrogen chloride, HCl. When HCl is dissolved in water, the resulting mixture is called hydrochloric acid. Not only is this mixture a very common laboratory agent, but it is also used in food processing and to treat the water in swimming pools.

[Earlier], we learned about the bond between hydrogen atoms in H_2 molecules. We saw that the 2 electrons in the H_2 molecule are shared equally between the atoms and can be viewed as an electron-charge cloud surrounding the hydrogen nuclei. This sharing creates a covalent bond that holds the atoms together. There is also a covalent bond between the hydrogen atom and the chlorine atom in each molecule of HCl. It is very similar to the covalent bond in hydrogen molecules, with one important exception.

The difference between the H-Cl bond and the H-H bond is that the hydrogen and chlorine atoms in HCl do not share the electrons in the bond equally. In the hydrogen-chlorine bond, the two electrons are attracted more strongly to the chlorine atom than to the hydrogen atom. The negatively charged electrons in the bond shift toward the chlorine atom, giving it a partial negative charge, $\delta-$, and giving the hydrogen atom a partial positive charge, $\delta+$. The lower case Greek delta, δ, is a symbol that represents *partial* or *fractional*.

When the electrons of a covalent bond are shared unequally, the bond is called a **polar covalent bond**. As a result of the unequal sharing of the electrons in the bond, a polar covalent bond has 1 atom with a partial positive charge, $\delta+$, and 1 atom with a partial negative charge, $\delta-$.

Bishop, M. *An Introduction to Chemistry,* "Equal and Unequal Sharing of Electrons," p. 100. (San Francisco: Bejamin Cummings, 2002). Reprinted with permission of Mark Bishop.

How do your marginal notes compare to the ones on the previous passage?

 DIY: Do-It-Yourself Activity

Make it a goal to read at least part of a newspaper every day. For one thing, reading daily will help you read more rapidly. As a runner gets faster by taking training runs, so does a reader become a faster and better reader by reading. Also, you will keep up with current events, which will help you to be a more critical participant in class and in the world around you. If you don't wish to purchase a newspaper, the library has many daily newspapers that you can read while you are there or online. Make it a habit!

Outlining

Outlining is another note-taking strategy you may want to try with certain textbooks. Outlining works best with very linear texts (biology, chemistry, and history, to name a few). The best type of outline, and the one that you are most likely to stick with, is the informal outline. Unlike a formal outline, which uses Roman numerals, an informal outline uses just bullets and dashes. With this type of outline, you identify main topics and then list the subtopics under each main topic. It is

• Previewing Your Textbooks

—

—

—

• Using Guide Questions

—

—

—

• To Highlight or Not to Highlight

—

—

—

• Annotating Your Textbook

—

—

—

generally easy to pick out the main topics and subtopics when reading a textbook. The best way to find them is to use the previewing strategy discussed earlier in this chapter. Look for boldface section headings, definitions, and terms. In some cases, the authors have already outlined the chapter for you. If so, use this outline as a starting point, filling in more details as you read the chapter. Above are the topics in this chapter so far; now you fill in the subtopics.

Summarizing What You Have Read

During college, you are going to be asked to write summaries. And even if you are not asked, you may want to write them because summarizing is a good way to assess whether you fully understand information you have read. Writing a summary is a skill that should be learned early and used often.

What is a summary? Think of it as a shortened version of what you have just read. It should include the author's thesis (main idea) and the author's major supporting points. A summary should not be encumbered by details (supplying details is what the original is for), nor should it be an exact replica of the original (why write it then?). A summary should be expressed in your own words, but it should not include your opinions. Let's say you just saw a new movie and a friend asked you what it was about. If you were to respond with every memorable detail, your friend might be pretty annoyed, and also, there would be no reason for her to see the movie. Most likely, you would summarize the main plot and add some information about the setting and characters. If you were asked for your opinion, you could give it, but that would not be a part of what the movie was about. This holds true for summaries. Summaries are going to be critically important to you in college. They are very basic and yet, for many students, very difficult to write. Here are the steps you can take to summarize what you read:

1. Preview what you need to read.
2. Identify the author's thesis (put the reading's main idea into your own words).
3. Annotate and underline the major supporting points.
4. Write a summary by:
   a. Writing the author's thesis in your own words (this becomes the thesis of your summary)
   b. Writing, in your own words, the author's supporting points.

Remember that a summary should be brief. A summary of a one-page article, for example, should be a single short paragraph. Also, the best way to focus on what should be in a summary (and what should be left out) is to *think of an umbrella.* The umbrella itself is the author's thesis, and the other sentences you write should express only what is covered by that thesis. What is not covered by the thesis should not be in the summary (the raindrops that fall around you, hitting the ground away from the umbrella, would include your personal opinions on the author's thesis or supporting points). Be brief. Be concise. You are not rewriting or editorializing; rather, you are highlighting the "gist" of what was said. It is that simple.

Read the passage on the next page, an excerpt reprinted in Bishop's *An Introduction to Chemistry,* and then examine the summary below. Take note of the format of the summary in order to see how a good summary is organized.

Summary: Read the following summary of the passage on the next page. Look for the thesis and supporting points. Also, does it fit with the "umbrella" concept?

Forensic scientists have improved the use of fingerprints in solving crime through new discoveries. First of all, they have identified three different types of fingerprints: plastic (prints left on soft material), visible (prints left with easily detectible materials like blood or ink), and latent (prints made with materials like oils or perspiration that cannot be seen until made visible by the addition of a substance). They have also discovered a difference between the prints of adults and the prints of children. They have found that adults have a higher concentration of molecules called esters, which cause strong attraction and low evaporation, making adults' prints linger longer at crime scenes. These discoveries have lead to a greater rate of crime solving and conviction.

Chemistry Gets the Bad Guys

We've all seen it on TV and in the movies … the detective arrives at the crime scene and stalks into the room wearing a trench coat. The area is taped off, and the experts from the crime lab are already "dusting for prints." In the movies, this usually means spreading black powder that will stick to the fingerprints, but in the real world, forensic scientists have developed new and better ways to make fingerprints visible and help identify "the perp."

There are three types of fingerprints. If the people investigating a crime are lucky, the fingerprints will be either *plastic* (impressions left in soft material such as wax or paint) or *visible* (imprints made by blood, dirt, ink or grease). Usually, however, the fingerprints are *latent* (invisible patterns that must be made visible before they can be of use). Latent fingerprints are composed of perspiration, oils, amino acids, proteins, inorganic salts (such as sodium and potassium chloride), and many other substances. In order to make latent fingerprints visible, the investigator covers the area with a substance that either sticks to them more than to the surfaces they're sitting on or, in some cases, reacts chemically with the fingerprint components.

A 1993 kidnapping case provided forensic chemists with a puzzling problem. An 8-year-old was kidnapped in Knoxville, Tennessee, but fortunately, she was able to escape and identify the car used in the kidnapping. When the car was checked for fingerprints, the investigators found many latent fingerprints of the car's owner, but they could not find any fingerprints of the kidnapped girl. Knowing that this would raise doubts in the minds of the jury, they began to study differences between the fingerprints of children and adults in hopes of finding an explanation. They found that an adult's fingerprints contain a relatively high concentration of molecules called esters that are produced by the oil glands on a grown person's face and then transferred to the fingers when they touch the face. These esters are not produced until after puberty, so they are not found in a child's fingerprints. The ester molecules are very large, with strong attractions that lead to low rates of evaporation. This discovery, which explained why the owner's fingerprints could be found even after the child's prints had evaporated, helped convince the jury that the car's owner was guilty.

Doris R. Kimbrough and Ronald De Lorenzo, "Solving the Mystery of Fading Fingerprints with London Dispersion Forces," used with permission from the *Journal of Chemical Education 75*, no. 10 (October 1998), 1300–1301. In Bishop, *An Introduction to Chemistry*, "Chemistry Gets the Bad Guys," p. 593. (San Francisco: Benjamin Cummings, 2002). Reprinted with permission of Mark Bishop. Copyright © 1998, Division of Chemical Education, Inc.

Assessing a Professor's Lecture Style—and What It Means for You

Rosario has five different classes this semester. Her writing and biology professors are both great. They are lively and entertaining and assign lots of hands-on and group activities. Her speech professor, on the other hand, acts as though he's giving a speech—the most boring speech in the world. He never looks up, speaks in a monotone voice, and reads directly from his notes. Her psychology professor lectures, too, and shows a lot of things on PowerPoint. Because of this, the professor turns the lights down, which makes it hard for Rosario to stay awake. Finally, her political science professor cracks a lot of jokes, sometimes teasing students in a good-natured way. Rosario finds this really helpful in keeping her attention.

Get Involved!

Speaking of reading, one of the places on campus where you will do a lot of it is the library. Why not consider working there? The campus library is a major student employer, and working on campus can provide you with many benefits. The obvious is extra cash, but less obvious may be that students who have a part-time job learn to manage their time better than those who have more free time. Also, a campus job can give you a chance to meet new people and expose you to things you knew little about. (In the library, for instance, you will encounter the map room, the children's literature collection, and the audio visual desk. Who knows, it may get you thinking about career possibilities!)

Anthony has five classes too, but he sees things a little differently. He doesn't like group activities much because he feels he ends up doing all of the work. His writing and biology professors "waste time," in his opinion, with all of these activities. He likes speech because he's a good note taker, and the professor speaks clearly and has a lot of good material in his notes. He loves psychology because the professor shows everything on PowerPoint, making it really easy to follow. Also, with the lights turned down, Anthony finds it easier to concentrate. He hates political science, though, because the professor gets off track making dumb jokes. Worst of all, Anthony hates to be embarrassed, and the professor sometimes makes fun of him.

Get the picture? Rosario and Anthony are in the same five classes, with the same professors, of course. Why the different perceptions? Because Rosario and Anthony are different people, and they like different things in their teachers. Rosario is a little more outgoing and likes to be active in her class. Anthony prefers a quieter class, with more direct instruction from his professors. Yet they both want—and need—the same things from their classes: to learn and to get good grades. If it is not possible for them to change to sections with other professors, does that mean they're out of luck? No. But first, note that sometimes you can change professors. How? If you do some research ahead of time—and you should do research by talking to friends and your academic advisor—you might be able to avoid some professors who just don't match your style. Naturally, your friends are going to have different perceptions than an academic advisor. But make sure the friends you consult about this matter respond to the same teaching approach that you do. After all, if Anthony relied on Rosario's advice about whose course to take, he'd probably end up with the exact opposite of what he was seeking. And academic advisors are probably going to be reluctant to criticize other faculty members, who are, after all, colleagues. In that case, read between the lines and think carefully about what your advisor is saying. For example, say you ask, "Should I take marine biology with Roth?" If his response is, "You might really enjoy Corgan," you might want to avoid Roth. In some cases, of course, you won't be able to avoid a particular professor, especially in your first year when you are often assigned most of your courses. What can you do to succeed in a situation like that?

First of all, to be certain what teaching styles you work best with, you need to know your own learning style, as we noted in Chapter 2. A visual learner is going to learn better with someone who uses overheads or the board. An auditory learner will learn best with the lecture style. And a kinesthetic learner? Hands-on activities. But just because you're strongest in one area doesn't mean you're unable to learn from other styles.

Second, you need to be aware of a few archetypes, or standard teaching styles, you're likely to encounter among your professors. No one can say one style is better than another, and you could have good and bad professors within any one of these styles. But understanding the styles is a first step toward understanding how to do well in any professor's class.

Here, then, are the three major teaching styles you are likely to encounter in college:

> **Traditional lecture style.** This professor gives information to you through lectures and expects you to take notes. There are variations within this type. For example, some lecturers ask a lot of questions and expect, even demand, responses. Others simply read their notes and expect little, if any, participation from members of the class. Another variation within this category is that some lecturers focus primarily on the facts, whereas others expect students to form opinions about the information being disseminated.
>
> **Collaborative style.** This professor uses a lot of group work and discussion and generally expects a lot of participation from students. Such a professor is more likely than others to notice an individual student—including one who is not participating.
>
> **Dialectic style.** This professor uses a form of teaching known as the Socratic Method. Here the professor asks questions and expects students to generate knowledge by becoming engaged in the question and answer process. Again, individual participation is going to be very important in a class like this.

Time-Out Tip

If you are having trouble catching all the information a professor is giving in lectures, ask him or her whether you can tape the lecture. Many professors (when asked) will allow students to tape lectures with a small, portable tape recorder. *But don't use the tape as an excuse not to pay attention in class. Replaying every lecture is time-consuming. Use the tape to "fill in the blanks" in your notes and confirm main ideas. If you are an auditory learner, listen to the tapes again while walking to class or driving to campus.*

Often, the nature of the class determines which style a professor uses. The professor who lectures to the 200 students in her Introduction to Chemistry class might be very collaborative in her 12-student senior seminar. Also, many times a professor will use a combination of styles even within the same course, depending on the material covered and the response of the students. No one style is necessarily better than another, it is probable that you, much like Rosario and Anthony, will find one style more to your liking than another. What can you do to adapt to other styles when necessary? Try these tips by tracing down from your professor's style along the top to your style in the left-hand column. In the box in which they intersect, you find a learning tip that is right for you.

If your professor's style is ⇒	Lecture	Collaborative	Dialectic
And your preferred style is ⇓ **Lecture**		▸ Actively participate in the group. ▸ Force yourself to take leadership roles. ▸ If you don't want to be a presenter, volunteer to play an active role by taking notes, putting together a poster, etc.	▸ Ask questions when you get a chance. ▸ Meet with the professor during office hours. ▸ Seek out a tutor with whom you can go over class notes and get hints on how you might be tested.
Collaborative	▸ Sit near the front so you can focus. ▸ Meet with the professor during office hours. ▸ Tape record with permission. ▸ Form a study group with other students in the class.		▸ Get involved in the question and answer; don't wait for questions to be directed to you.
Dialectic	▸ Sign up for a tutor with whom you can discuss the material.	▸ Form discussion groups within group activities.	

Quick and Dirty Note-Taking Strategies

Note taking is at the heart of the college experience. You bring a notebook to class, you take notes, and then you study for your test by—you guessed it!—reading your notes. Although most students know how to take notes—after all, you just scribble things down, right?—the real issue, and a far more important one, is whether they know how to take *effective* notes. How can you make the most of the time and effort you put into note taking? First of all, you can avoid some common mistakes:

Don't try to write down everything the professor says. If you're frantically trying to write everything down, you may fall behind and miss important information. If you have read the assigned chapters *before* class, listen for the information from the textbook that the professor also emphasizes in the lecture. Write this information down. If no reading is assigned, write down information that is not only mentioned but also presented on the board, on the overhead, or on PowerPoint. Otherwise, try to pick out cues such as repeated information, and of course write

What Worked for Me

"When I walked out of my first history lecture, I knew I was in for some work. I couldn't believe how much the professor covered in one class!" exclaimed Jack. "I made the decision right then and there not to get behind. What worked for me was that I reviewed my notes after every class and before the next one," Jack explained. "I am a history major, so I knew I had to do well in this class. And I didn't want to just cram information into my head the night before and forget it after the test. Reviewing notes allowed me to get the information into my long-term memory. I scheduled time on my calendar for these reviews—they didn't take more than half an hour." When asked what he did, Jack said that he simply reread what he had written, summarizing the information in the margins of his notebook. He also marked when he was missing information or had a question to ask during the next class. "It worked," Jack said. *Jack learned early that new information not reviewed within a day or so is lost. If he hadn't followed his plan, he would have had to learn all the information in his notes a second time when he prepared for the tests.*

down any information that the professor comes right out and says is important. Don't worry about not picking up this skill right away. You will develop it over time (and many lectures!).

Don't ignore the professor's opinions. If you do, you may miss out on some important clues to what will show up on the test. The professor's opinions can be especially important to know when it comes to essay questions. Although you certainly shouldn't be expected always to agree with the professor's opinions, you should know what they are so that if you disagree, you can make a strong case.

Abbreviations can be very helpful, but avoid using too many. In your hurry to take notes, how many times have you used an abbreviation—certain that you'd remember what it stood for—only to look over your notes later and have no clue? Although "Goodt" may make a lot of sense in class, it can be easy to forget that the professor was talking about the "German occupation of Dutch territory" and not some German general you're supposed to remember.

Reviewing Your Notes

Now that you've taken all of these notes, what are you going to *do* with them? Some students take the notes and barely, if ever, look at them again. Other students wait to look them over until right before the exam, when they "read" them again. Neither of these strategies is very effective. What's the problem? The problem in the first case, obviously, is that the student is assuming that just taking the notes is enough. It isn't. If you never look at your notes again, the whole exercise is pointless. In the second case, the student is waiting far too long between taking the notes and actually becoming engaged with them again. After all, if your course starts in early September and your first test comes in mid-October, by test time you

Teamwork Activity

The object of this activity is to practice your note-taking and evaluation skills. Gather three or four students from your class. Take turns being the lecturer and being note takers. Have the lecturer "give a lecture" using material provided to you by your instructor or from another class. The lecturer should read the material at a moderate pace, and the note takers should take notes. After the lecture is over, the lecturer will "grade" the notes for completeness and organization. Switch roles.

"Grading" Tips

▶ An "A" set of notes:
  ▷ main ideas with supporting ideas clearly marked
  ▷ examples set apart with "ex."
  ▷ clear, consistent system of organization
▶ A "B" set of notes:
  ▷ main ideas but may have a few missing supporting details or examples
  ▷ examples noted but not marked
  ▷ inconsistent system of organization
▶ A "C" set of notes:
  ▷ some main ideas and supporting details missing
  ▷ some examples missing
  ▷ no system of organization
▶ An "F" set of notes
  ▷ none of the above! Don't let that happen!

won't have looked at the earliest material in over a month. Some of the notes may be almost meaningless because you've lost the "context" of the material. Notes work best when you can put them in the context in which they were taken: You wrote them down while your professor was speaking, so they'll make the most sense when you can still recall your professor speaking. The best way to put them into context immediately is to read them over at least twice between the class in which you took them and the next class; this is known as the **After and Before Method:**

▶ Review your notes once immediately *after* the class, or at least sometime later that day.

▶ Review your notes a second time right *before* the next class meeting.

The first reading is important because the material is still fresh in your mind. You will still remember any unusual abbreviations; a sloppily written word will still make sense. The phenomenon that led you to write the notes—the class itself, that is—took place recently enough that you will be able to fill in any blanks in your notes. The second reading is important not only because it will help you learn the material fast but also because it will get you focused for the note taking you are about to do in *that* class. The best way to do this is to show up for class ten minutes early, take out your notebook, and see what your professor was talking about during the last class. Many professors start their lectures without any review or discussion of what they covered in the last class. While many students will spend the first few minutes of the lecture figuring out where they are, you will already have everything in context.

An added benefit of this approach is that it reduces your overall study time and enables you to avoid painful and ineffective last-minute cramming. Numerous studies have shown that learning material in small chunks over a long period of time is much more effective than trying to learn a large chunk of material in a short period of time. Another bonus is that because you are reviewing and learning your material as you go along, you will more readily grasp the context of the lectures as they progress in the course. If you put the "After and Before Method" to work, you will quickly find that you are having an easier time learning the material.

Combining Textbook and Lecture Notes for the Best Study Guide Ever

Putting it all together—that's the final goal here. In this chapter, you've learned about annotating textbooks, and you've learned about taking better notes in class. Now, how do you combine this knowledge to study more effectively and efficiently and, ultimately, to get better grades in your classes?

Studying for a test can be frustrating. Sometimes, of course, if you didn't go to class—or you did go but didn't pay attention—it's frustrating because you don't have anything to study. But it can be equally frustrating if you find yourself with *too much* stuff: piles of notes from class, scribbles in the margins of your textbook, index cards that you made while annotating your textbook. How do you organize all of this material?

Some of the preparation should be done ahead of time, as you're doing the work in the first place. For example, when you're taking notes in class, always write down the date for each session. This gives you an automatic organizer, and it will help you in a couple of ways: (1) It helps you remember when material was presented, and (2) if you need to see your professor with a question, it will help your professor figure out when he or she presented it.

One of the best ways to prepare as you go through your class and text notes is to try to predict what kinds of questions your professor is going to ask on the test. To this end, be sure to attend any review sessions your professor holds. Usually, professors will tell you the format of the test (that is, the combination of multiple-choice, true/false, fill-in-the-blank, short answer, and/or essay questions). Sometimes, professors will provide copies of old tests, which will give you an excellent idea of the types of questions they might ask. Another effective technique is to brainstorm potential questions with a study group.

The next step is to figure out what material is covered. Did the professor's lectures come straight from the book, or did they consist of new material? This is an important question. Some professors lecture and test almost directly from the book, whereas others consider the book as supplementary material. Sometimes, for better or worse, you'll have a professor whose lectures—and tests—have nothing to do with the book. (This understandably leads students to ask themselves, "Why did I have to buy this book?" One answer is that many professors feel students must expand their knowledge beyond what's covered in class.) The best way to find out what material is on the test is to talk to the professor.

Lifeline

If you are having trouble taking good notes in your lecture classes, ask another student or students in your class to get together for note review sessions. Such sessions really work because each of you may have gotten something the others missed. Likewise, you can confirm what each of you heard in the lecture and answer each other's questions.

If you have a learning disability, register with your campus ADA office. Through this office, if it is an appropriate accommodation for you, you can often get a copy (confidentially) of the notes of a hired note taker, another student in the same class who takes good notes.

Once you've gathered your material, there are a few things to look for in your notes:

► Recurring topics
► Key names and dates
► Both facts and opinions

This information can appear in either your text and/or the professor's lecture notes. And of course, when you notice information that appeared in *both,* you can feel pretty confident that you've identified material that is likely to appear on the test.

What do you do with this recurring information? One smart thing to do is to make one set of study notes to "clear the clutter" and really get you focused on what seems most likely to be on the test. If you prefer index cards, put the information that appears in both sets of notes on them, one point at a time. Putting too much information on any one note card defeats the purpose of using a note card (remember that they are flash cards). If you prefer outlines, take out sheets of lined paper and make one study outline from both sets of notes. You get the picture. Your objective is to put away the books, put away the disorganized lecture notes and miscellaneous scraps of information, and make one personalized study guide that you are very confident is the best study guide ever.

Finally, remember that your professors often make up tests the same way you study for them. That is, they look over what they've covered (in their lectures and in assigned readings) and then make up questions based on that material. A study guide is only as good as the questions it helps you answer. Practice making up questions and then practice answering them. Put yourself in your professor's shoes, and you'll take a giant step toward improving your results on tests.

Increasing Your Yield:

Readings for Practical Application

This chapter has covered reading and note taking at the college level. You have learned how to preview your textbooks, how to use guide questions, how to highlight, how to outline, how to annotate, and how to summarize to get the most out of your textbooks. Of course, college is not just about reading; it is also about going to lectures, so this chapter also helped you to assess your professors' lecture styles, how to take effective notes in lectures, how to review those notes, and, finally, how to pull your textbook and lecture notes together to be as prepared as possible for tests and exams. The practical strategies presented here have been widely studied and have been proved to work through experimentation.

Those of you who like practical, research based activities such as the ones presented in this chapter will probably do well in science courses that take a very linear approach to understanding the world around us. The readings that follow give you an opportunity to explore the physical sciences more closely—not only to apply the textbook reading strategies but also to consider whether a career in the physical sciences may be for you.

The "Textbook Case" reading in this chapter is about black holes. Taken from a physics textbook, this reading illustrates how scientists use facts, mathematical formulas, and deductive reasoning to determine that an object is a black hole. In essence, they combine strategies to successfully prove a theory, just as you must combine study strategies in order to achieve success as a student.

The "Life After College" reading gives you a look at one area of science, the developing field of biotechnology. Many new discoveries with applications ranging from food production to medical science are coming from research in this growing field.

Scientific breakthroughs don't always come without controversy. Genetic engineering is one area of biotechnology that has engendered some controversy. Another is cloning, the subject addressed in our "Current Issues" reading. Regardless of what you might think you know about cloning, this article about the use of cloning to save endangered species will probably challenge some of your assumptions about the issue.

Reading and Study Tips: Physical Sciences

Unique Features and Comprehension Strategies

Physical science textbooks feature short, staccato sentences and are loaded with to-the-point information. You may feel you can skip information in some textbooks, especially those that provide many examples for the same idea or concept, but you need to read the information in physical science textbooks more carefully. Almost everything you read will be important to note. **Study each sentence—it is very difficult to skim such technical information. Read the sentence, identify the key words and definitions in context, and then read the sentence again for the concept. Make note cards as often as necessary to reinforce your understanding of these key words and concepts.**

Physical science textbooks feature special vocabulary in each chapter. These terms usually appear in boldface type in the text discussion and are often included in a glossary at the end of the chapter. This placement shows how important these vocabulary words are in the textbook as a whole. **Resolve to keep up with the introduction of new vocabulary. You can avoid falling behind by making vocabulary flash cards. Put the word on one side and the definition and an example on the back. Make use of those extra free minutes that usually go to waste (waiting for the bus or for class to start) throughout your day to review a note card or two. Make them early and look at them often.**

There are two different types of approaches: traditional (teaches terms and concepts somewhat in the abstract) and issues-based (puts concepts in the context of real-world events). Try to figure out what type of textbook you have. This will affect how you read and study the material presented in the book. In the traditional book, it is more likely that you will be doing a lot of memorizing. You are also more likely to have objective tests based on the information. The second type of book requires you to understand the concepts in context. You will be reading about real-life examples and situations, and you will need to draw the scientific principles out of those examples. In a course based on such a textbook, you are more likely to see essay and application tests. **Be prepared to make flash cards for the first type of text, and for the second, be prepared to apply the theories and concepts you are studying to real-life examples of your own devising. The more you try to apply these ideas to things with which you are already familiar, the more sense you will be able to make of it all.**

Physical science textbooks assume at least some high school background in science. Don't expect to be walked though the basics in a college-level physical science textbook. Chances are that basic information will be covered quickly or not at all, the assumption being that you already know and understand it. **If you don't, you need to get tutoring or spend extra time reading to get caught up on the information you need.**

In physical science textbooks, the concepts build sequentially. You will begin to notice that one concept builds on another, just as one chapter builds on the one prior to it. This is important to notice right away, so that you will not be tempted to skip assigned readings or jump around in the text. **Outline the readings from the text and compare your outline to your lecture notes; outlining works best for science texts because scientists tend to think linearly. As we noted in this chapter, an informal outline will help you organize the concepts presented in the readings. Follow the steps suggested, from previewing the text to identifying main topics and subtopics and to then writing the actual outline. Outlining will emphasize just how the concepts are building on each other. The outlines will also give you handy review sheets to look at when you have a few extra minutes so that the information will stay fresh in your memory. You don't want to have to relearn a lot of science information right before a test!**

Do the assigned reading before the lecture so you can familiarize yourself with the technical aspects of your professor's lecture topic. Lectures in science courses are full of technical jargon and complex concepts, many of which, as we have said, build on previous concepts. **In order to understand new information that your professor presents, you need to read before and possibly even after a lecture.**

In your reading, if you do not understand a word or concept, do your best to figure it out with the help of your text's glossary and examples. Then, when you get to the lecture, you will understand it better because you will be encountering it for the second time. Moreover, you will be better able to formulate questions in the event that you are still confused.

Be prepared for quantitative information. Take math courses before science courses that require math applications (physics, chemistry, and geology, for example). The principles and concepts of science are often based on mathematical principles and concepts. **To understand the scientific concepts fully, you also have to understand the math behind them. Therefore, it is not the best plan to take math after science or even at the same time. Think about this when you are registering for your classes.**

Reading 1:   A Textbook Case

The following textbook excerpt is included here because this chapter discussed specific strategies for improving your reading and note-taking skills. Using specific strategies, scientists also seek to solve problems in the most direct way. Even if you have some idea what black holes are, you may not be familiar with the science behind the discovery of black holes. Do you know how scientists came to identify them? This textbook excerpt leads you through this process. Nearly all college students will take at least one physical science course, and if you decide to major in science, you will have many textbooks similar to the one from which this reading is taken. As you read this selection, underline, annotate, and, most importantly, outline (as explained above) to best organize the material for yourself.

BEFORE YOU READ

1. When you hear that the following passage is from a physics textbook, what are some thoughts that go through your mind? Do you feel confident? Anxious? Do you think you'll be able to understand the material?
2. What science classes did you take in high school? What other science background do you have: science camps, field trips? How prepared do you feel for college-level science courses?
3. As you learned in this chapter, preview the following textbook selection and then create guide questions to answer when you have finished reading.

Observations of Black Holes

A. Hobson

Gravitational forces become unimaginably large near [a collapsed star]. If you had the misfortune to get too close, you could not escape, because gravity would not let anything escape. If you were within a few hundred meters of the central point and you tried to throw an object away from the center, you would need to throw

---

SOURCE: A. Hobson, "Observations of Black Holes." In Art Hobson, *Physics: Concepts and Connections*, 2nd ed. (Upper Saddle River, NJ: Prentice-Hall, 1999), pp. 123–125. © 1999. Reprinted by permission of Pearson Education, Inc., Upper Saddle River, N.J.

it faster than the speed of light in order for the object to escape the star. . . . [O]bjects cannot be thrown faster than the speed of light. Nothing can get out of the immediate vicinity of the star's central point, not even light itself. Such an object is called a **black hole.**

Observations of Black Holes

We can detect black holes by means of their gravitational influence on things around them. The first probable black hole, Cygnus X-1, was discovered in 1972. This object is thought to be a double star, two stars orbiting around each other, held together by their gravitational attraction. One star is a visible giant star, and the other is an unseen compact (in other words, far smaller than a normal star) object. By observing its gravitational effect on the visible star, the compact object's mass can be deduced to be some 15 solar masses. Since theories indicate that a compact object of more than three solar masses can only be a black hole, astronomers believe that Cygnus X-1 is a black hole. Satellites in orbit around Earth detect X rays from Cygnus X-1 that further confirm that it is a black hole. Apparently the invisible object's gravitational pull is drawing gases from the visible star and accelerating them down into and around the black hole, a process that tears apart the gas atoms and causes them to emit X rays that we can observe.

It is difficult to believe that objects as exotic as back holes actually exist. Scientists don't go out of their way to invent strange ideas like this. To the contrary, they always look for the most natural, least strange, explanation of the observed data. For example, people once found it strange that Earth could orbit the sun, but astronomers such as Copernicus found that this was the most natural idea that could account for the data. In the same way, astronomers today find that a black hole is the most natural explanation for Cygnus X-1. If it is not a black hole, then this object is not compact, or it does not have a mass larger than 3 suns, or compact objects of greater than three solar masses do not always collapse to become black holes. Astronomers find it easier to believe that Cygnus X-1 is a black hole than to believe any of these three options. Science is conservative, always preferring the least-odd conclusion possible.

Using X-rays to identify possible black holes and then studying these candidates by more direct means, several objects have now been discovered that are believed to be black holes resulting from the gravitational collapse of a star.

Much more massive black holes are thought to exist at the centers of many galaxies. In some galaxies, confirmation of a central black hole comes from telescopic observations of the speeds of individual stars near the center. These stars are orbiting the center, indicating that something at the center is holding them in orbits. Measurements of the stars' orbital speeds enable the mass of the central object to be deduced from the law of gravity; faster speeds indicate a larger mass at the center. For example, observed orbital speeds as high as 1000 km/s near the center of our own Milky Way galaxy imply a black hole with a mass of about 2.6 million suns lurks at the center.

Such observations lead astronomers to conclude that many galaxies have black holes at their centers and that the distant and powerful galaxy-like objects called *quasars* are powered by massive black holes.

AFTER YOU READ

1. This passage discusses a phenomenon that can be detected only through deductive reasoning. What are some other such phenomena? What makes phenomena that can be proven in other ways more or less believable than black holes? Are there any that you don't believe in?
2. Write a summary of this excerpt in the manner recommended in this chapter.
3. How do scientists detect black holes? What kinds of information did scientists need before they were able to determine the existence of black holes? Although the author acknowledges that black holes can be difficult to believe in, what reasons does he provide for believing in them? Do these seem convincing to you?
4. The scientists discussed in this passage used a plan to argue scientifically their case for the existence of black holes. Describe their plan. How can you put together your own plan for studying? Present your plan to the class.

Reading 2:   Life After College

Science, although it is an academic discipline with an abstract dimension, also has many practical applications. It is one thing to enjoy science and science courses, but it is another thing to make a career out of science. Do you know all the possibilities for careers that involve science? The article below highlights one interesting and growing scientific field: biotechnology.

BEFORE YOU READ

1. The following passage discusses careers in biotechnology. What do you think of when you hear that term?
2. What are some other careers that require a science background? What do you think draws a person to those types of careers? Do you think that science careers attract a certain type of person?

Careers in Biotech: Inventing the Future

T. J. Wallis

Want to help feed the world, develop new medications, cure diseases, help keep our environment clean, and help solve crime? Then a career in biotechnology just might be for you.

Did you know that scientists have been able to turn skin cells into beating heart cells that could be used to repair a damaged heart? Did you know that scientists have found a way to turn human fat into cartilage, offering a good supply of repair materials for people with damaged joints? These and other medical breakthroughs hit the headlines weekly. And it's all the result of biotechnology.

Biotech includes a wide variety of sciences and careers. Here's some information to help you decide if a career in biotech is right for you.

What Is Biotech?

Biotechnology is the science of using living things to develop new products. These include pharmaceuticals, improved foods, medical diagnostics, and industrial products. It's important because it is the branch of science that is literally changing the world we live in. It crosses all industries. Experts are calling the 21st century the "biotechnology century"—and with good reason.

SOURCE: T. J. Wallis, "Careers in Biotech: Inventing the Future," *Career World 30* (April/May 2002), 6–10. Reprinted by permission.

Ed Uthman, M.D., a pathologist from Houston, Texas, explains biotechnology this way: "Science is about the relationship between humans and nature. It's not about hawking some product [or] attending boring sales meetings. . . . It's about uncovering real truths of the universe—how matter and energy interact to produce what we call life with all its complexity."

The biotech industry has more than doubled since 1993. According to the Biotechnology Industry Organization, there were almost 1,400 biotech firms in the United States in 2001. You can bet your Bunsen burner that biotechnology will be the branch of science that discovers ways to improve the diagnosis and treatment of hereditary diseases. It will provide us with safer drugs and more environmentally friendly herbicides and pesticides. Biotechnology will help us find cures for spinal cord injuries, come up with innovative new ways to solve crimes, help clean up the environment, and give us safer, more efficient industrial products. That's why the amount of money invested in the biotech industry increased a whopping 156 percent in one year, from 1999 to 2000.

Biotechnology is making headlines around the world—the Human Genome Project (HGP) and the **cloning** of human embryos are just two examples.

The HGP (which maps and studies the genes in human DNA) fuels the multibillion dollar U.S. biotechnology industry and is going a long way toward fostering the development of new medical applications. And now, with medical treatments needed for emerging diseases, biotechnology will no doubt be at the forefront of scientific research for a long time to come. Stem cell research and cloning are new technologies we will also be hearing more and more about.

All of these new discoveries will mean more demand for science and math lovers to do research or to support those doing the research.

Adam Frederick is one of those people with a love of science and math. He has a master's degree in environmental biology and works for Maryland Sea Grant, where he is an education specialist at the University of Maryland's Biotechnology Institute (UMBI). It's his job to translate the research

that takes place there into educational programs. He helps non-scientists understand how biotechnology works. One of the programs Frederick and his team have created focuses on oil pollution. The program demonstrates how biotechnology can be applied to assist in the cleanup of oil spills.

About 5,000 middle and high school students come to the UMBI Sci-Tech Education Program each year to get some hands-on biotechnology lab work. They might study biofilms and biodiversity in Chesapeake Bay or learn a little about DNA extraction or zebra fish embryology. Whatever lab they end up in, the students are able to test a hypothesis and come away with a better understanding of biology concepts.

Discover a New Career

There are two career tracks for biotech scientists. First, there is the academic track, where you work at a university or research institute, or teach in the classroom or lab. The second track is to work in private industry, where you might do research or hold a managerial position and be involved in the business end of running a biotech company. "There are always going to be people who are innately interested in science. Those are the ones who will become career scientists," Frederick explains.

Some of the main careers in the biotechnology field include scientists, technologists, and technicians. Here are a few of the positions held by people who work in this industry.

▶ Biological and Medical Scientists: These are highly educated individuals (usually with a doctorate degree) who study living organisms and their relationship to the environment. For the most part, they work in research and development, conducting research to advance our knowledge of living organisms, including viruses, bacteria, and other infectious agents. These are the scientists who help develop new vaccines and medicines. They are biochemists, botanists, microbiologists, physiologists, marine biologists, zoologists, and ecologists. Though each has a specialized area of interest, all study living organisms and their relationship to the environment.

The salary range for scientists varies dramatically, depending on their field of expertise and whether they are employed in the private or public sector. In 1999, the National Association of Colleges and Employers reported salaries for individuals with a doctorate started at about $45,700, with a master's degree around $34,500, and with a bachelor's degree at $29,000. Those who work for the federal government earn $55,000 or more per year.

▶ Clinical Laboratory Technologists don't need the same level of education as biological and medical scientists, but they play an important role in performing medical tests to detect and diagnose disease. They examine and analyze body fluids, tissues, and cells. They look for bacteria, parasites, and other microorganisms; analyze the chemical content of fluids; match blood for transfusions; and test for drug levels in the blood to show how a patient is responding to treatment. They must be accurate and reliable, have an interest in science, and be able to recognize their responsibility for human health and life. They have titles such as blood bank technologist, immunology technologist, histology (tissue) technician, and cytotechnologist (cell).

Usually, a bachelor's degree in medical technology or a life science is required to work in this field. Some people qualify with an associate's degree or a certificate from a technical school or the armed forces. Frederick points out that these workers may "start in this position and move up by getting a graduate degree."

The average salary for clinical laboratory technologists was $40,500 in 2000, according to the Bureau of Labor Statistics, though some individuals were earning more than $55,500 at the high end and some closer to $29,200 at the low end.

The American Society of Clinical Pathologists reports a continuing shortage of personnel in clinical laboratories.

▶ Science Technicians are the people who set up, operate, and maintain laboratory instruments, monitor experiments, make observations, calculate and record results, and often reach conclusions. They must keep detailed logs of all their work-related activities. These individuals have a strong background in science and math. Most employers prefer technicians to have at least two years of specialized training or an associate's degree in applied science or science-related technology. Technicians usually work under the supervision of scientists. Job titles in this category include biological or chemical technician, environmental technician, nuclear technician, and petroleum technician.

Science technicians earned between $13.02 (agriculture and food) and $28.44 (nuclear) per hour in 2000. The average annual salary for biological science technicians was $32,753 in nonsupervisory positions.

Wanted: Crime Solvers

A "hot" career right now, says Frederick, is forensic science, which uses the tools of biotechnology to solve crimes. Think "crime scene investigators" and "pathologists."

"There is a whole area [which uses] arthropods [insects, spiders, and similar creatures] for clues," says Frederick. "It requires a tremendous amount of knowledge. There are certain insects that only lay eggs after a certain period of time. If the [scientist] knows the different stages [of the insect's life cycle], he or she can tell how long a body has been there. There are very few experts in the field, but it is growing."

In fact, there are only nine forensic entomologists in North America. Dr. Gail Anderson is one of these. She was recently named one of the leading international innovators in the field of crime and punishment by *Time* magazine. Her expertise on insect activity on homicide victims allows her to pinpoint with great accuracy such details as time of death and whether a body has been moved. She has been involved in more than 130 homicide investigations. Dr. Anderson's interest in science is inherent. "How can you not be interested in science?" she asks. "It's life. It's how our bodies work."

When asked how it feels to play a role in solving a crime, Dr. Anderson responded, "It's very good. It's not just solving the crime. I can also help exonerate somebody too. To be able to make any step forward in the process of justice is wonderful, and you really know that your research means something."

Dr. Uthman teaches and writes on the topic of forensic pathology. He suggests that certain personality traits might come in handy if you want a career in pathology. He says you have to have a talent for and an interest in science, good communication skills, a strong stomach (as you will be routinely dealing with dismembered and decomposing bodies), and a thick skin, as you will be periodically challenged by local media and detectives.

The Scientific Advantage

If investigating, researching, and coming up with new discoveries and innovations appeal to you, consider a career in biotechnology. Frederick offers this advice to high school students wanting to enter this diverse and exciting field: Get a good background in math, chemistry, and obviously biology. Take a second and third course in chemistry. That will put you ahead of or on a par with others.

"And when you get to college," Frederick adds, "look for opportunities to do independent research as an undergraduate. If you're really serious about it, investigate a college. Find out who the professors are in the biology department and biochemistry department. Make it a point to talk with these professors and ask if you can do some work in the laboratory. If you get some independent research experience while in college, you will be far ahead of your peers when you graduate, and independent firms will snatch you right up."

Now that's an advantage! Are you ready to invent your future?

AFTER YOU READ

1. When do you think biotech advances and ethics collide? What are some controversies you've heard about regarding biotechnology? Provide examples. Explain your point of view on each.
2. What does it mean to be "innately interested in science"? Is such interest necessary for a successful career in biotech? Why or why not?
3. How would you describe the tone of this article? How does the tone advance the cause of attracting people to the field of biotechnology?
4. Why do you think the field of forensic entomology is growing? Identify a crime and crime scene that might require a forensic entomologist and explain why.

Reading 3: Current Issues

You have probably heard something about cloning in the news, but what do you really know about it? Do you know enough to form an educated opinion? Although it is certainly a technological advancement, cloning nevertheless is controversial. Science has always been associated with progress, and progress can lead to differing opinions. Scientists such as Galileo and Darwin formulated theories that provoked controversy for generations. The following article examines a subject that is currently controversial: cloning.

BEFORE YOU READ

1. Explain cloning as you currently understand it. Do you think it is ethically acceptable or not? Why?
2. Do you know of any animals that are endangered? What has caused their endangerment? Besides cloning, can you think of any other ways that these species could be saved?
3. Do you believe humans should use technology in order to save endangered animals? Why or why not?

Species on Ice
K. Wright

The high-tech, high-controversy attempt to save endangered animals with clones and surrogate moms

The Tabby crouched on the cage's platform is fiercely attentive, as if he's not sure whether he's the hunter or the hunted. Something's different about this cat: His big blue eyes are a little too close together, his nose a bit long, and his limbs on the rangy side—even for a tom. Among the dozens of friendly felines romping in a nearby corridor, this one stands out, as nervous and haughty as the last cat on Earth.

Actually, Jazz is the first of his kind, an endangered African wildcat born almost two years ago from a frozen embryo that was implanted in an ordinary house cat. Acting as midwife was Betsy Dresser, director of the Audubon Center for Research of Endangered Species, on the bayou near New Orleans. Dresser is a leading advocate of efforts to protect rare animals by cloning and other advanced reproductive techniques. Her controversial aim is to provide a last-ditch, high-tech redoubt for species that might otherwise vanish when their habitats do.

"We're a safety net for these species," explains Dresser. "I feel like I'm in the emergency room of the conservation movement."

Some conservationists say that such singular feats of assisted reproduction are unlikely to yield meaningful results for species survival. But no one disputes the fact that Dresser's compound is ground zero for such feats or that her new wildcat is the most conspicuous example yet. Jazz began as a twinkle in Dresser's eye back in the 1980s, when she first began considering the concept of frozen zoos—collections of sperm, embryos, and tissue samples from imperiled animals stored in tanks of liquid nitrogen. With technological advances, the frozen cells might someday be used to re-create populations of species that face extinction. Dresser knew that in order to effect such recoveries biologists would have to get humble surrogates to gestate embryos of exotic species. Using mothers of the endangered species could be impractical, if not impossible. The advantage of using surrogate mothers is that "you'd be able to make more babies because you're not using the endangered mothers themselves" she says.

The principle of interspecies surrogacy was first demonstrated in the 1970s, when an Asian mouflon lamb was born to a domestic wool sheep. In the early 1980s, Dresser and her colleagues at the Cincinnati Zoo coaxed a rare African antelope called a bongo from a doe of a more plentiful species, the eland. A few years later, the Cincinnati team shepherded the birth of a gaur, an endangered Asian ox, by a Holstein cow. In 1994, Dresser announced the live birth of a threatened Indian desert cat, delivered by a house cat that had been implanted with a fresh embryo. Jazz represents the next stage in Dresser's vision: living, purring proof that frozen embryos can remain viable after thawing and can develop normally in the womb of another species.

Because egg cells, unlike sperm, don't freeze well, Dresser needs fresh eggs to make her frozen embryos. But collecting fresh eggs or embryos from rare wild females is tricky, so scientists are developing a new cloning technology as an alternative. In ordinary cloning, the nucleus of an egg cell is replaced with the nucleus from a body cell of the animal to be cloned. A jolt of electricity then prompts the egg to begin dividing, after which it is implanted in a surrogate mother. To get around

SOURCE: K. Wright, "Species on Ice," *Discover 22* (September 2001), 28–29. This article first appeared in *Discover* magazine.

the problem of collecting eggs from endangered mothers, conservation cloning would have to involve two added twists: The egg cells, as well as the surrogate mothers, would be of a different species than the animal being cloned. Earlier this year, scientists at Advanced Cell Technology in Worcester, Massachusetts, announced the birth of the first such chimeric clone, a gaur calf that was produced from a skin-cell nucleus injected into the egg of, and nurtured in the womb of, an ordinary cow. The calf appeared healthy at birth but died from a bacterial infection two days later.

Meanwhile, Dresser's own attempts to clone bongos and wildcats in surrogate species have failed, and Chinese ventures to clone giant pandas are foundering as well. When scientists at Advanced Cell Technology cloned the gaur, they worked on 692 eggs to get one live birth.

That's not surprising, says David Wildt, head of reproductive sciences at the National Conservation and Research Center. Cloning and other assisted reproductive technologies won't save the panda or any other endangered species unless conservationists also develop detailed knowledge of each species's biology, he says.

"'It's easier to highlight these one-shot wonders than it is to address the huge need for basic knowledge of the reproductive biology of endangered species," he says. For example, artificial insemination has become critical to the captive breeding of pandas, black-footed ferrets, and cheetahs, but only after years of research on the reproductive mechanisms unique to each animal. Success in one species doesn't translate easily to any other. Fifteen years ago, Wildt hoped he could quickly adapt the breeding methods that had become routine in cattle to cheetahs. "We learned that cheetahs are not cows," he says.

Wildt and other critics fear that cloning encourages a false sense of hope and complacency where immediate action is needed. "There's a total misperception about what these reproductive services can offer," he says. He worries that surrogate programs like Dresser's, which tend to focus on species that are related to such well-studied mammals as cows and cats, divert attention away from the most threatened species and the preservation of their habitats. "The point is that there's 40,000 vertebrate species out there being ignored."Dresser says that by working with domesticated species and their relatives now, she can expand the reach of the program later. She plans to take her techniques out of the Audubon Center compound to the field, implanting bongo embryos in wild eland in Kenya, for example, so the offspring will learn to fend for themselves in natural surroundings.

In the meantime, some members of the conservation community may become more accepting of the center's approach. In an April talk at the American Museum of Natural History, research scientist Phil Damiani of Advanced Cell Technology emphasized the potential of frozen zoos for preserving the diversity of a dwindling species's gene pool. Instead of a two-by-two Noah's ark approach, genome banks could store tissue samples from thousands of individuals of each species. "I had people coming up and saying, 'We never really looked at cloning in that respect,'" says Damiani. "They take a second look at it when they realize we're not talking about creating a genetic bottleneck."

But Dresser says that the idea of keeping a species alive in a nitrogen tank rather than in the wild will never be appealing. It's a grimly pragmatic solution to the problem of encroaching humanity— realpolitik for the biosphere. "Some people say, 'If this is the way we have to save them, then I'd rather they went extinct,'" she says. "I don't agree with that at all."

Scientists have closely studied the reproductive biology of less than 1 percent of the 40,000 vertebrate species. Biologists understand only a few endangered animals—such as elephants, cheetahs, chimpanzees, and baboons— well enough to manipulate their reproduction.

AFTER YOU READ

1. What did you learn about cloning that you did not know before you read this article? Has this article changed the way you think about the issue?
2. Why do critics fear that cloning encourages a false sense of hope?
3. What are the obvious and not-so-obvious problems with interspecies cloning? Make a chart of these. Do you believe the potential benefits outweigh the problems and risks? Why or why not? Present your group consensus to the class.
4. Would you feel comfortable doing what Betsy Dresser does? Why or why not?

Compounding Your Interest: Further Readings

Buchanan, M. (2001). *Ubiquity: The Science of History . . . or Why the World Is Simpler Than We Think.* New York: Crown.

Dyson, F. J. (1999). *The Sun, the Genome, & the Internet: Tools of Scientific Revolutions.* New York: Oxford University Press.

Giles, J. & Knight, J. (February 20, 2003). "Dolly's Death Leaves Researchers Woolly on Clone Ageing Issue." *Nature.*

Hasty, P., et al. (February 28, 2003). "Aging and Genome Maintenance: Lessons from the Mouse?" *Science.*

"Researchers Hope to Use Cow Clones as Medicine Factories" (September 2002). From *Genomics & Genetics Weekly via NewsRX.com*

Shermer, M. (April 2003). "I, Clone." *Scientific American.*

Chapter 4

Earning the Grade on Tests

This chapter will cover the following topics:

Objective Tests
Subjective Tests
Other Types of Tests
Memorization
Cramming
Test Anxiety

Sooner or later, no matter how hard you try to avoid them, you will be faced with what many find to be one of the most dreaded aspects of the college experience: tests. Multiple-choice tests. Essay tests. Open-book tests. Take-home tests. The number and type can make your head spin. Like it or not, they are an inevitable part of the college experience.

You've taken tests before, of course, in high school and grade school, and you've taken many different kinds of tests, from spelling and math tests to the SAT or ACT tests that were part of your college admissions process. You may be someone who enjoys taking tests because you do well on them and you really feel they show your abilities. Or you may be someone who dreads tests because you "freeze up" on them and forget answers that you are certain you know. If you're in the first category, there are some strategies you can add to your repertoire that will improve your already strong abilities. If you're in the second category, there are numerous strategies you can employ that will build your confidence and increase your success on tests. You can earn the grade you want by employing a combination of hard work and strategizing for both studying and test taking.

An initial investment in good test-taking strategies at the beginning of your college career will pay off in college and beyond. Tests may also become not-so-dreaded after all. As so often happens in life, the more you put into preparing for tests, the more you will get out of them. There is no mystery to this. There are no short cuts either. There are, however, plenty of good strategies. That's the point of this chapter. After you read this chapter, you will realize that

Think About It

Answer the following questions in the space provided.

What test-taking strategies have worked for you in the past? Which ones have not worked? _____

_____

_____

_____

you can do well on the tests you will face in college and beyond. You will see that taking tests is just another investment in your future.

First Things First

Before studying for any test, you need to know what you are in for, so ask. That's right: If you don't know, ask. If the type of test and what will be on it are not a part of the syllabus, your professor should let you know. If you are not sure, however, you need to find out. Will the test be on the notes, the text, or both? Will it be essay or multiple-choice? Will it be comprehensive or not?

Next, you need to think about what professors want from tests. Some professors want to see that you've been paying attention to the facts and details presented in the readings and the lectures. Others are more interested in applied knowledge. One professor might be interested in your writing ability on an essay, whereas another might be more interested in seeing that you covered the main points.

The bottom line is that you need to be prepared. There is no point in studying unless you know what you are studying and how you should be studying. Once this is clear, the rest of this chapter will be much more useful.

Objective Tests

The type of test that you will encounter most often is the objective test. This is the black and white test, the right or wrong test. You either love them or hate them. Some students say, "Give me an essay test any day. I can write my way around any answer." Other students say, "Give me multiple-choice. The answer is already there." If you are more like the first group of students, it is time to learn your way around an objective test.

Multiple-Choice Tests

Multiple-choice tests present you with a question or statement, followed by a choice of four of five answers, some of which can be similar or confusing. Some multiple-choice questions are strictly related to definitions or to your ability to recognize facts or identify people:

The type of test that provides the test taker with more than one answer to choose from is called:

   a) a take-home test

   b) a comprehensive test

   c) a multiple-choice test

   d) a headache-inducing test

Others, however, call for the application of material, ideas, or understandings. They are not always as straightforward as they might seem:

Which of the following is the best example of responsible student behavior when it comes to preparing for a biology test?

   a) The student asks around to see what other students know about what will be on the biology test.

   b) The student checks the syllabus. If the information about the biology test is not on these, he assumes the professor does not want the students to know.

   c) The student visits the professor during office hours. He asks what types of questions will be on the test and what he should focus on in his studying.

   d) The student goes to see a tutor, hoping the tutor will tell him what will be on the test.

The best way to prepare for a multiple-choice test is to practice *taking* a multiple-choice test. What does this mean? If your textbook has practice tests at the end of each chapter, you are in luck. Even if your professor doesn't assign them, take them! You will get used to seeing the course content in the multiple-choice format. Seeing answers next to other possible answers, and having to distinguish among them, is a lot different from staring at a straightforward set of notes. Think about it. Your notes don't have four or five possible choices. There is only one. But when you take a multiple-choice test, you have to pick that answer out from a list of several alternatives. This could get confusing, especially if two answers are very similar or if one of the answers is indeed a correct answer—but to another question! Think of it as being in a forest and having to find one particular variety of maple tree among other types of trees or even among similar, but not identical, maples. If you have only looked at maples, and have never looked at birch trees or willow trees, you are going to have a tough time. That's why taking practice multiple-choice tests is the best way to prepare. If your textbook does not include practice tests, talk to your professor. Sometimes he or she can provide supplementary texts that offer them. Some professors also keep old tests on file, either in the office or in the library. Taking these tests as practice enables you to "get into the head" of the test maker.

   Here are the steps to follow when taking multiple-choice tests:

1. Read the question carefully and then read every possible answer.
2. Practice the process of elimination. Remember that good test takers look for the wrong answers and eliminate them. The right answer remains. This works especially well for questions with two very similar answers.

3. Once you have made a decision, re-read the question, following it with your chosen answer. Does it make sense? Is it grammatically correct?

*A special tip for students who **really** hate multiple-choice tests:* Turn the questions into fill-in-the-blank or short-answer questions. Do this by covering up all the choices. Then read the question and write an answer down on the paper. When you have done that, look at the choices to see whether your answer is there. (This tip is helpful for students who experience anxiety when they look at the choices before deciding on an answer.)

True/False Tests

As a student, you have one distinct advantage with true/false tests: You have a 50/50 chance of getting each question right. Nevertheless, true/false questions can be very tricky, and you need to keep in mind the following tips.

▶ Watch out for questions that contain negatives, especially if they contain a double negative.
▶ Watch for key words in each statement.
▶ Pay attention to words that may indicate that a statement is true (these include *some, few, many,* and *often*).
▶ Pay attention to words that may indicate that a statement is false (such as *never, all, every,* and *only*).
▶ Remember that if any part of a statement is false, the entire statement is false.

Fill-in-the-Blank Tests

Although you see these kinds of tests less frequently in college than in high school, you will still come across them occasionally. Here are some tips:

▶ Read the entire statement carefully so that you are clear about what should go in the blanks.
▶ Give the same number of answers as there are blanks.
▶ Never assume that the length of the blank has anything to do with the length of the answer.
▶ Pay attention to the word that precedes the blank.
▶ Look for key words in the sentence that may trigger a response.

Matching Tests

The positive thing about matching questions is that all of your answers are right in front of you. The challenge is getting them all in the right place. Here are some tips:

▶ Read each column before you answer.
▶ Determine whether there are the same number of items in each column. If there are more answers than questions, then you will have some answer choices left over.
▶ Determine whether you may use an answer only once or more than once.

- ▶ Match what you know first.
- ▶ If you are not going to be using any answer more than once, cross off answers that have already been used.
- ▶ Use the process of elimination for answers you might know.
- ▶ Look for logical clues.
- ▶ Use the longer statement as a question; use the shorter statement as an answer.

Subjective Tests

Some students love subjective tests, and others dread them. What makes them different from objective tests? First of all, the answer isn't somewhere on the test. It is in your head, waiting to be formulated. Also, these types of tests aren't "black and white." Although an answer can certainly be wrong, no answer will look the same on every test taker's paper. Some students see this as license to write everything they know, but it is unwise, and wasteful of time, to cover the paper with irrelevant information. The key to success on subjective tests is to understand the questions and to provide brief, direct, and well-supported answers. That's all, you ask? It is not as bad as you think.

Every different test you take requires a different plan of attack for studying. The best thing you can do is to study by doing the very thing you will be doing on the test. This makes sense. Can you imagine being on a football team whose practice sessions consist only of watching tapes of people playing football? Can you imagine practicing for a piano recital by looking over the notes on the sheet of music and hearing the tune in your head? Hardly. The football team that watches people play but never hits the field is doomed to be trampled. The piano player who never tickles the keys will end up quite embarrassed at the recital. In these cases, it makes sense to practice by doing. Why, then, do many students ignore this principle when studying for tests? Does the following lament sound familiar? "I don't know why I flunked the sociology test. I studied for five hours last night. I looked over my notes at least five times." This student put some time into studying, but it was time not well spent. Like our hapless football player and piano player, this student did not prepare by doing. What did she not do? She did not *write*. If you are taking a test that requires writing, you need to prepare by writing. Here are some tips on how to do that:

- ▶ Review your text and class notes. (See Chapter 3 for ways to make them great!)
- ▶ Turn your notes into specific questions.
  - ▷ Think about what the professor stressed during lectures.
  - ▷ Look for main ideas in your notes.
  - ▷ Become your professor. What questions would he or she ask?
  - ▷ Come up with both questions that could be tackled in a few sentences and questions that would require a brief essay.
  - ▷ Meet with your professor during his or her office hours to get feedback on your questions. You want to make sure you are on the right track.
- ▶ Put each question on a separate index card.
- ▶ After a sufficient amount of review time, take out the question cards and answer them on a separate piece of paper.

▶ Time yourself. Remember that you have only a limited time to take a test. Get used to working under a time constraint.

▶ Check your answers against your notes.

▶ Check your answers again.

▶ If possible, find a good student or two from your class. Form a study group. Have each person make up test questions, and then exchange them. You never know what another student will come up with that you may have missed. There is strength in numbers!

Short-Answer Tests

Short-answer tests consist of questions that can be answered in no more than a few sentences. Sometimes, you don't even have to write a complete sentence, just the key words. Make sure you know before you start whether this is permissible, and if you're not sure, ask your professor.

Here are two examples of short-answer question formats that you are likely to encounter:

1. Identify two physical characteristics of the American goldfinch that aid in its survival. Be sure to name the characteristic *and* identify the benefit.
2. Define the term "homeopathic" and provide an example.

Easy enough? Well, you have to remember that since you have only a sentence or two, no word can be wasted. The key to a winning answer on a short-answer test? Be direct. Look at the question. Formulate a brief answer. Check your grammar and punctuation. If you have prepared for a short-answer test by writing, this should be no problem.

 DIV: Do-It-Yourself Activity

Find out what the top professional journals are in your field of study. Make a habit of reading at least a couple of articles a month from those journals. This will help you learn what "conversations" are going on in that field and will familiarize you with its special vocabulary, or jargon.

Essay Tests

Essay tests are an expanded version of short-answer tests. The questions are more complex. The answers are a little longer. The problem that an essay test presents, then, is that students often write "around" the answer before getting to the point or, worse, never really get there at all. How do you avoid this? Think of this analogy: An essay answer is a *sandwich,* not a *pot of soup.*

What can go into a pot of soup? Just about anything. And everything gets mixed together. To make chicken soup, for example, you boil the chicken, make the stock, add vegetables and noodles, and simmer it all together. The final result is good, but the flavors blend into a whole. To find one taste or one ingredient, you have to dig through the others. Now compare this to an essay answer formulated like a pot of soup. Let's say you have just written down everything you remember or everything you think might be related to the question. The professor has to try to find the answer in the soup. More often than not, however, the professor will give very little credit (if any at all) to an answer that did not directly answer the question.

The better alternative in answering an essay question is to build a sandwich. When you make a sandwich, you begin with the bread. When you answer an essay question, the first piece of bread is the direct answer to the essay question. It is the foundation for the rest of your answer. Once you have given a one-sentence answer to the question, you have to support that answer—through examples, discussion, definitions, and the like. Think of these main ingredients as the turkey, the ham, the cheese, the lettuce, the tomato. Smaller, more specific points (salt and pepper?) may also be layered in a precise order on the bread. The sandwich is then finished off with the second piece of bread, which functions as your conclusion. Your conclusion should sum up what you said; it should reflect the answer you stated in the beginning. Thus the opening sentence and the conclusion frame your answer, just as the two pieces of bread hold the sandwich together.

Below is a sample essay question:

1. Identify and discuss three techniques a good student would use to prepare for a test in a new course.

Note two very different responses to this question:

Weak Answer

I hardly ever studied for tests in high school. I just went in and tried to see what I could get away with. However, I can't do that in college because the tests are too hard. So I have had to learn a lot of stuff. I have to use note cards when I study and go over them all the time. My roommate always asks his friends if they had the class and tries to get information from them. He is also a good basketball player so he knows a lot of people. But I have to really study for my tests. I sometimes get people to quiz me.

In conclusion, taking tests in college is really hard. Students really need to prepare for them more than in high school.

The foregoing essay is weak for a number of reasons. If you recall the soup analogy, you can see that this student has merely thrown in a number of items without explicitly connecting them. In addition, the student has added irrelevant information, such as the fact that his roommate is a good basketball player. This student has not clearly answered the question by making the three items that are requested "jump out" at the reader. Now let's look at a stronger essay.

Strong Answer

There are three major things that good students would do in preparing for a test in a new course. First, they would find out what kind of test to expect. Second, they would meet with the professor to discuss strategies. Finally, they would come up with practice questions and take practice tests.

Finding out what kind of test to expect is a key part of being successful. It is important to know what kind of test it is so a student can prepare accordingly.

This information is often on the syllabus; if not, students need to find out from the professor. Preparing for an objective test is much different from preparing for a subjective one.

Meeting with the professor is a good idea for many reasons, but it is particularly important when preparing for a test. Often, the professor will provide you helpful tips. As an added benefit, the professor will appreciate the effort.

Making up practice questions and answering them is a great way to prepare for a test. For one thing, it involves active learning. Furthermore, students can often predict what is actually going to be on the test so that it is familiar when they see it. Also, you are practicing what you will be doing—writing—whereas if you are just reading over your notes, there is no guarantee that you will be prepared.

If applied, these strategies will help students do well on their tests. Finding out what to expect, meeting with the professor, and practicing taking tests will all pay off. Tests in college are hard but do not have to be impossible.

This essay is strong because it is like a sandwich. The student introduces the question first as the foundation (the first piece of bread). The sandwich (essay) is next filled with strong supporting ingredients in an orderly fashion. The sandwich is then completed with the conclusion (the other piece of bread). When an essay question is answered in this way, the professor does not have to search for the answer.

How do you write a strong essay answer yourself? You can follow some very easy steps when you first get the questions, even before you start to write. You can also take definite steps to stay on track when you write the answer. These steps are listed below.

Before you start to write:

1. Read the question carefully at least two times. Make sure you understand every part of the question.
2. Note the key words that tell what kind of answer to write.
   a. *Compare and contrast* means to explain similarities and difference between two or more things. (Example: Compare and contrast the presidencies of Kennedy and Reagan.)
   b. *Discuss* means to present a reason or argument. (Example: Discuss the effects of school uniforms on the behavior of public elementary school students.)
   c. *Trace* means to show the steps in a process. (Example: Trace the development of an "A" answer on an essay exam.)
   d. *Define* means to explain the meaning of a word or idea. (Example: Define the term "subjective" in the context of types of tests.)
   e. *Explain* means to tell how or why. (Example: Explain the change from lecture to web-based instruction for college writing courses.)
3. Make an outline or concept map before you start to write. (*Note*: This does not waste time; it actually saves you time because you won't lose track of where you want to go. Also, if you run out of time, some professor may give you some points for the information in your outline.)

Lifeline

If you think you might need help studying for an essay test, there is help on your campus. Most campuses have tutoring centers or offices where students can sign up for peer tutors. You can find a tutor for the subject and go over possible test questions. After you practice writing out essay answers, request help from a writing tutor to see whether you understand how to organize a good essay answer. Arming yourself with a few writing tips can help you go from just "getting something down on paper" to writing a winning answer. It works!

When you start to write:

1. Answer the question in the first sentence of your essay. (Don't make the professor hunt for the answer!)
2. Use the rest of the essay to prove what you said in the first sentence. Use your outline to stay on track with your first point, second point, third point, and so on.

After you write:

1. Check your answer against your outline or concept map to be sure you didn't omit anything you really wanted to include.
2. Read the answer as one complete unit to make sure it flows well and would make sense to your professor. You can add any transitions you think would be necessary.

Other Types of Tests

Take-Home Tests

The professor says the test is a take-home. Sounds easy, right? Not so fast. Although a take-home test means you will have access to all of your materials and a lot of time to complete the test, the challenge comes from two areas: (1) Your professor is going to expect a much more detailed answer, often with citations, and (2) you have to structure your time carefully so that you will give the test your very best effort.

The steps to success on a take home-test are as follows:

1. Find out exactly what your professors' expectations are. Do they want three pages or ten pages? Do they expect to have formal citations or can you use

informal references? Do they think you'll need 2 hours or 12 hours? How do you find this out? Ask.

2. Organize your material. Take-home tests require you to use all of the material you've used in class plus supplemental material. That's a lot. Before you even start the writing process, you need to figure what you're going to need and then gather it all in one place. That will make the actual time you are taking the test much more productive.

3. Structure your time. If you have a weekend to do the test, schedule the time you will work on it just as you would schedule, say, an appointment with the dentist (though we hope the test-taking experience will be more pleasurable!). Figure out when you're going to do it, and put it on your schedule.

4. Do it. Just putting it on your schedule is not enough. Follow through by doing what you promised yourself.

The good news is that take home-tests are less artificial in that they give you a little more breathing room to allow you to show what you know. Students who suffer from test anxiety in the traditional exam setting will find that take-home tests help them avoid those feelings of anxiety. The key to doing well is to get organized from the beginning. That is, develop a plan and then follow through on it.

Open-Book Tests

The good old open-book test. Open-book tests, much like take home-tests, often sound easier than they really are. More often than not, professors make open-book tests much more difficult than closed-book tests. And for good reason. The answers are right in front of you. But like a dollar bill misplaced on a messy desk with papers piled up all over it, the information in a book may not be so easy to find when the time comes. Many students do poorly on open-book tests because, although the material is there in front of them, they aren't able to access it in the time allotted because their notes are simply too messy. But there is a way to deal with this problem. It is to organize your book and your notes. Here's how:

▶ Buy some sticky notes in various colors. Mark important sections of each chapter with them, writing the topic on each sticky note. Use particular colors for particular types of information—for example, green for definitions, pink for formulas, yellow for important people, and so on.

▶ Highlight, underline, and annotate your text and notes. As you learned in Chapter 3, you need to *do something* with your text, not just read it. This is never more important than in a class with open-book tests.

▶ Anticipate test questions. Write them down. Have a "Table of Contents" for these questions. In other words, write down the page number that corresponds to the answer to each question.

Speaking and Listening Tests

Speaking and listening tests, though not as common as, say, multiple-choice tests, shouldn't catch you off guard. These tests are often given in language classes such as Spanish or French or in music courses. For example, such a test may require you to listen to a selection from a larger work by a particular composer. You may be asked to identify the work, the composer or certain characteristics of the music. In a language course, you may be asked to answer a professor's question out loud in the language, or you may listen to a recording and have to answer questions about it. Speaking and listening tests may also be administered in other courses. Some professors give tests individually and ask you to speak about a certain topic. Their goal, as in any other test, is to see how much of the material you've learned. Listening tests are given as part of the Praxis teacher exams (described in more detail below), and they can also be incorporated into a variety of classroom settings.

Here are some important steps to follow for success on speaking tests:

1. Prepare for such a test as vigorously as for any other test. Don't think you can just wing it because you don't have to write anything down.
2. *Listen!* This may sound obvious, but you must carefully listen to the material. Pay attention. Often, the material will be read aloud or played only once. If you miss it, it's gone.
3. Organize your answers in your head just like an outline. Don't be afraid to think about the question before answering it. Your professor would appreciate the fact that you're giving serious thought to your answer.
4. If it is permitted, take notes while the material is being played or read. This will give you a reference point.
5. Don't get frustrated if you miss something. Doing so may cause you to miss the next set of material that is being read or played. Stay focused.
6. Don't get off the topic. Blathering on and on about irrelevant material is just wasting your professor's time. Don't think she or he is not going to see through it.

What Worked for Me

"The minute I left my first biology lecture," Maria said, "I knew I was in a whole new world. Although I had taken biology in high school, it seemed like we covered a whole year in one day. Plus, there were 130 students in my class—that was the size of my whole senior class. I didn't think the professor would ever know my name." Maria had to develop a plan. "I knew that I couldn't just do what I had done before. I had to try something new."

First, she signed up with a biology tutor. "She showed me some strategies that worked for her when she took the class. That built up my confidence." When Maria ran into some problems that the tutor couldn't help her with, she decided to go see her professor. "I was really nervous about it because this professor didn't really know me at all. But she turned out to be really nice one-on-one, and she gave me some tips on how to study for the test." Applying these strategies made all the difference for Maria in that course. "Don't get me wrong, I'm not planning to become a biology major, but I ended up with a B in the class, and I learned a lot about what I could do as a student."

Career/Professional Tests

If you think your testing days will be over when college is a happy memory, think again. There are many tests that you may take in your career down the road. Lawyers must take the bar exam, counselors must fulfill licensing requirements throughout their careers, and even doctors take periodic exams to ensure that their knowledge is up to date. But even before you get to that point, you may have to take exams toward the end of your college career that will help you get into graduate school or law school, say, or to become certified as a teacher. Here are some of the exams you might be taking:

- ▶ **GRE, the Graduate Record Examination.** This is the test that is required by most graduate schools. The test has three parts: Quantitative, Analytical, and Language Skills. Also, you might have to take a subject area test.
- ▶ **Praxis I and II.** In most states, you must take Praxis exams in order to be certified as a teacher. The Praxis I series consists of reading, writing, math, and listening. Praxis II consists of specialized tests based on your area of certification.
- ▶ **GMAT, the Graduate Management Admission Test.** This is the test you'll take if you're considering getting an MBA.
- ▶ **LSAT, the Law School Admission Test.** As the name implies, this is the test you'll take if you want to go to law school. It features multiple-choice questions and a writing sample.
- ▶ **MAT, the Miller Analogies Test.** Some graduate schools require this in lieu of, or in addition to, the GRE. It features analogies: A is to B as C is to ____.
- ▶ **MCAT, the Medical College Admission Test.** This is the test that applicants to medical school take.

What can you do now to prepare for such tests? First of all, develop good test-taking skills. This will help you gain the skills and confidence necessary to be successful on these types of exams. Second, you need to learn your material thoroughly. If you're cramming for every test now and forgetting the material as soon as the test is over, that's not going to help you much on a test you're taking two or three years from now. The fact is that everything you are doing now is preparing you for tests like these. And if you know already that you want to go to law school or medical school, buy a test prep book now just so you can see what kind of information will be on the test. You can never start too early.

Comprehensive Exams

If you don't know already, you will soon learn that some courses and some degree programs have something waiting for you at the end of the line: the dreaded comprehensive exam. These exams, although they seem overwhelming in the scope of information they cover, don't have to be the end of the world. With the right preparation, you can do well. Comprehensive exams come in two types:

1. Exams that cover material learned in one course throughout the entire semester (such an exam may be called a final)
2. Exams you take in your major in order to graduate.

If you need to take a comprehensive exam at the end of one course, you may find that it is a combination of many of the tests we have described: multiple-choice, true/false, matching, and essay. The difference between a regular test and a comprehensive one in a course is that you need to remember everything from the beginning of the semester. Here are some steps for doing well on comprehensive exams in a course:

1. Keep good notes from the very first day of class.
2. Don't miss class, or at least limit your absences.
3. Make note cards throughout the semester for frequent and periodic review.
4. Save all your other tests if your professor returns them. You can use these to review.
5. Meet with your professor after exams to see where you went wrong if you did not do as well as you had hoped. Such a conversation will help you discover how to do better on the next test.
6. Study in groups. Each group member can come up with questions to ask the other group members. Also, the group members may be able to fill in gaps you may have in your notes.
7. Make up practice tests, and practice taking them!

A comprehensive exam at the end of your college career can be very intimidating. Obviously, you have a lot riding on it because you are about to graduate, and that adds to the stress level. But don't become overwhelmed. Here are some steps for success on a comprehensive test that is a requirement in your major:

1. First, speak with your advisor about what the main topics or questions will be. This information can really narrow the focus of your studying. You will not have to remember everything. Also, find out what format the test will be in. Most likely, this test will consist of essay or short-answer questions, because you will be applying and synthesizing information.
2. Once you have the general topics and format, form a study group with other students in your major. Each group member can be assigned to research and review a different major topic and then report to the rest of the group. This will save a lot of time.
3. Have the group members ask each other questions.
4. Practice writing out answers to possible questions.

Teamwork Activity

The object of this activity is to predict potential test questions. Gather three or four students from your class to form a study group. Using your knowledge of the professor's testing style and the format to be used (often your professor will tell you the format of the test), have each member of the group write down several potential test questions. For example, if the test format is all multiple-choice, write down as many multiple-choice questions as you can think of at a time. If it is a short-answer and essay test, write down questions in that format. You will be surprised how many of the questions you can predict. Naturally, you will also find that it's much easier to recognize the answer if it's "your own" question.

Memorization

To memorize or not to memorize? This is a difficult question. It is often better to really understand information, to be able to apply it, to have it become a part of your everyday life. Sometimes, however, memorization really is necessary. Definitions. Vocabulary in a foreign language. Parts of the body for an anatomy course. But the more meaning you can give to what your need to remember, the better. Anyone can learn to remember information better. It is a matter of knowing a few tricks of the trade.

Here are some tips to improve your memory skills:

▶ **Pay attention!** We remember better that which we focus on in the first place. Don't just take notes in a lecture. Really listen. Note the emphasis the professor places on certain points. Note good examples that the professor gives of concepts.

▶ **Mnemonic devices.** A mnemonic device is a way of remembering material through the use of unrelated words and phrases. They can be silly and even nonsensical, but they are a very effective way of remembering information. For example, if you were to have a test on this chapter and had to remember all the types of tests discussed, you could make up a mnemonic device like this: **My teacher forgot my sandwich even though other students couldn't care.** The first letter of each word would remind you of each type of test: **m**ultiple-choice, **t**rue/**f**alse, **f**ill-in-the-blank, **m**atching, **s**hort-answer, **e**ssay, **t**ake-home, **o**pen-book, **s**peaking and listening, **c**areer/professional, and **c**omprehensive. You probably still remember some mnemonic devices you've used in the past.

▶ **Make memorable associations.** One student had to remember the name Lemieux. It was unfamiliar to him, but he remembered it by associating it with the cartoon character Pepe LePew.

▶ **Try to make a mental picture of something you are trying to remember.** For example, you could remember that Augusta is the capital of Maine by picturing a gust of wind knocking over the mainsail on a ship. You say to yourself, "The Maine problem was Augusta wind."

▶ **Repeat, repeat, repeat.**

▶ **Use a multisensory approach.** Use different senses: Write it down, read it, have someone tell it to you, and see it on a flash card or picture you've drawn.

▶ **Use flash cards.** Write down important information and test yourself. Bring a few cards along with you every day. When you have a few free minutes while waiting for class to start or waiting in line at the bank, grab a card and review it. This strategy really works.

▶ **Study often for short periods of time rather than cramming right before a test.**

Cramming

The best advice about cramming? Don't do it! As we have already seen, in college it is often necessary to retain information well beyond the test itself. It may show up again in a later test in that class, or the information might be the foundation

for something you're expected to know in a future class. This is particularly true if the course serves as a prerequisite for another course.

Cramming is best avoided, but in a pinch, it's better to cram than to do nothing. If you're faced with this situation, you have to realize that you're not going to be able to learn it all, so you need to decide what's most important. Review the most important information first. Recite it until you're out of time. Write down important information over and over. Try to relax; anxiety just gets in the way. Try to get a good night's sleep. Pulling an all-nighter may be a college tradition, but it's not a very effective one. Too often, students who pull all-nighters crash just before the exam.

Test Anxiety

Although anxiety is a natural part of test taking, some students have so much anxiety that it interferes with their ability to take the test. In some cases, a student may even have a clinical case of anxiety. If you think that might be you, your best bet is to seek help from a counselor. In certain cases, you might be legally entitled to accommodations through the Americans with Disabilities Act (ADA). If you have severe anxiety and want more information, seek help from the ADA coordinator on your campus.

Some general tips for test anxiety, particularly milder cases, are the following:

▶ Do some relaxation exercises—deep breathing, for example—right before the test.

The Hard Way

"Now that I am back again after leaving school a year ago, I know I will not study more." Alex, a 20-year-old sophomore psychology major was discussing his plans with a few friends in the cafeteria. They stared at him in disbelief. How could someone who got .83 GPA at the end of freshman year say he was not going to study more? They thought he was headed for trouble again ... until Alex explained. "I am not going to just study more. I am going to study smarter." What Alex had learned the hard way was that just looking at notes, just looking at the book, doesn't get anyone anywhere. He knew, first hand, that he had to take an active role in his studying. He recalled, between gulps of soda and bites of pizza, how, in his general psychology class his first semester, he thought he had everything under control. "I went to class. I took notes. I read my book. But it pretty much ended there. Right before a test, I would take out my notes and my book and skim though them again. Sure I remembered all the stuff. It was right there in front of me! I looked at my notes for a few hours before each test. What I also did was listen to music, watch television, and check out the action below my dorm window. What I didn't do was practice taking tests." Alex learned the hard way how not to study. "I went to my psychology tests and froze. Nothing looked familiar anymore. Nothing had really sunk in. The same thing happened in all my classes." Looking back now, Alex learned a valuable lesson. "Finally, at the end of the year, with a lousy .83 GPA, I left college thinking I would go work. I got a job at a grocery store near my house. After a few weeks, I noticed a woman studying in the break room. She told me she was going to the community college for business. After I sat down to eat my lunch, I noticed she was taking what looked like a test. Turns out that she had made up her own test from her notes and flash cards. She wanted to see if she really knew it. After that, I also enrolled in the general psychology course at the community college and got her to help me study. I ended up with a B. The difference that time was I took an active role in my studying. I wrote information on note cards, I made up practice tests, I had her quiz me. I even talked to the professor about what would be on the test. I now know taking tests is not that hard—once you learn to do it the right way."

▶ Visualize yourself taking the test and being successful.

▶ Be fully prepared. If you've done everything you can to prepare for the test, you'll be more confident and more relaxed.

With these new test-taking tools at your disposal, you'll be at your best the next time you have to take an exam.

Increasing Your Yield:

Readings for Practical Application

In this chapter, we have covered one of the most critical elements of your college education: taking tests. From objective and subjective test to career and professional tests, the chances are that, like it or not, you are going to be taking quite a few tests in your college career. We also talked about test anxiety—what it is and how to deal with it. Learning the art of test taking will make you even more effective in navigating this experience.

A lot of what we know about how to do well on tests is based on research from the field of psychology, and this chapter's "Textbook Case" reading deals with one of the key elements of good test taking: memory. This description of memory is a technical one, examined through the lens of psychology.

In the second section, "Life After College," the career of a lawyer is examined, and the issues of job satisfaction and meaning are discussed. Here you will discover that life after college doesn't mean an end to tests and other professional challenges. The author also talks about how you have to sell your own success to others. You do that in an interview—convincing the interviewer that you have what it takes—but you also do it once you have the job. You have to convince others that you deserve that raise or that promotion.

In the "Current Issues" section, we take a look at the politics of language and how something as seemingly simple as word choice can affect people's feelings. Is using a term such as *sportsmen* simply part of tradition, or does it reinforce male/female stereotypes? Are people who complain about it justified, or are they merely taking things too seriously?

Reading and Study Tips: Psychology

Unique Features and Comprehension Strategies

Psychology textbooks feature discipline-specific vocabulary. Psychology is the scientific study of human mental processes. As a unique area of study, it has its own unique vocabulary. Terms drawn from this vocabulary often appear in boldface type at the point where they are introduced and defined, and they may also appear in a glossary at the back of the book. **Internalize vocabulary. You will be learning a great deal of new and unfamiliar terms in your reading. If you have to look up every word every time, it's going to take you a lot longer to read, and it's going to be much harder to understand. When you come across a new vocabulary word, take time to understand it thoroughly before reading on. Stop for a moment, say it to yourself, and then say the meaning. If you don't know the meaning, look it up in the glossary or in a dictionary, or try to pick up the meaning from the context. By doing this, you will be more familiar with the word the next time you come across it.**

Much of what is covered in psychology textbooks is research-based. Much of what you will learn about human behavior from psychology textbooks is a result of studies that have been done by people in the field over a large span of time. Statements about human behavior, then, will often be followed by evidence supporting the statement. This evidence will be in the form of specific research studies that are cited in the text. The researchers and the specific studies will be noted. It is important to understand that this evidence is part of the whole picture the textbook represents. **Look up the primary research. Your textbooks collect information from many different sources, including studies that are considered primary research. If you are interested in one area, or you want to understand how a theory was developed, use the list of references in your textbook to locate the sources. This is also a good idea if you have been assigned a research paper. Use your textbook as a starting point for your research.**

Psychology textbooks provide examples of the application of concepts. Because psychology is the study of human behavior, theories and concepts are applied in order to explain behavior. Textbooks present theories, concepts, ideas, definitions, and terms and then show their application in the "real world" or to situations with which you are familiar. These applications help to reinforce and make more concrete the abstract information presented. **Think of your own applications for the definitions, theories, and concepts presented. These applications will be easier for you to remember, and coming up with them will ensure that you really understand the subject matter involved. Furthermore, exams and tests often require you to apply concepts or theories, so you need lots of practice doing this.**

Psychology textbooks often provide chapter outlines. Because psychology textbooks are presenting concepts rather than telling a story, the authors generally provide an outline to help guide you through the readings. Remember that the authors themselves probably used this outline to guide their writing. **Read chapter outlines and summaries before reading the chapter. This will help you in comprehending unfamiliar material. Look for outlines at the beginning of each chapter. You will find these helpful in getting a picture of what's coming, which in itself will help you comprehend the material better. This general outline can also help you create a more specific outline on your own.**

Psychology textbooks often use graphical illustrations. There are some principles in psychology—Maslow's hierarchy of needs, for example—where an illustration is the best way to explain the ideas involved. **Study such illustrations and even redraw them for yourself. Doing so will help you understand the material and remember it better.**

Material in psychology textbooks is not always presented in a linear fashion. Because of this, you will find that annotating the text will help you understand the "big picture" better. There are clear sections in psychology textbooks. The text presents a concept or theory, explains it, and then gives an example. Often, the text will go right on to another term or concept. Because the texts present material in small chunks, you will find annotation much easier in a psychology textbook. **You can read a small amount of material at a time in a psychology textbook. When you come back to where you stopped before, you can use your annotations for a quick review, and then continue on to the next section.**

Reading 1:   A Textbook Case

This excerpt from a chapter in a psychology textbook is included here because of the connection between learning and studying and psychology. In many cases, knowing why certain study techniques work (or don't work) for you can be as important as knowing what they are. Why? Because in college you will be called on to adapt your study skills in new ways in order to meet the challenges posed by college-level classes. Applying the *exact same* study strategy that you used in high school may prove unsuccessful. But if you understand how the strategy works, you will be able to adapt it to new modes of learning. The following selection examines memory, one of the basic building blocks of studying. As you read, think about the many ways in which you have used your memory since you have arrived in college.

BEFORE YOU READ

1. What techniques do you use now to try to remember information? What type of information do you tend to remember best and why?

2. Have you ever had some piece of information—a phone number, somebody's name, a favorite tune—on the tip of your tongue but have found yourself unable to recall it? How did that make you feel? What finally helped you recall the information?

The Nature of Memory

D. A. Bernstein and P. W. Nash

How does information get turned into memories?

Memory is a funny thing. You might be able to remember the name of your first-grade teacher, but not the name of someone you just met five minutes ago. Mathematician John Griffith estimated that in an average lifetime, a person stores roughly five hundred times as much information as can be found in all volumes of the *Encyclopaedia Britannica* (M. Hunt, 1982). Keep in mind, however, that although we retain a great deal of information, we also lose a great deal (Bjork & Vanhuele, 1992).

Memory plays a critical role in your life. Without memory, you would not know how to shut off your alarm, take a shower, get dressed, recognize objects, or communicate. You would be unaware of your own likes and dislikes. You would have no idea of who you are (Craik et al., 1999). The impressive capacity of human memory depends on the operation of a complex mental system (Schacter, 1999).

Basic Memory Processes

A psychology professor we know sometimes drives to work and sometimes walks. He once drove to his office, forgot he had driven, and walked home. When he didn't see his car in its normal spot the next morning, he reported the car stolen. The police soon called to say that "some college kids" must have stolen the car, because it was found on campus (next to the psychology building!). What went wrong? There are several possibilities. Memory depends on three basic processes: encoding, storage, and retrieval. Our absent-minded professor might have had problems with any one of these.

First, information must be put into memory, a step that requires encoding. **Encoding** is a process that puts information to be remembered into a form that our memory system can accept and use. We use *memory codes* to translate information from the senses into mental representations of that information. **Acoustic codes** represent information as sequences of sounds, such as a tune or a rhyme. **Visual codes** represent stimuli as pictures, such as the image of a person's face. **Semantic codes** represent the general meaning of an experience. Thus, if you see a billboard that reads "Huey's Going-Out-of-Business Sale," you might encode the sound of the words as if they had been spoken (acoustic coding), the image of the letters as they were arranged on the sign (visual coding), or the fact that you recently saw an ad for Huey's (semantic coding). The type of coding we use influences what we remember. Semantic coding might allow you to remember that an unfamiliar car was parked in your neighbors' driveway just before their house was robbed. If there were little or no other coding, however, you might not be able to remember the make, model, or color of the car.

The second basic memory process is storage. **Storage** refers to the holding of information in your memory over time. When you recall a vacation taken in childhood or find it possible to use a pogo stick many years after you last played with one, you are depending on the storage capacity of your memory.

The third process, **retrieval**, occurs when you find information stored in memory and bring it into consciousness. Retrieving stored information such as your address or telephone number is usually so fast and effortless that is seems automatic. The search-and-retrieval process becomes more noticeable, however, when you read a quiz question but cannot quite recall the answer. Retrieval involves both recall and recognition. To *recall* information, you have to retrieve it from memory without much help; this is what is required when you answer an essay test question or play *Jeopardy!* In *recognition,* retrieval is aided by clues, such as the response alternatives given on multiple-choice tests and the questions on *Who Wants to Be a Millionaire*. Accordingly, recognition tends to be easier than recall.

Types of Memory

In which hand does the *Statue of Liberty* hold her torch? When was the last time you made a phone call? What part of speech is used to modify a noun? Your attempt to answer the first question is likely to elicit a visual image. To answer the second, you must remember a particular event in your life. The third question requires general knowledge that is unlikely to be tied to a specific event. Some psychologists suggest that answering each of these questions requires a different type of memory (Baddeley, 1998). How many types of memory are there? No one is sure, but most research suggests that there are at least three basic types. Each is named for the kind of information it handles: episodic, semantic, and procedural (J. B. Best, 1999).

Any memory of a specific event that happened while you were present is an **episodic memory**. It is a memory of an episode in your life. What you had for dinner yesterday, what you did last summer, [and] where you were last Friday night are episodic memories. **Semantic memory** contains generalized knowledge of the world—such as that twelve items make a dozen—that does not involve memory of a specific event. So you would answer the question "Are wrenches pets or tools?" using your semantic memory, because you don't have to remember a specific episode in which you learned that wrenches are tools. As a general rule, people convey episodic memories by saying, "I remember when . . ." whereas they convey semantic memories by saying, "I know that . . ." (Tulving, 1995). **Procedural memory** involves knowledge of how to do things, such as riding a bike, reading a map, or playing tennis. A procedural memory often consists of a complicated sequence of movements that cannot be described adequately in words. For instance, a gymnast might find it impossible to describe the exact motions in a particular routine.

Many activities require all three types of memories. Consider the game of tennis. Knowing the official rules or the number of sets needed to win a match involves semantic memory. Remembering which side served last requires episodic memory. And knowing how to hit the ball involves procedural memory.

Recalling all three kinds of memories can be either intentional or unintentional. When you deliberately try to remember something, such as where you went on your last vacation, you are relying on **explicit memory**. In contrast, **implicit memory** involves the unintentional recollection and influence of prior experiences (D. L. Nelson, 1999; D. L. Schacter, Chiu, & Ochsner, 1993). For instance, while watching a movie about a long car trip, you might begin to feel slightly anxious because you subconsciously recall a time you had engine trouble on such a trip. Implicit memory operates automatically and without conscious effort. In fact, people are often unaware that their actions have been influenced by previous events. Because some influential events cannot be recalled even when people try to do so, implicit memory has been said to involve "retention without remembering" (Roediger, Guynn, & Jones, 1995).

AFTER YOU READ

1. The authors give an example of the professor who thought his car was stolen when, in fact, he had just forgotten that he had driven it to work. Have you ever done anything similar? What have you learned about memory that could help you avoid doing something like this?

2. How can understanding the psychological nature of memory help you to improve your own memory skills? Use specific examples from the reading.

3. Provide your own examples of each of the different types of memory that you learned about in this selection.

Reading 2: **Life After College**

We've all seen films and television programs about lawyers, which usually focus on the drama of the courtroom. What they don't show, however, is the years of preparation, all of the hard "leg work" and research behind the scenes, and the office politics that affects who gets what case and who is promoted in the firm. In this chapter we talked about test taking and the challenges and stress associated with it. As this article hints, challenges and stress don't disappear once you graduate from college. In many cases, they grow, and in most careers, you will have a fair share of both. Consequently, if you develop effective strategies now for handling challenges and stress, the benefits will almost certainly carry over into your professional career.

BEFORE YOU READ

1. What were some of the tests you had to take in order to get into college? What kinds do you think you will need to take to get into your chosen career? How have you prepared? How will you prepare?
2. What is your impression of the legal profession? What depictions of it have you seen on TV and in movies? Are they generally positive or negative? How realistic do you think they are?
3. What is "an associate" in the context of this title? How can you figure it out before reading the article?

Don't See Yourself as an Associate?

G. Cutter

Welcome to the firm! You've toiled most of your life to reach this point—buckling down in high school to improve your chance of Ivy League admission, tailoring your college curriculum to showcase your pre-law promise and mastering abstruse logic games to ace the LSAT. The reward for all that hard work? Three years of Socratic fear and loathing with a bar exam chaser. It's time to be happy, right?

After keeping your nose to the proverbial grindstone and deferring fun and frivolity to reach this day, you are now a first-year associate at a prestigious firm. The digs are great, the pay is incredible—but did you have to check your dreams at the door?

Lawyers are by their nature a serious and hardworking bunch, experts at delayed gratification. Most understand that the "brass ring" is elusive, and the first years of practice can offer large doses of tedium interrupted by occasional infusions of sheer panic. But given the sacrifices one must make to enter the profession, financial and temporal, where is the payoff?

Certainly, our choices in life and their consequences are given context by the times in which

we live. In other words, timing is everything. Just days after I launched my Wall Street legal career in the fall of 1987, Black Monday happened—the largest stock market drop in history, when the Dow lost almost 23 percent of its value in one day. That was a jarring introduction to the impact of markets on corporate firm practice, but it didn't dampen my enthusiasm for transactional practice.

That stock market "correction"—while it appeared cataclysmic at the time—was a ripple in the pond compared with the aftermath of the events of [September 11, 2001]. Having observed the first anniversary of the attacks, career decisions, like all life's choices, stand in sharper relief. While no one discounts the importance of planning for the future, we are all struck by the sense that each of us must make today matter.

A Wonderful Life

That's just what my Columbia Law School classmate Matt Leonard did in his short lifetime. A Cantor Fitzgerald lawyer who perished on Sept. 11, Matt always gave 110 percent to every endeavor. Though he was a smart guy—great grades, top firm job and a prestigious Southern District of New York

Gail E. Cutter, "Don't See Yourself as an Associate? No One Else Will Either. Finding Fulfillment as a Lawyer Begins by Giving 110%," *Texas Lawyer* 18 (October 14, 2002), 26. This article is reprinted with permission from *Texas Lawyer*. ©Texas Lawyer.

clerkship—more important to Matt than making a lot of money was doing good. Maybe it was his Jesuit upbringing or perennially sunny outlook, but Matt came closer to embodying the values of "It's a Wonderful Life" than anyone I've ever seen.

When Matt dedicated countless hours to pro bono organizations, ultimately earning a seat on the board of MFY Legal Services Inc., recognition was the furthest thing from his mind. He volunteered to chair his 15th law school reunion, not for the fabulous networking opportunity it would offer with his now-successful classmates, but because he genuinely enjoyed bringing people together. When Matt stopped on a snowy street corner to sing Christmas carols with a homeless man, he didn't do it to win points—just dimes and quarters for his duet partner. The federal judge for whom Matt clerked said of him, "He was probably one of the kindest law clerks I ever had. . . . It is a loss beyond the measure of comprehension." Imagine inspiring that kind of eulogy.

Lately, stories of compassion, courage and heroism appear alongside accounts of greed, fraud and cover-ups by accountants, lawyers and other corporate fiduciaries. Where can today's junior associates look for role models? How can a novice professional align her moral compass in a world where integrity and honesty seem to be in short supply?

In counseling hundreds of law students and lawyers over the past decade, I've observed that our profession is, on the whole, full of closet idealists. Law school is an affirmative choice over business school largely due to a desire for deeper purpose. In spite of steadily climbing starting salaries, most law students say they pursued a legal education to "make a difference." Many gladly would forgo some of the money for a greater sense of purpose—they just don't know where to start. More disturbing, they believe that career choices are binary and that good comes only in the form of public interest and sacrifice; working in a firm is viewed as "selling out" and utterly incompatible with deriving meaning from practice. Where is the archetype of the public-private partnership? When did the term "corporate citizen" become an oxymoron?

Somehow, the associate position has become a professional way station, a means to an end. Law students assume that private practice will not provide job satisfaction, but will somehow magically transport them after a few years to a more desirable and meaningful career destination. The familiar law student refrain "I don't see myself staying in a firm too long" is usually followed by "I want to keep my options open."

Focus, Learn, Observe

Happily, the search for a meaningful start in legal practice and the pursuit of career mobility can both find resolution in the same approach. Simply put, the best way to plan for tomorrow is to strive for excellence in all you do today. It might sound like a Hallmark card, but a real investment in and commitment to your current responsibilities and relationships will lead to future opportunities. As mom used to say, nothing succeeds like success.

The best way to keep your options open is to see yourself as an associate. Devote yourself to private practice, and to your chosen employer, 110 percent. Why bother, you ask, if you're a short-timer?

In the first place, your firm has earned your commitment, given how much it is paying you. More important, your clients will demand and deserve all of the energy, focus and skill that you can muster. You might not think that Megacorp A's skirmish over market share with Megacorp B is "meaningful," but it certainly is to the employees whose livelihood is tied to the outcome of the case, not to mention the shareholders whose 401(k)s are heavy in Megacorp A stock. Lives may not depend on the accuracy of your research or the precision of your due diligence, but you should care as if they did.

Start now to define your professional identity. From this day forward, everyone you encounter, from opposing counsel to court clerks to clients to firm partners, will be drawing conclusions about you as a lawyer and as a person. If you don't see yourself as a successful firm associate, neither will anyone else. You may think that your antipathy to private practice is invisible to all but your closest friends. Think again. Partners and senior associates can spot apathy from a mile away, and they are much too busy to waste their valuable time and energy training and mentoring uncommitted associates.

If your goal is mobility, remember that successful firm associates have many options and unsuccessful ones have few. Every day of your firm life is an audition—you don't even know for whom and for what role. Your supervisors, colleagues, adversaries and clients are constantly sizing you up—judging your competency, attitude and future prospects. While you are yawning through some mid-level's interminable drafting session or doodling during a deposition, you are being observed. Even that game of Nerf basketball to break up the monotony of due diligence does not go unnoticed.

Be a Sponge

Learning is an attitude, and observation is an active process. Think of yourself as a sponge, and seek opportunities for soaking up information, skills and professional lessons. Trapped in a partner's office while he argues with co-counsel on an unrelated matter? Instead of silently seething or playing Tetris on your Palm Pilot, learn from this lesson. Consider the attorney's negotiation style. What can you observe about this pro's approach? What would you do differently? Try to be inconspicuous. Don't smile, nod at his good points or hold up score cards rating his performance, but take notes. Test your own firm lingo. How many buzzwords does the partner use that you don't understand? Make a discreet note of them (on that trusty legal pad you are never without) and look them up later.

Real substantive training and meaningful feedback are not your birthright. They are the reward for your hard work and for winning the confidence of more-experienced attorneys at your firm. Associates who view the world with a sense of entitlement do not inspire the loyalty and helpful guidance of partners. And a junior associate without a partner or influential senior associate to watch his back often "falls through the cracks"—ending up with too few assignments and facing obscurity, if not outright dismissal, come evaluation time.

Record Your Highs and Lows

You'll never be able to identify your dream job—let alone obtain it—until you know where your passion lies. Keep a detailed record of your projects—not just substance and skills, but highlights and lowlights. Note accomplishments by the firm's standards, as well as your own. Take a daily reading of your emotional barometer. Note the sources of your ups and downs, what comes easily and what is sheer torture, and what is a struggle but provides real satisfaction. Over time, this information will provide the road map to your dream job. The process even might reveal that you derive more meaning and satisfaction in your daily firm grind—in the little things—than you ever expected.

Your best lessons in professionalism also will come from the day-to-day things. Treat every client encounter, meeting with opposing counsel or conference call as if it were an encounter with a future employer—it could be. Picture yourself being hired by your firm's biggest client. Envision earning a recommendation for a public sector job from your pro bono supervisor. Visualize your former partner referring a case to your new solo practice. It could happen; in fact, it happens every day.

Move to a client's legal department, and you may one day become your supervising partner's client. Instead of conjuring up revenge fantasies, focus on practical ways to strengthen your current professional ties; they will last a long time.

Strive to be known as a person of integrity. Resist the urge to start lying in little ways. The five minutes you "round up" on your time sheet today or the phony excuse to put off a deadline tomorrow could devolve into much more serious matters later on. Surely the professionals embroiled in corporate fraud today did not start out their careers with the aim to deceive. Never lose sight of what is honest and true.

Write a letter to yourself now to crystallize your hopes and dreams in the law. Divulge your most treasured hopes about your professional future, your expectations and your greatest fears. Review this letter every year at evaluation time to keep yourself on track. Your goals and aspirations may change because you've gained greater self-knowledge, but don't give up on your dreams.

In his 15 years of practice, my friend Matt built a life any lawyer would be proud to emulate. He followed his heart instead of his wallet. He always made time to do legal work for the poor, even when he worked on the 104th floor of the World Trade Center as a high-powered securities litigator. He never forgot where he came from, that first job as a janitor, and he always treated everyone with respect. He represented the best the profession could be. And Matt always remembered to follow his bliss; he never stopped singing.

As you strike out on your own path, remember why you became a lawyer. Approach every project, no matter how mundane, as if your professional reputation depended on it. Find time to offer legal help—80 percent of Americans cannot afford it. Preserve and protect what is best about your character; don't let the practice or profession change you into a person you no longer respect. And most important, never forget to sing.

AFTER YOU READ

1. What is the author's main point about a law career? What does she mean by deferred gratification?
2. Why, according to the author, is every encounter—whether with a judge or with a clerk—important? How can you apply this philosophy as a college student?

Reading 3: Current Issues

The following excerpt discusses the issue of gender in language. In college, you are studying information from many different sources, some new, some old. As you look at the following essay on an aspect of language, think about how the English you're reading in today's textbooks is different from what you might read in a source that is a hundred years old—or four hundred years old. It's still English, but it has changed. Why? What factors lead to change? What factors discourage change?

BEFORE YOU READ

1. What does the term *political correctness* mean? What are some of the positive and negative connotations?
2. When have you been offended by what someone said? How did you react?

The Great Person-Hole Cover Debate

L. Van Gelder

I wasn't looking for trouble. What I was looking for, actually, was a little tourist information to help me plan a camping trip to New England.

But there it was, on the first page of the 1979 edition of the State of Vermont *Digest of Fish and Game Laws and Regulations*: a special message of

welcome from one Edward F. Kehoe, commissioner of the Vermont Fish and Game Department, to the reader and would-be camper, i.e., me.

This person (i.e., me) is called "the sportsman."

"We have no 'sportswomen, sportspersons, sportsboys, or sportsgirls,'" Commissioner Kehoe

Lindsy Van Gelder, "The Great Person-Hole Cover Debate." In A. Cassebaum and R. Haskell, *American Culture and the Media: Reading, Writing, Thinking* (Boston: Houghton Mifflin, 1997), pp. 144–146. Originally published in *MS.* Magazine. Reprinted by permission of the author.

hastened to explain, obviously anticipating that some of us sportsfeminists might feel a bit overlooked. "But," he added, "we are pleased to report that we do have many great sportsmen who are women, as well as young people of both sexes."

It's just that the Fish and Game Department is trying to keep things "simple and forthright" and to respect "long-standing tradition." And anyway, we really ought to be flattered, "sportsman" being "a meaningful title" being earned by a special kind of dedicated man, woman, or young person, as opposed to just any hunter, fisherman, or trapper."

I have heard this particular line of reasoning before. In fact, I've heard it so often that I've come to think of it as The Great Person-Hole Cover Debate, since gender-neutral manholes are frequently brought into the argument as evidence of the lengths to which humorless, Newspeak-spouting feminists will go to destroy their mother tongue.

Consternation about woman-handling the language comes from all sides. Sexual conservatives who see the feminist movement as a unisex plot and who long for the good olde days of *vive la différence,* when men were men and women were women, nonetheless do not rally behind the notion that the term "mankind" excludes women.

But most of the people who choke on expressions like "spokesperson" aren't right-wing misogynists, and this is what troubles me. Like the undoubtedly well-meaning folks at the Vermont Fish and Game Department, they tend to reassure you right up front that they're only trying to keep things "simple" and to follow "tradition," and that some of their best men are women, anyway.

Usually, they wind up warning you, with great sincerity, that you're jeopardizing the worthy cause of women's rights by focusing on "trivial" side issues. I would like to know how anything that gets people so defensive and resistant can possibly be called "trivial," whatever else it might be.

The English language is alive and constantly changing. Progress—both scientific and social—is reflected in our language, or should be.

Not too long ago, there was a product called "flesh-colored" Band-Aids. The flesh in question was colored Caucasian. Once the civil rights movement pointed out the racism inherent in the name, it was dropped. I cannot imagine reading a thoughtful, well-intentioned company policy statement explaining that while the Band-Aids would continue to be called "flesh-colored" for old time's sake, black and brown people would now be considered honorary whites and were perfectly welcome to use them.

Most sensitive people manage to describe our national religious traditions as "Judeo-Christian," even though it takes a few seconds longer to say than "Christian." So why is it such a hardship to say "he or she" instead of "he"?

I have a modest proposal for anyone who maintains that "he" is just plain easier: since "he" has been the style for several centuries now—and since it really includes everybody anyway, right?— it seems only fair to give "she" a turn. Instead of having to ponder over the intricacies of, say, "Congressman" versus "Congressperson" versus "Representative," we can simplify things by calling them all "Congresswoman."

Other clarifications will follow: "a woman's home is her castle". . . "a giant step for all womankind". . . "all women are created equal". . . "Fisherwoman's wharf.". . .

And don't be upset by the business letter that begins "Dear Madam," fellas. It means you, too.

AFTER YOU READ

1. Van Gelder mentions a passage she found in the 1979 edition of the State of Vermont *Digest of Fish and Game Laws and Regulations.* Do you think the current edition of that guide still uses the term *sportsman* universally? Why or why not?

2. How does the author use humor to make her point? How does she turn the opponent's arguments against them? Do you think her techniques are effective? Use some examples from the passage to explain.

3. Before reading this article, we asked about the term *political correctness.* How does it apply to this article? Has your opinion on the issue changed in any way?
4. How may the language you use to answer questions in class and on a test affect the way the professor perceives you as a person and the quality of your answer? Has this ever happened to you? Have you known it to happen to someone else?

Compounding Your Interest: Further Readings

Morrow, D. (October 13, 1996). "'What's my line? Good Question' (The use of aptitude testing in corporate America)." *New York Times.*

Smith, G. (April/May 2002). "Survivor—College Style." *Career World.*

_____. (September 1997). "What you need to know about pre-employment tests." *Career World.*

Chapter 5

Critical Thinking Strategies for the Academic Investor

This chapter will cover the following topics:

"For there is nothing either good or bad, but thinking makes it so," Hamlet muses in Shakespeare's play of the same name. In a sense, this is exactly the point of critical thinking. You, the critical thinker, have the ability to determine what you think about issues, about what you've read, and about what you see or hear. You may make an initial judgment on the basis of a first reaction, but it is in looking more closely at something that you can really determine its merit. To be an effective critical thinker, you must base your judgments on sound principles.

As an academic investor, you want to be as aware as possible of potential pitfalls that could put your academic investments (such as time, effort, and reputation) at risk, and you also need to be able to recognize a good investment opportunity when you see one. How do you do this? By being a critical investor. At the college level, what this really means is being a student who applies critical thinking skills in all aspects of his or her college career.

Critical thinking is "the careful, deliberate determination of whether we should accept, reject, or suspend judgment about a claim, and the degree of confidence with which we accept or reject it" (Moore & Parker, 1997). As a critical thinker, you are called upon to make judgments about many things you encounter in everyday life and in your academic pursuits. You cannot accept everything you read, hear, and see at face value. The mere fact that something is in print does not make it true or valid. Just because someone says something happened does not make it a fact. Likewise, something that is a fact is not an opinion. But you may have an opinion about it. Confused? That may not be a bad thing.

Think About It

Answer the following questions in the space provided.

Why might a tobacco company be a biased source of information for a research project on second-hand smoke? What are some other examples you can think of in which a company or other organization might be biased? What problems may this cause, and what can you do to be sure you receive as much objective information as possible? _____

_____

Admitting that discerning fact from opinion is a complex—and sometimes confusing—process is often one of the first steps to becoming a critical thinker. This chapter will help you work your way through the confusion so that thinking critically becomes second nature.

First Things First

Are you not yet convinced that you need to be a critical thinker? Let's say you are writing a research paper on the effects of second-hand smoke for your health class. On the basis of the results of some quick searching on the Web, you are arguing that second-hand smoke isn't really that bad. Sounds okay, right? Hold on. Where did your get your research? If in looking back at the Web pages you visited, you discover that your main source was a major tobacco company, you could have a problem. Not that the results are automatically negated, but you have to be aware of the possibility of bias. Even if you don't notice it, your audience will, and that can lead them to question your entire argument. Did you think critically about your sources? If not, you may soon find out that your investment of time and effort was ineffective. To avoid this problem in the future, you need to learn how to think more critically.

Becoming a Critical Thinker Every Day

Critical thinking is not just a classroom exercise. You need to be a critical thinker in all aspects of your everyday life, from having conversations with friends, to watching television, to choosing the best major or career. Every day you must make decisions that require you to understand thoroughly what is going on, what your options are, and what the best choice may be. It could be as simple as what to eat for dinner. It could also be as complicated as ending a long-term relationship or transferring to another college. Once you begin to see critical thinking as an everyday activity, it will become second nature. Here are some examples of everyday situations that require good critical thinking skills:

It is almost midterm and you are failing your biology class. The class is required for your major, and you need it now to stay in the proper sequence of courses. You feel like you will never pass it, however, and wonder if you should drop it.

You have gotten in the habit of eating fast food in the cafeteria and have gained weight and feel lethargic. You contemplate a change in your diet and wonder if you should seek professional guidance.

Your friend has all but moved into your room because she doesn't get along with her roommate. You want to help her, but these constant visits are keeping you from getting your work done.

You are having trouble keeping up with your classes because you are in a difficult major. You really want to try out for the lacrosse team, however. You wonder whether or not you can be a good student and a lacrosse player at the same time.

A friend has recently been telling you that he is contemplating suicide. You have spent several sleepless nights helping him and have missed a number of classes as a result. You don't want to abandon your friend, but you also don't want to flunk out of school.

It is almost election time, and you have done little to keep up with the candidates and the issues. One of the candidates visits your campus and says that, if elected, he will provide more financial assistance for college students. You wonder if you should vote for him on the basis of this one statement.

A friend of yours is working an overnight shift at a local warehouse in order to earn enough money for expenses. Lately, though, she has been missing her two morning classes because she's too tired. She told you recently that she is probably going to fail both of those classes.

You recently returned to college after dropping out ten years earlier. Since then you have had two children who are now in elementary school. Although you thought that you would have more time now that your children are older, the opposite is proving to be true. With all of their homework and activities, you barely have enough time to attend to their needs and the needs of your spouse, let alone do enough for the three college classes in which you are enrolled. You are beginning to think that going back to college was a mistake.

At a couple of recent parties, you drank heavily and blacked out for parts of the evening. You were told by friends about some of the embarrassing things that you did. You don't want to get a bad reputation, but you also don't want to stop having fun.

A credit card company has set up a stand in the student union building. The company representatives are offering some great free gifts for signing up. You'd like the gifts, but you are afraid that if you get the card you will overuse it, and you don't even have a job.

At the student union, you and your friends are sitting around talking about a professional athlete who has been charged with sexual assault. One of the friends says, "I know he's guilty. I can see it in his face."

Obviously, you will have many assignments in college in which you will analyze and develop arguments, but it is just as clear that you can't stop thinking critically when you leave the classroom. The above scenarios are real-life problems in need of real-life solutions. Later in this chapter, you will be exposed to specific problem-solving strategies that can be applied to these problems, as well as to other problems you will encounter while in college.

Fact versus Opinion

A dolphin is a mammal. Pearl Harbor was bombed on December 7, 1941. Harvard University was founded in 1636. Everyone needs a college degree in this current employment climate. A Granny Smith is a type of apple. Is there an opinion among these sentences? Which one is it? If you said the opinion is "Everybody needs a college degree in this current employment climate," you are correct. Why? Because an opinion is a belief that needs support. It can be argued about and debated. You, as a college student, may feel one way, and your friend, who joined the army, may feel another way. You can both go out and gather evidence to argue one way or the other. A conclusion may never be reached. Think about it. Your friend may offer as an example someone such as Bill Gates, who never finished college but is one of the wealthiest people in the world. You may be able to find evidence of college graduates being less susceptible to layoffs than those with little or no college. Your friend may counter with statistics on the healthy job climate for plumbers and electricians, both of whom do not need a college degree to work in their field. It can go on and on.

A fact, however, cannot be argued. It can be proved. A statement of fact does not include evaluation or judgment. A fact can be verified by tests, measurements, historical records, or other sources of information. If you indicated that all the other sentences at the beginning of this section were facts, you were correct. Why? You can prove each one. Let's begin with the dolphin. You can prove it is a mammal by citing scientific documents that list the characteristics of a mammal and showing that a dolphin exhibits those characteristics. It would also be very easy to find historical documents indicating the date that Pearl Harbor was bombed. You may even still be able to speak with eyewitnesses. To prove when Harvard University was founded, you could also turn to historical documentation. As far as the Granny Smith is concerned, you can find proof that there is a type of apple called a Granny Smith.

Here are some things to remember about facts and opinions:

▶ Words contained in statements of facts and opinions are often very different. Facts contain concrete words referring to specific things, dates, and information that can be proved. Look for words such as *17 pounds, 1974, 68 degrees, oak tree.* Opinions, on the other hand, contain abstract words that are hard to measure, such as *hot, cold, hate, tall, short, beautiful.*

▶ Statements that show attitudes toward something are opinions because they cannot be proved as absolute fact. For example, when a student says, "College algebra is a waste of time," he or she is expressing a personal opinion. This student, if engaging in a debate about this topic, would need to provide support for this opinion in the form of examples or reasons why, in his or her particular case, an algebra course is a waste of time. This student may be an art major who feels that more art courses are more important than math; a business major, by contrast, might not have as much support for such an opinion.

▶ Students need to be able to distinguish between facts and the interpretation of facts. One of the most widely studied events of the last fifty years is the assassination of President John F. Kennedy. Experts agree that he was killed on November 22, 1963. That is a fact. It was captured on videotape and witnessed by countless numbers of people. It has become a matter of historical record. The interpretation of that event, however, varies widely. Many accept that a single gunman was responsible, whereas others speculate that the assassination was part of a conspiracy. These are opinions—neither has been proved. The *fact* remains, however, that Kennedy was killed on November 22, 1963.

▶ Be aware that many little facts do not always add up to one big fact, because that big "fact" may still remain an opinion. Let's go back to the opinion asserted earlier that everyone needs to go to college in this current employment climate. You may be able to prove that the average starting salary of a software

Teamwork Activity

The object of this activity is to help you work together with your classmates in distinguishing facts from opinions. Being able to do this will help you as you take more classes and conduct more research in college. It is one of the most basic skills of a good critical thinker.

Break into groups of three or four. As a group, read and discuss the statements listed in the table below. After you have discussed each one as a group, enter a check mark to indicate whether the statement is a fact or an opinion. Then, in the space provided, enter a brief reason why you answered as you did.

	Fact	Opinion	Why?
Biology is the best major to prepare for medical school.			
Dr. Gramley teaches Bio 101 at 8 a.m. on Tuesdays and Thursdays.			
The turkey wrap in the cafeteria is a healthful alternative to a hamburger.			
The math text for Math 105 was written by a professor at this school.			
Speech is the best course to take as a first-semester freshman.			

engineer with a bachelor's degree is higher than the average starting salary of a factory worker at a large automobile plant. You may also be able to prove that the lifetime earnings of people with bachelor's degrees are a significant percentage higher than those of people with a high school diploma. You may even be able to prove that certain jobs are available only to those who have earned at least a bachelor's degree. You may have gathered all these facts, but these facts do not make the original assertion that a college degree is necessary in the current employment climate any less of an opinion. Why? Well, what about the facts that your friend will marshal to support the other side of that argument? He or she may show that jobs not requiring a college degree are more plentiful in a certain geographic location. He or she may also show that the cost of college and the income loss while in college will not be made up by the possible higher salary. Both sides offer good arguments. Remember, an opinion is something that can be argued. But all the evidence that can be gathered does not transform the opinion into a fact.

Arguments

What are we talking about when we discuss argument? In this context, we're not talking about the type of argument two people might have if they are angry at each other. What we are talking about is forming an opinion or making a claim about an issue and using evidence to support it. Still, what does that mean? For you as a college student, making an argument, especially in the context of a college-level paper, is expressing your particular belief about a topic and being able to substantiate that belief. You can have an opinion about computer-based registration procedures, such as "That's not going to work" or "This is a better way." In order for that to be an argument, however, you need to back it up with research (in other words, you've done some homework on the issue) and proof that your view has support. Therefore, instead of simply "That's not going to work," you can say, "That's not going to work because there are not enough computer terminals that will have access to the online registration." This contention would be followed by evidence. (For example, your discovery that there are only 200 computers to serve 5000 students.)

To review, every argument is about some issue (in the case above, computer-based registration). The person making the argument about an issue, then, actually makes a claim, which is his or her own belief about that issue (computer-based registration will not work yet because there are not enough computer terminals on campus that will have access to the registration). The claim, however, is not the end of an argument. You will note that a claim must be accompanied by supporting evidence in order for an argument to be a strong one.

Evidence comes in many forms, and the type of evidence needed to support a claim depends on the type of claim you are making. For example, if someone has claimed that fraternity membership has a negative effect on grades, you should expect to see evidence such as data, which may consist of actual grades of students before and after they joined a fraternity on your campus. You may also see that the person making the claim has researched other studies done on the same topic and has cited those researchers' results. Anecdotal evidence from personal experience may also be offered (and can be an effective way of persuading), but it would not in itself be enough to support the claim. Thus you can see that evidence can take many forms, but you also need to be aware that evidence should not be biased.

It is important for you to understand the information you have just read about the construction of an argument so that you can better recognize the arguments of others (which is an important skill in college) as well as formulate your own. The ability to do both helps you to be a better critical thinker. Throughout your college career, you will be bombarded with information from many different sources.

Much of this information will be in the form of arguments made by others. Your first step in learning to think critically about this information is being able to recognize an argument when you see one. Next you want to be able to recognize a *good* argument when you see one. You also want to be able to "argue the argument"—in other words, to be able to agree or disagree by constructing an argument of your own.

Making an Effective Argument

Of course, just recognizing strong arguments is not enough. You need to be able to construct arguments of your own. How do you do that? You have already tackled the first step, which is to understand what makes a good argument. Your own argument should have a topic (which is a focused issue) and a claim.

A topic for an argument is sometimes assigned to you by a professor. At other times, you will be given a choice. Either way, the topic should be manageable in the amount of time and space you have to make it. If you are writing a two-page paper, for instance, you cannot expect to argue effectively a topic such as genetic modification of foods or nuclear waste disposal (although you may be able to narrow these topics down further for longer papers). A better topic for a two-page paper might be something closer to home, such as life in the residence halls or campus dining.

The claim, however, is not the end of an argument. You have a right to a claim about a particular issue, but you must be prepared to back up that claim. To do that, you need to gather evidence. Support in the form of evidence is vital.

Once you have chosen a manageable topic, you have to be specific in terms of what your focus will really be. Even a focused topic can have many different facets, and you don't necessarily want to address them all. Take the topic of life in the residence halls. What specific aspect of life in the residence halls do you wish to tackle? There are certainly many aspects of residence life, and you can't cover them all in a two-page paper. Through the process of brainstorming, you could identify one important issue, such as the use of curfews for students in the residence halls. That is much more specific.

Finally, what is your opinion about curfews in the residence halls? There are certainly many opinions about them. What is yours? If you felt that curfews don't improve student safety in the residence halls on your campus, that would be your claim.

What is the next step? Evidence. First, you could gather from the campus safety office data such as crime statistics, which are public information. You could compare the statistics for residence halls that have curfews to the statistics for those without curfews. You could also read studies that have been done on the issue by researchers on other campuses and cite these studies as evidence. Personal experiences could be used, but not as your sole source of evidence. You should also remember that any argument has more than one side. Research the opposing view of your argument, and be prepared to counter the opposite side as well as to accept what valid points are made in support of it. No evidence or argument that you

Get Involved!

Tammy knew that one of the hardest things for her as a future high school history teacher would be to get her students to go beyond wanting to just memorize the facts for tests to get an A. She wanted to be able to get students to ask questions, to form opinions, and to formulate arguments. "I saw some of my best teachers and professors do it. I wanted to be able to be that kind of teacher myself." In her junior year, one of her history professors suggested that Tammy become a Supplemental Instruction leader—who facilitates group tutoring sessions—for the World History I class. She jumped at the chance to get some more experience in teaching. What she discovered is what she had learned from many of her professors: You learn best what you teach. She was becoming a better teacher because she was helping her students learn how to ask better questions, anticipate test questions, and form opinions for essay tests. She was also learning the history material better, which helped her prepare for her comprehensive exam in her senior year.

offer should be biased. If it is, it is not going to be very effective in persuading anyone who does not already agree with you.

Let's walk through the building of another argument:

Think of a topic related to your major or possible major.

_____

What specific part of this broader topic is of interest to you?

_____

What about it? What is your opinion?

_____

What evidence can you gather in support of this topic? (List some specific types of evidence you think you will need.)

_____

_____

_____

Recognizing Bias in Arguments

Everyone has a point of view that is based on his or her own experience. People can form a prejudice or attitude toward something, sometimes without even realizing it. These points of view, attitudes, and prejudices form what is known as bias. Bias can play a major role in how an argument is perceived by the audience. Remember that bias is not automatically a negative thing. For example, the director of a foster care program might argue for more funding to help the organization place the increasing number of children in need of foster care. You might expect this person to be biased in favor of more funding, but this bias may also reflect a genuine passion for the work that needs to be done.

Let's look at another example that shows how bias works. On a pre-game show for a professional football game, a sports reporter goes up to a fan who is dressed in a New York Giants jersey, with his face painted blue and red. She asks, "Who do you think is going to win this game?" Predictably, he shouts, "Giants!" Later, the reporter asks a respected analyst and former player and coach, who answers, "Based on the performance of the quarterback, the offensive line, and that unstoppable running back, I'd have to go with the Giants." Which respondent are you more likely to believe?

Bias can be everywhere, from a conversation with a friend to a lecture in college. The better you are at detecting it, the better you will be at thinking critically. In dealing with arguments, detecting bias is especially important. When you analyze an argument, you have to be aware of the bias of the speaker or writer. Here are some ways you can try to recognize bias:

▶ **Determine the relationship of the speaker to the topic**. For example, if the topic is the health benefits of green tea and the speaker is the president of a tea company, you may expect some bias. On the other hand, if the speaker is a nutritionist who is not employed by a tea company, you may expect more objectivity. Bias can be difficult to spot, so you may have to do some digging. If you were researching the role of consumer lawsuits against the fast-food industry, you might come across the Center for Consumer Freedom. Although this may sound like a consumer group, with a little digging you will discover that it is a restaurant lobbying organization. That doesn't discount what the group says, but it certainly changes one's perspective on its members' comments.

► **Be aware of any stereotyping by the speaker or writer**. For example, if the topic of a town meeting is controlling rowdiness by college students in the town bordering campus, and the speaker gets up and says, "All college students are heavy drinkers," you need to be alert to the possibility that the speaker is biased against college students and is not ready to engage in an objective argument. Although some students may drink heavily, certainly not all of them do. This would be a hasty and misleading generalization. In fact, some town residents may be heavy drinkers, too, but neither fact directly addresses the problem at hand.

► **Be alert for highly charged, emotional statements or name calling in an argument**. A person who is highly emotional is unlikely to respond to a rational argument at that time. Likewise, an emotional person has a more difficult time being objective. At the same town meeting, another person gets up and says, "Someone told me that a drunken college student rode up on her front lawn and smashed into her garage door. These kids are animals! If she had been in her yard, she could have been killed! College kids should stay on campus and leave us alone!" Such emotionalism often weakens the argument of the speaker in the eyes of the listener. The emotional speaker may get some audience members charged up initially, but the argument itself is weak. You need to be aware of emotional speaking and writing, and you should avoid resorting to biased emotions in creating your own arguments.

► **Determine whether the speaker or writer is using accurate and complete information**. For example, a speaker might tout the benefits of an acne medication on the basis of the results of one study but fail to share the information that four other studies were inconclusive and that, in fact, one study showed harmful effects from the medication. When you present an argument, be sure to research your topic thoroughly, providing perspective on both sides of the issue while arguing for your side.

 ## DIY-Do-It-Yourself Activity

Choose a topic you believe to be controversial: the health risks of fast food, privacy rights, gun control, or the like. Now find one website related to the topic. In order to determine the legitimacy of using information gleaned from this website in a research project, ask yourself the following questions about the website:

1. What is the main focus of the website?
2. What individual or organization is the primary author or sponsor of the website?
3. Is the website primarily presenting facts or opinions?
4. Does the website contain research findings? Who conducted the research?
5. Do you think the website is biased? Why? Why not?

You should also be aware that many sources of information, as well as many writers and speakers, have biased perspectives that are a part of who they are. For example, a child of divorced parents may, as an adult, argue against marriage because of his or her own negative experience. Being a child of a difficult divorce is a part of who the adult becomes. This may be his or her built-in bias. There is nothing wrong with this bias unless you are not aware of it—and that is your responsibility as a critical thinker. You too may have your own bias, but in building academic arguments, you need to be as objective as possible.

Fallacies

Just as bias can weaken argument, so can a fallacy. What is a fallacy? A fallacy is a deceptive and erroneous argument. In other words, the argument is not valid and won't stand up to the tests of logic. The deception involved is important to understand because fallacies can be deployed to build convincing arguments, and the best way to avoid being taken in is to examine what's going on. The individual statements in the fallacy may be true, but the weak argument that they make does nothing, in the eyes of the informed listener, but damage the credibility of the person presenting the argument. Whether you are writing an argument or evaluating someone else's, you need to be aware of fallacies so that you can both avoid and detect them. Understanding fallacies is another important skill of an effective critical thinker.

Some of the most common fallacies are:

Ad hominem   This is an attack on the person without addressing the real problem or issue. For example, a presidential candidate attacks an opponent's defense plan by saying, "You didn't serve in the military so what do you know about defense?" The opponent's defense plan could be very strong regardless of his or her own military record.

Let's take another example. Say a student receives a low grade on a test. Instead of addressing what went wrong on the test, he goes to his professor's department chair and argues that his professor is a poor teacher who doesn't care about the students. The problem, however, may have been the student's lack of preparation or misunderstanding of the questions. Immediately attacking the professor is just a way of avoiding the real issue.

Ad populum   This fallacy claims that if the majority of the people support an argument, then it must be valid. For example, if an ad for peanut butter states that four out of five moms choose it, a consumer may think it must be the best. But does just the fact that more people buy it make it the best?

In the student union, you hear a group of engineering majors saying that education is the largest major on campus and therefore it must be the easiest to get into because they'll take anybody. Other engineering students also agreed because the majority of the group said it. But the number of students in the major, of course, does not determine its quality and certainly doesn't mean that it's automatically the easiest major to get into or the best major for you.

Appeal to authority   Also known as *ad verecundiam,* this common fallacy is often used in advertising and political campaigns. In a political campaign, you might see an ad like this: "These ten Nobel Prize-winning economists support Candidate X's plan." It may sound impressive, but Candidate Y might have ten Nobel-prize-winning economists supporting his or her plan, too. Neither one is using a logical argument.

In explaining to all of the business majors program changes that will require many of them to take more courses, the dean of the business college states that this is a great plan because the president of the university supports it. This appeal to authority is a fallacy because, first, the president may not have considered the students' point of view, and, second, the president could be wrong.

Appeal to tradition   This fallacy suggests that just because things have always been done one way, they should continue to be done that way. You might hear something like this: "Back in my day, the men worked, and the women stayed at home and took care of the kids. And everybody was happy with it." The mere fact that this person had that experience does not mean that it's the only way or that it takes everyone's perspectives into account. Perhaps the women wanted to do something different but didn't have the opportunity.

Let's look at another example. Luis has returned to college after working for several years as a computer technician because he feels the degree will increase his chances of getting a better job. He and a group of other computer science majors have just completed summer internships in the field. They feel that the curriculum should have more programming courses. When they talk to the department chair, he says that the curriculum has been working well for years and that 90% of the college's graduates get jobs in their field within six months. What's missing from the department chair's argument is that what's happened in the past may not hold true for the future.

Bandwagon   The bandwagon approach implies that something should be done simply because everyone's doing it. Commercials often use this technique by implying that everyone is using a certain product and, therefore, you should also use it.

In the residence hall, you may hear that "everybody is going to the party, so you should go, too." Just because everyone is going doesn't mean it is a good idea. Let's say the party ends up being raided and the students all get citations for underage drinking. Just because everyone was there didn't make it the best place to be. This is a form of peer pressure.

Begging the question   To beg a question is to accept or assert some assumption as a "given," or foregone conclusion, without offering any evidence to support it. For example: "The increasing number of SUVs on the road will inevitably lead to greater traffic fatalities because of rollovers." The statement alone is powerful, but there is no evidence in the statement to support it. As a reader, you are left with more questions than answers.

You might hear, "If you join a sorority, you're going to become a snob and never hang out with anyone who's not in your sorority." Whether that happens or not, there is no evidence in the statement that shows that joining a sorority in itself will make it happen.

Circular reasoning   This fallacy occurs when an author or speaker restates a point in such a way as to make it seem that the restatement provides support for the point itself. A stockbroker might say to a client, "You really need to buy some shares of this stock. The telecom industry is a good place to put your money. This is the stock for you to invest in now." The statement is full of positive words, but the stockbroker has not given any evidence to support an argument for purchasing the stock.

At your college, you might hear an RA say, "We must enforce quiet hours in the residence halls. Quiet hours are important for students living on campus. Noise can be a real problem, and quiet hours are necessary." Where in this statement is there any support for the claim that quiet hours should be enforced? All three sentences are essentially just repeating the claim that quiet hours are needed without providing any reason why.

Hasty generalization   This is the fallacy of drawing a conclusion in the absence of any supporting evidence. Stereotypes are a good example of hasty generalizations. At the checkout counter, you see a grocery store tabloid with a cover story about the relationship between two movie stars. A woman next to you says to her friend, "That will never last. Those Hollywood relationships never do." Indeed the relationship may not last, but it's a hasty generalization to say that this particular relationship won't last simply because the two are movie stars.

Let's say you are doing poorly in your physics class. There is one older student in the class who has been getting A's on every test. You hear some other students grumbling that she is messing up the curve and that older students always do better and make it tougher for the other students to do well. They've made a hasty generalization based on one person's grades in one class.

Plain folks   This fallacy aims to create the illusion that the speaker is just an ordinary person like his or her audience, when in actuality he or she may not be. Political candidates frequently portray themselves as representatives of the "working man" or the "middle class." In reality, a large percentage of politicians at the national level are millionaires. By presenting themselves as "one of you," the politicians aim to persuade you to agree with their views.

Let's say a student was suspected of throwing a keg party in the residence hall. The hall director has the student in her office for questioning. In order to elicit a confession, the director says, "You can tell me what happened. I know what it's like in college. We used to have parties, so I can sympathize. Just let me know what happened, and I'll try to cut you a break." The director is using a plain folks argument here.

Red herring   The approach here is to avoid the main issue by introducing irrelevant material that might sway the intended audience into agreement. A teenager is arguing with her boyfriend, who has told her he can't go to the movie with her because he has to meet his friends. She says, "You should go to the movie with me like you promised." He responds, "Come on—I helped you with your math homework yesterday, so give me a break." He has introduced an entirely unrelated issue that has nothing to do with his promise to go with her to the movies.

Let's say a professor accuses a student of cheating on a test by looking at another student's test. The accused student responds by saying, "Everybody was cheating—I saw a student with a cheat sheet on his water bottle." The student is merely deflecting attention and has not addressed the real issue—his own cheating.

Slippery slope   This is a claim that something should be avoided because if it isn't avoided, something worse is going to happen. The slippery slope fallacy is really a scare tactic. For example: "If you give drug addicts clean needles at a needle exchange, you are encouraging drug use. Next thing you know, there'll be drug addicts on every corner, and young people will feel free to experiment with drugs all they want." The statement itself contains no evidence that this would happen.

A parent might say to a student, "I'm giving you this credit card only for emergencies. If you use it for anything else, you're going to end up sinking into debt, you're going to have to quit school to pay your bills, you'll never finish college, and you'll end up working at minimum wage for your whole life."

Straw man   The approach here is to misrepresent an opponent's argument in such a way that it is unappealing to anybody. Essentially, through this misrepresentation, one is attacking an opinion that a person doesn't really hold. Politician A supports a temporary moratorium on the death penalty until some systemic problems are investigated—including the recent execution of a person who was later determined to be innocent through DNA testing. Her opponent, Politician B, later attacks her for being soft on crime and wanting to let murderers roam the streets.

Two students have received a number of tickets for parking in spots designated for people with disabilities. They appeal the tickets to the student conduct board, which is made up mostly of students. In their appeal, they claim that the campus police ticketed them only because they were parking there to distribute leaflets protesting a campus expansion plan and that the tickets were an attack on free speech.

Time-Out Tip

If you have a problem that is causing you to have an emotional reaction, step back and try to treat your problem as an assignment to solve in which you could be totally objective. What would you do if you had an assignment instead of a problem? First, you would do research, ask others what they have done in your particular situation, and learn what their outcomes were. Write a pro/con list for each possible solution, and then, when you've done as much as you can, act on the basis of knowledge rather than emotion.

Fallacies can be tricky to recognize and are often used unknowingly. This is another important reason why you want to be able to recognize and avoid them. If you use one and an opponent recognizes it, it can destroy your audience's overall perception of the validity of what you are saying. Try to recognize fallacies in your own and other's arguments. Can you think of any that you've heard or read recently?

Gathering Evidence

On a dig, an archaeologist will look under the surface of the earth to find artifacts of life from many thousands of years ago. In the process of gathering evidence, he or she will build a case to explain how a certain culture rose and fell or how a particular animal's extinction occurred. The case must be made meticulously. When you prepare an argument, you are digging beneath the surface for evidence that will support your views when you present them to an outside audience. You have a right to a certain view, but in a formal argument, you must be able to show why your view is indeed a strong one. After all, the mere fact that you are convinced that you are right will in itself do nothing to convince anyone else that you're right. The ultimate reason for making an argument is to convince an audience. And the most valid way to convince them is with strong evidence.

How do you gather appropriate evidence? The traditional methods you may have used for writing papers in the past are a good starting point. The library is full of resources that can be used to bolster your argument. Newspapers and periodicals, as well as scholarly journals and government documents, all contain material that can be used as evidence. The scholarly journals and government documents will contain results of studies on just about any issue. With these, you can check the primary source of a study that may have been cited in a newspaper or magazine (and you can see whether it was properly referenced). On the Internet, millions of resources are at your fingertips—just be sure to check the source of the information. You can interview an expert in the field. Create your own survey by polling fellow students on an issue. Local agencies (Red Cross, social services, hospitals) are another valuable resource that you can access.

The Hard Way

Too good to be true? Jack found something that was. He liked to work out every afternoon after classes but before dinner. "Trouble was," Jack says now, "so did everybody else on campus." Jack felt like he spent half his time in the gym just waiting for machines. In the campus newspaper, Jack saw an ad for a new gym opening right next to campus. The ad showed dozens of exercise machines instead of the one or two that were available at the gym on campus. "It looked great. The best part was that if I could just come up with $125 up front, as a special deal, I wouldn't have to pay any membership fee all year." Jack visited the new gym, which was just nearing the end of its renovations, and signed up. The manager told him he had nine other gyms in another part of the state. "The opening day was supposed to be February 1st, but when I went over there, they were still waiting for the equipment." A week later, when Jack went by, the place was shut down. "I was so angry. For me, that $125 was a lot of money. And there was nothing I could do about it." He filed a complaint, but the owners were nowhere to be found. "Thinking back, the whole thing was just ridiculous. If I'd thought more about it, I could have just saved a lot of money by going to the campus gym at a different time. Or, if I'd looked into it just a little bit, I would have found out that this guy didn't have any other gyms. He was pulling the same scam all over the place. I've learned my lesson." Jack's experience shows that applying critical thinking skills is not something that is useful only in the classroom.

What Worked for Me

By the second semester of her freshman year, Reese, a chemistry major, was ready to change majors. She studied hard, attended all her classes, got help from her professors, and went for tutoring. "Still," she says, thinking back, "I was barely passing some of my courses." Candace, Reese's roommate, said, "Why don't you major in psychology with me? I think it's really fun. Plus, I'm getting mostly A's and B's." If Reese had not been a critical thinker in her everyday life, she might have fallen for that one. (Here are just a few of the questions we would need to answer before we could assess the relevance of Candace's recommendation: Was Candace's major just easy for her? Did she have a good background in it? Were the professors she had taken so far easier graders than others she might encounter later? Did she cheat?) Instead, Reese decided to ask some critical questions and conduct some very important research. First of all, she took a major/minor finder inventory and a career assessment test. "The tests kept telling me I should major in chemistry!" she laughs. She also spent a few hours talking with her advisor, who told her it was not unusual for chemistry majors to do poorly the first year, as they adjust to the rigors of college chemistry, but then to see their grades improve in the sophomore year. And he recommended a few ways to study that she had not tried before. Reese also knew she did not want to deviate from her plan to be a researcher in the pharmaceutical field. Consequently, instead of jumping ship when the going got rough, she thought critically about her major, asked the right questions, and decided to stick it out. By the time she was a senior, she had a 3.1 GPA.

As you build your case, you may come across material that has a different viewpoint. Don't ignore information that doesn't match your view. It is both more forthright and more effective to acknowledge competing information and then explain why you disagree with it.

As you gather this evidence, you should first determine which information is relevant to your argument. You may find that some of what you've dug up just doesn't belong. For example, say you are researching the issue of paying athletes at Division I schools. In the process, you come across an article about how recent high picks in the draft have fared in their first years in the NFL. This is obviously not relevant.

Then you need to check to see whether the evidence you have found is legitimate and complete. Is the information coming from reliable and unbiased sources? Is there more than one relevant study or article on an issue that helps support your view? Have you effectively addressed information that contradicts your viewpoint? When you have gathered the appropriate evidence and cited the appropriate sources, you can feel confident that your argument will stand up to close examination.

Solving Problems in the Real World

Let's face it—in life, you are going to be faced with problems. In college, problems can occur in a number of different situations—academic, social, physical, and otherwise. With the added stress of being in college, problems can sometimes seem overwhelming. Problems, however, can also be seen as opportunities to grow as a person if you apply your critical thinking skills. Every problem may have more than one solution; it is up to you to find out which solution is best in your particular case. Let's consider the following example:

1. **Identify the Situation:** Markita, a geography major, has been doing well in all of her classes except psychology. After the midterm exam, she realizes that she currently has an F in this course.

2. **Identify Possible Problems:** Initially, you may think that her problem is that Markita has an F in psychology, but her F may just be a symptom of another problem. Certainly, the F is not a good grade, but Markita really needs to understand why she has an F in this particular class when she is doing well in all of her other courses.

3. **Examine Possible Problems:** A critical approach for Markita would be to look at some factors that may be causing her to do poorly.

She decides to examine the following:

- ▶ The professor and his teaching style
- ▶ The number of students in the course: 300
- ▶ The type of exams: multiple-choice
- ▶ Where she sits in class: toward the back because her friends sit there
- ▶ The text itself
- ▶ Her background in psychology
- ▶ The time of the course meeting: 8:00 a.m. MWF

She examines these factors one by one. She realizes that she is okay with the professor and his teaching style. Clearly, in a class this size, he is going to have to lecture, but that is not different from many of her other classes. She also has a biology course with 250 students, and she's getting a B in that class. She doesn't feel like she's just a number; she has participated in spite of the numbers, and the teaching assistant is always available during her office hours. She has always done well on multiple-choice exams, so she decides that's not a factor. Sitting toward the back has not been a problem in any of her other classes, and the professor has a microphone, speaks clearly, and uses PowerPoint presentations that are easy to read. The text seems accessible enough, and for the most part she has kept up with her readings. She took a psychology course in high school, and she did fine. So far, so good.

4.   **Identify the Key Problem:** The last factor on her list, she realized, was creating some problems. The psychology class was her only 8:00 class, and she is not a morning person. Also, she had missed a number of Monday morning classes because she would go home on the weekends to see her boyfriend and make the two-hour drive on Monday mornings to get back. Sometimes she ran late and missed psychology. She also stayed up late on weeknights with her friends and would wake up at 7:30 or even later, drag herself to class, and not be very alert or focused.

5.   **Examine Possible Solutions:** When Markita realized that her problem was the time of the class, she went to discuss the situation with her advisor. Her advisor told Markita that she would need to try to do better in the class she had because it was too late in the semester to switch to a psychology class at a different time. Markita had thought that might be an easy solution but realized she needed to investigate some others. Her advisor looked over her syllabus to see how her grades were distributed. As of the middle of the term, only 30% of the grade had been determined because she still had two major tests coming and a final. Her advisor thought she still had time to get a better grade.

6.   **Implement the Best Solution:** One of Markita's friends suggested she get a tutor because she still had time to pull the grade up with those three tests. She also talked to her roommate, and her roommate agreed that they would try to get to bed earlier on the nights before her 8:00 class. Since she was getting more sleep, she was able to get up at 7:00, take a shower, and have breakfast before class started. She was refreshed and focused, and instead of rushing in right at 8:00, she would arrive a few minutes earlier and review her notes. Finally, she realized that if she wanted to go home on the weekends, she would have to start coming back on Sunday nights to ensure that she would not miss any more classes. Markita was able to pull her grade up to a B. The next semester she was able to avoid taking any 8:00 classes because she knew that wasn't the best time of day for her.

How can you incorporate Markita's problem-solving strategy to deal with some of the problems you are facing? Remember the steps:

1. Identify the situation.
2. Identify possible problems.
3. Examine possible problems.
4. Identify the key problem.

5. Examine possible solutions.
6. Implement the best solution.

Practice this problem-solving strategy now so that you will be better prepared when you need it. Here are some possible situations you may be dealing with (feel free to work with your own situations as well):

▶ You and your roommate are not getting along.
▶ Your team is practicing all the time, and you never seem to get anything else done.
▶ You have gained ten pounds in the first two months of school, and you feel awful.
▶ You are a commuter and can't seem to make any friends because you don't spend a lot of time on campus.
▶ You don't think you are cut out for the major you have chosen.
▶ You feel like the only adult student on campus, even though you know there are others. You just don't know where to find them or how to find your place on campus.
▶ You are feeling homesick and wish you hadn't chosen a college so far from home.
▶ English is your second language and you are having difficulty keeping up with the reading and are not doing well in your writing courses.
▶ You can't understand your math professor.
▶ You keep getting bad grades on your essays.

If one of these situations sounds familiar, apply the problem-solving strategy as you work through the steps below. Or work through them to address a different situation that you are experiencing now.

Lifeline

If you want to learn more about critical thinking, sign up for a critical thinking course. Many philosophy departments offer such courses, and they may count in your major as a general elective. You will have the opportunity to immerse yourself in this topic and will reap the benefits in your other courses. It may be best to take such a course as early as possible in your college career.

1. Identify the situation.
   _____
   _____

2. Identify possible problems.
   _____
   _____

3. Examine possible problems.
   _____
   _____

4. Identify the key problem.
   _____
   _____

5. Examine possible solutions.
   _____
   _____

6. Implement the best solution.
   _____
   _____

Reading and Watching the News Critically

Two hundred years ago, when a new president was elected, it took months for most of the country to get the news. Now, for better or worse, news is transmitted instantaneously. We now get the news every day from many different sources: newspapers, news magazines, the Internet, television, radio. With the push of a button or the click of a mouse, we are inundated with more information than we may even care to have. That is why, now more than ever, we have to read and view the news with a critical eye and ear.

There are more sources of news now than ever. That is why you need to be aware of the fact that not every source is objective and that many have a built-in bias. Here are some things you can do to be sure that you are reading and watching the news critically:

Read from multiple sources. Watch different networks. If you are trying to keep up with world events, for instance, it would be wise not to get all of your information from one network or one newspaper. Doing so might cause you to have only one view of an event or situation. Your task is analogous to that of a police detective investigating a crime scene—a bank robbery that took place at a busy shopping mall. She would not rely on one witness to get a view of what happened. She would, instead, interview as many witnesses as possible. Witness A and Witness B may have seen different things, but all of their information is pertinent to the detective's effort to determine what happened. The same thing is true of understanding the news. You need to consult a number of sources before you can feel confident that you know what happened.

Learn the slant of different sources—some are more liberal, some are more conservative. Different sources usually present the news in slightly different ways. Many news sources have a bias of some kind (even if it's a slight one), but few will openly say so. Having a bias is not necessarily a bad thing, but as a consumer of the news, you must take it upon yourself to be aware that news stories may be spun in a certain way.

Try to understand the bias of the speaker, presenter, or writer. Often, news sources feature people who are leaders in different areas. Sunday morning talk shows, for example, frequently feature leading politicians. Naturally, leading politicians are going to do their utmost to represent their own viewpoints. Newspapers have an op-ed (opinion-editorial) page where writers express their own viewpoints on a subject. Certain writers almost invariably take a particular slant—be it conservative or liberal. Again, as a reader, you need to be aware of the author's slant. Often, news sources include both "pro" and "con" essays in the editorial section. Read both so you will know what advocates on both sides of an issue think.

Understand the difference between a news article and an editorial. News articles are generally meant to be at least somewhat objective. Editorials, on the other hand, are specifically meant to convey the author's views on a subject. It's important that you know where each is placed in a newspaper; you certainly don't want to mistake an editorial for a news article when you are citing a source.

Don't automatically assume that statistics are correct. For some reason, statistics have a ring of authority to them. They sound impressive. You may hear, "Three out of five Americans support the president's view on taxes." Sounds okay. But what isn't clear is what the source is. If it's a Gallup poll, that would be pretty neutral. If it's a poll commissioned by the president's party, it may not be so neutral. After all, the president's own party is unlikely to publicize a poll that is not favorable. Also, you don't know what the rest of the poll says. For example, three out of five Americans might have said they support the president's view on taxes if the deficit is taken care of first. What the speaker said originally, in this case, left out some important information.

Pay attention to retractions. News organizations are made up of people, and people make mistakes. Whereas a big story may appear on the front page or at the beginning of a newscast, retractions—where news sources correct mistakes—are often buried inside the paper or right before a commercial break. Obviously, you are not getting the whole story if you miss the retraction.

The most important thing is to pay attention to what's going on in the world outside of your own environment. As we noted before, becoming a well-informed person will make you a better student overall. However, in doing so, be sure to apply what you have learned in this chapter so that you don't take any news source at face value. Be critical as you are becoming informed.

Increasing Your Yield:

Readings for Practical Application

This chapter has covered various aspects of critical thinking, one of the key skills you need to develop as a college student. You have learned the key differences between facts and opinions, how to recognize and avoid bias and fallacies, how to make effective arguments, how to gather evidence, how to apply critical thinking skills to solving problems in your own life, and how to think critically in a world with ever-increasing outlets for news coverage. You should now understand the importance of being a critical thinker every day and everywhere—not just in the classroom, but in all aspects of your life.

This chapter has also addressed how to use critical thinking skills when you need to make an argument. *In college, you may be called upon, whether in a speech course or in a course in your major, to give a speech to argue a point instead of writing a paper.* Accordingly, our "Textbook Case" reading comes from a public speaking textbook. After examining the strategies for reading a speech communications textbook, you can apply them to the selection.

The "Life After College" reading in this chapter, "For These ESPN Aides, Every Night a Highlight," gives a behind-the-scenes look at what it is like to be an intern at the top-rated cable sports network. It shows how being able to think on your feet, make split-second decisions, and practice good communication skills can land you a dream job.

Finally, the "Current Issues" selection from Neal Gabler's book *Life: The Movie* looks at what fame, occasioned by increasing media coverage, can do to average people. This is an interesting exercise in critical thinking. It invites you to think in some depth about the role of the news in covering current events and making temporary celebrities—for good or ill—of unknown people. This reading gives you a chance to put into practice the strategies suggested in the "Reading and Watching the News Critically" section of this chapter.

Reading and Study Tips: Speech Communications

Unique Features and Comprehension Strategies

Speech communications textbooks combine theory with how-to strategies. Although you may see a speech communications textbook largely as a practical guide to preparing for and giving a speech, you need to understand the theory behind the instructions. Speech communications textbooks often provide this theory. **Read and understand the theory before jumping into its application. Don't overlook this important aspect of your speech communications text.**

Speech communications textbooks are generally broken down into major topics related to developing and presenting an effective speech. The organization of the textbook helps you to understand how to organize the preparation, writing, and delivery of your speech (in other words, what you need to do before, during, and after). **Put the concepts and suggestions that you encounter to work in your own speeches so that you are immediately reinforcing what you are learning.**

Remember that speech communications textbooks are, first and foremost, how-to books. As soon as you learn the concepts, apply them. They will become second nature.

Speech communications texts are usually organized to show that giving speeches is a process much like writing. Putting together a good speech is similar to putting together a good paper. **You need to have a clear idea of the purpose of the speech and understand your audience, and you need to narrow your topic, research and provide support for your ideas, and be sure you are well organized. Look at the examples your text provides. Take each step of the speech-writing process very deliberately, thinking about what you are doing and learning.**

Speech communications textbooks often provide a chapter outline. You can use this outline to prepare yourself for what will be in the chapter. **Read the chapter outline first. Doing so will help you prepare for what is to come. Also, you will see that the order in which the topics are presented in the text is the order in which you yourself will attack the steps in the process of developing and delivering a speech. Pay attention to this order. Make your own outlines from chapter material. If you outline the chapter material, you will gain practice in outlining for your own speech, which is an important part of speech writing. You should also outline any discussion of theory or key sample speeches so that you will be well prepared for tests.**

Diagrams are used to illustrate communications theory. Visual learners especially should take advantage of the diagrams that often accompany the text in a speech communications textbook. Sometimes it is easier to understand the steps in a process when they are graphically illustrated than when they are explained in words alone. Moreover, diagrams make it easier to remember complex material, such as you may find in discussions of communications theory. **Carefully examine diagrams to help you understand the abstract theory presented. You may want to recreate diagrams as a study tool to see whether you understand and remember the concepts presented. If, for example, the text is discussing the levels of influence of behaviors, attitudes, beliefs, and values, a diagram will help you understand how they interact.**

Speech communications textbooks use many real-life examples. Speeches are not restricted to academic settings. They are given in everyday life, whether by politicians soliciting your vote or by businesspeople making a sales pitch. Textbooks provide examples both of famous addresses and of effective lesser-known speeches. Be sure to read these examples and learn from them. **Read all examples to make concepts seem more accessible. The examples that are presented in speech texts are particularly helpful in illustrating the abstract concepts in the text. You may also want to watch out for good speeches made on television or on your campus and note what you think makes them particularly effective based on what you learned in the text.**

Many speech communications textbooks contain website access or CD-ROMs that have sample speeches from well-known speakers. Hearing and seeing a good speech is often even more valuable than reading one. **If your textbook provides these added features, take advantage of them, even if your professor does not assign them. Much of the effectiveness of a speech lies in the subtleties of the delivery: hand motions, eye contact, variations in pitch, and facial expressions, to name a few. You can always learn to improve your own delivery from watching the delivery of those who have perfected their craft.**

Your professor may pick and choose sections for you to read. Speech textbooks tend to be fairly comprehensive, so your professor may focus on some chapters or even on certain parts of different chapters. **Pay close attention to what is emphasized. Make sure you clearly understand which material is being emphasized, because your professor will have those guidelines in mind when she or he evaluates your presentations, and this material is more likely to show up on any tests.**

Speech textbooks often provide a highlighted list of information to enforce ideas presented in the text. These lists are great study guides for you to review major concepts and review them quickly. For instance, if a chapter presents guidelines on how to avoid plagiarism, the textbook may also review these guidelines in a list at the end of the chapter. **Review any such lists carefully. You may even want to copy them onto note cards for further review.**

Reading 1: A Textbook Case

The following excerpt from a textbook chapter is included here because of the connection between ethical speaking and what you learned in this chapter about avoiding bias and gathering credible and thorough supporting evidence. A good critical thinker is able to find and choose evidence to support his or her argument, while also remaining objective about the subject. Chapter 6 covers writing papers in college, and evaluation of your written papers will be of great importance in your college work. Hence, you will often be called upon to formulate an argument in a paper, but you will also be called upon to prepare an argument when you give a speech or some other oral presentation. How you form that argument and present it to an audience should be based on the critical thinking skills you learned in this chapter. When you speak in front of an audience, you have a responsibility to be truthful and thorough. A critical thinker will be an ethical thinker, who will, in turn, be an ethical speaker.

BEFORE YOU READ

1. Think of several speakers you have heard (in person, on a news show, or in a class) who you think were biased. What made them biased? How did this bias affect your attitude toward them and their speeches? How is the bias displayed in these speeches tied to ethics in public speaking?
2. Refer to the "Gathering Evidence" section in this chapter. Why do you think giving accurate and complete supporting evidence is important in public speaking?

3. If you were asked to give a ten-minute speech about a topic important to you, what topic would you choose? Why? How do you think you could make other people agree with you?

Ethical Speaking

G. L. Grice and J. F. Skinner

Maintaining strong ethical attitudes and standards requires sound decision making at every step in the speech making process. In this section we present seven guidelines to help you with these decisions.

Speak Up About Topics You Consider Important

First, ethical public speakers make careful decisions about whether or not to speak. In many public discussions outside of the classroom, silence is often an option, and if the issue is trivial, sometimes it is the best option. There are times, though, when people have an ethical obligation to convey information or when they feel strongly about an issue or an injustice. *Ethical communicators speak up about topics they consider important.* Our nation's history has been shaped by the voices of Thomas Jefferson, Frederick Douglass, Susan B. Anthony, Martin Luther King, Jr., Cesar Chavez, and other advocates. That shaping continues today in the voices of Jesse Jackson, Marion Wright Edelman, Colin Powell, and Elie Wiesel, among many others. You may not have the impact of those famous speakers, but you do have an opportunity to better the communities of which you are a part. This class provides you with an opportunity to share information your classmates can use to help them get more from their college experience or to help them function better in their careers and personal lives. You also have a chance to educate others about problems you feel need to be confronted. We remember one student who showed special sensitivity in addressing a topic she opposed on ethical grounds.

Pam, a sophomore public relations major, had been an animal welfare advocate for a long time, but she knew from class discussions and conversations before class that a number of her classmates hunted for sport or for food. She realized that if she turned her ten-minute persuasive speech into a general sermon against killing animals she would only make a number of her classmates feel defensive. She wanted to speak on some aspect of animal welfare but knew she had to narrow and focus the topic.

As a volunteer worker for several animal protection agencies, Pam had become aware of the problems associated with the use of steel leg-hold traps. Inside city limits, they posed a threat to pets, children and adults who did not know where they had been set. She also opposed their use in the wilderness because, she said, they inflict pain and suffering and kill non-target animals. Pam delivered a well-documented speech to persuade her listeners that

---

SOURCE: G. L. Grice and J. F. Skinner, "Ethical Speaking." In *Mastering Public Speaking,* 4th ed. (Boston: Allyn and Bacon), pp. 26–30. Copyright © 2001 by Pearson Education. Reprinted by permission of the publisher.

the use of these traps should be outlawed. Her carefully worded thesis was not that killing animals is wrong, but that the use of this particular trap is cruel and inhumane. She even discussed two other types of traps as humane alternatives. The class listened intently to Pam, and toward the end of her speech she was gratified to see that many of her classmates, hunters included, were nodding in agreement with her.

Much of your speaking in this class and later in life may not be on significant social or political issues. Yet this class provides you with the training ground to hone your skills as speaker and listener. Use these skills as you move from involvement in class and campus issues to improvement of your community.

> *A speech is a solemn responsibility. The man who makes a bad thirty-minute speech to 200 people wastes only half an hour of his own time. But he wastes 100 hours of the audience's time—more than four days—which should be a hanging offense.*
> *—Jenkin Lloyd Jones*

Choose Topics That Promote Positive Ethical Values
Second, *ethical speakers choose topics that promote ethical values.* Selecting a topic is one of the first ethical choices you will make as a speaker. Unless you are assigned a topic, you can choose from a wide range of subjects. In a real sense, you give your topic credibility simply by selecting it. As an ethical speaker, your choice should reflect what you think is important for your audience.

In the course we teach, many student speeches have expanded our knowledge or moved us to act on significant issues. But consider this list of informative speech topics:

    How to get a fake I.D.
    How to "walk" (avoid paying) a restaurant check
    How to get a faculty parking permit
    How to beat police radar
    How to get out of a speeding ticket

We have heard speeches on each of these topics. Even though they were informative rather than persuasive speeches, each one of these how-to topics implies that its action is acceptable. We do not know why students chose these topics, but we suggest that all of those speakers disregarded their listeners, failed to consider the values they were promoting, and presented unethical speeches.

Speak to Benefit Your Listeners
Third, *ethical public speakers communicate in order to benefit their listeners.* Speakers and listeners participate in a transactional relationship; both should benefit from their participation. As the Jones quotation [above] suggests, listeners give speakers their time; speakers should provide information that is interesting or useful in return.

You may often speak for personal benefit, and this is not necessarily unethical. You may, for instance, speak to a group, urging them to support you for president of the student body. There is nothing wrong with pursuing such personal goals, but ethical speakers do not try to fulfill personal needs at the expense of their listeners. As one popular book on business ethics states, "There is no right way to do a wrong thing." Speakers whose objective is to persuade, for example, should do so with the goal of benefiting both the audience and themselves. Even informative speakers have an ethical obligation to benefit their audience. Here's an example of how this can work in your public speaking class.

> Assigned to give an informative speech demonstrating a process or procedure, plant lover Evelyn decided to show how to plant a seed in a pot. Her instructor, who had asked students to write down their topic choices, was privately worried that this subject was something everyone already knew about. Evelyn was, after all, speaking to college students who presumably could read the planting instructions on the back of the seed packet. The instructor did not want to discourage Evelyn but wanted the class to benefit from her speech.
>
> Without saying, "You cannot speak on this topic," the instructor shared her concerns with Evelyn. She found out that Evelyn had several other plant-related topics in mind. Evelyn agreed that a more unusual topic would be more interesting to the class and more challenging for her to deliver. On the day she was assigned to speak, Evelyn presented an interesting speech demonstrating how to propagate tropical plants by "air layering" them. Evelyn got a chance to demonstrate her green thumb, and her classmates learned something most had never heard of before.

Notice how Evelyn finally paid attention to her audience. At her teacher's suggestion, she rejected the simple, familiar topic that would probably not have taught her audience anything.

Use Truthful, Accurate Supporting Material

Fourth, *ethical speakers use truthful, accurate supporting materials and valid reasoning.* Listeners have a right to know not only the speaker's ideas but also the materials supporting those claims. Ethical speakers are well informed and should thus test their ideas for validity and support. They should not knowingly use false information or faulty reasoning. Unlike the commercial cartographers we mentioned at the beginning of this chapter, they should not deliberately include false information in their speeches. Yet we sometimes witness students presenting incomplete or out-of-date material, as in this example:

> Janet presented an informative speech on the detection and treatment of breast cancer. Her discussion of the disease's detection seemed thorough, but when she got to her second point, she said that the only treatments were radical mastectomy, partial mastectomy, radiation therapy, and chemotherapy. She failed to mention lumpectomy, a popular surgical measure often combined with radiation or chemotherapy. Her bibliography revealed that her research stopped with sources published in the early 1990's, explaining the gap in her speech content.

Janet did not necessarily act unethically; she was simply uninformed and ended up being embarrassed. But what if Janet had known of the lumpectomy procedure and had just not wanted to do further research to find out about it? Then we would question her ethics.

In this case, certain listeners did not notice the factual errors and the lapses in content while others did. Not getting caught in a factual or logical error does not free the speaker of ethical responsibility to present complete, factual information. If you speak on a current topic, you need to use the most recent information you can find and try to be as well informed as possible.

Reveal Your True Motives for Speaking

Fifth, *ethical speakers make their intentions clear to the audience.* In other words, they do not intentionally manipulate the audience. Allan Cohen and David Bradford define manipulation as "actions to achieve influence that would be rendered less effective if the target knew your actual intentions."

We are familiar with one company whose sales strategy matched that definition of manipulation. This company relied on door-to-door salespersons, especially college students, and instructed new employees to make a list of friends who might be interested in purchasing the product. The employees were told to contact these friends and tell them the good news about their new job. The company also coached employees to say that part of the job involved making presentations to potential customers and to ask if they could practice giving their presentation to the friend in order to get some helpful feedback. In addition, because the company wanted to encourage its workers to succeed, employees offered each volunteer "critic" a gift. However, the company also told their salespeople confidentially that the presentations were actually a test to see if they could sell the product, and that they should take advantage of these sales opportunities.

We consider this strategy manipulative and unethical. The salespersons made the appointments under false pretenses. The company exploited its employees' friendships; the employees in turn exploited their friends' willingness to be helpful. These helpful critics might not have participated if they [had known] . . . their friends' real intent. A public speaker may try to inform, convince, persuade, direct, or even anger an audience. Ethical speakers, however, do not deceive their listeners. They are up-front about their intentions, and those intentions include benefiting the audience.

Consider the Consequences of Your Words and Actions

Sixth, *ethical speakers concern themselves with the consequences of their speaking.* Mary Cunningham observed, "Words are sacred things. They are also like hand grenades; handled casually, they tend to go off." Ethical speakers have a respect for the power of language and the process of communication.

It is difficult to track, let alone to predict, the impact of any one message. Statements you make are interpreted by your immediate audience and may be communicated by those listeners to others. Individuals may form opinions and behaviors because of what you say or what you fail to say. Incorrect information and misinterpretations may have unintended, and potentially harmful, consequences. If you provide an audience with inaccurate information, you may contaminate the quality of their subsequent decisions. If you persuade someone to act in a particular way, you are, in part, responsible for the impact of the person's new actions.

Strive to Improve Your Public Speaking

Finally, *ethical speakers strive to improve their public speaking.* Speakers who use the guidelines we have presented accept their obligation to communicate responsibly in the communities of which they are a part. Their ideas have value, are logically supported, and do not deceive their listeners. We would argue, however, that this is not enough.

Ethical speakers are concerned not only with what they speak, but also with how they speak. As a result, they work actively to become more effective communicators. This course provides you with an opportunity to begin mastering public speaking. You will learn how to select, support, evaluate, organize, and deliver your ideas. Your professional and public life beyond the classroom will extend your opportunities to speak publicly. Speakers have "the opportunity to learn to speak well, and to be eloquent [advocates of] truth and justice." If they fail to develop these abilities, they have not fulfilled their "ethical obligation in a free society."

Responsibilities of an Ethical Speaker

1. Speak up about topics you consider important.
2. Choose topics that promote positive ethical values.
3. Speak to benefit listeners.
4. Use truthful, accurate supporting material and valid reasoning.
5. Let the audience know your true motives for speaking.
6. Consider the consequences of your words and actions.
7. Strive to improve your public speaking.

AFTER YOU READ

1. Do you think that Pam, the animal rights advocate, was true to her beliefs? Why or why not? Do you agree with her decision about what to cover in her speech? Why or why not?
2. Do you believe it is important to reveal one's motives for speaking? Why or why not? Can you think of a situation in which you or someone you know did not reveal such motives? Was that decision acceptable or not? Why?
3. What can you do to be sure you are always providing complete and accurate information in a speech?
4. What do you think is the most important responsibility you have to an audience when you give a speech? Why?

Reading 2:   Life After College

Have you ever wondered who picks the highlights for the evening sports report? At ESPN, they are recent college graduates. The article that follows was chosen because the ability to speak in public and to conduct research thoroughly can lead to some pretty exciting job possibilities. Indeed, the ability to do research, to speak in public, and to think on your feet is even more important in life outside the classroom than in class. The world of work demands those skills every day. You might decide to put your skills to work in a job such as a sports reporter, one that will be easier to obtain if you get your foot in the right door.

BEFORE YOU READ

1. Think of a career or two in which you have some interest. What are some "first-step" jobs you might take to get into that field? Write down your ideas. Along with your fellow students, tape your ideas up somewhere in the classroom. Your instructor will then lead a discussion with the rest of the class to get some feedback on how feasible these ideas are.

2. You've probably heard a phrase similar to this: "Even college graduates have to pay their dues." What do you think this means? Provide some examples. How do you think you might have to "pay your dues"? Have you "paid some dues" already? Explain.

3. Many careers have a reputation for being glamorous. A TV anchor job, for example, might seem glamorous, whereas the behind-the-scenes jobs in TV might seem a bit more mundane. Do you see yourself as more attracted to the glamour or to making a contribution behind the scenes? Why?

4. What kinds of jobs do you think especially demand good public speaking skills? Formulate a list to which you can refer later.

For These ESPN Aides, Every Night a Highlight

S. Donohue

It's June in a place called "the campus," and about 30 young production assistants—most right out of college—are glued to small television sets in the highlight room, watching baseball, hockey and basketball games.

Finally, after spending five hours at ESPN's Bristol headquarters trying to find out what makes its "SportsCenter" series fly, it's as if you'd discovered the secret of the operation.

There they were, eating ice cream and slurping soda through straws in a room that hits visitors like a cross between a sweat shop and a college computer lab. But the papers these PAs work on are highlight log sheets, recording every hit, field goal or hockey fight they see.

There are 106 PAs working at ESPN and executives there call them the "heart and soul" of the network. Because as much as the clever quips of anchors Stuart Scott and Dan Patrick, the highlights they find are the signature of ESPN's flagship show, which draws 25 million households a month.

College Spirit

"It's the most important job we have here—I've always said that," said Norby Williamson, himself a former PA, now senior coordinating producer overseeing "SportsCenter" and shows such as "Baseball Tonight."

The PAs working on the highlights will have a relatively quiet period surrounding the All-Star break this week, but usually, they work 12- to 14-hour days. Most of the PAs live five minutes away in the same apartment complex. Some date each other, and many are roommates, paying $490 for a two-bedroom in the complex. They call it "the dorms."

SOURCE: Steve Donohue, "For These ESPN Aides, Every Night a Highlight," *Electronic Media 18* (July 12, 1999), 1–2. Reprinted with permission.

"It's like college all over again," said former PA Melissa Beasley.

ESPN only keeps 65 percent of the PAs after a six-month trial, so they like that their landlord lets them sign a six-month lease.

"SportsCenter" is ESPN's most profitable show. More PAs work on the show than [people in] any [other] . . . job category. And with many PAs starting out at less than $10 an hour, it's easy to see why ESPN makes so much money from the program.

Running live at 6:30 p.m., 11:30 p.m., 1 a.m. and 2 a.m. (ET), "SportsCenter" drew an average 2.68 Nielsen Media Research cumulative rating in ESPN's universe and 2 million households in June.

The 2 a.m. show, which is repeated from 5 a.m. to 1 p.m., averaged a 0.38 rating and 292,000 households for each rerun.

The Next Generation

ESPN gets more than 50 applications a month for the PA jobs. A stint at ESPN is the logical start for any college kid hoping to get into the sports television business. And ESPN gives its PAs more responsibility than other networks, letting them pick the highlights, edit them and run the graphics for their shows.

"What we're really looking for here is to identify the next generation of ESPN producers," said Al Jaffe, vice president of production recruitment, who sometimes feels "like the admission officer at Harvard."

ESPN recruits PAs with diverse backgrounds, from history students to pre-med majors. But most of them graduated from broadcast journalism programs at schools such as Syracuse University, Boston University, Northwestern University, the University of Missouri and Emerson College, Mr. Jaffe said.

Many ESPN producers started as PAs, including Mark Sumner, associate producer of "Baseball Tonight," who strolled into the highlight room after his show ended at 12:30 a.m. to thank the troops.

"This room is an absolute zoo. These guys are the people that no one sees," said Mr. Sumner.

"I'm all for being in the credits," jests PA Daryl Lewis, one of those with the laborious job of watching three-hour baseball games to come up with 45-second highlights for the network.

Ed Schizel, coordinating producer of the 11 p.m. "SportsCenter," says he gives new PAs a pep talk. He tells them: "The trick is to give the viewer every night something that reminds me why I got to watch 'SportsCenter' tonight . . . because they always tell me at least one or two things that make me sit up and say, 'Wow,' or make me run to the phone to add somebody to my rotisserie team."

Effortless Ad Lib

And their handwriting better be good enough for anchors to be able to read names such as NHL star Vaclav Varada off the shot sheet out of one eye while watching the highlight with another.

Mr. Patrick demonstrated the technique last month. When the Sabres-Stars Stanley Cup opener ended a few minutes before his "SportsCenter" telecast ended, viewers at home saw only the video and heard Mr. Patrick's voice with the late-breaking story. It was all done on the fly.

Of course, it's not all like that. At 5 p.m. that day, Rich Eisen, an anchor on the 1 a.m. and 2 a.m. "SportsCenter" shows, was sitting in his cubicle writing copy for his show, like he does most days.

Dressed in gray khakis and a blue polo shirt, 6:30 p.m. anchor Bob Ley was likewise in the newsroom putting some final touches on his script and rapping with "Baseball Tonight" analyst Peter Gammons.

Mr. Eisen says he and all the other anchors write all of their own copy, but he acknowledges producers sometimes come up with some of their best lines.

Producer Gus Ramsey is credited with coming up with the idea of quoting the film "A Few Good Men" when an outfielder robs a home-run shot at the wall, and it's become one of Mr. Eisen's signature calls.

As the fielder reaches for the ball, he says: "You want me on that wall, you need me on that wall." Then he adds "You can't handle the truth," as the video cuts to the batter's reaction.

Timing Is Everything

With only a few plays making the highlights from any given game, the PAs have the timing down. PA Pete Watters notes that a home-run highlight usually takes 10 seconds, while a double will typically last 14 seconds.

Highlight supervisor Stephanie Druley adds that the typical highlighted play snippet lasts for eight to ten seconds, and a few of those are stitched together from nearly every game. Putting those seconds together is what makes "SportsCenter" what it is. It's exhausting work.

And the days and nights are long. At 3:30 a.m. one June morning, the last of the PAs head out the door after a long shift.

There's little to do in Bristol, perhaps at all times, but certainly at this time of night.

"The two options are going to Denny's or going to bed," says Mr. Lewis, one of the PAs. He's going to bed.

AFTER YOU READ

1. Do you think the ESPN aides are taking a big risk by taking a job like this? Why or why not?
2. Has this chapter—and this reading specifically—changed your attitude and opened your eyes about job possibilities and the skills necessary for you to get the kind of job that you may want? If so, how? If not, why not?

Reading 3: Current Issues

The following excerpt is from a nonfiction book that offers theories about how celebrity plays a role in our society. Consider how you might define celebrity at this point. The article you've just read about ESPN aides brings to mind the celebrity status of many people in television news: The anchors become celebrities who are sometimes part of the news themselves. This piece specifically talks about how often the line between news and entertainment blurs. Just as anchors often become celebrities, so do people in the news often become a source of entertainment for viewers. The following section shows what happens when everyday people become celebrities. As we discussed in this chapter, a good critical thinker needs to apply critical thinking skills to reading and watching the news. This excerpt will give you an opportunity to use your critical thinking skills to analyze what you are reading.

BEFORE YOU READ

1. Refer to the "Reading and Watching the News Critically" section in this chapter. Apply the suggestions from that section to the following questions: Can you think of any "regular person" who has been part of a news story recently and has been "overexposed"? How has this overexposure affected the objectivity of the news reporting and the purpose of the media in reporting that particular story?
2. Watch a half-hour news show. Using the suggestions in the "Reading and Watching the News Critically" section, look for any indications that the program is blurring the line

between news and entertainment and/or is losing its objectivity. Consider your findings when reading the following excerpt.

3. What might the author mean by "the other side of the glass"?
4. In your opinion, how does fame change people?
5. What do you think are some positives of being famous? Some negatives?
6. Watch an "entertainment news" program like *Entertainment Tonight* or *Access Hollywood*. What is their "take" on celebrity? Why do you think they approach it from this angle?

The Other Side of the Glass

N. Gabler

[*Note: Arthur Bremer, the man who shot 1972 presidential candidate George Wallace and had originally targeted President Richard Nixon, wrote in his diary about his plans to kill in order to become a celebrity. He wanted to be the subject of a television movie.*]

What had become apparent to Bremer had also become apparent to virtually everyone living in the late twentieth century: that if you weren't part of the life movie itself, then you were relegated to being part of its vast anonymous audience. To many, this was too terrifying a prospect to contemplate. Not to be in the movie, not to be acknowledged, was the profoundest form of failure in the entertainment state. As the writer George W. S. Trow analyzed the situation in *Within the Context of No Context,* America was now divided into two grids. One was the grid of the popular—the grid, broadly speaking, of entertainment. The other was the grid of the intimate—the grid of one's personal life. Everyone belonged to one or the other—everyone, that is, except celebrities. "Celebrities have an intimate life and a life in the grid of two hundred million," Trow wrote. "For them, there is no distance between the two grids in American life. Of all Americans, only they are complete."

But everyone naturally sought completion. "I know I'm nothing," longtime pornographic film star Nick East told Susan Faludi of *The New Yorker.* "Though most of the world has seen my face, I'm nothing because I didn't do anything." Still, East looked forward to a day when he would make himself "worthy" of public recognition, a day "when I'm on the talk shows—the next O. J. Simpson, not that I'm going to kill somebody, but the next media sensation—when all the 'Hard Copy' shows, when the world is going to pay attention." It was the new American Dream. As director/choreographer Michael Bennett once said, "Unfortunately in America today, either you're a star or a nobody."

"Everybody wants to be famous," actor Bruce Willis told Jay McInerney in his *Esquire* interview, following Bennett's line of reasoning, but Willis doubted it had always been that way and he attributed the change to what he called television culture. On television ordinary Americans daily saw the benefits of celebrity and the adoration that celebrities received. At the same time, television helped nurse Americans' own sense of inadequacy, not only in the face of celebrity but in the ordinary course of life where dissatisfaction was one of the major engines of advertising; you bought things because you had to compensate for what you didn't have. In a society that often encouraged a lack of self-worth, if only to force people to spend money to ameliorate the situation, "the 'star' provided an accessible icon to the significance of the personal and the individual," as cultural analyst Stuart Ewen put it. Indeed, the subliminal message of every

---

movie icon in every movie was the importance of being important.

The trouble was that the icon didn't live in our quotidian space. Despite the insistence on the basic democracy of celebrity and despite the fact that the public could exercise its power to drag celebrities back across the threshold, it was a central tenet of the mythology of celebrities that they inhabited their own special world. Leo Braudy called it a "mystic community of other famous people, a psychic city of mutual respect for each other's individual nature." Writer Tom Wolfe, labeling it the "Center," described it as "the orbit of those aristocrats, wealthy bourgeois, publishers, writers, journalists, impresarios, performers, who wish to be 'where things happen,'..." And Andy Warhol cited access to this world as the "best reason to be famous": so you can read all the big magazines and know everybody in all the stories." As far as the general public was concerned, its existence was never doubted, only envied. "I know who they are," novelist Jacqueline Susann once said of her readers, "because that's who I used to be. They want to press their noses against the windows of other people's houses and get a look at the parties they'll never be invited to, the dresses they'll never get to wear, the lives they'll never live."

But that didn't stop them from hoping that they might yet gain access to that world, that they might yet get to the other side of the glass. The question was how. The answer, increasingly, was television, which was itself on the other side of the glass, the glass of the television tube that separated the celebrated from the anonymous. The great unspoken egalitarianism of celebrity was that because it was *human* entertainment, one didn't necessarily need any talent to attain it. All one really needed was the sanctification of the television camera. That was in part why people immediately reacted whenever a television camera caught them, however briefly, in the lens. Even at sporting events fans would leap and wave and mug as the cameras panned the stands during breaks in the action, though it was never clear exactly to whom they were waving or for whom they were mugging. Had they told their dear ones to stay glued to the set on

the off chance they might make an appearance? Or was it simply that for one split second they were on the other side of the glass themselves in that blessed world of celebrity?

It was the desperation to get to the other side of the glass, the understanding of what it took to get there and what it conferred once one arrived, that director Martin Scorsese captured in his 1982 film *The King of Comedy*. Rupert Pupkin (Robert DeNiro) is an aging celebrity aspirant addled by dreams of fame. He spends his evenings in his basement holding imaginary conversations with celebrities and hosting his own talk show with cardboard cutouts of Liza Minnelli and Jerry Langford (a fictionalized Johnny Carson). When Pupkin actually manages to meet Langford (played by comedian Jerry Lewis) and asks him for an opportunity to do his comedy routine on Langford's television show, Langford delivers the old show business bromides about hard work and tells him he will have to start at the bottom.

But Pupkin knows enough about celebrity to know better. He and an equally addled accomplice, whose dreams are of star romance, not fame, kidnap Langford. The ransom? An appearance by Pupkin on *The Jerry Langford Show.* "That's the only way I could break into show business—hijacking Jerry Langford," Pupkin jokes to the audience, which doesn't know yet that he is not kidding. And Pupkin ends his routine with the new American truth: "Better to be king for a night than a schmuck for a lifetime." Of course, once he kidnaps Langford, Pupkin has in fact broken through the glass. His stunt makes him a celebrity. He graces the covers of *Time, Newsweek* and *People*. He signs a one-million-dollar book contract for his life story, which becomes a best-seller and is sold to the movies. When last we see him, he has served his jail sentence and is making a television appearance as the "king of comedy."

Similarly, in the 1995 film *To Die For* a beautiful young woman named Suzanne Stone (Nicole Kidman), stuck in the improbably named town of Little Hope, New Hampshire, dreams of escaping the monotony some day by becoming another Barbara Walters. "You aren't anybody in America if you're not on TV," she declares as she angles for a job as a local television personality. When Suzanne manages to lasso a dim-witted teenage girl into a scheme to murder her husband so that she can more aggressively pursue her career, the girl compares their friendship to "living in this really great movie," though she finally comes to recognize the paradox of Suzanne's lust for celebrity: "If everybody were on TV all the time, we'd be better people. But if everybody were on TV all the time, there'd be nobody to watch"—unless it is life, not TV, that is the medium.

What Rupert Pupkin had solved, with perverse ingenuity, was the matter of how to get on television. Statisticians speak of a cocktail party effect, by which they mean that in order to get heard at a cocktail party, a guest must talk more loudly. This in turn prompts another guest to talk even more loudly, which prompts yet another guest to talk more loudly still and so on, until there is cacophony. In a sense, Americans at the end of the twentieth century lived within the cocktail party. Anyone wanting to be heard had to adopt the celebrity variant of the bigger, louder, faster aesthetic that drove conventional entertainments, but this set off a chain reaction of one-upmanship, forcing would-be celebrities to become ever more outrageous to be seen amid the clamor and heard above the din.

As Scorsese had dramatized, some people were willing to do almost anything to get to the other side of the glass for their moment of beatification, and the media were just as eager to grant it. One drunken fan who fell twenty-five feet while catching a point-after touchdown at a Chicago Bears game appeared on *The Late Show with David Letterman* and had already signed with an agent for speaking engagements and commercials. Others, who had absolutely nothing to barter for fame but their private lives, closed the gap between the grids and passed to the other side of the glass by revealing their innermost secrets on daytime television exploitation talk shows. Since there were nearly two dozen of these programs in the mid-1990s, and each program consumed roughly eight guests an hour, some one thousand people each week were

engaging in the cocktail conversation, trying to shout over the others, with thousands more waiting in the foyer. The truth was, though, that shouting was no longer sufficient. Real entertainment demanded combat. As one producer admitted, "For a show on rape, it used to be enough to interview the victim. Now you need the victim and the perpetrator. You need her to come face to face with her rapist."*

And these thousands ready to expose the worst of themselves, ready to endure humiliation for a visit to the other side of the glass, were not even the most devout flagellants. Others gave more to celebrity. Appreciating the entertainment value of death, they gave their lives. Comedian Freddie Prinze committed suicide because, according to a friend, he saw it "as a way of becoming immortal—you know, getting your face on the front page of every newspaper. He planned it." In the same way, pornographic film star Cal Jammer killed himself because, surmised a former girlfriend, he saw the attention the media devoted to the suicide of a female porn star. "I wonder if Savannah reached such a high level of fame after her suicide that he thought that was the way to do it," said the girlfriend. But unfortunately not even the tabloid television shows picked up his story. He gave his life for fame and still didn't make it to the other side of the glass.

It was in truth an occupational hazard for putative celebrities. No one knew exactly what it took to pass. You could kill yourself and not make it. You could look sensational and not make it. You could do outrageous things and not make it. You could commit unspeakable crimes and not make it. ("How many times do I have to kill before I get my name in the paper?" a serial murderer once complained.) There was so much caprice involved, just as there was so much caprice involved in

---

*The progenitor of these programs, *Donahue,* left the air in 1996 after thirty years, conceding that the entertainment envelope had been pushed beyond its ability to compete. Said an executive of *Donahue*'s television syndicator, "The kind of show he [Phil Donahue] wanted to do is not the show the average person wants to watch anymore. They want to be entertained and not his way. They want more craziness." (New York Times, January 18, 1996, p. A19).

determining which conventional entertainments succeeded. And the most exasperating part of it for those who wanted to become human entertainment was that the celebrities and the celebrity wannabes really were often indistinguishable from one another. With talent no longer a prerequisite, it was luck as much as anything that put some people on one side of the glass and some people on the other, making celebrity yet another example of chaos theory.

Yet even for those who were lucky enough to make it, there were perils. In 1987 Robert O'Donnell was a thirty-seven-year-old fireman paramedic in Midland, Texas, when he pulled eighteen-month-old Jessica McClure from an abandoned well in full view of the world watching on the Cable News Network after baby Jessica had been trapped for nearly sixty hours. "It was the greatest moment of Robert's life," said his mother, "and it was the worst thing that ever happened to him." O'Donnell immediately passed to the other side of the glass, becoming a nationally recognized hero who was soon squabbling with fellow rescuers over the movie rights to the story.

What he had not bargained for was that his stay there would be temporary. As *New Your Times* reporter Lisa Belkin put it, he was "a man so changed by fame that he no longer belonged in his world, but not changed enough that he could leave that world behind." Angry that his celebrity hadn't brought him greater reward, O'Donnell began suffering severe migraine headaches, for which he sedated himself with painkillers. In short order, he lost his job, was sued for divorce, bounced from one situation to another and then finally killed himself with a shotgun blast on a barren West Texas road. O'Donnell had been addicted to fame, and the true cause of death was his withdrawal from it. As has happened to so many others, his scenes had been left on the cutting room floor of the life movie. In taking away his celebrity, they had taken his reason to live.

AFTER YOU READ

1. This piece was published in 1998, before the explosion of "reality television." What are some of the ways in which reality television plays on our desire to be on "the other side of the glass"? Think of specific examples from shows that you have seen.

2. Why do you think our society values people on the other side of the glass? Identify and discuss at least two people who have gone from one side of the glass to the other side of the glass, and explain what you see as the positive and the negative aspects of their experience.

3. Analyze one case of a person who, like Jessica's rescuer Robert O'Donnell, has gone from one side of the glass to the other. Apply the critical thinking strategies you have learned in this chapter. Specifically, what are the ethical obligations of reporters to someone like O'Donnell? What are the ethical obligations of the reporters to their viewers and readers?

4. Do you think that Robert O'Donnell was predisposed to having trouble dealing with fame? Why or why not?

5. Did this passage help you understand why people want to get to the other side of the glass?

6. Have you seen or read about people (such as former child stars or once-popular musicians) who seem to be desperate to stay on the other side of the glass? What do you think drives them?

7. Do you think that people who are the subject of news stories have a right to expect their celebrity to continue? Why or why not? If you had the chance to be a celebrity, would you do it? Why or why not? How would you deal with celebrity?

Compounding Your Interest: Further Readings

Browne, M. N., & Keeley, S. M. (2000). *Asking the Right Questions: A Guide to Critical Thinking,* 6th ed. Upper Saddle River, NJ: Prentice-Hall.

Lewis, H. W. (1997). *Why Flip a Coin? The Art and Science of Good Decisions.* New York: Wiley.

McCoy, C. M., Jr. (2002). *Why Didn't I Think of That? Think the Unthinkable and Achieve Creative Greatness.* Upper Saddle River, NJ: Prentice-Hall.

Paul, R., & Elder, L. (2000). *Critical Thinking: Tools for Taking Charge of Your Learning and Your Life.* Upper Saddle River, NJ: Prentice-Hall.

Paulos, J. A. (1995). *A Mathematician Reads the Newspaper.* New York: Anchor Books.

Reference

Moore, B. N., & Parker, R. (1997). *Critical Thinking.* New York: McGraw-Hill.

Chapter 6

Being Prepared to Write Papers and Give Presentations in College

College isn't just studying; at some point, you have to produce. What this means is that although learning itself is a process, your professors will eventually call on you to deliver a product. This requirement could come in the form of a quiz, a test, or an out-of-class assignment. And it could come in the form of a paper or an oral presentation. Most students have experience with these in high school, but many of them find out it's a whole new story in college. The expectations are greater. The assignments are more open-ended, requiring more independent thinking on the part of the student. The stakes are often higher. With presentations, you're frequently in front of a larger group that you don't know well. Therefore, these kinds of assignments can lead to a lot of anxiety. However, doing papers and presentations can go much more smoothly if you prepare yourself for this inevitable college experience. And you might even enjoy the process.

Learning to write and give presentations isn't just a means to an end such as getting a good grade and graduating from college. Writing and presenting well are skills that will also help you get a job, keep a job, and excel in a job. Many students who feel they have a weakness in one or both of these areas try to avoid confronting their shortcomings. Sadly, instead of improving their performance and overcoming any shortcomings, they end up, at the completion of their college careers, pretty much where they were at the beginning. This doesn't have to be the case. This chapter is designed to help you realize that writing papers and giving presentations are not only manageable tasks but worthwhile ones as well.

This chapter will cover the following topics:

Understanding the Assignment
Brainstorming
Narrowing Your Topic for a Paper or Presentation of Realistic Scope
What a Thesis Statement Really Should Be
Organizing Your Supporting Paragraphs or Points
Using the Computer to Do Research
Tricks of the Trade: Refining and Delivering the Product
Citing Sources
MLA and APA Guidelines: What You Need to Get Started

Think About It Answer the following questions in the space provided.

What part of writing a paper do you find the most difficult? Why? _____

_____

_____

_____

_____

First Things First

You wouldn't think of replacing your car stereo without first learning how by either reading the directions or talking to someone who knows how to do it. Likewise, when it comes to writing papers or planning oral presentations in college, you need to know a few things before you begin. First of all, the level of expectations for the finished product has changed now that you are in college. What was acceptable before won't make the grade now. Also, to complicate matters, different professors may have different expectations. An A paper for one professor might be a C paper for another because they are simply looking for different things. You need to find out, before you even begin, what your professor wants. Some professors will provide you with written guidelines and sometimes even a grading rubric that explains how points will be distributed. If this is not the case—and it may not be—it is still your responsibility to find out by asking your professor. As far as oral presentations go, you should be sure to get important information such as how much time you have; whether or not you need sources, visuals, or handouts; and, just as for a writing assignment, who your audience is (your fellow class members or an imaginary audience such as the Senate). The information provided in the rest of this chapter will be genuinely helpful only if you fully understand the assignment.

Understanding the Assignment (for a Paper or Presentation)

The Paper

This seems like a no-brainer, doesn't it? In order to get a good grade on a paper, you must fulfill the requirements of the assignment. In other words, you must do what the professor asks you to do. This doesn't mean that you have to *say* whatever you think your professor wants you to say. That's just pandering. But it does mean you have to follow the professor's instructions carefully. Following directions is an important skill, too. You don't need to be mindless about it, but in the future, when your boss asks you to put something together in a specific way, you will be expected to do so. Surprisingly, many students do poorly on papers not because they aren't good writers or don't have good ideas but because they simply haven't met the professor's requirements. Let's look at the following typical mistakes.

Writing too little. If your professor requires six pages, you should write six pages. If you can only manage three, then you clearly haven't put enough time or effort into the assignment. And don't try stretching three pages into six by using 16-point font, bold type, and three-inch margins. Believe it or not, after reading thousands of papers, your professor probably has a pretty good idea of whether you have the required numbers of words and pages. Incidentally, a good rule of thumb is that a typed page has around 250 words. Thus, if your professor asks for 1000 words, your paper should be about four pages long.

Writing too much. Too much? Yes. If your professor asks for five pages and you write ten, chances are you might just end up antagonizing her. Guess what? You're not the only student in the class. And that class is probably not the only one your professor teaches. Maybe she gave a five-page assignment because she has forty students in your class and two sections of that course, with all of the papers coming in at the same time. Get the picture? She has four hundred pages of student work to read, critique, and grade. If you really think you have to go significantly over what the professor asked for, check with the professor first. Some will authorize the overrun. Others won't. You just need to know in advance. Another issue to consider is whether you are writing too much because you are having trouble making your points clearly and concisely. Learning to get to the point is very important, not least because it is a crucial skill in the workplace.

Not answering the question. This is one of the biggest mistakes students make. They write a decent paper, but it doesn't answer the question the professor has asked. For example, the professor asks for a paper giving five reasons why the United States became involved in World War II. The student writes a paper about Pearl Harbor. Yes, the student has written a paper about the war, but it doesn't come anywhere near fulfilling the assignment. If you turn in papers like this, your professors may wonder whether you even took the trouble to read the assignment. Or they might even suspect that you just took an old paper from another class, borrowed a paper from a friend, or bought your paper on the Internet. In any case, failing to answer the professor's question is likely to lead to a failing grade. If you're not sure about the assignment, read the requirements in the syllabus or handout more closely, talk it over with a friend, and always ask the professor for clarification (after all, your friend might have it wrong, too).

Not using enough sources. Sometimes, when asked, "How many sources do we need?" a professor will say, "As many as the paper demands." In other words, if you need two sources, use two. If you need ten, use ten. More often than not, though, you will be given a minimum—at least two, at least four, or the like. Be sure to use that many and then maybe a couple more. We've talked about plagiarism already, so you know that when you use four sources, you must cite four—even if only two were "required."

Not using the right kinds of sources. With the explosion of the availability of information on the Internet, more and more professors are giving you specifications not only on how many sources to include but also on what types. You may get instructions that say something like, "A minimum of five credible secondary sources. At least two must be from books, at least one from an academic journal, and a maximum of one from the Internet." Do not fail to follow these guidelines, which are frequently very important to the professor. Professors want you to use different sources so that you will be exposed to all of them. They want you to read articles in academic journals that are meant for a scholarly audience so that you can see how this style differs from that in a popular magazine. Also, be aware that professors often limit Internet sources because students frequently have a hard time (or don't spend enough time) differentiating between credible sources (such as cnn.com and msn.com) and not-so-credible sources (Joe's Edgar Allan Poe Fan Page).

The Presentation

Many of the problems that students have in preparing effective presentations are similar to the problems they have with papers.

Length. Obviously, if your professor asks for a five-minute presentation, and you run out of material after a minute and thirty seconds (yes, they often time you), you are going to have a problem. Also, if you prepare a speech and never time yourself, you

might be surprised to find that you are way over the limit, which is also a problem. And not just for the professor. By exceeding your allotted time, you are also likely to incur the wrath of other students, particularly those who are waiting to "go on."

Organization. A presentation is not like a rambling conversation. Like a paper, a presentation must have a clear organizational plan behind it. In some ways, it needs to be even better organized, because your listeners generally do not have an outline in front of them, and they cannot flip back to something they didn't quite get the first time around—as they could in a paper. So get your act together before you're in the spotlight. Many professors give sample outlines for a presentation; if they don't give you one, ask. There's no worse feeling than being in front of an audience with nothing to say.

Creating Interest for the Audience. A presentation makes available many opportunities that a paper doesn't offer you. For instance, you can create a PowerPoint presentation to enhance your spoken content. You can pass out handouts or use other visual aids (posters, pictures, graphs, charts) that clarify your message for the audience. Remember your audience when you're speaking. Make it clear why they should be interested in what you're saying. Connect what you are saying with their interests or with things they need to know.

Following the Guidelines. Frequently, professors will give you specific guidelines for presentations. Some requirements, such as length and organization, have already been discussed. Always read these guidelines carefully. Do your professors require you to use two visual aids and one handout? Do they require you to refer to authority figures to substantiate your points? Do they expect you to prepare for a question-and-answer session with your classmates? Many students overlook these secondary requirements because they are so focused on the presentation itself.

Get Involved!

Brett is a senior about to graduate with a major in meteorology and a minor in communications. "Yeah, people always joke, 'So you want to be a weatherman?'" Brett laughs. "I had never thought about it before college. I came in as a geology major and then just became interested in weather. I also had a great communications class—just a gen ed class, really—that got me interested in maybe being on TV. So it's a natural combination." When Brett decided to pursue his interest in becoming a meteorologist for a TV station, he realized he needed to polish his presentation skills. "Doing the weather, people want to see more than just the temperatures; they want to see your personality, too, so they come back to you every night. I was already working for the campus TV station, but I felt I needed more." A floor meeting in his residence hall gave him another idea. "They said they were looking for campus tour guides. I knew the campus, and I thought it was a job that would be fun and would help me work on my presentation style. I got the job, and it not only helped me with my skills but was also a great way to learn to speak to a different kind of audience. After all, in class you're just talking to other students. But with this, I was talking to potential students, their parents, brothers, sisters, aunts, uncles. A lot of the parents were alums, too, so I really had to know my stuff. It's been a great experience that has set me up for doing well at the next level."

Brainstorming

Sometimes, in their hurry to get started, students skip the process of brainstorming, thinking they'll save time. Many students feel that they are making progress only when they are putting words on the page. Big mistake. The truth is that if you fail to take time to think carefully about what you are doing, you could be *adding* a lot of time to your project while hurting your chances of getting a good grade.

Brainstorming is, after all, merely a form of thinking, and it's hard to have any brilliant ideas if you haven't spent time thinking. Also, your first idea is often not your best. In brainstorming, one idea builds upon another. Often, the fourth or fifth—or even tenth—idea is the one that works best—and it may have little or nothing to do with your first idea.

Take a look at this brainstorming session that several students conducted when given the assignment of *identifying a problem and finding what they thought was the best solution.* The requirement was to respond in the form of a short essay and an oral presentation to the class. At first, many students were overwhelmed by the assignment, primarily because they were choosing topics that were far too broad for the scope of a 2- to 3-page paper and a 3-minute presentation. Some of the topics they first considered were

- ▶ Paying college athletes
- ▶ Guns in schools
- ▶ Swapping music on the Internet: Is it stealing?
- ▶ Euthanasia
- ▶ Use of dietary supplements

The instructor then told the students to "think smaller" by writing about "what they know." This led to the following topics:

- ▶ Credit card debt
- ▶ Car insurance rates
- ▶ Student loan debt
- ▶ Failing a course
- ▶ Roommate problems
- ▶ Poor cafeteria food
- ▶ Overcrowded dorms

Getting these topics (or complaints!) on paper led the students to some more specific topics:

- ▶ From the overcrowded dorm topic, a student decided to write and speak about having two roommates instead of one and why that is a problem.
- ▶ From the same topic, a student wrote and spoke about parking problems near the dorms—and suggested a solution.
- ▶ From the topic of poor cafeteria food, a student decided to write and speak about the problem of there often being few healthy options and to propose a solution for her own campus.
- ▶ From the topic of debt, a student decided to write about the burden of taking out too many college loans and a way to lighten the load by seeking campus employment, instead, to offset college costs.

The list went on and on. And the students began to see that brainstorming plays an important part in the planning of writing and presentation assignments. In the

What Worked for Me

"I used to be terrified when I had to give a speech," Tran said as she sat in the student union building. "I hated it so much that I would get nervous the night before and almost feel physically sick. It was driving me crazy." As an education major, Tran knew she had to overcome her fear. "I really wanted to be a teacher, but I was definitely starting to wonder if I was going to have to switch majors." A few bad experiences in front of her speech class weren't helping her, either. "I would forget what I was saying, and my mouth would get dry. I felt totally unprepared." Tran stumbled upon a new plan unexpectedly. "The girl down the hall who was in my speech class was talking to me and saying how much she hated to give speeches, too. I'd felt so embarrassed, but now I realized I was not alone. We decided to practice our speeches in front of each other. Soon, we added a few other people. It really helped. I was able to get a lot of my nervousness out of the way, and the others would point out problems. If I was boring, they'd tell me, or"—she giggled—"if I was looking at my shoes. I still feel a little bit nervous, but working with a group ahead of time has really changed the way I feel about giving presentations."

rush to get done, many students just start writing. These same students often have to stop and begin again after they realize the topic is just too big. Or worse, they turn in an unwieldy paper and get a poor grade for not meeting the requirements of the assignment. On the other hand, many students who don't brainstorm procrastinate because they don't think they can come up with "anything good" to write about. Brainstorming is a procrastinator's best solution. A few bad ideas will eventually give way to a good one. The point is just to put something down. Next time you have a paper or presentation to plan, brainstorm first.

Narrowing Your Topic for a Paper or Presentation of Realistic Scope

Think big. Have you heard that expression before? Our culture promotes the concept of Big-ness. The bigger the better. Super-sized. Biggie fries. Big Red. Big Mac. The Big Gulp. Perhaps bigger is sometimes better, but in college you're going to be far more successful by thinking small, at least where paper and presentation topics are concerned. Far too many students make the mistake of trying to tackle too comprehensive a topic on too small an assignment. A two-page paper explaining the complete works of William Shakespeare. A three-minute presentation describing the causes of the Civil War. Arguing against the death penalty in two paragraphs. The Complete History of Einstein's Theory of Relativity in Five Minutes or Less. Entire books have been written on topics like these! All of these students would have been far better served by narrowing their topics to sizes appropriate for the assignment. Instead of a paper on the complete works of Shakespeare, how about a discussion of Hamlet's relationship with Ophelia? Instead of a talk on the causes of the Civil War, how about a discussion of the Gettysburg Address? After all, part of what you are trying to do in college is to understand things in detail, to get beneath the surface. If you pick topics that are too big for the assignment, you're going to end up merely skimming the surface, generalizing, giving the watered-down encyclopedia version. Furthermore, you're going to find it much harder to write or speak on over-sized topics because you will have to waste a lot of time and energy trying to figure out *how* to water it down. Why do so many students gravitate to bigger topics? There are several reasons.

Lifeline

Having trouble with a paper? Most colleges have a writing lab or tutoring center where trained staff are available to help you. They certainly will not write the paper for you, but they can help you get over the hump—whether it's picking a topic, narrowing one, structuring it, or whatever. Be aware that most writing centers are not editing shops set up to proofread your paper. They will expect you to take an active approach to your writing and to use their assistance to learn to become a better writer.

▶ The big topics are more obvious and therefore easier to think of in the first place.

▶ Students think they can avoid the challenge of actually learning anything more about the topic if they keep it vague and confine it to superficial things that they already know.

▶ They often think they won't have enough to say if the topic is too small.

The Inverted Triangle Method of Narrowing Your Topic

An effective way of concretely taking a large topic and whittling it down to a manageable size is to put your ideas on paper in the form of an inverted triangle, which has its "base" at the top. This larger end of the triangle is your big topic, the one you started out with on the assignment. The middle section breaks it down a little further, separating it into several different aspects of that larger topic. Finally, the point on which the inverted triangle balances, or the smallest part, is the specific aspect that you choose to tackle for the assignment. Start big and work your way down. When you get to the point of the triangle, you should have a topic that is manageable for a short paper or presentation.

Take, for instance, an assignment to write a 3-page paper on any aspect of William Shakespeare's work. You would *start out* with the complete works of William Shakespeare in the top section of the inverted triangle. It's a broad topic, so you use the broadest space. From there, you might want to take one specific work that you liked the best—let's say *Hamlet*. This would go directly below the complete works. Of course, the play *Hamlet* is also too broad a topic for a 3-page paper. So now you ask yourself, "What about *Hamlet* would I like to explore?" Using the brainstorming method discussed earlier, you can think of a number of aspects: characters, setting, symbols, dialogue, relationships, performance, and so on. Soon you've narrowed it to performance on stage or film (which you list as the next entry below on your triangle). Performance includes such categories as staging, history, the play on film, and famous actors. As you ponder these alternatives, you remember being really drawn to the play after seeing Mel Gibson's performance as Hamlet. Finally, you decide to compare Mel Gibson to Laurence Olivier in the title role. As you begin to outline your thoughts and to write, you may find that you want to narrow your focus even further (comparing, for example, the two actors' delivery of the soliloquies or the extent to which each introduced comedy into certain passages), but at least you have arrived at a starting point of reasonable scope.

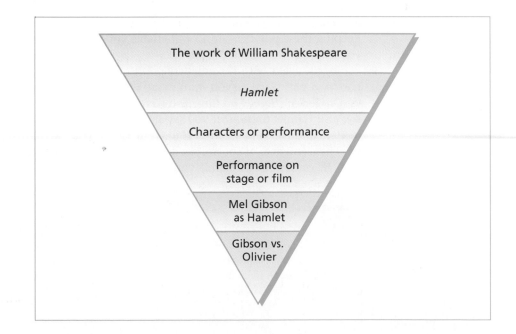

The work of William Shakespeare

Hamlet

Characters or performance

Performance on
stage or film

Mel Gibson
as Hamlet

Gibson vs.
Olivier

Teamwork Activity

The object of this activity is to practice narrowing topics for papers or presentations. Get together with three or four other students from your class. Take turns choosing a "big" topic (reality television, binge drinking, making more fuel-efficient vehicles). The other students draw an inverted triangle and try to narrow the topic down to manageable size for a paper or presentation. The person who chose that topic then evaluates how successful the other students were at narrowing it down. If you have a paper or presentation coming up soon, this might be a good way to get some help from your classmates in choosing the topic.

What a Thesis Statement Really Should Be

Just as an umbrella has to cover you in the rain to be effective, a thesis statement has to cover the material in your paper or presentation. In a typical college paper, a thesis statement is one sentence. It is also a statement that needs to be proved. In other words, it's not just a fact, such as "Light travels at 186,000 miles a second." A thesis statement answers a question posed by the assignment. On an essay test, it is usually obvious what the question is because the professor has provided it. But in assigning a paper or presentation for a course, your professor may not ask a specific question. You may receive, instead, only general guidelines from which *you* need to form a question. When you narrow your topic, you are left with a smaller subject from which you need to form and answer a question. This answer, which becomes your thesis, needs to reveal the subject of the paper or presentation *and* what you are saying about it. (After all, if the thesis were merely a fact, there would be nothing left to say.) What you are saying about the subject of your paper is your *opinion,* one that you need to argue through your supporting paragraphs or points. Keeping these points in mind will enable you to formulate a thesis that will help you organize the rest of the paper.

Begin again with the smallest point of your inverted triangle. What is your narrow topic? What do you want to say about the topic? Look at the topic "Gibson vs. Olivier" in *Hamlet* on film. You have not yet written a thesis. What *about* Gibson and Hamlet on film? If you say simply that "Olivier portrayed Hamlet on film in 1948 and Gibson portrayed Hamlet in 1991," you have written a very poor thesis. This sentence, of course, needs no further discussion. It is simply a matter of fact. If, on the other hand, you say that "Although Olivier and Gibson both

 DIY-Do-It-Yourself Activity

If you haven't tried it already, learn how to use PowerPoint or some other type of presentation software. Another student may be able to help you, or you could consult the audiovisual services on your campus. It is fairly easy to learn to use these types of software, and being familiar with them will make you more confident because you will have more tools to draw on in your presentations.

credibly portrayed Hamlet, Gibson's version would appeal more to a contemporary audience," you have written an effective thesis. Why? Because it both reveals your subject and says something about the subject. And what you said about it is an opinion that needs to be substantiated through the rest of the paper.

Organizing Your Supporting Paragraphs or Points

If you've ever moved, you know that one of the challenges is organizing all of your possessions. And you know that packing boxes the right way saves you a lot of trouble in the long run. If you label a box "kitchen supplies," for instance, you know that you should put in it only things that belong in the kitchen. You won't misplace something by packing it in the wrong box, and when you move in, you simply put that box in the kitchen, and you are ready to unpack. Writing an organized essay is a lot like packing boxes. If you plan ahead, separate your ideas into "boxes," and put sentences in the boxes according to the labels, you will find the job much easier to handle.

Think of each paragraph in an essay as a box, with each box holding a different idea or concept. Look at the five boxes that follow, and imagine them as five paragraphs in an organized essay. The first box would be your **introduction.** The middle three would be the **body paragraphs**, in which you explain the points mentioned in your introduction. Finally, the fifth box would be your **conclusion.** Clearly, you might be assigned longer or shorter essays, but we'll use this is as a standard starting point. Thinking in terms of boxes can be very useful because students often have difficulty deciding where points or ideas go in an essay. If you think about putting those points in separate boxes, you keep your paragraphs focused and avoid letting any of them become long, rambling, or unclear. Also,

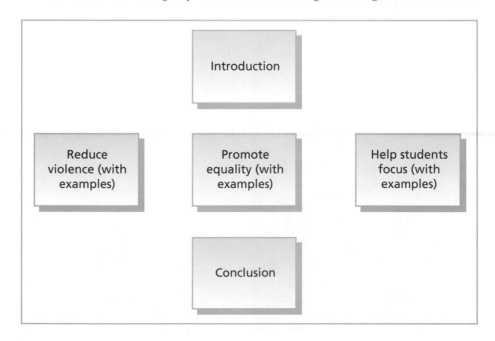

when you think in terms of boxes, you are free to move the boxes (or paragraphs) around until you get it right. Moreover, if you draw a few boxes before you start to write, you can create a very quick and painless outline to use as a guide. Let's say you have been assigned to write an argumentative essay advocating uniforms in public schools (sometimes professors ask you to take a certain position whether you agree with it or not—they may want you to demonstrate that you can work on it from any angle). Your thesis statement is "School uniforms reduce violence, promote equality among students, and help students focus on academics." The thesis statement belongs in the introduction.

The sample use of boxes shown on the previous page illustrates how using boxes to organize your essay writing will help you stay on track. This concept applies to presentations as well. When you put together a presentation, you must stay focused, too. Whether you use index cards or an outline for a speech, the key is to be organized.

Using the Computer to Do Research

If you have just recently graduated from high school, chances are you probably never had to change a typewriter ribbon or make a carbon copy. Even if you don't have a cell phone, you've certainly seen someone using one. Some of you may never even have gone to a photo shop because you use a digital camera and print out pictures on your computer. Technology has affected nearly every facet of life, and the process of doing research is one of the things that has been profoundly changed through technology. Before you jump right into doing research on the

computer, remember that books still exist, and sometimes books are better. Not everything is on the Internet, and it's not always easier to find information on the Internet than in a library. Never discount the idea of just wandering around the library and doing traditional research. When you do decide to use the computer in your research, the following tips will make your research go more smoothly:

▶ Go to your college library's homepage to find out what resources are available online. Many research tools are available only to subscribers, and colleges often subscribe in a way that covers all of their students. Some of the subscriber-only features that you may find on your library homepage are search engines such as EbscoHost and Lexis-Nexis. These can provide not only article titles but also, in many cases, full-text versions of these articles that you can print out right from your computer. You can also search by subject area for such fields as pre-med, education, and literature, among others.

▶ For Internet searches, be sure to know how credible your source is. As mentioned earlier in this chapter, some sources are better than others. You need to know who has written the material and must use your critical thinking skills to assess the credibility of the information.

The Hard Way

J osie had always thought of herself as a good—even an excellent—writer. "Everyone had always told me that, too. My teachers, my friends. I wrote for the high school paper. It was an area where I guess I had a lot of confidence." Coming into college, Josie felt certain that her skills would be a great help. "I thought that since I had gotten A's on all of my papers in high school, why shouldn't I in college?" Needless to say, she was shocked and disappointed when she started getting back papers in the C range. "I felt personally hurt, as if my professors just didn't like me. And their comments were so general, even confusing. I remember one that said, 'Well-written but needs more development.' I didn't even know what that meant." At first, she focused on her hurt feelings. "I thought, 'They just have it in for me. There's nothing I can do about it.' Then I decided I couldn't just feel sorry for myself." At that point she decided to take an active approach. "Talking to my professors was the first step. I had to get their perspectives. What they told me is that although my skills were good, I had to get beneath the surface, to really develop my ideas. One professor even told me, 'Don't just try to hide behind your strong technical skills as a writer. You've got to show me that you can think.' I've come to realize that they were really teaching me how to become better. The skills I had were good, but if I didn't improve and develop, I would just be a good high-school-level writer. I had to continue developing my strengths so I could get better and better. Now, I'm getting A's again on most of my papers, and I know it's not just because of the writing but also because of what I have to say. That's a good feeling."

You, as the receiver of information, need to be able to distinguish legitimate sites from sites that may not be providing the most accurate information. Ask yourself questions like these:

▷ Who is the author?

▷ With what organization is the author affiliated?

▷ Does the source acknowledge any affiliation? Failure to do so is often a sign that the source is shaky.

▷ Does the source seem to be independent, or is it supported by outside money that may influence its content? (Much information—but less objectivity—may be offered by a politician's website, a lobbying group's website, or a study on the health benefits of eating potatoes that is sponsored by the potato growers association.)

▷ Does the site refer to any other authoritative sources for its information?

The bottom line is that there are a lot of sources out there for any subject you could possibly think of researching. The key is to find the best, most reliable sources for your work. If you have any doubt in your mind about whether a source is reliable, check with your professor or with your college's reference librarian.

Tricks of the Trade: Refining and Delivering the Product

Gathering your information—whether it's for a research paper or a presentation— is a key part of success, but it's only the first part. To be truly successful, you need to refine that information into a finished product for your professor.

For papers:

▶ Always proofread your work at least twice. This means you should read each word carefully, checking for errors in grammar, punctuation, and spelling. In addition, it is helpful to have someone else look at your paper; after a while, you can miss mistakes just because you've looked at the same words over and over.

▶ Follow any guidelines given to you by your professor. If he or she wants a cover sheet, put on a cover sheet. And we have already discussed the issue of length. Make sure that you are also aware of any guidelines related to formatting style and that you follow through completely. If you have been asked to use MLA style, use it not only for the citations but also for headers, page numbers, spacing, and margins.

▶ Make sure that the ink in your printer is not running low, that your paper isn't wrinkled, and that you haven't spilled coffee on it. Appearance *is* important.

For presentations:

▶ Practice. Many students fail to prepare adequately for presentations. The dynamics of speaking in front of an audience can affect you; you must practice thoroughly. Simulate that environment by speaking in front of a couple of friends. You should also speak in front of a mirror or videotape yourself to get an idea how you look.

▶ Just as you'd want your paper to look good, you should dress neatly for a presentation. This doesn't necessarily mean that you must wear a suit (unless you are specifically asked to do so), but don't pull a grungy t-shirt out of the laundry pile, either.

▶ Eye contact is important. So are volume and speed. Some students—especially those who are not thoroughly prepared—look at the floor and talk quietly and quickly. Not surprisingly, they don't do well and feel even more nervous the next time out.

▶ Visual aids give your presentation a little extra punch. Enhancing your presentation in this way shows that you have put in the time and effort, it appears more polished, and it gives your audience something else to look at during your presentation. (An added benefit is that it can be a relief to know that not everyone's eyes are riveted on you at every moment.)

▶ Be prepared on the day of the presentation. Don't forget your material (note cards, overheads, handouts); you don't want to appear as though you don't want to give your speech or as though you aren't ready.

Keeping these things in mind will help you take your papers and presentations one step further. You will have the polish that will separate your work from that of students who didn't put in as much effort. At the end of the day, these hints won't save a paper or presentation that lacks substance (or just isn't very good). But they will help a good paper or presentation shine in the best possible light, and that light will reflect favorably on you.

Time-Out Tip

 Giving a speech can be nerve-wracking. There's no doubt about it. If you're feeling especially nervous right before a speech, try a technique known as diaphragmatic breathing. You can actually do this while sitting in your seat, and no one will even know you're doing it. Deep breathing sends oxygen to the brain and muscles and can help you relax. Start by sitting up straight with your palms resting on your thighs. Take a few slow breaths deep into your diaphragm, and wait a few seconds before releasing it. Doing this for thirty seconds can help you feel much more relaxed and focused.

Citing Sources

When it comes to writing papers or giving presentations, if you use an idea that is not your own, you must always cite the original source. Always. *Always.* It is that simple. Sometimes students think that if they change the wording, they do not have to cite the source. Remember, however, that you are citing the idea. Thus you have a responsibility to make the reader or the audience aware of the fact that you did not come up with the idea yourself. If you keep this basic rule for citing sources in mind, you will avoid plagiarizing in a paper or presentation.

Here are some basic tips for citing sources:

▶ When you quote from a source directly, cite that source according to the format you have been told to use (MLA, APA, or the like). (In all cases, when you quote directly you must put the text in quotation marks, except for longer passages that you indent.)

▶ When you paraphrase a section of a source, cite it according to the format you have been told to use. Remember that paraphrasing is taking a piece of text and putting it in your own words. If you find yourself writing three or more words in a row that are the exact words used in the original source, you need to go back and either reword your paraphrase or quote directly instead. Furthermore, it's not enough simply to change words to synonyms (as when the author says "larger" and you change it to "bigger"); this, too, is a form of plagiarism. If it's that close, simply quote it.

▶ When you cite a source in the body of your paper, remember to include bibliographical information on that source in your "Works Cited" section or on your "References" page. If it is in your paper, it must appear on this page as well.

▶ If you have lost track of a source but still want to use the information, do not make up a source. This is another from of plagiarism. Either find the original source again or use a different source.

▶ Keep track of page numbers as well. If you quote directly in MLA format, for example, you need to provide the page on which that quote appeared. This is one reason why it is important to keep track of all of your sources and of what information you took from each source.

▶ Always cite your sources in accordance with a format you have been told to use. If your professor does not assign a particular format, choose the one you are most familiar with and stick to it. Always be consistent. In the next section, you will find a basic overview of MLA style and APA style—two of the most common formats for writing research papers. Become familiar with these formats. Keep handbooks on hand. Using such a format is not difficult. You just have to resolve to *do* it.

MLA and APA Guidelines: What You Need to Get Started

Different disciplines require different formatting styles. The two styles you are most likely to come across in college are APA (American Psychological Association) style and MLA (Modern Language Association) style. Usually, your professor will specify which format you should use. But if he or she doesn't, here are some general guidelines about which one you should use. In the liberal arts (English, history, philosophy, etc.), you are usually going to use MLA style. In the social sciences (education, sociology, psychology, etc.) and the hard sciences (biology, physics, etc.), you are probably going to use APA. You will frequently cover the basics of these styles in your composition class, but nobody expects you to memorize all of the rules. Most professors don't even know all the rules. What they *do* know, and what *you* need to know, is where to find the information. Most writing handbooks contain a fairly detailed summary of the rules regarding both of these formats. Here are some of the things they will give you:

▶ Format for citing sources—including complex rules for Internet sources—both in the text of your paper and in your bibliography at the end.

▶ Format for headers, footers, page numbers, cover pages, margins, charts, graphs, photos, and the like.

▶ Guidelines for using outside sources properly. An outside source is any source that provides information you did not write or create. For example, outside sources include books, magazines, journal articles, and websites.

As a college student, you would be well advised to keep some kind of writing handbook by your side as you write your papers (in many first-year composition classes, you will be required to purchase such a handbook as one of your textbooks). If you have particularly detailed questions about formatting, go to the original source:

▶ American Psychological Association. (2001). *Publication Manual of the American Psychological Association.* Washington, DC: American Psychological Association.

▶ Gibaldi, J. (1999). *MLA Handbook for Writers of Research Papers.* New York: Modern Language Association.

Alternatively, you can consult the respective websites: www.apa.org and www.mla.org.

year of publication to the latest to reflect a historical progression. Alternatively, it may be organized by genre (type of writing), being divided into short stories, poems, and plays. Some literature textbooks are instead organized by theme, such as patriotism, courage, loss, or hope. **Read the table of contents carefully to determine what approach your book takes. Understanding this at the outset will help you avoid confusion later. Your notes should also reflect this organization because your tests may reflect it — you may be asked to put literature into historical perspective, or you may be asked to compare two poems, for example.**

Literature textbooks are not necessarily linear. You may find yourself jumping around quite a bit, depending on what readings your professor assigns. **Use a variety of strategies. Different types of writing in literature textbooks require different strategies. You may be able to read a short story quickly, but it often takes two or three readings to understand all the facets of a good poem. Also, a short story is easier to summarize than a poem, which may not tell a story. Instead, a poem may capture an image or set a mood. Looking for key words in poems can help you appreciate the full meaning. A play may best be understood when read aloud. You might consider getting a group of friends together to act out a play you need to understand. Also, try to summarize every so often. Put the stories, plays, or poems in your own words so you can check your comprehension. See the tips for annotating in Chapter 3.**

Reading 1:   A Textbook Case

This short story is included here because in a literature class you will be exposed to many different forms of writing, of which one is the short story. The short story may seem the most "comfortable" to read because it is more direct than a poem or play. Poems may have many layers of meaning that may not seem immediately accessible, and plays are generally meant to be performed, not just read. This short story is one you may very well see in an introductory literature course. Even though it was written in the late nineteenth century, it contains some universal and timeless ideas. As you read this short story, look for the irony and the foreshadowing. Underline the passages in which these elements appear, and write brief notes to yourself in the margin. When you have finished reading the story, summarize what happened in a brief paragraph in your own words.

BEFORE YOU READ

1. The main character in the story that follows is a woman living in the late nineteenth century. What do you know about women's roles at this time? How has life changed for women between then and now?
2. When is an hour a long time? When is an hour a short time?
3. Have you ever been confronted by a shocking piece of information? What was your reaction and how did you digest this information?

The Story of an Hour

K. Chopin

Knowing that Mrs. Mallard was afflicted with heart trouble, great care was taken to break to her as gently as possible the news of her husband's death.

It was her sister Josephine who told her, in broken sentences: veiled hints that revealed in half concealing. Her husband's friend Richards was there, too, near her. It was he who had been in the newspaper office when intelligence of the railroad disaster was received, with Brently Mallard's name leading the list of "killed." He had only taken the time to assure himself of its truth by a second telegram, and had hastened to forestall any less careful, less tender friend in bearing the sad message.

She did not hear the story as many women have heard the same, with a paralyzed inability to accept its significance. She wept at once, with sudden, wild abandonment, in her sister's arms. When the storm of grief had spent itself she went away to her room alone.

There stood, facing the open window, a comfortable, roomy armchair. Into this she sank, pressed down by a physical exhaustion that haunted her body and seemed to reach into her soul.

She could see in the open square before her house the tops of trees that were all aquiver with the new spring life. The delicious breath of rain was in the air. In the street below a peddler was crying his wares. The notes of a distant song which someone was singing reached her faintly, and countless sparrows were twittering in the eaves.

There were patches of blue sky showing here and there through the clouds that had met and piled one above the other in the west facing her window.

She sat with her head thrown back upon the cushion of the chair, quite motionless, except when a sob came up into her throat and shook her, as a child who has cried itself to sleep continues to sob in its dreams.

She was young, with a fair, calm face, whose lines bespoke repression and even a certain strength. But now there was a dull stare in her eyes, whose gaze was fixed away off yonder on one of those patches of blue sky. It was not a glance of reflection, but rather indicated a suspension of intelligent thought.

There was something coming to her and she was waiting for it, fearfully. What was it? She did not know; it was too subtle and elusive to name. But she felt it, creeping out of the sky, reaching toward her through the sounds, the scents, the color that filled the air.

Now her bosom rose and fell tumultuously. She was beginning to recognize this thing that was approaching to possess her, and she was striving to beat it back with her will—as powerless as her two white slender hands would have been.

When she abandoned herself a little whispered word escaped her slightly parted lips. She said it over and over under her breath: "free, free, free!" The vacant stare and the look of terror that had followed it went from her eyes. They stayed

SOURCE: K. Chopin, "The Story of an Hour." In E. V. Roberts and H. E. Jacobs, *Literature: An Introduction to Reading and Writing*, 6th ed. (Upper Saddle River, NJ: Prentice-Hall, 2001), pp. 393–405.

keen and bright. Her pulses beat fast, and the coursing blood warmed and relaxed every inch of her body.

She did not stop to ask if it were or were not a monstrous joy that held her. A clear and exalted perception enabled her to dismiss the suggestion as trivial.

She knew that she would weep again when she saw the kind, tender hands folded in death; the face that had never looked save with love upon her, fixed and gray and dead. But she saw beyond the bitter moment a long procession of years to come that would belong to her absolutely. And she opened and spread her arms out to them in welcome.

There would be no one to live for her during those coming years; she would live for herself. There would be no powerful will bending hers in that blind persistence with which men and women believed they have a right to impose a private will upon a fellow-creature. A kind intention or a cruel intention made the act seem no less a crime as she looked upon it in that brief moment of illumination.

And yet she had loved him—sometimes. Often she had not. What did it matter! What could love, the unsolved mystery, count for in the face of this possession of self-assertion which she suddenly recognized as the strongest impulse of her being!

"Free! Body and soul free!" she kept whispering.

Josephine was kneeling before the closed door with her lips to the keyhole, imploring for admission. "Louise, open the door! I beg; open the door—you will make yourself ill. What are you doing, Louise? For heaven's sake open the door."

"Go away. I am not making myself ill." No; she was drinking in the very elixir of life through that open window.

Her fancy was running riot along those days ahead of her. Spring days, and summer days, and all sorts of days that would be her own. She breathed a quick prayer that life might be long. It was only yesterday she had thought with a shudder that life might be long.

She arose at length and opened the door to her sister's importunities. There was a feverish triumph in her eyes, and she carried herself unwittingly like a goddess of Victory. She clasped her sister's waist, and together they descended the stairs. Richards stood waiting for them at the bottom.

Someone was opening the front door with a latchkey. It was Brently Mallard who entered, a little travel-stained, composedly carrying his grip-sack and umbrella. He had been far from the scene of the accident, and did not even know there had been one. He stood amazed at Josephine's piercing cry; at Richards' quick motion to screen him from the view of his wife.

But Richards was too late.

When the doctors came they said she had died of heart disease—of joy that kills.

AFTER YOU READ

1. What event foreshadowed the ending of the story? Did the ending surprise you?
2. How do you explain Mrs. Mallard's reaction to her husband's death? Do you feel her reaction was justified? Why or why not?
3. Identify at least two examples of irony in this story and explain why they fit the definition of irony.

4. What emotions does Mrs. Mallard experience on the first floor, and what emotions does she experience on the second floor? How does the setting contribute to the story?

5. As a group, draw a timeline of the story. Identify key events and shifts in emotion. From this timeline, try to write a summary, in the group members' own words, to see whether you understand the story.

Reading 2: Life After College

Those of you who have ever contemplated a career as a writer, and those of you who have thought at all about writers and what they do, may have assumed that it is all about writing "the great American novel." A typical stereotype of a writer is a person alone in a room churning out what will eventually be the next best seller. Although this is a possibility for some would-be writers, there are many other options from which to choose. As with any career, making good choices involves learning as much as you can about what opportunities are out there. This article discusses some "hot jobs" for writers. As you read it, picture yourself in one of these jobs. Does this article open your eyes to possibilities you never thought of before?

BEFORE YOU READ

1. What are some popular conceptions of what writers are like?

2. Who are some fictional characters who are writers you see on television sitcoms or dramas, in movies, or elsewhere in popular culture? As they are portrayed, how do they fit or defy the stereotype?

3. If you could be any type of writer, what type would you be and why? If you cannot envision yourself in a job that requires writing, what aspect of it does not appeal to you? What can you do to change your attitude toward writing?

Hot Jobs for Writers

A. Gibson

Love to write? Here are some jobs that can turn your love of words into a marketable career.

Jake wrote his first poem at age 5, started a neighborhood newspaper at 12. His favorite subject in school is English, and in his spare time he writes copy for the high school yearbook. In short, he loves to write. He can't imagine having a career that doesn't call for him to be typing away at the computer keyboard.

But how can Jake actually make a living at this art? There are hundreds of jobs that rely on the craft of writing, and several avenues to venture down. There are writers who:

► sell or persuade with their words—advertising copywriters, public relations specialists
► break the latest news—newspaper and magazine reporters, television and radio broadcasters
► explain and inform—corporate or technical writers
► enlighten and entertain—entertainment and magazine writers, television or film scriptwriters.

SOURCE: A. Gibson, "Hot Jobs for Writers," *Career World 27* (January 1999), 29–31. Reprinted by permission.

The salaries and opportunities available in these individual writing fields vary. Some of these writing careers, though somewhat high-profile and glamorous, won't necessarily make you rich. Newspaper reporters, for example, rarely earn the big bucks. And as for novelists? Well, not everyone can be the next Anne Rice. Competition is fierce to get a book published, or a script put on the screen. However, several writing-related careers allow you to build a savings account while satisfying your creative urge to write.

High-Tech Hires

You love the creativity of writing but also like chemistry classes. Did you know that there's a career out there that combines the two fields?

Dawn Perry didn't know that until she accepted her first job out of college as a technical writer. Technical writers write about complex scientific ideas in simple, clear, everyday language. They write for an audience of experts as well as for nontechnical people. Many technical writers work in the electronics, aviation, aerospace, weapons, chemical, and pharmaceutical fields. Some work for a company full- or part-time. Others, free-lance writers, work on a per-assignment basis. They may write the user's guide to your computer and other instructional manuals, catalogs, instructional aids, books, articles, or even advertising copy.

Perry works for the National Center for Genome Research, a nonprofit organization that uses computers to analyze genetic information. Her job duties include writing product manuals and text for the organization's Web site. Readers may be people within her organization, scientists, or students. For example, her software manuals are geared toward biologists or graduate students who understand science but may not be familiar with the computer software.

Technical writers must be organized and flexible, able to learn quickly and work on their own, Perry says. Like all writers, they must have a tough skin to handle criticism and feedback on their writing. Editors will make changes to a piece of writing to make it more effective, and can often see need for changes that the writer can't. Perry, who has a

background in communications rather than science, enjoys her job because it allows her to write while learning about new topics—in this case, biology. Not only is the work interesting, but Perry says that technical writers are in high demand. Their jobs generally pay better than others in the journalism field.

A Nose for the News

Do you think a 9-to-5 desk job would bore you to tears? Do you have a hunger for digging out the truth in life? Then look no further. Try the fast-paced field of news reporting. Writing opportunities exist at newspapers, magazines, radio and television stations, and with on-line publications. Because news is always breaking, these writers often are "on call." Reporters might find themselves covering a city hall meeting at 8 a.m. or a house fire at 11:45 p.m.

News reporters gather information by attending meetings, conducting interviews with sources, and doing research at libraries, courthouses, and so on. They often write stories quickly on deadline, delivering the news in a concise, reader-friendly manner. Because news reporters are required to write objectively, they must take accurate notes and must not take sides on an issue. The best reporters aren't shy. They must be assertive and persistent to get information necessary for their news stories.

Because the journalist's craft takes time to learn, new hires often start out at the bottom rung of a news organization. But they can climb up over time for greater prestige and salaries. Beginning news writers might start out, for example, as proofreaders or copy editors at newspapers, or as editorial assistants at magazines. Reporters can advance to editors, who oversee, edit, and determine the content of a publication.

One of the up-and-coming areas of news reporting is writing for on-line services and electronic publications as on-line content developers/writers. Not only are newspapers and magazines creating on-line versions of their publications, but new publications that exist solely in cyberspace are popping up on the World Wide Web. The rise in popularity of the Internet and the boom in electronic publishing are creating a greater demand for people who can develop virtual and verbal content for on-line publications.

Persuading the Masses

One of the ways news reporters find out about the latest scoops is from public relations specialists. These professionals write materials that promote the image and reputation of an organization or public figure. They spread "good news" to create a favorable public impression of their employer or client. They may work directly for one company, government agency, or nonprofit organization. Or, they may work for a public relations firm that handles many different clients.

Rob Roth, a senior associate with international public relations firm BSMG Worldwide, has helped spread the news about many different clients. For example, he and the company got a small financial lending business 135 mentions in the media in the first year, including a quote in the *New York Times*.

This public relations professional promotes everything from new food items to real estate projects for his clients. But with each project, the strategy is similar. First, Roth learns all about the company, who its customers are, and what message it wants to send out. To be successful in the public relations campaign, he must show the media and public why the company's latest project is important. Roth then determines who should receive the information.

This is where his writing skills come in. Roth may write any number of news releases (short, informational pieces for news reporters) and media advisories to get the word out. He also may create business plans and presentations, and may instruct clients on how to respond to the media's questions.

Public relations specialists must be self-confident, assertive, enthusiastic, and creative. Roth says his work environment is fast-paced, and he often juggles more than a dozen projects in a month.

With that routine, Roth is never bored. He enjoys working closely with the movers and shakers of the world. Handling various projects, he's learned a lot about many issues and subjects. That, however, also can be a bit of a downside to the job, he says. "While it's never boring, you also have to hop around. You wish you could put more time into a specific project," he says.

Searching for Slogans

"Got milk?" "Want some?" "Where do you want to go today?" Heard these phrases before? These ad slogans, promoting milk, Taco Bell fast food, and the Microsoft company, seem to pop up everywhere. That's the point. Advertising copywriters specifically created them to stick in your head.

Advertising copywriters are similar to public relations specialists in that they deal with persuasive writing. Copywriters focus on creating memorable, eye-catching sales messages—a combination of images, slogans, and text. Their goal: to encourage you to buy a company's product. The job requires a mix of sales skills and creativity.

The copywriter works with several people. Perhaps the most important is the account executive, who works directly with the client needing the ad and determines what the client wants. The art director is then called on to create an art concept that goes along with the text the copywriter has written.

Finally, the team consults with a media expert—someone who decides the best places for ads to run. The ad may appear on radio or television, in magazines or newspapers, on billboards, or even on the Internet.

Write-fully Yours

Most careers for wordsmiths will be on the rise in the coming years. The technical writing field is rapidly expanding, with opportunities available for talented writers with some education in the science fields. Competition for public relations jobs is expected to be intense, as it's considered a glamorous, popular field. But those with solid academic backgrounds, media experience, and skill with new technologies, such as the Internet, will have an edge. The outlook is good for ad copywriters, too, with the best opportunities in big cities such as New York, Chicago, Washington, DC, and Los Angeles.

Think "small" if you're considering a career as a news reporter. The number of large daily newspapers is on the decline in the nation's cities, so the opportunities will be best at small-town or suburban publications. In the broadcast field, hiring at big television networks is expected to decrease. But small stations, new cable networks, and new radio stations will continue to need writers. The Internet also will offer increasing opportunities for on-line content developers and writers.

It's never too early to start honing those writing skills. Take English and journalism classes. Write for the school newspaper, yearbook, or literary magazine. And get a well-rounded education—as a writer you'll be called upon to become a mini-expert on many topics. Learning about new things is another of writing's many rewards—perhaps a reason why Jake, and maybe you, got into it in the first place.

For More Info

Society for Technical Communication
901 North Stuart Street, Suite 904
Arlington, VA 22203-1854
Brochure: "Careers in Technical Communication," single copy free. Call (703) 522-4114. Or visit the STC website at *www.stc-org.org*.
National Newspaper Association
1627 K Street NW, Suite 400
Washington, DC 20006
Pamphlet: "A Career in Newspapers." Write or call NNA for free single copy at (703) 907-7900. Or visit the NNA website at *www.nna.org*.

AFTER YOU READ

1. Which of the writing careers discussed in this article were new to you?
2. According to the article, creative writing is a competitive career. Why is this? What do you think students can do to get an edge in this competitive field?
3. Identify some of the differences among the different types of writers. Which of them appeals to you the most? Which has the least appeal?
4. According to the author, what is the career outlook in this field? What are some skills that you would need? How do you think the skills needed are different in the various fields of writing? Gather your answers to these questions as a group; then prepare and present a brief career seminar for future writers.

Reading 3: Current Issues

Later in this text, in Chapter 10, we will examine the role of technology in the classroom and in society at large. As college students, all of you use technology to make your personal and academic lives easier. One of the ways in which you use technology is for writing and researching papers. Although technology can be helpful in this process, some technological short cuts can lead to bad habits that can be detrimental to your writing. In the following passage, we take a look at the relatively new phenomenon of text messaging.

BEFORE YOU READ

1. List all the ways (or at least as many ways as you can think of) in which you have used technology in the last week. How do you think your life would be different without technology?
2. Think about the role of instant messaging and text messaging in communication. Do you think these types of messaging hinder or help communication? Why?

R ur txt msgs :(or OK?

MILWAUKEE, Wisconsin (AP)—The text messages on Margarete Stettner's cell phone are filled with shortcuts—like "G2G" for "got to go" and "LOL" instead of "laugh out loud." Even when she isn't using her phone, the lingo sometimes makes its way into what she writes.

"It does affect, sometimes, how I do my schoolwork," the 13-year-old from Hartland, Wis., said as she shopped in a mall, where cellular phones are as common as low-cut jeans. "Instead of a Y-O-U, I put a U."

That alarms some linguists, who worry that the proliferation of text messaging—where cell phone users type and send short messages to other phones or computers—will enforce sloppy, undisciplined habits among American youths.

Other experts, though, don't think the abbreviations will leave their mark on standard English.

In June 2001, wireless phone users sent 30 million text messages in the United States, according to the Cellular Telecommunications and Internet Association, an industry trade organization. By June 2002, that number had increased to nearly 1 billion.

The method is most popular among teenagers, according to Upoc Inc., a New York-based firm that helps users of mobile devices share information on everything from the rapper Bow Wow to celebrity sightings. A study by Upoc in 2001 found 43 percent of cellular phone users ages 12 to 17 used text messaging, compared with 25 percent of those 30 to 34.

Those teenagers, hampered by limited space and the difficulty of writing words on numeric phone keypads, helped create the text-messaging lingo.

Words were abbreviated ("WL" for "will") and common phrases became acronyms ("by the way" turned into "BTW").

> **FACT BOX**
> **Abbreviated words:**
> "G2G" (got to go)
> "LOL" (laugh out loud)
> "WL" (will)
> "BTW" (by the way)
> "AFAIK" (as far as I know)
> "SOL" (sooner or later) or (sadly out of luck)
> "W" (what?)
> "PXT" (please explain that)

There are even dictionaries to sort out the meaning of, say, "AFAIK" ("As far as I know").

"SOL" can mean "sooner or later" or "sadly out of luck," but if you're unclear on which was meant, simply message back a "W" (what?) or "PXT" (please explain that) for a clarification.

Jesse Sheidlower, principal editor of the U.S. office of the Oxford English Dictionary, said text messaging is going through the natural progression of language.

Much text-messaging lingo was first used in instant-messaging programs on personal computers, and some phrases, such as "SWAK" for "sealed with a kiss," have been used for decades, Sheidlower said.

As text messengers discover and share new abbreviations and acronyms, the language becomes familiar to a growing population of cell phone users. And as more people use the lingo for text messaging, Sheidlower said, it is more likely to spill into speech or writing.

That worries American University linguistics professor Naomi Baron, who said text messaging is another example of a trend in written communication.

"So much of American society has become sloppy or laissez faire about the mechanics of writing," Baron said.

SOURCE: "R ur txt msgs :(or OK?" cnn.com. Retrieved on December 28, 2003 from *http://www.cnn.com/ 2003/ TECH/ptech/02/13/text.messaging.ap/*. Reprinted with permission of The Associated Press.

Problems arise when people use the casual language in other forms of written communication, such as e-mail, in which the sender may not receive the message for some time, or writings in which the reader may not even know the author, she said.

But other linguists said a simpler, more relaxed vernacular is acceptable for talking or text messaging.

"Language and languages change," said Carolyn Adger, director of the Language in Society Division of the Center for Applied Linguistics in Washington. "Innovating with language isn't dangerous."

And besides, Adger said, text messaging, like e-mail and instant messaging, is making it easier for people to communicate.

"I think that all of this stuff is really wonderful, because it's expanding the writing skills of people," she said.

Text messaging hardly appears to have hurt written language in Europe, where 10 billion text messages are sent each month, said Charles Golvin, senior analyst with Forrester Research.

In fact, as more adults began using text messaging in Britain and Germany, the lingo fell out of favor, said Alex Bergs, a visiting linguistics professor at the University of Wisconsin-Milwaukee. Even teenagers use the language for only a while, he said.

One teen in Milwaukee, college student Jeremy Rankin, spends quite a bit of time using wireless devices in his job at a cell phone store. The 18-year-old admits he sometimes finds himself abbreviating when he types.

"I might do it by accident, but I don't think that's a problem as far as school papers go," he said. "I proofread my stuff."

AFTER YOU READ

1. According to the article, what are some of the ways in which technology is changing our language?
2. What technological innovations have changed our language in the past? How?
3. List as many words as you can that didn't exist ten years ago. Can you list some that didn't exist twenty years ago? Thirty years ago? Discuss what caused the development of these words.
4. The article quotes experts on both sides of the issue of the effects of text messaging on our language—some who are very concerned and others who are not. First explain their respective arguments, and then indicate which outlook you agree with and why.

Compounding Your Interest: Further Readings

Daniel, M.H., & Edwards, A. (October 1997). "Speak Up!" *Essence.*
Jefferson, M. (July 8, 2001). "We Are All Tourists." *New York Times Book Review.*
King, S. (2001). *On Writing: A Memoir of the Craft.* New York: Pocket Books.
Strunk, W., & White, E.B. (2002). *The Elements of Style,* 4th ed. New York: Allyn & Bacon
Welty, E. (1984). *One Writer's Beginnings.* Cambridge, MA: Harvard University Press.
Zinsser, W. (2001). *On Writing Well.* New York: Quill.

Chapter 7

Keeping a Balance

This chapter will cover the following topics:

Gaining Confidence as a Student and as a Person

Your Social Life and Your Academic Life: A Balancing Act

Diversifying Your Experiences: Taking Advantage of the Diversity on Your Campus

Service Learning / Volunteering

I n gymnastics, the balance beam event requires the gymnast to perform on a beam four inches wide four feet above the ground. If you've ever seen or participated in the event, you know that the gymnast doesn't simply walk back and forth on the beam (after all, many people could do that) but must perform flips and handstands while always maintaining balance. If you were to ask the competitors what it takes, one word would probably come to mind: focus. If the gymnasts lose focus, they will fall off the beam, risking injury and losing the competition. College can be like a balance beam. Lose focus, and you're likely to hit the mat: fail a class, party too much and study too little, flunk out of school. All kinds of negative things can cause you to lose focus. But to maintain your focus, you must have balance in your life—balance among school, work, and leisure time. This means that although studying is good, it shouldn't be the only thing you do. Likewise, relaxing by playing video games or going to a party can be good, but you still have to get your work done. During your first year in college, however, finding a balance may be easier said than done. There are a lot of distractions. You're responsible for keeping your own schedule, often for the first time. You are experiencing freedom, but you're still getting used to the responsibilities that come with it. A college campus, with all of the things that are going on, is buzzing with activity and opportunities. Perhaps at no other time in your life will you be so much immersed in new cultures and ideas, with opportunities to meet people with such widely varying backgrounds and diverse opinions. In the midst of this whirlwind of activity, you need to find a way to keep yourself focused on your own goals, even as those goals might change, while still taking advantage of everything college has to offer you. Achieving that kind of balance is the point of this chapter.

Think About It

Answer the following questions in the space provided.

Are you living a balanced life right now? If so, why? If not, why not? _____

_____

_____

_____

_____

What Worked for Me

"I was drowning," computer science major Damian says. "Too many parties, too many hangovers, too many wasted days." Now a junior, Damian has made it a priority to refocus his time and energy. When a few of his friends graduated, he realized that he himself was going to be out of school in not very long and that he needed to be ready. One of his friends had a tough time finding a job with a 2.1 GPA in a competitive field. Another had no campus activities on his résumé—and couldn't very well put down "going to parties." With a newfound perspective, Damian realized that he needed to get involved in the right kinds of activities. During the week, he works at the computer help desk, where he is also able to do his own work when he is not busy. He saves partying for Fridays and Saturdays if he gets his work done by then. He has improved his GPA significantly, while maintaining a balance between work and fun.

First Things First

In thinking about keeping your focus, it is important first to identify what your focus actually is. What do you want to get out of college? Are you focused on preparing for a specific career? Are you focused on earning the grades you need to get into graduate school? Are you in college to explore different possibilities? Are you in college because you didn't know what else to do? Think about this issue. Your honest answers will help you determine what your focus will be. And knowing what your focus is will make actually focusing a lot easier!

Gaining Confidence as a Student and as a Person

College is a time of opportunity. A time to gain confidence in yourself as a student and as a person, an individual with strengths and weaknesses, with talents and knowledge to apply to problems, jobs, and everyday life.

Confidence comes from taking responsibility for your own life. When you take responsibility for yourself, you discover that you can handle obstacles and learn from them. You may already have encountered learning opportunities in your own social life in college, in taking care of your health, and in meeting new people. No one can give you confidence. You have to go out and gain it yourself.

Here are some suggestions for gaining confidence as a student and as a person while in college:

Challenge Yourself. What are you afraid of? What do you wish you could do that you can't do right now? Think about it, and then think about how you can overcome the fear or learn to do something that seems almost impossible right now. But don't try to confront the whole problem all at once; rather, break it down into manageable pieces. Let's say you are afraid of speaking in front of people. You wouldn't decide to overcome your fear by being a speaker at your college's graduation, in front of hundreds or thousands of people. Instead, you can begin small. First, try to answer questions in class if you didn't do much of that in high school. Little by little, you will see it is not so bad to be the focus of attention in class. You

may also think about joining the debate club. You will learn to speak in front of people in a smaller group setting, and you will get a lot of practice doing it.

Meet New People. College is one of the best times in your life to meet new people. Try to meet as many new people as you can. Of course, that is not the same as being friends with all of them. Gaining confidence in meeting new people will help you when you interview for jobs and when you start out as the new person at a company right out of college. One of the things you want to do in college that is different from what you may have experienced before is to meet people of differ-ent age groups, different ethnic groups, different religions, and different back-grounds or ways of life. Why? Because in the work world, you will be expected to interact with people from all backgrounds. Also, you can enrich your own life by opening yourself up to the experiences of others.

▶ Try to meet and really get to know people outside your age group. The easiest place to start is with your professors. Some students are afraid to talk to their professors outside of class. However, most professors are very approachable. You may see them in a different light when talking to them in their offices or interacting with them in a student organization. Besides helping you get bet-ter grades (because your professors know you and know you care), you will also learn how to interact with people in authority. This will prepare you for job in-terviews and for feeling comfortable in a job where you must work with or in-teract with people on all levels of the organization.

▶ Be open to meeting people from different backgrounds, ethnic groups, and religious affiliations. It is natural for people to gravitate to other people with similar backgrounds. However, remember that gaining confidence isn't about doing what is comfortable; it is about doing something new or difficult. Seek out opportunities to become a part of cultural activities that celebrate diversity: dinners, musical events, movies, festivals. You will not only meet new people but also learn about new cultures—and a little bit more about yourself.

Be Curious. In college, you should open your mind to new experiences, new points of view, and new ways of examining the world around you. If you are not curious, you end up doing the same things over and over. Then, when it comes time to do something new, you may lack the confidence to do it. Curiosity is a great confidence booster. Curious people reach out. They ask questions. They challenge assumptions. They look at something old in a new way. These activities generate a sort of mental energy that translates into confidence because you see what you can do—and you are doing many things! You also see that you can deal with problems that come along because you are more alert and are accustomed to seeking out new solutions.

▶ Care about the political process. Learn as much as you can about any elections going on when you are in college. Be aware of the issues. Argue them with friends and faculty. Don't accept the received wisdom. Think for yourself. Vote.

▶ Read the local paper. Learn as much as you can about the community that is home to your college or university. This goes for reading the college paper as well. Be involved with what is happening on your campus.

▶ Ask questions in class.

▶ Try some foods that are completely new to you. You never know when you will be able to talk about these food experiences. And you never know whom you will meet while trying these new foods. Think raw fish sounds disgusting? Try some sushi. You might like it. Or maybe you will like latkes better. Don't know what latkes are? Go find out.

▶ Learn to play a musical instrument or figure out what golf or lacrosse is all about.

Take Courses to Explore New Interests. Every major has specific requirements when it comes to which courses you must take. But there is room in almost every degree program for some "free" electives. Take advantage of this. Pick a course not because you have to take it but because you want to take it. It will be a whole new learning experience. Maybe your grandmother speaks German and grew up in Germany. You may want to visit some day. Learn the language. Perhaps you have always been a movie buff. Take a course in film appreciation and learn about the way movies are made and the different periods in which they have been made. Learn the language of film and how to talk about movies. Who knows, you may end up with a new major or minor that evolved out of a course that you took "just for fun." You will gain confidence from knowing that you can learn new things. And as you become a "specialist" of sorts in a new area, you will become a better conversationalist.

Lifeline

If you are inter-ested in a career that requires travel, skills in another language, or an ap-preciation for other cultures (such as international busi-ness or teaching), consider spending a semester abroad. Most campuses of-fer programs in which a stu-dent, for about the same tuition, can enroll in a uni-versity in another country. This is a great way to im-merse yourself in another language, gain a new per-spective on the world, and become more independent. To find out more about such programs, you can begin with your advisor.

Travel. Your college years may be one of the best times to travel. Even if you don't have a lot of money, there are many opportunities for budget travel with campus groups. Start out simple. Student activities offices often sponsor cheap or free trips to local attractions such as ball games, amusement parks, and museums. If you net-work well, you might be selected to represent your college at an event in another state or even another country. Studying abroad is a great way to combine travel with academic credits. And it is a lot less expensive to travel to a foreign country as a student than as a tourist. Students stay in dorms and pay the usual student fees. Many side trips are also included in the fees. Traveling is one of the best ways to get a new perspective on your world. Also, being exposed to new people and en-vironments, and having to learn how to acclimate yourself, is a great way to gain confidence.

Meet the Goals You Set. There is nothing more satisfying than accomplishing what you resolved to do. Set reasonable goals and work at them bit by bit. When you have reached them, you will have a sense of satisfaction that will give you more confidence to set and achieve other goals in college and beyond. For example, say that after a rough first year, you start to get your footing academically. You decide to try to make the Dean's List the second semester of sophomore year. Naturally, if you achieve this goal, you are going to feel especially good because you will know how far you have come. Having the goal will help motivate you during the tough times in the semester. Even if you don't achieve the goal the first semester out, if you have been working at it, you are getting closer, and you may do it next time.

Putting some of these suggestions into practice will help you build your confidence. And even if you're brimming with confidence already, you will still benefit by opening yourself up to new experiences. Take some chances in college. That's what the whole experience is about.

DIV: Do-It-Yourself Activity

On a piece of paper, write down the question "What do I want to get out of college?" To answer this question, set three goals for yourself (for example, I want to get accepted into medical school, I want to meet many new people, and I want to be a chemical engineer with a company overseas). Discuss your answers with your advisor and seek some suggestions from him or her.

Your Social Life and Your Academic Life: A Balancing Act

It may have been many years since you were in a playground, but surely you re-member the see-saw. Sometimes you and a friend "worked" well together, going up and down. But if your friend suddenly jumped off, or the weight was not evenly distributed, the see-saw ended up unbalanced. For a see-saw to work, everything has to be in balance. This is true of your time in college. Without balance, you can quickly come crashing down.

How do you achieve balance? By looking at two major areas of your college ex-perience: your social life and your academic life. Think of them as riding on either end of that see-saw. They should be weighted evenly and should work together to keep your college experience a positive one.

The meaning of academic life is probably clear to you by now, but what does having a social life really mean in college? Different people might answer that question differently, but a healthy social life typically includes such areas as the following:

▶ **Personal growth.** The person you are right now as you start college is not the person you will be when you graduate. The experiences that you are having and will have are shaping who you are. They are changing you, and they will make you a different person. Even though your life right now may seem consumed by assignments, tests, and deadlines, college is also a wonderful time to grow in ways that only experience outside the classroom can provide. Personal growth is not something you're likely to be conscious of on a daily basis, but there are things you can do to foster it. For instance, college libraries tend to have wonderful collections of nonacademic reading materials, such as current novels and nonfiction books. Take advantage of this access to such a wealth of reading materials in areas that interest you. Reading for pleasure can improve your ability to read your college textbooks. Similarly, while at the library you may pick up a DVD of a film you wouldn't normally see at the multiplex. You could also take the opportunity to try something different, such as a pottery class, downhill skiing, or cooking.

▶ **Free time.** A healthy social life includes time just to unwind. Sometimes it's good to do nothing: Walk around town, stop in on friends, have a cappuccino at the coffee shop, hang out and daydream. The energy you restore during those times can help you out when things get hectic.

▶ **Family time.** Don't neglect your family! They can be a great source of support, and spending some of your free time with your family can be a very worthwhile break from the stresses and strains of college.

▶ **Friendships.** Don't neglect your friends, either. Friends you've made in college, as well as those you had before you entered college, are an important part of your social life.

▶ **Hobbies.** A good hobby can be a great stress reliever. If you brought a talent with you to college, develop it. Or you can develop a new hobby that could be a source of satisfaction throughout your life.

Remember what you learned in Chapter 2 about managing your time. Coming up with a good time management plan is as good a place to start as any when trying to achieve a balanced college life. You should look first at how much time you will need for your courses—the time in classes, the time allotted for studying, the time for long-term projects and papers. Then you have to consider the hours you may need for a job. What you have left (after eating and sleeping) are the hours you can give to a social life.

And a social life may be just as important as your academic life in making your college experience enjoyable and meaningful. For one thing, the personal connections you make and the people you get to know may be as crucial to your success in the future as what you learn in your classes. Even more important, the friends

Time Out Tip

If you are worried about doing too much or too little at college, talk to an **upper class student in your major, a student who has survived the first year of college.** Upper class students can tell you the truth about what is good to be involved in and what is a waste of time. They can also tell you how much work to expect in certain courses to help you properly balance your time and budget the time needed for difficult classes. There are many out there who have lived through what you are going through, and they will be happy to tell their stories!

you make in college may be the best friends you will ever have and some may be your friends for the rest of your life. Friends help friends find jobs. Some friends stick with you after college when you want to move to a new city or try a new experience. You also learn new things about yourself when making new friends. Likewise, when the going gets tough, and it does sometimes in college, having friends helps you in countless ways. Thus taking the time to make friends in college is definitely a worthwhile investment!

Just be careful where you make your investment. It is no secret that some people come to college just to have fun and don't really even imagine actually graduating. Likewise, many students arrive with emotional baggage or get into trouble during college and unknowingly pull others down with them. For more advice on relationships, see the website.

Diversifying Your Experiences: Taking Advantage of the Diversity on Your Campus

Wan-Chen, an international student from Taiwan, was speaking in Mandarin with her friend from home, Han-Li, in the cafeteria. They were discussing the picnic they attended the previous Saturday. As they were talking, they noticed a couple of American students listening in on their conversation from the table next to them. Suddenly, the guy on the right stood up and said, "Why don't you learn to speak in English? If you can't, you should just go back to your own country!"

Laurie and Felicia were sitting together on a bench outside the science building talking about the notes that Felicia missed the class before. Laurie joked to Felicia that her short, spiky hair was getting too long. As they got up to leave, two guys walked out of the building laughing, and one of them looked at Felicia and shouted, "Dyke!"

Sue and Jordan were walking home from a party one night downtown and noticed a group of black students up ahead. Sue recognized Darren in the group. He was in her biology class, and she had often heard him talk to other guys about a gang from his town. Before the group could get any closer, Sue said to Jordan, "Let's cross to the other side of the street."

By definition, diversity is the quality of being different or an aspect in which things differ. When you leave college, the so-called real world will be filled with differences: different people, different religions, different jobs, different bosses, different environments. When you invest your money, one of the oldest pieces of advice is to diversify your assets, which means not putting all your money in one place. You want to spread your investments around to reduce your risk. For instance, if you have all of your money in high tech and the market falls, the value of your entire portfolio will fall. If, however, you have spread your investments among bonds, energy stocks, real estate, and manufacturing, you have a better chance of making some profit or at least not taking a loss. The same is true of making an investment in your future in terms of how you spend your time on campus. Spending time with the same group of people or doing the same activity over and over is like putting all your money into one sector. On the other hand, when you invest some time and effort in expanding your experiences, meeting people from

Teamwork Activity

Work in groups of three or four students each. Have each team member identify a characteristic about himself or herself that has sometimes been stereotyped (for example, blond hair, football player, art major). One group member (not necessarily a female!) should act as secretary to write down the stereotypes. After the stereotypes have been identified, the group members will discuss possible sources for the stereotypes and ways in which these stereotypes could be challenged and eliminated on campus. Each group will then make a brief presentation to the class.

different backgrounds (and we are not speaking only of race and religion, as we'll discuss in a moment), you are diversifying your portfolio of experiences. These experiences will yield dividends when you apply for a job or for admission to graduate school. Seeking out new and diverse experiences is just as important as pursuing the knowledge necessary to understand your chosen profession. They are both important; they are just different kinds of investments.

But just what do you think of when you hear the word *diversity*? Race? Religion? Both are part of it, but they are by no means the whole story. And not knowing the whole story often leads to blind acceptance of stereotypes.

In the investment world, people are often swayed by "hot tips," when someone inflates the potential profit of buying a stock or other investment. An investor may invest, thinking he or she will otherwise miss out on a golden opportunity, when in fact that "opportunity" could be a major pitfall. Without research, the investor really doesn't know whether the hot tip is a legitimate investment opportunity or a rumor. Stereotypes too are dangerous because they keep the individual from gaining information beyond what appears on the surface. Diversity encompasses all differences among people, places, and things. Race and religion appear on the list that follows, but so do some other items that you might not have thought of as aspects of diversity:

Race: Latino/a, Asian, Arabic, Native American, Caucasian, African American, Indian, and many combinations thereof. Race is a key identifier because it affects not only our background but also the way we look and how others perceive us. According to *The Chronicle of Higher Education,* in 1999 fully 30% of college students were nonwhite, a 50% increase over 20 years earlier.

Religion: Judaism, Islam, Christianity, Buddhism, Hinduism, to name just a few. Chances are you will meet many students whose religious backgrounds are different from your own. You will probably also encounter students who are atheists or agnostics and students who are still searching for a religion to call their own. Perhaps that description fits you. College is a time of exploration for many students. Be open to and respectful of the religious convictions of others and you will gain a valuable learning experience.

Culture: Another key identifier is culture. Two people of the same race could have significant differences in their culture: foods, religion, social customs, and the like.

Even though cultures stem in many ways from geographic locations, there are also many situations in which different cultures exist very close to one another.

Gender: Males and females certainly have their differences. Often, one group believes that the other group cannot do something (women aren't strong enough, men aren't sensitive enough) and ascribes that stereotype to *every* member of the opposite sex. But people who think primarily in terms of gender, instead of looking at members of the opposite sex as individuals, may have trouble working together in a classroom or work situation in which males and females are on equal footing.

Sexual Orientation: Lesbians, heterosexuals, gays, bisexuals, transsexuals. Sexual orientation is not always readily apparent, and rumors about individuals may circulate without any factual basis. Sometimes, people are afraid of others in a different category. Differences in sexual orientation can be the source of intense prejudice and even discrimination that is often based on fear and lack of knowledge.

Socioeconomic Class: Money. One student may be taking the bus from home every Sunday and get off at the same time another student is pulling up in the Mercedes her father gave her when she graduated from high school. College affords an opportunity to see much variation in income, from the student whose entire education is being paid for by his family, to the student on a full scholarship, to the student going to school part-time while working in a sandwich shop to make ends meet. Negative attitudes toward people of different income levels may arise, partly out of a lack of understanding of what others' experiences have been. But, of course, it is often more than money. A student may be in college because his father sits on the board or his grandmother endowed a scholarship. Those who know this may have preconceived notions about the student, just as they may have preconceived notions about a student who won a scholarship to play football.

Disabilities (physical, learning, mental): It is often difficult for students without disabilities to place themselves in the position of those with disabilities. Sometimes it is easier not to help. Sometimes they just don't now how. Likewise, students with disabilities may feel alienated because of their need for special accommodations, or they may feel uncomfortable having to ask for such accommodations for fear that they will be singled out or not seen as earning a grade on their own merit. A student with an unseen disability with implications beyond the classroom, such as depression, can be misunderstood by peers and professors. Many more disabilities exist, and many more people cope with them every day than most college students realize.

Age: Age? That's right—age. One thing that surprises a lot of students who come to college right out of high school is that they are suddenly in class with people of all different age groups. In nearly all public, private, and preparatory schools, students are divided into classes by age. In college, it's a different story. It may surprise some students to hear that 38% of college students are 25 or older, according to *The Chronicle of Higher Education.* A 19-year-old sophomore could be sitting next to a 30-year-old accountant who has returned to school to take an extra class for work. The 30-year-old accountant might be sitting next to a grandmother who has returned to school to finish a degree program that she had quit decades ago to have her children. In addition to dealing with students of different ages, college students have to learn to work with professors and staff members on a different basis. Also, you have to learn to work with professors and staff members in a more professional way—college is training you to be a member of the community on a more egalitarian basis than in high school.

Environment (rural/suburban/urban): Even in a relatively small area, you can see major differences in environment. Within a hundred miles, you could go from some of the largest urban centers, through the suburbs, to farm country and wilderness. Naturally, such disparate environments evoke different responses, especially if the environment is different from the one in which a person grew up. For example, a student from a small rural community may fear life in a large city. A student from the city may think that there is "nothing to do" on a small suburban campus.

Types of Music: Although you may not think of it in this way, music is a particularly potent form of identification for many college students. Heavy metal. Rap. Pop. Country. Rock. Folk. Classical. Alternative. For many students, there is a way of life, including clothes, slang, and hairstyles, associated with each type of music. And many students dislike other types of music fully as much as they enjoy their favorite variety. Unfortunately, students are sometimes unfairly pigeonholed on the basis of the music they listen to the most. For instance, some may say that heavy metal fans are "into Satan," or that country fans are "all hicks." Students with little knowledge of a certain type of music may buy into stereotypes rather than really learning what it is all about.

Major: A student's choice of major may also lead other students to label him or her. An engineering major may be seen as "smarter" than a student majoring in sports management. An art major may be seen as a nonconformist. A business student may be perceived as only into money, whereas the student majoring in classical literature is seen as having no grasp on reality beyond the "ivory tower." These labels persist because they have been around longer than the students themselves. They imply that the major itself defines the whole person, when in reality, any student can have many more interests outside of those that are related to his or her major.

Hobbies/Clubs: Even though campus hobbies and clubs are very positive, they can be perceived by others in negative ways. For example, those who don't play chess and don't know much about it may assume that every student who is in the Chess Club is a geeky math major with little in the way of a social life. Never mind that several of the Chess Club members are also on the lacrosse team and are attracted to chess because of its unique competitive nature. The chess-playing student may also like the diversity of others in the club.

Personality Types: There are almost as many personalities as there are people, but there are some general categories that you may encounter. It is important to remember that even such general traits do not define the whole person. For example, just because someone is an introvert does not mean he or she does not want to socialize. It may just mean that he or she prefers to be alone some of the time but can enjoy company or a party with good friends as much as the next person. An extrovert may feel more comfortable meeting new people or being in a room with many people, but this doesn't mean he or she does not need to be alone or to be serious some of the time, instead of always being the center of the fun. Sometimes conflicts arise between opposite personality types because one or both of the people find it hard to understand how the other person thinks or feels.

Cliques ("jocks," "preps," "geeks," "skaters," etc.): When you were in high school, you may have seen or been a part of a clique, which really is a group of people who are pretty much the same. The problem with cliques is not only that they leave people out, but also that those on the inside are often prevented from learning about a lot of other people. Cliques tend to label people strictly in terms of one quality (jocks are only into sports or geeks are only into computers), when people are a lot more three-dimensional than that. Cliques are less obvious on a college campus, in part because students are more mature and the campus is a much larger environment. However, it is still easy to fall into groups of people who are very similar—on the same team, in the same major or fraternity, or with the same taste in music. It is not bad to have friends who are similar to you, but think about adding some diversity too.

Body Types: Often too much emphasis is placed on outward appearances. There is really no denying that. Thanks to the images of the "perfect" man and woman promulgated in the media and popular culture, college students are under a lot of pressure to live up to those images. This kind of pressure can have many negative consequences, such as eating disorders and steroid use, and it can also result in negative attitudes toward those who do not live up to the ideals. Furthermore, a negative self-image can lead to a lack of confidence, which in turn may discourage others from getting to know the individual who falls short of society's artificial standards.

Food Preferences: Maybe you didn't expect to see this item in a section about diversity. If you went to a high school that was not very diverse, most people probably ate pretty much the same way you did. In college, however, you are likely to encounter foods you have never seen before because you will meet people from many different backgrounds, religions, and cultures. You may meet some students who have chosen a vegetarian lifestyle. Sometimes both vegetarians and meat-eaters can "get in each other's faces" about what they are eating or not eating before even talking about the choices they have made and why. If you have never seen anyone eat dried squid before, for example, you may want to turn away. But it might be more interesting to ask the person about it and maybe give it a try.

Difference doesn't mean that we don't have things in common. And it certainly doesn't mean that the differences are the most important things about us. But it is important to acknowledge differences so that we can discover what is similar about us. Doing so can prevent preconceptions from keeping people from really getting to know each other and can encourage appreciation of the very differences that once made us uneasy.

Why is a college campus an especially good place to experience diversity? One reason is that you often start with a clean slate in college. You may be the only student from your high school at your college, or you may be one of only a few from the same high school who chose to go to your large university. The clique you might have been in doesn't exist anymore, so you have a chance to get to know people very different from the people you knew before. Also, colleges and universities tend to be a microcosm of the world around them, with students from widely disparate backgrounds—from different parts of the country and from all over the world. Your professors have specialized in different disciplines and have had all kinds of experiences before coming to work at the college. In high school, most students were more or less the same age in each grade, whereas in college you will have students in your classes from all kinds of age groups.

What are some of the best ways to invest your time in diverse experiences? Here are some suggestions:

- ▶ Attend a multicultural banquet.
- ▶ Attend musical events, dances, and plays that celebrate other cultures, and attend events traditionally associated with your own culture to see how others react.
- ▶ Take multicultural courses such as African literature, Asian art, women in history, Islamic religious history, Greek mythology, any foreign language, and international studies.
- ▶ See a foreign film with subtitles.
- ▶ Join a committee to plan a multicultural event.
- ▶ Volunteer to be a reader or note-taker for a student with a disability.
- ▶ Volunteer for Special Olympics.
- ▶ Be a volunteer to help international students get acclimated to the campus and community.
- ▶ Volunteer for Habitat for Humanity.
- ▶ Volunteer at a local nursing home.
- ▶ Eat at a restaurant that offers a cuisine you have never tried before.
- ▶ Read a major Sunday newspaper every week. Be sure to read sections that you don't normally read, such as world news, book reviews, or editorials.
- ▶ Join a multicultural organization on campus.
- ▶ Read and learn about the history of your own campus and the community in which it is located.
- ▶ Go to lectures or listen to guest speakers on topics such as gay/lesbian issues, disability law, affirmative action, and various cultures.

Being a college student means you have access (and much of it is free access!) to more cultural and educational activities than you will ever have again. It is up to you to take advantage of these opportunities. Remember that being educated goes

Get Involved!

How can getting involved help you keep a balance? Ask Carlos. "I always felt overwhelmed with work. Then, in one of my classes, we were asked to analyze what we'd done with our time in the last 48 hours. I realized that there were big chunks of time when I was just sitting on my bed watching TV." The problem, Carlos recognized, was not only that he was wasting time watching TV but also that it was sapping a lot of his energy. "After sitting there for 3 hours, I hardly had the energy to go to the dining hall. If I hadn't changed my habits, I wasn't going anywhere." A friend told Carlos about the Latino Student Alliance. "Before, I didn't like to do anything that seemed to identify me as 'different,' but in college, with so many different types of people around, I was happy to get a little bit of my native culture—not 24/7, but just every once in a while. In the alliance, we do presentations at local schools, have dinners together, meet with other student groups, and even play pick-up basketball in the gym once a week." Carlos is graduating on time at the end of next semester. "Honestly, I don't know where I'd be right now if I hadn't gotten involved. I really don't think I would have stayed in college. In retrospect, it was the best thing I could have done, and I'd recommend the same thing to any other student."

beyond the classroom. It includes combating stereotypes, meeting new people, and learning about unfamiliar places and customs. College gives you a rare opportunity to open yourself up to diversity. It is one investment worth making.

Service Learning/Volunteering

Another way to become involved with the rich diversity of your campus and surrounding community is to volunteer. You may feel that you're so busy sometimes in college that you think, "How can I afford to volunteer?" A better question might be "Can I afford not to volunteer?" As a college student, you will have opportunities to get involved in many activities, but one of the most valuable to you may be becoming a volunteer. How is it valuable? One of your goals in college is to tap into different interests and explore different opportunities in your community, while building up your résumé. But volunteering adds another dimension to the picture you present of yourself to a potential employer or graduate school. Volunteering can show a true commitment to your field. For example, a potential teacher who has volunteered for Big Brother/Big Sister or for America Reads shows that he or she doesn't see teaching just as a paycheck but also as an opportunity to make a difference in the lives of children. Moreover, it really is intrinsically a valuable learning experience. As a volunteer you're not just giving; you're receiving a great deal in return.

Sometimes you can sign up for a course that has a service learning component. For instance, you may find a psychology course where the professor assigns a project in which students serve a certain number of hours at a local charity. You may be able to sign up for a first-year composition course in which a major assignment

is to volunteer at, say, a local food bank or after-school program and then write about the experience.

Here are some other good ways to find volunteer opportunities:

▶ Visit your campus volunteer or student activities office.
▶ Join a campus organization that does volunteer work (fraternity/sorority, Circle K, student professional association, and so on).
▶ Call or visit the local chapter of the YM/YWCA, United Way, Red Cross, or other organization that is likely to welcome volunteers.
▶ Look into an "alternative" spring break, where you work for Habitat for Humanity or another organization during your time off.

The following are some success stories of student volunteers whose efforts paid off for them and the people they helped.

Ashley, a marketing major, started out volunteering at the local soup kitchen during her first year in connection with one of her sorority's service projects. While there, she met another volunteer who just happened to work for one of the large local marketing firms. This led directly to an internship with the company, one which helped her land her first job.

Phil started as an elementary education major. He volunteered at a local day care center to get required observation hours for the major. While working there, he became interested in how family dynamics affected the children with whom he was working. After reflecting on this interest, Phil talked to his advisor and eventually

The Hard Way

Maya enrolled in a state university about an hour from her home, partly because of the reasonable cost, but also because many of her high school friends enrolled there. "I was not as afraid to go to college back in August because my roommate was my friend from high school, and she had a car, so we knew we would be able to come home every weekend," said Maya. This seemed like a great idea at the beginning of her first year, but by April, she felt very disconnected from the campus and was thinking about dropping out. She went to see her advisor and explained her problem: "I didn't make any new friends here this year, and my roommate and I are not going to live together next year. I did not get involved in any social activities because I went home every weekend. I feel like I don't belong here." Maya's advisor encouraged her to consider ways to improve her situation without leaving school. One of his suggestions was that she stay on campus in the summer to work in the orientation program for new students. She was worried that she would be homesick but decided to give it a try. By the end of the summer, she realized that she did not have to go home every weekend, and she had made some new friends. In fact, some of the people she met over the summer helped her get involved with another program: America Reads. Now in her sophomore year, she spends a few hours a week tutoring students at the elementary school. As a future teacher, Maya now realizes that she should not have shut herself off from her new environment.

changed his major to psychology. He now plans on going to graduate school and preparing for a career as a family therapist.

Gina was a junior studying architecture. Gina's roommate, Stephanie, decided to take part in an alternative spring break program and teach on a reservation in rural South Dakota and asked Gina to go with her. Gina ended up loving the experience and decided to join the Peace Corps after college. Now, working at an architecture firm back in the United States, she feels that her experience in South Dakota changed her life for the better. It expanded her view of the world and helped her make other decisions as she was completing college.

Increasing Your Yield:

Readings for Practical Application

In this chapter, you considered the importance of balancing work and leisure, classroom learning and opportunities outside the classroom. You learned how to take advantage of the many opportunities on campus to help you gain the confidence you need to succeed in college and beyond. You found that there are many ways for you to gain experience and personal growth through volunteering. Likewise, recognizing and embracing the diversity of your college campus will open many doors for you, help you learn more about the world, and, ultimately, discover a lot about yourself. Few places offer as many free cultural activities as a college campus. Plays, art exhibits, film festivals, and lectures are there for you to enjoy. You may even decide to become a part of such cultural events by trying out for a play or musical or exhibiting your work or reading your poetry. In fact, becoming involved in the arts can help you to grow in ways that can build your confidence for contributing to any field in which you are interested. The focus on the readings for this chapter, then, is the arts.

You have seen how texts in various disciplines approach their respective subjects. Nearly all liberal arts colleges require students to take humanities courses, and many specify at least one art course, usually a class in art history. The "A Textbook Case" reading that follows is an excerpt from an art history textbook. Read the strategies suggested for approaching such a text, and then invest some time and effort in reading this excerpt in order to prepare for future readings in this unique discipline.

If you are contemplating becoming a visual or performing arts major, you will be reading textbooks in the field as well as practicing your art through such pursuits as painting, photography, acting, dancing, or singing. If you are considering such a major, you may be wondering what the future holds for you in terms of possible jobs and career paths. The "Life After College" reading will give you a glimpse into the activities of two curators as they prepare a major exhibition.

If this chapter sparked your interest in service learning or volunteering, you may be eager to read more about it. The "Current Issues" reading enables you to explore the positive aspects of volunteering and even the possibility of volunteering as a career path.

These readings together will give you an opportunity to explore the unique discipline of the visual and performing arts, while also expanding on the content of the chapter. Invest in these readings and discover future growth opportunities.

Reading and Study Tips: Visual and Performing Arts

Unique Features and Comprehension Strategies

Textbooks in the visual and performing arts include visual and graphical displays. One of the unique features of such texts is their extensive use of visuals and graphics to help readers immerse themselves in the works, the ideas, and/or the plays that are illustrated. Textbooks in other disciplines may have photos, graphs, and diagrams, but these texts do not rely on them to such a degree. In textbooks in the visual and performing arts, these illustrations are essential to giving the reader a comprehensive perspective on the material. Not only can you read about a work of art, a play, or a dance, but you can also see a reproduction or a photograph. Be certain that you do not ignore the visual nature of these texts. **Take notice of which works are presented prominently, as signaled by reproduction in full color rather than black and white and by large reproductions or full-page photos. Such prominence is a clue to what may be the most important artistic works to be discussed in any chapter. Pay attention to works of art that are illustrated in the text. Those, particularly if they are focused on in the lectures, tend to be important on the test. Not all works of art in a visual or performing arts text are represented by a photo or diagram, so pay careful attention to the works that are. These are important, and they may show up on a slide exam in which you have to identify title, artist, subject, and/or date for various works of art. Listen carefully to material covered in the lecture. Ask yourself, "Is the professor focusing more on the names and dates, or is he or she focusing more on the concepts and the historical context?"**

Art tends to be full-color. Art textbooks are often expensive because of full-color reproductions or photographs. Again, it is important for you to view the art in the text and really study it; words alone would not convey everything you need to note. These full-color reproductions may appear again on an exam, and you may be asked to discuss the works. Study not just the content but the colors as well. **For art history texts, take notes as you read and make sketches of important works of art. Also, make sketches of works shown on slides during lectures. The process of making these sketches—no matter how crudely they are drawn—will help you grasp and recall the material. In the textbook reading on Islamic art included here, you will see an illustration of the Dome of the Rock. Being able to sketch it yourself, however roughly, will help you to remember its unique features, especially when you see it again on a test and need to identify it.**

Important artists and works are presented in boldface type in many textbooks. Just like books in other disciplines, such as psychology or science, visual and performing arts textbooks may have bold headings or bold terms, names, places, and dates. These bold items will help you to understand what is important when you are reviewing for a test. Know the terms and definitions. Be able to provide examples. In those texts that do not call your attention to key points via boldface type, you must identify that information on your own. Listening carefully to what the professor stresses is important and paying attention to visuals in the texts will help you identify the main ideas. **If your textbook has a glossary, use it. Look up the important terms in the glossary. Make note cards for each word. Try to rewrite a definition in your own words so that you will be able to remember it better. Make flash cards. Photocopy the textbook photos of the paintings and sculptures, cut them out, and paste them onto index cards. On the back, write down the name of the artist, the title of the work, and its period or date. You can then carry these around as flash cards to do regular reviewing. Ask a friend to quiz you. Have him or her hold up the cards and see how much you can remember. Use other memory aids as well. Try to make associations and silly or unusual connections to help you remember. For example, you might need to remember a painting that was done in 1808. When you count the figures in the painting, you find that there are eight of them. Those eight figures can help you remember the date. In a textbook reading on Islamic architecture, you will see illus-**

trations of different mosque plans. One type is the *central-plan* mosque. A good way to recall and identify this plan is to remember that it has a circle in the *center*. The other plans do not.

Studio arts texts tend to focus on procedures. If you are taking a studio course, such as printmaking, pottery, or dance, you may have a textbook to help you understand not just the discipline itself but also specific techniques employed by practitioners. **Watch for lists of instructions. The photos are there to help you understand the steps better and get a clear sense of what you need to be doing. Again, looking at photos, in addition to reading, is very important. Compare your technique with the photos. When learning the processes and procedures covered in studio arts texts, don't wait too long between reading the material and practicing it. The whole point is to be able to apply the information. Use the texts as tools, just as you would a brush, a costume, a dance shoe, or paint.**

Visual and performing arts textbooks lend themselves to both objective and subjective tests. The content in visual and performing arts textbooks covers facts such as dates, periods, and artists, but these textbooks also examine how periods and artists affected and were influenced by one another. For example, in a class on Northern Renaissance Art, your professor could give you a test consisting of multiple-choice questions about artists and the dates when they produced particular works. On the other hand, your professor could give you an essay test asking you to make connections between the art and the politics of the time. **Find out whether your professor gives primarily objective or subjective tests. This will dictate to a certain extent what type of material you need to focus on as you study. If you are going to have objective tests, be sure to learn such things as names, dates, titles of works, major artistic periods, and the qualities characteristic of the styles prevalent in those periods. If you know you will have an essay test or essay questions, you want to step back and look at the larger picture. Look at the major time periods and their unique characteristics. Then be ready to cite major artistic works as examples. You need to see connections and be able to compare and contrast major periods and artists. Really try to understand what makes a certain period, artist, or work of art unique. Be able to compare one period of art with another, for instance, or one artist with another. For example, in the selection from an art history text that follows, you will learn about Islamic architecture during the early caliphates. When you have finished reading, you should be able to discuss in what way Islamic architecture of that time was unique and what made it such an important artistic endeavor. Look deeper than the examples and the dates.**

Reading 1: A Textbook Case

The following excerpt is from an art history textbook typical of those used in general art history classes for students who are not majoring in art. Many college students with general elective requirements in the humanities decide to take at least one art history course. This textbook excerpt focuses on ancient Islamic architecture, but you will notice that it also provides a brief history of Islam in order to put the architectural principles in context. On a related note, we have often discussed the importance of keeping up with current events related to your major and your career choice in order to be prepared for interviews. Similarly, keeping up with current events can help you get the most out of your textbooks. After you read this textbook selection, think about how familiarity with current events can help you understand the reading better.

BEFORE YOU READ

1. What do you know about the religion of Islam? From what do you draw your information?
2. What does art mean to you? How would you define it? What is your background in art? Do you consider architecture art? Why or why not?
3. Preview the textbook selection that follows, noting the boldface type and the illustrations that accompany discussion about important works of art. Then formulate guided reading questions to answer as you read. You may want to compare notes and answers to your questions with others in your class.

Art During the Early Caliphates: Architecture

M. Stokstad

The caliphs of the aggressively expansionist Umayyad dynasty ruled from their capital at Damask (in Modern Syria). They were essentially desert chieftains who had scant interest in fostering the arts except for poetry, which had been held in high esteem among Arabs since pre-Islamic times, and architecture. The building of shrines and mosques throughout the empire in this period represented both the authority of the new rulers and the growing acceptance of Islam. The caliphs of the Abbasid dynasty, who replaced the Umayyads in 750 and ruled until 1258, governed in the grand manner of ancient Persian emperors from their capitals at Baghdad and Samarra (in Modern Iraq). Their long and cosmopolitan reign saw achievements in medicine, mathematics, the natural sciences, philosophy, literature, music, and art. They were generally tolerant of the ethnically diverse populations in the territories they subjugated and admired the cultural traditions of Byzantium, Persia, India, and China.

Architecture

As Islam spread, architects adapted freely from Roman, Christian, and Persian models, which include the basilica, the martyrium, the peristyle house, and the palace audience hall. The Dome of the Rock in Jerusalem, built around 687–691, is the oldest surviving Islamic sanctuary and is today the holiest site in Islam after Mecca and Medina (fig. 8-2). It stands on the summit of the Temple Mount (Mount Moriah) and encloses a rock outcropping (fig. 8-3) that has long been sacred to the Jews, who identify it as the site on which Abraham prepared to sacrifice his son Isaac. Jews, Christians, and Muslims associate the site with the creation of Adam and the Temple of Solomon. Muslims also identify it as the site from which

SOURCE: M. Stokstad, "Art During the Early Caliphates: Architecture." In *Art History*, Vol, 1, rev. 2nd ed. (New York: Harry N. Abrams, 2005). © 2005. Reprinted by permission of Pearson Education, Inc., Upper Saddle River, New Jersey.

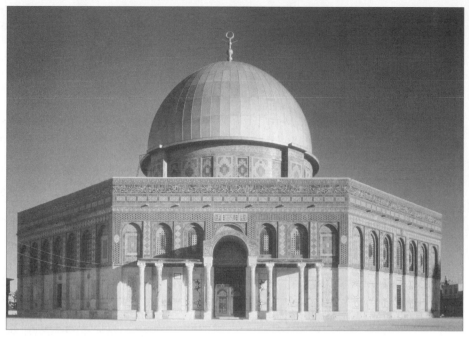

Figure 8-2

Figure 8-3

Muhammad, led by the angel Gabriel, ascended to heaven in the Night Journey, passing through the spheres of heaven to the presence of God.

The Dome of the Rock was built by Syrian artisans trained in the Byzantine tradition, and its centralized plan—octagons within octagons—derived from both Byzantine and early Christian architecture. Unlike its Byzantine models, however, with their plain exteriors, the Dome of the Rock, crowned with a golden dome that dominates the Jerusalem skyline, is opulently decorated both outside and inside. The central space is covered by a dome and a tall **drum** supported by an arcade. Concentric aisles enclose the rock. As at San Vitale in Ravenna, interior surfaces were originally decorated with marble **dadoes** at ground level and glass mosaics above. Remains of the mosaics show Byzantine-style foliage combined in a new style with jewel-like Sassanian Persian insignia. This imagery consists of a double-winged motif often associated with Sassanian royalty. The more than 700 feet of Arabic inscriptions on the structure are a distinctly Islamic feature. Written in one script on the interior and another on the exterior, these inscriptions include the references to Jesus Christ in the Koran. Later Islamic architects built similar domed octagonal sanctuaries and saints' tombs from Morocco to China.

The Umaayyad caliphs, disregarding the Prophet's advice about architectural austerity, built for themselves palatial hunting retreats on the edge of the desert. With profuse interior decoration depicting exotic human and animal subjects in stucco, mosaic, and paint, some had swimming pools, baths, domes, and private rooms. One of the later desert palaces was begun in the 740s at Mshatta (near present-day Amman, Jordan). Although never completed, this square, stone-walled complex is nevertheless impressively monumental (fig. 8-4). It measured about 470 feet on each side, and its outer walls and gates were guarded by towers and bastions reminiscent of a Roman fort. The space was divided roughly into thirds, with the center section containing a huge courtyard. The main spaces were a mosque and a domed, basilica-plan audience hall that was flanked by four private apartments, or *bayts*. *Bayts* grouped around small courtyards, for the use of the caliph's relatives and guests, occupied the remainder of the building.

Unique among the surviving palaces, Mshatta was decorated with a **frieze** that extended in a band about 16 feet high across the base of its façade. This frieze was divided by a zigzag molding into triangular compartments, each punctuated by a large **rosette** carved in high relief (fig. 8-5). The compartments were filled with intricate carvings in low relief that included interlacing scrolls inhabited by birds and other animals (there were no animals on the mosque side of the building), urns, and candlesticks. Similar designs in both

Figure 8-4

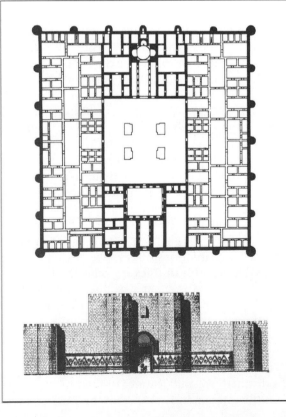

Figure 8-5

sculpture and mosaic adorned the interiors of Roman and Byzantine buildings but were never on exterior surfaces, and the designs were not so densely interwoven. Beneath one of the rosettes, two facing lions drink from an urn from which grows the Tree of Life, an ancient Persian motif.

With the development of mosque architecture during the early Umayyad period, the characteristic elements of this place of communal worship began to emerge. There were facilities for ritual cleansing before entering the consecrated space, a *sahn*, or courtyard, and a large covered space to accommodate Friday prayers. Worshipers prayed facing the **qibla** wall, which was oriented toward Mecca. A niche called a **mihrab** differentiated the qibla wall from the others. The imam delivered a sermon from the minbar, near the qibla wall. Some mosques included an enclosure called a *maqsura* near the mihrab for dignitaries. Muezzins, or criers, called the faithful to prayer from one or more of the towers, or minarets (literally "lighthouses"), on the exterior. Some early mosques were housed in modified pre-Islamic buildings.

When Abbasids overthrew the Umayyads in 750, a survivor of the Umayyad dynasty, Abd ar-Rahman I (ruled 756–788), fled across North Africa into Southern Spain (known as "al-Andalus" in Arabic), where, with the support of Syrian Muslim settlers, he established himself as the provincial ruler, or amir. The Umayyads continued to rule in Spain from their capital in Cordoba for the next three centuries (756–1031) and were noted patrons of the arts. Thus one of the finest surviving examples of Umayyad architecture, the Great Mosque of Cordoba, is in Spain.

Figure 8-6

This sprawling structure was begun on the site of a church in 785. Repeatedly enlarged until the fifteenth century, when it returned to Christian use, it combines Umayyad, Abbasid, and pre-Islamic influences into a distinctive Western Islamic style. The marble columns and capitals in the **hypostyle** prayer hall were recycled from the ruins of classical buildings in the region, which had been a wealthy Roman province (fig. 8-6). Two tiers of arches, one over the other, surmount these columns; the upper tier springs from rectangular posts that rise from the columns. This double-tiered design, which was widely imitated, effectively increases the height of the interior space and provides ample light and air within it. The distinctively shaped **horseshoe arches**—a form known from Roman times and favored by the Visigoths, Spain's pre-Islamic rulers—came to be closely associated with Islamic architecture in the West. Another distinctive feature of these arches, also adopted from Roman and Byzantine precedents, is the alternation of pale stone and red brick **voussoirs** forming the curved arch. In the view of one art historian, the overall effect of these features transforms the hall into a "wild three-dimensional maze, a hall of mirrors in which the constant echo of arches and the unruly staccato of colors confuse the viewer, presenting a challenge to unravel the [mosque's] complexities" (Dodd, pages 12–13).

Figure 8-7

Figure 8-8

In the final century of Umayyad rule, Cordoba emerged as a major commercial and intellectual hub and a flourishing center for the arts. It surpassed Christian Europe economically and in science, literature, and philosophy. Beginning with Abd as-Rahman III (ruled 912–961), the Umayyads boldly claimed the title of caliph. Al-Hakam II (ruled 961–976) made the Great Mosque a focus of royal patronage, commissioning costly and luxurious renovations that disturbed many of his subjects. The caliph attempted to answer their objections to paying for such ostentation with an inscription giving thanks to God, who "helped him in the building of this eternal place, with the goal of making this mosque more spacious for his subjects, something which both he and they greatly wanted" (cited in Dobbs, page 23). Among al-Hakam's renovations was a new mihrab with three bays in front of it. The melon-shaped, ribbed dome seems to float over a web of intersecting arches that emerge from their supporting piers (fig. 8-7). Lushly patterned mosaics with inscriptions, geometric motifs, and stylized vegetation clothe the domes in brilliant color and gold.

In the eastern Islamic world, the caliphs of the Abbasid dynasty ruled from Baghdad for more than a century after they seized power from the Umayyads. In 836, however, Caliph as-Mutasim (ruled 833–842) established a heavily fortified new capital at Samarra, about 60 miles north of Baghdad. In the mid-ninth century, Caliph at-Mutawakkil (ruled 847–861) began construction of the great Mosque of Samarra (fig. 8-8). In ruins today, it was for a long time the largest mosque in the Islamic world. It featured a hypostyle prayer hall 525 feet wide at the qibla wall and 25 perpendicular aisles. The fortress-like wall enclosing the complex was more than 8 feet thick and about 33 feet high, with curved buttressing and round corner towers. The façade may have had mosaic decoration. An unusual spiral-ramp minaret, perhaps inspired by the **ziggurats** of the ancient Near East, rises more than 160 feet next to the mosque wall.

AFTER YOU READ

1. From where did Islamic architects get their inspiration? Provide a specific example.
2. What is the relationship between the Islamic religion and its architecture? Provide examples.
3. Identify the characteristic elements of mosque architecture during the early caliphates. Develop a chart to list these characteristics, giving specific examples from the text for each. What characteristics of mosque architecture make it unique? Develop two possible test questions from your chart.
4. Choose three art works for which to make flash cards. Photocopy the illustrations, paste them to an index card, and then provide the necessary information on the back of each index card (see the comprehension strategies suggested in this chapter). Also, make flash cards for the major terms in this chapter. Then write at least three test questions from your flash cards.

Reading 2: Life After College

The art history textbook reading in this chapter is a good example of material that an art history major would read. You may take only one art history course in school, or you may decide to make art history your major. If you have a love of art history, or even a curiosity about it, the following article will be of interest. It profiles a career tailor made for art history majors. This chapter also discussed networking as a way to land jobs and internships. This article discusses networking of a different sort: networking to borrow paintings in the course of putting an exhibition together. Both types of networking, however, are about building connections. This article explains how a major art exhibition is planned and describes the role that curators play in seeing the project through from beginning to end. If you have ever wondered how exhibitions at art galleries or museums come to be, read on. This article may also give you a chance to think about a career you might never have considered.

BEFORE YOU READ

1. What is a curator? What do you think a curator does? As a class, develop on the board a list of the essential duties of a curator. After reading the article, see how accurate your list is, and then refine it by adding and subtracting items as appropriate.
2. What do you know about Edgar Degas? Have you ever seen any of his work? How would you describe it?

3. Write about a memory you have of visiting an art museum or gallery. Was it a positive or a negative experience? Why? If you have never been to an art museum or gallery, how have you been exposed to art work? Do you like looking at art? Why or why not?

"Degas & America": Career Canvas for Curators

M. Hunter

Horses and jockeys, ballerinas and women engaged in life's daily tasks–all beckon from French Impressionist Edgar Degas' works. Nearly 80 precious objects quietly demand investigation, each carefully selected and meticulously arranged in vivid galleries of yellow and teal.

"Degas & America: The Early Collectors" studies the United States' discovery of the work of Edgar Degas—through the careers of curators David Brenneman and Ann Dumas. This 1865 work is "A Woman Seated Beside a Vase of Flowers (Madame Paul Valpincon?)" from the Metropolitan Museum of Art's H. O. Havemeyer Collection.

SOURCE: M. Hunter, "'Degas & America': Career Canvas for Curators," cnn.com, March 6, 2001. Retrieved on December 28, 2003 from http://www.cnn.com/2001/CAREER/trends/03/06/degas/index.html. Reprinted by permission of CNN ImagiSource.

Those trademark dancers pirouette, horses canter, women comb their hair: It's as if a slice of late 19th-century French life was brought to Atlanta's High Museum of Art, when a new show opened there on Saturday.

"Degas & America: The Early Collectors," is at the High through May 27 before traveling to Minnesota's Minneapolis Institute of Arts. It's the first show to explore North Americans' response to Degas' work when they became aware of his paintings and sculptures 120 years ago. The exhibit is also an unprecedented chance for museum-goers in the Southeast to examine, firsthand, such a large collection of Degas' paintings, sculptures, drawings and prints.

And while concentrating on one response to the artist's fabled career, the show reflects the efforts of two art historians—who put "Degas & America" together at a fevered pace.

"On the one hand, we're trying to produce a very well-rounded, balanced and varied selection of Degas because this is the first major Degas exhibition there's been in Atlanta," says Ann Dumas. She's an independent curator and Degas scholar from London and has been instrumental in the exhibit's development. "At the same time we're trying to tell the story about the history of Degas in America."

She has worked in this instance with colleague David Brenneman, the High's curator of European art, the two of them assembling the collection and telling the story of how the United States embraced Degas more than a century ago.

The story begins in 1878, when New York's young Louisine Elder (later Louisine Havemeyer) acquired what is believed to be the first Degas to be bought by a North American collector. The show goes on to trace the progress of American acquisitions through 1936, when the first Degas retrospective had its debut.

Wheeling, Dealing

Dumas and Brenneman worked for two years putting the exhibition together—a time frame considered all but breakneck for a major exhibition, which more frequently takes four or five years to stage.

The team began working in earnest in 1999, with extensive research to determine the show's concept and shape. And then the wheeling and dealing began.

A flood of letters went out to potential lenders, explaining the exhibition and requesting loans. Dumas and Brenneman traveled the country to lobby museum officials face-to-face to "squeeze the pictures out of them," according to Dumas.

The personal touch worked best, Brenneman says. "It's really amazingly effective, actually showing up," he says. "It's a lot like being a traveling sales guy."

"There are so many exhibitions now," Dumas says, "particularly in this very popular area of 19th-century French painting, that you're always in competition with other people. And if you can really turn up and make your case, it really makes a big difference from just writing the letters."

With loans of art approved from large and small institutions across the U.S., Dumas and Brenneman then returned to the books. They had

Among the works seen in "Degas & America" is "The Ballet Class," ca. 1880, an oil on canvas from the Philadelphia Museum of Art

to research and write contributions to the exhibition's catalog, which serves as a scholarly record of the show long after the works have been returned. Then, and only then, could the nuts and bolts of assembling the show begin.

Some parts, they say, didn't always fit so smoothly.

Brenneman recalls the week before the exhibition's planned press preview on February 27. Works were still in crates, two important paintings from the Metropolitan Museum of Art in New York hadn't arrived, and High officials were staring at blank walls where paintings should be.

"You just can't visualize the exhibition fully until you actually see them up on the walls," he says.

The work did make it to the walls in time, though, and the exhibit opened to a warm reception. "It is a pleasure to see (Degas') stature reaffirmed in this beautifully installed and well-thought-out exhibition," writes Catherine Fox for the Atlanta Journal-Constitution. The show is, she writes, a "panoramic vision" of the "adventurousness of this quintessential Parisian."

Getting Started

Degas brought Brenneman and Dumas together for the Atlanta show, but different paths led each to a career in art.

Brenneman's interest in art started early and was cultivated by visits to museums with his parents.

"I went to college wanting to be an art historian, which was very strange," he says. "I think I was probably unusually focused at about 17 or 18."

A master's degree and Ph.D. from Brown University followed an undergraduate degree in art history from Pennsylvania State University. While working on his doctorate, Brenneman was an intern at the Fogg Art Museum at Harvard University and worked as an assistant curator of paintings for two years at the Yale Center for British Art at Yale University.

He finished his doctoral studies and came to the High Museum in 1995, where he found a job he says he considers challenging.

Edgar Degas, an auto-portrait, 1857.

"There's a kind of juggling that's always going on between what's temporary and needing attention, and the ongoing needs of the permanent collection," he says. "But these exhibitions help us a great deal because people come to the museum (who) wouldn't normally."

Dumas' work isn't centered as much as her peer's on permanent collections.

As an independent art historian, she focuses almost exclusively on temporary exhibitions. Dumas pursues her engagements while serving as an adjunct curator at the Royal Academy of Arts in London. She says she likes it that way.

"You have a lot of creative freedom in that you can come up with ideas and write proposals to a number of museums and eventually one of them may take you on," she says. "And there's a lot of variety because you get to work with different institutions and different colleagues.

"The downside of it is that there's not the security of a regular job, and you don't always have that sort of institutional backing," says Dumas, a former Mellon Fellow at the Art Institute of Chicago. "But it suits me. I enjoy it."

Dumas received a master's in art history from the Courtauld Institute of Art at London University and then served as an assistant curator of European painting at the Brooklyn Museum of Art in New York.

"A Love of Objects"

Art historians train to develop a sophisticated eye.

"You really have to have a love of objects and a desire to learn about them and share that with other people," Brenneman says.

Museums look for a special talent when scouting curatorial help, says Philip Verre, deputy director of the High. When assessing a candidate for a curator's job, Verre says, he tries to "get a sense of the quality of the eye of the individual. Ultimately, we rely on curators to provide that finely tuned aesthetic eye."

Verre looks at candidates' expertise in the field—their awareness of the literature and collections—and at their connections.

In the world of curators, as in so many other professions, it's who you know in a network of peers, says Verre. He wants employees who can "use the network to the advantage of the institution."

Networking is essential, Brenneman says. "It's very helpful if you can call a friend up and say, 'Could we please borrow this pastel? I know you never lend it, but this is an important project.'"

A Ph.D. is becoming increasingly important to career art historians, although it isn't impossible to find a job in the field without one, says James McCredie, director of the Institute of Fine Arts at New York University. Two-thirds of the institute's art history graduates get a master's and then look for jobs in their field, he estimated.

"It has become more and more necessary, though you don't have to get a Ph.D., to do something in the history of art," McCredie says. "But, yes, it's becoming more and more necessary to have the label."

Building a Career

Pursuing a career in art history is not for the fainthearted and retiring sort, say insiders. Job competition is keen.

"The problem is that a lot of people want to study art history; far more people study it than there are available professional opportunities later," Dumas says. "But I think for the ones that are really serious and really stay on and do interesting work at graduate level, there will continue to be opportunities."

Dumas and Brenneman have already built a strong foundation for their collaborative reputation. Prior to the Degas exhibition, the two worked together on the High's 1999 public and critical success "Impressionism: Paintings Collected by European Museums."

And these exhibitions, say Dumas and Brenneman, benefit all. The public is exposed to more art. Museums get to showcase treasures from near and far. And the historians who package these shows gain in professional stature each time another exhibit bows.

"With each one (exhibition) you do, you build on a sort of critical mass of a reputation, which counts for quite a lot," Dumas says. "With each show it counts for more."

AFTER YOU READ

1. What did you learn about being a curator that you did not know before you read this article? Refer to the list of job duties that the class generated before reading this article.
2. According to this article, why is a degree in art history expected as training for this profession? What type of person would do best as a curator?

3. What role does networking play in the work of a curator? What role did research and networking play in putting together the Degas exhibit?

4. What can you do now if you are interested in being a curator or want to find out whether such a career might be for you?

Reading 3:   Current Issues

This chapter covered volunteering as a way to gain experience and learn more about a possible career path while helping others. The following article is included here because it delves deeper into volunteering: the reasons why people volunteer, the importance of volunteering at a young age, and the opportunities for people to begin their own charitable organizations or to go into nonprofit work as a career. As you read this article, take the time to consider the role of volunteering in your own life.

BEFORE YOU READ

1. Consider the following questions before you describe your feelings about volunteering: Have you ever done any volunteering in the past? What kind? Are you considering any volunteer work now? What would you like to do? Answer these questions and think about the role volunteering has played or could play in your life.

2. Visit your campus volunteer or student activities office (or find out who coordinates volunteer activities on your campus). Find out as much as you can about what volunteer opportunities are available on campus and in the surrounding community.

Growing Up as a Volunteer

I. Wilhelm

When Laura E. Lockwood started attending Manatee Community College two years ago, she couldn't leave behind her first love: the ManaTeen Club, a program in Bradenton, Fla., she and her sister had founded in 1994 to organize teenage volunteers.

Ms. Lockwood, who started ManaTeen at age 12, remained with the group during college as a member of AmeriCorps—the federal national-service program—and is developing a Junior ManaTeen program that will encourage children ages 8 to 11 to participate in charitable efforts.

"Getting out in the community can really make you feel better," says Ms. Lockwood, now 20. "It's hard work, but it's worth it."

Ms. Lockwood's example underscores a key reason why many charities and foundations are

SOURCE: I. Wilhelm, "Growing Up as a Volunteer: Influence of Charity Work Is Long-Lasting," *Chronicle of Philanthropy* 15 (January 9, 2003), 22–23. Reprinted with permission.

seeking to encourage young people to volunteer: Volunteering as a teenager often inspires passion for charitable work as an adult.

Studies on giving and volunteering indicate just how influential an experience like Ms. Lockwood's can be. People who started volunteering in their youth are twice as likely to volunteer as adults than those who did not volunteer when they were younger, says a recent report by Independent Sector and Youth Service America, both in Washington.

"It's an experience that hooks people," says Steven A. Culbertson, president of Youth Service America. "It's something they don't drift away from."

Increased Coïmmitment

For some adults, the commitment to charitable causes they were involved with when they were young increases with age. William T. Gallagher, a 37-year-old physician in Washington, has spent almost 20 years volunteering with an American Red Cross chapter in Pennsylvania. At 16, Mr. Gallagher participated in the charity's weeklong summer camp to build leadership qualities in teenagers; now he helps to organize the effort.

He says he now spends about 1,500 hours a year on volunteer work. "Sometimes volunteering just sucks you in," Mr. Gallagher says, noting that his charitable efforts are made possible because he works as a doctor only part of the week and has a flexible schedule.

Involvement with a charity as a youth also affects how adults donate money. Mr. Gallagher says his experience with the Red Cross has motivated him to give more money to charity than if he hadn't been involved with the group. He and his wife give about $10,000 a year to the Red Cross, food banks, cancer-research-and-treatment organizations, and their church's social-service efforts, he says.

Mr. Gallagher's experience echoes the report by Independent Sector and Youth Service America showing that adults who worked with charities as youths are more likely to donate to charity, and

they typically donate larger amounts of money as well.

For example, the study found that for U.S. households earning between $25,000 and $44,999, those that include adults who volunteered as youths on average give $232 more to charities a year than those households whose adult members did not volunteer as youths.

Professional Choices

People who start their own charity programs at a young age often do more than just donate and volunteer. "They tend to move toward the non-profit field as a profession," says Mr. Culbertson. "I don't know too many investment bankers who say, 'Yeah, I started this nonprofit and then I decided to go out and make money.'" He estimates that about 80 percent of teenagers who are heavily involved in charitable programs, such as founding a charity, decide to work in the nonprofit field.

With two years of college left, Ms. Lockwood, of the ManaTeen Club, says she may choose a career working with charities. "I'm planning on studying archaeology," she says, "but I really also want to take classes in nonprofit management."

Yet an early experience establishing a charity doesn't automatically equate to a career in the nonprofit arena.

At 13, Charlie Shufeldt started an Atlanta non-profit group called Free Bytes, which fixes computers and donates them to charities. But after graduating in June from Stanford University with a major in economics and a minor in computer science, he opted to work at Bank of America in San Francisco.

Now 23, Mr. Shufeldt says he wants to be involved with the charity he founded, but the distance between California and Georgia is too great to bridge. "I was frustrated because there was so much more I wanted to do, but I couldn't really do it 2,000 miles away," he says.

While Mr. Shufeldt doesn't currently volunteer with nonprofit groups—he says he is still getting settled in his new job—he . . . wants to work with charities [again] because his time with Free Bytes was an eye-opening experience.

"It was good for me to get perspective on the world," he says. "I went to a private high school in Atlanta, and it was a relatively sheltered community. When we'd work with someone like the YWCA, and show the kids how to do something on the computer and see how excited they'd get, it was a pretty gratifying experience."

Mr. Shufeldt says in the future he may volunteer his computer skills at an organization that provides technological aid to poor countries.

Free Bytes remained active after Mr. Shufeldt's departure because he was able to persuade a local foundation to grant the charity $30,000 to hire an executive director. Recently, Tech Corps Georgia, a charity dedicated to giving poor Georgians access to computers, acquired Free Bytes and plans to continue the group's programs.

Charities Shut Down

Unlike Free Bytes, a number of charities started by teenagers close because the founders leave to attend college or move on to other things, says Youth Service America's Mr. Culbertson. He estimates that about 20 percent of charities started by people under 18 shut down after the founder leaves or for other reasons. Other charities, he says, get taken over by a larger group, like Free Bytes and Tech Corps Georgia, while some manage to grow to the point where they can hire employees and become well established.

While Mr. Culbertson encourages young people to start their own charities, Trevor Ferrell, who at 11 established Trevor's Campaign for the Homeless, in Philadelphia, cautions youths "not to take it to the extent that I took it because I lost a good bit of my childhood."

During the 1980s, Mr. Ferrell's involvement with the nonprofit organization, which provides temporary housing to homeless people, made him the celebrity poster child for youth philanthropy. He received awards and praise for his efforts from former President Reagan, Pope John Paul II, and Mother Teresa. He starred in several documentaries, and CBS and HBO made television movies about him.

"At the age of 11, I was flying around the country and to India, Africa, and the Soviet Union," he says.

But in 1993, Mr. Ferrell quit the group he founded. "A big motivator in leaving was just to be able to go out and be a regular person, get away from the publicity, not do interviews, not do public speaking," he says. Trevor's Campaign for the Homeless remains open and continues to use his name, despite the parting.

Today, Mr. Ferrell, now 30, directs Trevor's Endeavors, in Philadelphia, which provides donated furniture, lamps, kitchen appliances, and other household items to homeless people who are moving into homes. Although he regrets parts of his childhood, Mr. Ferrell remains dedicated to the charity work that inspired him as a kid.

Says Mr. Ferrell: "When someone comes here and I get to help furnish their house and see how happy they are, that feeling is like a drug."

AFTER YOU READ

1. According to this article, why do organizations want young people to volunteer? Do you think these are good reasons? Why or why not?

2. According to this article, what are some pluses and minuses of volunteering? As a group, develop a list of pros and cons to present to the class. Use specific examples from your own experiences to add to the list.

3. The article described several people who started their own charities. What charity would you start if you had the ability, time and resources? Why? What would this charity do? Do you think that such a charity could actually get started and thrive? Explain your answers as best you can.

Compounding Your Interest: Further Readings

Brown, H. (February 19, 2003). "Art History." *Education Week.*

Conhaim, W. W. (March 2003). "Virtual Volunteering." *Information Today.*

Gregg, G. (April 2003). "What Are They Teaching Art Students These Days?" *Art News.*

McEnro, J. C., & Pokinski, D. F. (2001). *Critical Perspective on Art History.* Englewood Cliffs, NJ: Prentice-Hall.

Mosser, T., et al. (January / February 2003). "The Arts Communications." *Careers & Colleges.*

Chapter 8

Banking on Your Health

It has been said that that if you don't have your health, you don't have anything. This is very true in college. All the studying in the world won't make a difference if you are not well enough to make it to class, take a test, or finish that project. Likewise, decisions you make now could affect your health for the rest of your life. College presents a world of possibilities, but it also presents a good number of health risks. Understanding these health risks and learning how to remain healthy now and in the future is one of the best investments you can make—as important as the investment you make in your textbooks or extracurricular activities.

First Things First

Your good health begins today. Right now. No more saying, "I'll worry about it tomorrow." And getting healthy or staying healthy is not as hard as it seems. What one thing can you do today to get on the road to good health? It may be as simple as eating a piece of fruit or drinking a few glasses of water. It may be trying to get a couple more hours of sleep instead of staying up until 3 a.m. and dragging yourself bleary-eyed to your 8 a.m. class. It could be walking to class instead of driving across campus or taking the stairs instead of the elevator. Your health really can begin with first things first—taking it one step at a time.

This chapter will cover the following topics:

Staying Healthy When the Going Gets
    Rough
NEWS: Nutrition, Exercise, Water, Sleep
Understanding the Health Risks
    of College Students
    Alcohol/Drug Abuse
    STDs
    Meningitis and Other Communicable
    Diseases
    Tobacco Use
    Violence/Date Rape
    Depression/Suicide
    Side Effects of Tattooing and
    Body Piercing
    Eating Disorders

Think About It

Answer the following questions in the space provided.

What healthy habits do you currently have? What unhealthful ones? _____

_____

_____

_____

_____

Staying Healthy When the Going Gets Rough

Being a college student, as you can see, is hard work. And when the going gets rough, the first thing that may suffer is your health. It is easy to let your healthful habits slide during the hectic times of your first semester in college. You don't maintain a regular sleep pattern or get very little sleep (One day your first class may be at 8 a.m. and the next day you may not have a class until 12 noon). You get to the cafeteria or food courts and are confronted with pizza and burgers and nachos. You hang out in your friend's room instead of going to the gym to work out. You stay up for three nights straight because you left a research paper until the last minute. You share a cup with your friend at a party and you both come down with a cold. The list could go on and on. Being in college puts you at particular risk for health concerns even though you are, in general, the healthiest you will be in your life. For the most part, college students are healthy. But staying healthy may take some extra effort on your part.

As we said before, coming to college right out of high school, you may be faced with doing many things on your own for the first time. The key to staying healthy in college is arming yourself with the information you need for self-care. You are the one who can make sure you stay healthy.

NEWS: Nutrition, Exercise, Water, Sleep

To stay healthy as a college student, it is as easy as keeping up with the **NEWS:** **N**utrition, **E**xercise, **W**ater, **S**leep.

Nutrition

Healthful food is one of your best weapons against illness in college. And if you eat well, you will also feel a lot better and have more energy. You may have already heard of the "freshman fifteen." That really is not a myth. Many freshman do gain weight because they go from eating balanced meals at home to eating whatever they want—and mostly junk food—at any time of the day or night. What, then, can you do to be certain you are eating right? Keep in mind that you should make sure you get adequate protein, fruits, and vegetables every day. Also, resolve to limit the amount of junk food and fat in your diet. Specifically:

- ▶ Eat and drink low-fat or nonfat dairy products.
- ▶ Choose chicken or fish more frequently over red meat.
- ▶ Eat a salad instead of a sandwich made with lunchmeat.
- ▶ Choose tomato sauce for your pasta over high-fat cheese sauces.
- ▶ If you eat pizza, choose plain cheese or veggie over sausage or pepperoni.
- ▶ Eat pretzels or air-popped popcorn instead of chips for a late-night snack.
- ▶ Whenever possible, choose broiled or baked food over fried food.
- ▶ Eat unsweetened cereal instead of presweetened cereal, even if you have to add a little sugar. Alternatively, mix the two together to get less sugar.
- ▶ Make a sandwich with wheat bread instead of white bread.
- ▶ Eat more beans for fiber.

▶ Eat five servings of fruits and vegetables a day (put fruit in your cereal, have a salad at lunch, eat some corn at dinner—it is not too difficult).

▶ Learn to eat less butter on your toast and rolls. You may not even miss it if you cut it out all together.

▶ Learn to cut down on salt. Don't add it to your foods at the table. Once you have cut back, excess salt actually may taste terrible to you. This healthy step is really worth a try.

Here is a sampling of some healthful meal choices, whether at home, in your residence hall or apartment, or in the campus cafeteria or food court:

Breakfast	Plain yogurt with fresh fruit added, oatmeal with nonfat milk, wheat toast with jelly instead of butter, fresh orange juice, water
Lunch	Salad with low-fat dressing, turkey sandwich on whole wheat bread with lettuce and tomato (skip the mayonnaise), an apple or an orange, water
Dinner	Grilled or broiled chicken or fish, salad with low-fat dressing, steamed vegetables, brown rice, wheat roll without butter, frozen low-fat yogurt
Snacks	Peanut butter on celery or low-fat cracker, corn without butter, oatmeal cookies, low-fat granola bars (sweets in moderation!)

Exercise

Staying active when you are under stress is another great way to stay healthy. Active people tend to get sick less than sedentary people, and they feel better! Staying active is not difficult once you make it a habit. Even if you have never exercised

What Worked for Me

"I couldn't believe I gained twenty pounds in my first semester," Rita lamented when she went home for semester break. For Rita, the freshman fifteen had turned into the freshman twenty, and she wanted to do something about it. When she looked back on her semester, she realized that she just didn't make "eating healthy" a priority. She skipped breakfast, ate fast food for lunch and dinner, and often snacked late at night with her friends while they were studying or watching television. She also never exercised, rationalizing that her work and campus activities were more important. While she was home over break, she went to see a nutritionist, who started her on a healthful eating plan. She had been worried that she would lapse into her old habits when she went back for the spring semester, but she found ways to make her new plan work. "Every morning I make sure to get up in time to eat a healthful breakfast instead of grabbing a candy bar on the way to class. I eat cereal and fruit almost every morning, and I actually feel full and energetic until it is time for lunch." She also learned that the cafeteria and food court actually offer healthful alternatives that taste good: salads, grilled chicken, soups, and fruit. "I still treat myself now and then, but I make sure that I don't eat only junk food." She also learned to make time after classes to get to the pool to swim laps. She has more energy now and believes that even when she slips back into her old habits, she will return promptly to eating with good health in mind.

a day in your life, you can still do a few simple things to keep from being a college couch potato. But if you always exercised regularly in high school or before coming to college, stick with your routine as much as possible. Your body will thank you for it! And so will your mind; the stress you relieve through exercise will help you concentrate better, and your grades will improve. Just as you need to find a balance between school work and social activities, you need to strike a balance in terms of the physical activity you get on a regular basis.

Fitting exercise into the busy life of a college student is not as difficult as it may seem. Walk to class even if you have a car on campus. Resist the urge to drive to every building. Ride your bike to class and walk up and down stairs instead of taking the elevator. Take a walk after dinner each night with a friend to ease the stress of the day and burn off a few calories. Get involved in an organized exercise activity at least once a week (aerobics, swimming, golf, and the like). Use the fitness equipment available on your campus (weights, exercise machines, and so on). Many college campuses are a great place to jog or run (if you run at night, always have a running partner and wear light or reflective clothing). Try to raise your heart rate through exercise for at least thirty minutes at a time, three times a week. If you're worried about having too much work to do, combine exercising with studying. For example, you can listen to taped notes on a headset while you are walking or jogging, or you can review notes while on a Stairmaster.

Water

"Water, water everywhere, and not a drop to drink." This line from Samuel Taylor Coleridge's *The Rime of the Ancient Mariner* refers to sailors being surrounded by an ocean of undrinkable salt water. In college, however, many students neglect to

Teamwork Activity

The object of this activity is to help each other learn how to eat healthful meals in college. Organize yourselves into groups of three. Within your group, assign each student to a different campus office to interview a key person. Have one student go to meet a dietitian in the cafeteria. Have another student meet with a nurse in the health center. Have the third student interview a health or physical education professor. In the interviews, ask the following questions:

▶ What is a good breakfast to get a college student through the day?

▶ What are some healthful choices in the typical cafeteria line-up?

▶ What are some foods to avoid? What are some eating habits to avoid?

▶ What are some healthful snacks to stock up on in the dorms?

▶ What types of drinks are the most healthful?

▶ What's a good dinner choice at a food court?

When interviews are done, come back together to create an ideal menu for one week. Copy your menu to distribute to the class. Discuss what choices you made and why.

drink enough water on a daily basis even though there's plenty of it around. Being dehydrated causes you to function at less than your best. Even mild dehydration can cause fatigue or muscle soreness, and it can definitely affect your sleep. Prolonged dehydration can cause more serious medical problems, such as digestive tract infections and kidney stones. On average, your body functions best with the equivalent of eight 8-ounce glasses of water a day (that's a half gallon!). There are many ways to make sure that you get enough water. First, drink a glass of water with every meal. Bring a water bottle with you every day and refill it at the water fountain (don't use a water bottle for too long without washing it with soap and hot water). Add lemon, lime, or orange slices to your water to spice it up. Choose water over sports drinks when exercising. Have water before a sugary drink. If you still want the sugary drink, then have it after the water. Drink a glass of water after a meal. This actually helps clean your teeth and freshen your breath.

Sleep

For many college students, complaining about lack of sleep is nearly as popular as complaining about cafeteria food. The all-nighter is part of college lore. Staying up and talking until the early morning hours is one of those experiences that comes with the newfound freedom of living away from home. But beware. A lack of sleep will catch up with you, and if you're not careful, the price you pay could be your grades, your health, and your own sense of well-being. You may find yourself drifting off to sleep during class, unable to focus when studying, and not having the energy to exercise or enjoy social activities. Ideally, you should be getting seven to eight hours of sleep a night. And for some of you, that number may need to be higher. Listen to your body.

Make sure that you assign sleep the high priority it deserves in your life. First, you need to prepare for sleep. If you want to be in bed by 11:30, you need to start getting ready at least half an hour earlier. Give your body a chance to wind down.

Establish a regular routine for this (brushing your teeth, washing your face, reading a book for pleasure, and the like). Also, if you have a roommate, this will let him or her know that you're getting ready for bed. Avoid caffeine and alcoholic beverages for a few hours before bed. Although alcohol can make going to sleep seem easier, it will interrupt your sleep and affect how deeply you sleep. A warm shower can help you relax. Don't eat a heavy meal or snack before bed. Your body will be busy digesting the food and keep you from sleeping. If you have a roommate, work out an arrangement regarding what lights will be on, the nighttime noise level, and so on. Remember to be considerate. If you find that you and your roommate have lifestyles at opposite ends of the spectrum, you may want to request a roommate change. Don't exercise too late in the day. Avoid sleeping pills because you can become hooked on them, causing your body to forget how to sleep on its own.

DIY: Do-It-Yourself Activity

Keep a sleep journal for three days. To do this, every morning, before you begin your day, write down what you did to prepare for sleep the night before; what you did in the two hours before you went to bed; what, if anything, you ate before bed; what time you went to bed; and what time you woke up in the morning. Then write a few sentences about how you feel in the morning. After three days, look at your sleep habits. What healthful habits do you have? Which ones are not so healthful? What do you need to change?

The Hard Way

"After missing the second semester of my freshman year, I think I have learned a few lessons," Nancy said to her advisor the first week of the new semester. When Nancy moved into the residence hall, it was her first time away from home. "I unfortunately didn't know how to take care of myself. My Mom always nagged me about staying healthy—eating right, sleeping well, reducing stress, even drinking enough water." "Almost immediately," Nancy recalled, "I got caught up in the freshman schedule of actually no schedule at all. My roommates and friends would stay up until two in the morning one night, sleep until noon on another day, and sometimes just order pizza delivery instead of making it to the cafeteria. I don't even want to get into how I stopped running on a regular basis and consumed way too much junk food. Soon I was coming down with a cold every other week," Nancy lamented. "I missed too many classes because I either slept through the alarm or was just too tired to bother. By the end of my first semester, I came down with mono and went home." Nancy decided not to return to school the next semester. She is now back, living in an off-campus apartment with one roommate, and committed to maintaining a healthful lifestyle. "I learned my body wanted me to take care of it. My health and my grades go together."

Staying healthy when the going gets rough is not as hard to do as it may seem. If you can just focus on the basics, you'll be fine. Remember that investing in your health is as important as investing in your academic success. If you're not healthy, you're not going to have a productive or enjoyable academic experience.

Understanding the Health Risks of College Students

As a college student, you may be experiencing one of the healthiest stages of your life—you are young, active, and aware. Because you are a college student, however, you are also at risk for specific health concerns that come with the territory. As part of your education, it is important for you to learn as much as you can about those health risks that are especially high for college students—and to lessen them as much as possible. As we have said before, one of the best places on campus to gain valuable information is the health center. Don't wait until you are sick, injured, or worried. Go early and often to seek out information and guidance. You will be glad you did. In addition, the information that follows is a roadmap for this journey to wellness during your college years. The sources listed below each topic will provide additional information. The health center on your campus can also provide you with information on any of the topics you wish to know more about. It is always better to discuss any of these topics with a health care professional. Do not rely just on websites or on your friends for information; not all of it is likely to be accurate or up-to-date.

Alcohol/Drug Abuse

Partying with alcohol and other drugs has long been associated with the culture of college. This aspect of the culture has been memorialized in movies from *Animal House* to *Road Trip*. Many students, away from home for the first time, feel that partying is part of the experience they are supposed to have in college. Also, no parents are there to notice if they come home drunk or if they spend all day in bed with a hangover. Partying and having a good time are meant to be part of the college experience, but you have to use your head and think of the consequences of making alcohol and/or drugs the centerpiece of such experiences. In recent years, binge drinking—drinking five or more drinks in one session or drinking just in order to get drunk—has become a growing concern, particularly among female students. Binge drinking increases the chances of immediate health risks such as injury, unwanted sex, and alcohol poisoning. It also can become a habit that leads to alcohol abuse long after college. The abuse of alcohol and drugs can have serious consequences academically, legally, and in terms of one's personal health. Twenty-five percent of college students have reported lower grades and other academic problems associated with drinking (Wechsler et al., 2002). This same study reports that 5 percent of students have been involved with the police as a result of drinking. On an even more serious note, each year 1400 college students die from alcohol-related injuries. Half a million are unintentionally injured, and 600,000 are assaulted. Seventy-thousand students have been victims of sexual assault or date rape in alcohol-related incidents (Hingson et al., 2002).

Drug and alcohol abuse is one of the leading causes of academic failure among college students nationwide. Students who are more focused on partying than on studying inevitably lose track of what's important. A student may miss a class because of a hangover, then a test. Soon he or she doesn't hand in a paper. Next thing you know, he or she has failed the entire class. Many students who are dismissed from college are sent packing not because they couldn't handle the work but because they never showed what they were capable of as students as a result of their abuse of alcohol and drugs.

The legal consequences of alcohol and drug abuse can follow you around for a lifetime. Drinking under the age of 21 is illegal in the United States. Drug use is illegal. Many colleges have zero-tolerance policies. Get caught once, and you're no longer allowed to live on campus, or you may be expelled from the school outright. Beware of abusing prescription drugs as well; naturally, obtaining prescription drugs with false documents or by similar means is illegal. In some states, students arrested and convicted of underage drinking may be barred from becoming teachers, lawyers, or law enforcement officers. DUI (driving under the influence) convictions can result in serious penalties. And if someone is injured or killed while you are driving under the influence, the legal ramifications—including serious jail time—are likely to be overshadowed be your own feelings of guilt and regret. Drug possession and/or distribution charges can also result in serious jail time. Many states have mandatory sentencing guidelines with long terms in some very unpleasant prisons. Needless to say, not many companies are interested in hiring a person with a drug conviction. And many companies require drug tests for applicants, so even if you've never been caught, you could find yourself out of the running for a job. Also, be aware that if you are caught providing alcohol to minors or drugs to anyone—particularly if there is an injury or death—you could find yourself facing serious legal problems as well.

The health risks of alcohol and drug abuse are well known, but it is up to you, the college student, to make the right choice at some key moments. The peer pressure to drink and, depending on who your friends are, to do drugs, can be enormous. Know who your real friends are. Know where you stand on drinking and drug use before you are confronted with a decision. Know what your limits are before you get into a situation—and then stick to them. You don't want to end up as another sad story or statistic.

Many students don't recognize that they are on the verge of big trouble. Some signs that you may have a problem are the following:

▶ When you are under the influence of alcohol or other drugs, doing things that you wouldn't normally do
▶ Using drugs or alcohol to loosen up socially
▶ Passing out
▶ Having blackouts while under the influence of alcohol or drugs
▶ Drinking or using drugs to alter your mood—particularly if you are using the substance to make you feel better or to lighten up when you feel depressed
▶ Using in order to "get away from it all"
▶ Driving while under the influence

▶ Having unwanted sex while using
▶ Binge drinking—drinking just to get drunk
▶ Avoiding friends who don't support your use or abuse and hanging out only with other users
▶ Drinking alone

A lot of students who have ended up with problems started drinking or using drugs socially and suddenly found that it had gotten out of their control. If you have exhibited any of the above behaviors *even one time,* you may have a problem. Often, dealing with a problem requires extra help. If you need some help, visit your health center or campus counseling center right away.

Sources

Keeling, R. (March 2002). "Binge Drinking and the College Environment." *Journal of American College Health.*

Lederman, L., et al. (January 2003). "A Case against 'Binge' as the Term of Choice: Convincing College Students to Personalize Messages About Dangerous Drinking." *Journal of Health Communication.*

www.collegedrinkingprevention.gov

STDs

STDs—Sexually Transmitted Diseases—range from the embarrassing and mildly discomforting to lethal. College students are at high risk for contracting such diseases because of the nature of the college experience. College is a time of transition, and many students will have numerous sexual partners during their college years. Combine that with the abuse of alcohol and drugs, and one can easily see how STDs become a major issue among college students. Certainly, the best way to avoid contracting STDs is to practice abstinence (although in cases of date rape, even that may not be enough protection). For sexually active students, the best method of preventing STDs is a properly utilized condom. Your college health center will often supply information on condom use and may even provide condoms themselves. Also, you need to know your sex partners—after all, you are, in essence, having sex with everyone *they* have had sex with, particularly if you are having unprotected sex. Don't buy into lines like "I'm only doing this with you because I love you" or "Just this once, let me do it without a condom because it's more comfortable." "Just this once" is all it takes to contract an STD that can last a lifetime. If you are sexually active, get regular check-ups to be sure that you aren't carrying any STDs that you could unknowingly transmit to someone else. Having to tell your boyfriend or girlfriend, "I'm sorry, but I think I gave you genital warts" is not a great way to impress your partner.

One of the biggest spreaders of STDs in college is careless sex under the influence of alcohol or drugs. It goes without saying that substance abuse can affect people's judgment, resulting in a normally sensible student having unprotected sex, sometimes with a partner he or she barely knows. But you must be careful with sex *all the time*. You don't want an embarrassing one-night stand you'd rather forget leave you with the lifetime souvenir in the form of an STD.

Most STDs are contracted through vaginal, oral, or anal sex with someone who has the disease. Many can be spread even when the person is asymptomatic (shows no signs of the disease). Some STDs, such as HIV/AIDS and hepatitis B, can also be spread through the sharing of infected needles. Some of the most common STDs are briefly described in the following table.

STD	Time from Contact to First Symptoms	Symptoms and Diagnosis	Some Complications
Human papilloma virus (HPV) (also called genital warts, condylomata acuminate) Cause: virus	1–8 months	Itching and irritation; often looks like ordinary skin warts; diagnosed through examination.	Very contagious and may be linked to cervical cancer in women.
Chlamydia Cause: bacterium	1–4 weeks	Generally, there are no symptoms. Sometimes indicated by discharge and/or pain during urination. Diagnosed through examination and screening test.	Can cause pelvic inflammatory disease in women. Can cause sterility in both men and women. Can infect infants during birth.
Herpes Cause: virus	Up to 2 weeks	Blisters on genitals or lips. Diagnosed through herpes culture, pap smear, examination.	Linked to cervical cancer. Can cause serious problems or death to infants infected during birth.
Gonorrhea (also called dose, clap, drip) Cause: bacterium	2–10 days; sometimes 30 days	Yellowish-green genital discharge, burning during urination; sometimes produces no symptoms in men and women. Diagnosed through screening test and examination.	Can cause pelvic inflammatory disease in women. Can cause sterility in both men and women. Also linked to arthritis and blindness. Can infect infants during birth.
AIDS (acquired immunodeficiency syndrome) Cause: human immunodeficiency virus (HIV)	2–5 years or more	Purplish discolorations on arms and legs, weight loss, extreme fatigue. Diagnosed through blood tests.	Can lead to severe psychiatric problems and death. Can be transmitted from mother to fetus.
Hepatitis B Cause: virus	1–9 months	Sometimes without symptoms. Flu-like symptoms, fatigue, jaundice.	Can cause permanent liver damage.

(Continued)

STD	Time from Contact to First Symptoms	Symptoms and Diagnosis	Some Complications
Syphilis Cause: spirochete	10–90 days; usually within 3 weeks	Appears in two stages: first, painless sore; second, rash, fever, and flu-like symptoms. Diagnosed through examination and blood test.	Can cause brain damage, insanity, paralysis, heart disease, and death. A pregnant woman can pass on the infection.
Trichomonas (Also known as trich, TV, vaginitis)	Varies 1–4 weeks	Discharge, itching of genitals, painful intercourse, usually no symptoms in men. Diagnosed through Pap test, examination, urinalysis, and wet mount preparation.	Can cause gland infections in women and prostatitis in men.

(Adapted from Pennsylvania Department of Health (2000), "Common Sexually Transmitted Diseases.")
SOURCES: Brody, J. (1/21/2003). "Facts of Life: Condoms Can Keep Disease at Bay." *New York Times,* P F7; *http://www. niaid.nih.gov/factsheets/stdinfo.htm*

Meningitis and Other Communicable Diseases

Meningitis, an infection of the tissues and/or fluid around the brain and spinal cord, is a serious concern for college students. According to the journal *Current Health 2,* the number of cases of meningitis has doubled in the last decade among people between the ages of 15 and 24. According to the Centers for Disease Control and Prevention, those most at risk include college freshmen living in dormitories.

Time-Out Tip

Try to get into the habit of never leaving your glass unattended when you are at a party. It is always best to keep it in your hand instead of setting it down, especially if you walk away, even briefly. In just a few minutes, someone else could take a sip from your glass (or even slip something into it). Also, if you lose track of your glass, you may end up drinking from someone else's. All this could lead to anything from a common cold to something much more serious, such as meningitis. Or you could end up ingesting a date rape drug. You just never know—unless you always know where your own glass is.

College students do need to be aware of meningitis, of behaviors and conditions that increase the risk of contracting it, and what they can do to keep from becoming a victim. Meningitis is a highly contagious disease that thrives in an environment such as a college campus, in which students are living together in close quarters and possibly sharing cups, cigarettes, and other items.

According to the National Meningitis Association, there are two major divisions of meningitis: viral (caused by a virus) and bacterial (caused by bacteria in the throat or nasal passages). Bacterial meningitis is more dangerous—the disease progresses rapidly and can be fatal. Those who recover may suffer long-term effects, including amputations.

It is very important to learn and remember the symptoms of meningitis. They may include severe headache, fever, vomiting, numbness, stiff neck, confusion, seizures, and purple spots on the skin.

There are ways to prevent meningitis, and they begin with washing your hands regularly. Also, be careful not to share any items that have been in, or have been touched by, someone else's mouth. Finally, consider getting vaccinated (many colleges require it). The vaccine—Menomune—may prevent many types of bacterial meningitis. There is no vaccine for viral meningitis. Remember too that a vaccine is not a sure thing. Even if a vaccine has been administered, you still need to take preventive steps and watch out for symptoms.

Meningitis is one of the most severe communicable diseases to which college students are exposed, but a number of others, such as strep throat, the common cold, the flu, and mononucleosis, are more common. For more information on these, visit the website.

Sources

Centers for Disease Control and Prevention (www.cdc.gov)
Gard, C. (April/May 2003). "What Is Meningitis?" *Current Health 2*.
National Meningitis Association (www.nmaus.org)

Tobacco Use

In our culture, for many complex reasons, smoking and tobacco use have been associated with rebellion. For one thing, it's considered an adult prerogative, something forbidden to children. For another, the "cool factor" of smoking is reinforced in countless movies and TV shows, where rebellious anti-heroes smoke cigarettes or cigars (often, tobacco companies pay movie producers a fee for these "product placements"). Tobacco companies also carefully market to college students and teens. College is, of course, a time of growth, of moving into adulthood, and of rebellion, in some cases. Thus smoking a cigarette at a party or while sitting on the balcony with friends can seem like the cool thing to do. The problem is that what is little more than a social cigarette with friends can turn into a long-term habit that can be difficult (and, for some, impossible) to break. Some experts have found that the nicotine in cigarettes, cigars, and other forms of tobacco (dip, snuff, and chewing tobacco) can be more addictive than heroin. And the health consequences can be devastating and deadly. According to a 1998 report from the National Institute on Drug Abuse, "Tobacco kills more than 430,000 U.S. citizens each year—more than alcohol, cocaine, heroin, homicide, suicide, car accidents, fire, and AIDS combined." For information on the short-term and long-term effects of tobacco use, visit our website.

Considering how powerful an addiction tobacco can be, and the serious and even deadly consequences of long-term use, the best plan is to avoid using tobacco altogether. Peer pressure related to smoking, just as with alcohol and drugs, can be a major factor. Think ahead of time about what you will say if someone offers you a cigarette. If you don't want it, don't take it. Say that smoking gives you a sore throat or that you know someone who died of lung cancer. Say whatever it takes. Smoking is also a very expensive habit. If you are a smoker, just be aware that this is a habit that you're probably going to want to break before too long (at a certain point, it loses its glamour and becomes just a need). The sooner you do so, the easier it will be to stop and the better your health will be for the rest of your life.

Sources
www.cdc.gov/tobacco

Violence/Date Rape

College is meant to be an idyllic time in life, one in which you can focus on learning and making friends and having a good time. Many college campuses fit the idyll, their bucolic campuses filled with ivy-covered buildings and towering trees. Others are more streamlined and urban in appearance and setting. Sadly, however, colleges are not immune to the kinds of things that affect the rest of the world. Crimes—both violent crimes and "crimes against property," such as theft—exist on college campuses just as they do anywhere else. And this holds true for rural and suburban campuses as much as for urban campuses. In some ways, college students are even more vulnerable because they may live in an illusion of safety. The campus itself begins to feel like home—safe and familiar—and students often end up taking risks without even knowing it. Colleges are now required by law to issue a report on the crime rate on their campuses. Look into it to see where your college stands. Whatever you discover about the crime rate on your campus, here are some simple things you can do to reduce your risk of being a victim of violent crime.

▶ Walk in pairs or groups if you're out late at night.
▶ Call for a safety escort if you must walk alone at night. Nearly all college campuses have this kind of service. If yours doesn't, request that one be created.
▶ Be aware. If you have to go to your car in the parking lot, especially at night, check out the area carefully. Have your key ready. Walk to your car with a purpose.
▶ Report any suspicious activity to campus police.
▶ Avoid situations that can lead to violence. If a party you're attending is getting out of hand, leave before it does. Often, assaults and other types of violence occur in such situations.
▶ Stick to well-lighted walkways.
▶ Let someone know where you are and when you expect to be back.
▶ Carry a mobile phone for emergencies if you are frequently alone on campus.

Doing these things won't completely eliminate any risks, but it will reduce them.

One type of violence that is all too common on college campuses is date rape or acquaintance rape—rape perpetrated by someone the victim knows. Often, alcohol or drug use is involved in such situations. Some additional tips for avoiding date rape follow.

► Avoid drinking to the point where you lose track of your actions. Watch out for a date who is pushing drinks or drugs on you.

► Avoid being alone in a place where no one else could reach you or hear you if you shouted for help.

► If an acquaintance seems to be drunk or high, leave and say that you'll see him or her when he or she is sober.

These situations can't always be avoided, but again you can increase your chances of avoiding them. In recent years, there have been many reports of some new menaces: rohypnol and sodium gamma hydroxybutyrate (GHB). Rohypnol, also known as "roofies" or the date rape drug, and GHB are drugs that cause the victim to lapse into a state of semi-consciousness. Predators—sometimes even someone that the victim knows—have used this on unsuspecting victims and then raped them. If you are the victim of a violent attack or a date rape, report it. Too often, students are afraid of doing anything—particularly in the case of date rape—and this leaves the police in a position where they can't do much about it.

Sources
http://www.4woman.gov/faq/rohypnol.htm

Depression/Suicide

Mental health is also a major issue in college. College is a time of significant transition in the lives of young people. For traditional college students, this may mean leaving home and moving on to adulthood. For nontraditional students, it can mean balancing the obligations of college with home life. When the demands and challenges start to seem overwhelming, students can experience feelings of depression. Depression can also be caused by chemical changes that even now aren't always fully understood. Genetics is believed to play a role. Also, substance abuse can lead to depression. Most students feel down at times, but there are some things to watch for when those negative feelings become more serious and turn into what is known as clinical depression.

Here are some warning signs that indicate you might be suffering from depression:

► Disturbed sleep patterns—either excessive sleep or insomnia
► Overwhelming feelings of sadness or despair
► Feelings of euphoria alternating with feelings of gloom
► Strong and inappropriate emotional reactions
► Crying for no apparent reason or with little stimulus
► Feelings of loss of control

There are different levels of clinical depression, ranging from mild to severe. Treatment can range from therapeutic counseling to prescription drugs. If you think you may be suffering from depression, or if you have a friend who might be, seek professional help from your college's counseling center.

Thoughts of depression can also lead a student to contemplate suicide, the most serious consequence of depression. This is clearly one of the most serious health risks to students because obviously, in a completed suicide, the consequences are irreversible. Suicide is a permanent solution to a temporary problem. Even someone who attempts suicide only as a means of calling for help may inadvertently succeed. If you have been contemplating suicide or know someone who has, seek professional help immediately. You cannot help yourself on your own, and you are not qualified to take care of a friend who is entertaining thoughts of suicide. If you want to help someone else, the best thing you can do is get that person to a professional counselor or psychologist. Sometimes, in attempting to help a friend, students get in over their heads, taking on a responsibility that there is no way they can or should assume. One of the clearest warning signs of suicide is that the individual talks about it. Many times, those with suicidal thoughts talk openly about their plans. Other times, they will write about their intentions. Don't assume that someone is just joking. You can't take that chance. Other signs are persistent depression, giving away prized possessions, and even saying goodbye to people the individual knows. Again, don't take a chance—get help even if you only think there might be a problem.

Sources
http://www.nimh.nih.gov/publicat/depressionmenu.cfm

Side Effects of Tattooing and Body Piercing

Walking across many college campuses these days, you are likely to see quite a show of colorful drawings and metalwork. But this artwork isn't the sculptures or student paintings you might expect to see in a public setting. It is artwork in the form of tattooing and body piercing, both of which have become very popular among college students. In almost every college town, or somewhere near a college campus, you can find a place to get a tattoo or pierce a body part. Before you get a tattoo or body piercing, however, there are things you should consider.

▶ Tattoos are permanent (unless you consider expensive, difficult, painful, and time-consuming removal procedures—many plastic surgeons now spend a great deal of their time removing unwanted tattoos). What you decide to get tattooed on your body after a night out partying may not look as good to you the next day, or two years down the road.

▶ Piercing can sometimes lead to infections. Some parts of the body are riskier than others. The area needs to be kept clean.

▶ Getting a tattoo or body piercing can lead to serious infections if an unsterilized needle is used. These infections include hepatitis B and C and HIV.

▶ Make sure the shop you go to is licensed. Don't let anybody tattoo or pierce you in an unsanitary environment.

▶ Make sure the shop has an autoclave to sterilize equipment.

▶ Make sure the person doing your tattoo or piercing opens a new set of tools in front of you.

▶ Tattoo ink should be fresh and new for each customer. Be sure you do not get used ink.

For more information, visit our website.

Source

U.S. Food and Drug Administration Center for Food Safety and Applied Nutrition (www.vm.cfsan.fda.gov)

Eating Disorders

In our culture, there is an enormous amount of pressure on teens and young adults to be thin and fit. Tanned, trim, and toned bodies scream out at college students from nearly every magazine cover. Female models wearing bikinis smile happily. Nowadays, young men are feeling the pressure, too, as male models with "six-pack" abs appear on more and more magazine covers. The problem with these images is that they imply for many students that no other look is acceptable. Each person has a natural weight that has as much to do with genetics and bone structure as with diet. Everybody knows someone who can "eat anything she wants" without gaining a pound. Others struggle to keep their weight under control even when on a strict diet. In order to achieve what society considers acceptable, many students resort to unhealthful or potentially dangerous dietary supplements such as ephedrine. Other students develop eating disorders such as anorexia, bulimia, and binge-eating disorder (BED). **Anorexia** is characterized by extreme weight loss or starvation accompanied by obsession with body weight and its relation to self-image. This disorder can lead to serious complications and even death. **Bulimia** is characterized by binging followed by purging through vomiting or the use of laxatives. Finally, **binge-eating disorder** is characterized by binging followed by extreme guilt. People who are binge eaters can range from very thin to obese.

The "freshman fifteen" is not a myth. Many students do experience weight gain during their first year of college. Because of changes in diet, irregular eating habits, and impromptu socializing (those midnight pizza parties), students are susceptible to putting on a few pounds. Nevertheless, the best way to get a healthy body weight is to first figure out what that weight is (it's probably not what the models on the magazine covers weigh). Then, if you're overweight, develop a sensible diet (you

Get Involved!

J udith *was* involved in campus life, but her involvement left her little time for exercise. She was never involved in sports in high school and didn't plan on becoming involved in sports in college. She knew, however, that she needed to exercise. "I started to feel really sluggish and knew I was getting out of shape, but I didn't want to start a traditional exercise program or give up my social activities." Her friend Lindsay told her about the hiking club, and Judith knew she had the answer. "I don't have to go on every hike, and it is not competitive. I can go for the fun of it." She enjoys getting out with the group on a Saturday morning and exploring the mountains near campus. "I have made new friends and found a form of exercise I can stay with for a long time."

might want to work with a dietitian or physician), and lose weight slowly and safely. Rapid weight loss can cause major health problems that can affect your heart and digestive systems—and it rarely results in a long-term weight loss. Typically, those kinds of dieters quickly gain back the weight they have lost.

Sources

Grassi, A. (May/June 2001). "The College Environment and Eating Disorders." *Healthy Weight Journal.*
www.nationaleatingdisorders.org

Increasing Your Yield:

Readings for Practical Application

In this chapter, you have learned about understanding health risks and staying healthy in college. The readings that follow will help you learn more about your personal health and responsibilities while you are reading about another important discipline that nearly all college students encounter. That discipline is history. Just as you learn from your current experiences, so do you learn from the past. Likewise, you will be exposed to the past in reading history texts, learning about the career paths and contributions of those who have gone before you, and learning about past health concerns that have shaped the steps we now take to stay healthy.

In the first reading, "A Textbook Case," you will read about black republicanism during the slave era in the early 1800s. Before you read this excerpt, you will find some helpful tips for reading history texts. Apply these tips to the reading to help arm yourself with good reading strategies for your future history courses.

If you are contemplating majoring in history, you may be wondering what the future holds for you in terms of possible jobs and career paths. Although teaching may seem an obvious path, it is certainly not the only one, as you will learn in the "Life After College" reading about a Native American student pursuing his dream of preserving his own college.

This chapter also covered health risks to college students, among them communicable diseases. In the "Current Issues" reading, you will learn about SARS, severe acute respiratory syndrome.

These readings expand on what was covered in this chapter and give you a chance to apply the strategies you have learned to reading and understanding college-level material. The readings delve into subjects of intrinsic interest and offer some practice in reading text material in the discipline of history.

Reading and Study Tips: History

Unique Features and Comprehension Strategies

History texts tell a story. Even if the story is a complicated one, it is still a story. History textbooks are full of interesting true stories with many characters you may already know. Your previous knowledge of these characters can be applied to your textbooks, just as though you were reading a series of novels with continuing characters. The unique feature of history textbooks is that you can get to know characters and follow the events in the stories, as opposed to strictly memorizing information. **Approach your history textbooks as you would a good novel. Let yourself go back into the past. Keep in mind that these are real people and real events. See them as three-dimensional and worthy of getting to know. By doing so, you will become more involved in what you are reading, and this can help you remember the information better. History textbooks also force you to think critically. Use the critical thinking skills discussed in Chapter 5 to take your understanding to a higher level. Don't just try to memorize what happened. Instead, keep asking yourself, "Why did it happen?" "What did it mean?"**

You will then become engaged in the story, and it will make more sense. The answers to these questions will also become answers to essay questions you will encounter.

Many history textbooks provide an outline of every chapter. Chapter outlines are very helpful in most textbooks, but they are especially meaningful in history textbooks because they act as timelines of the events to unfold in the chapter. You will know what comes first, second, and so on, and you will know at what point the coverage in that chapter ends. These timelines prepare you for what you are about to read, as well as illustrate how the events that occurred flowed from one to another. **Read the chapter outline first, if one is provided. This will give you a sense of where the chapter starts, where it goes, and where it ends. Study the outline for a preview of what you will learn about and also to note the relationship between the outline and the order of events in the story you are about to read. Avoid merely scanning the outline. Instead, to get a head start in your understanding of the chapter, consider testing your prior knowledge of the period covered in the chapter by turning some of the outline entries into questions. You can also choose sections in the chapter to preview in more detail. Be sure to review the outline after you have read the chapter as well. You can test yourself on what you remember from each section as you review the outline. Make your own outlines and timelines! Take a cue from the authors of your history textbooks, and when you have finished reading, organize what you have read in your own personalized outlines and timelines. Doing so will help you see what you remember and will also help you organize your thoughts as you study for tests. The timelines will be great visual aids if your primary learning style is visual or tactile. The act of drawing out the timeline is a form of review. Your own timeline will always be more helpful than one provided for you, because you will be not only testing what you know but also reviewing what you don't. Moreover, you will have a better chance of actually "seeing" your timeline in your head when you are taking a test and must recall the order of events.**

Guide questions often appear throughout chapters in history textbooks. You may see guide questions throughout the chapters in your history textbooks. They are there to alert you to major ideas and themes and then to test your understanding of what you have read. If you can answer the question, you have a good sense of your comprehension of the information. **Practice using the guide questions to *guide* your reading. Read the questions first, and then, as you are reading, make sure you understand the content well enough to answer the questions. The questions also set up the major themes in the section that you'll be reading. Take note of these major themes. They may form the basis for some essay questions on tests. After you have read each chapter, write down the guide questions and give yourself a practice essay test. Go back and review the chapter to evaluate your answers.**

History textbooks are not set up for strict memorization because history is a continuum; in other words, you have to understand how what came before affected what came after. Unlike some textbooks that introduce new concepts throughout the book, history textbooks are really set up on a continuum. This can be both negative and positive: negative because you cannot decide to goof off for a few weeks and then drop back into the class when a new topic is introduced; positive because the information keeps building on itself. This is good because what you have learned before acts as a schema (framework of prior knowledge) in terms of which to assimilate and interpret what is to come. Having prior knowledge always increases your comprehension. **Read any given chapter all the way through once—but not in depth—just to get the general idea. This will give you a real sense of the story and keep you moving through it without getting bogged down by trying to remember names and dates. Then read it through a second time to get a more in-depth understanding of the material. Students who read their history textbooks two or three times—as opposed to once or not at all—tend to do much better on tests because they have a deeper understanding of the material and have not just skimmed it or done superficial memorization. Think about rereading major sections again as you review for tests. Remember the hint about creating practice essay tests. Rereading will help you to see whether your answers are not only right but also go into enough depth to demonstrate your complete understanding to your professors.**

History textbooks are not generally characterized by boldface type and definitions in boxes (although some do include these features). Most consist of continuous text, broken up by a few subheads, of course. It is up to you to discern the most important topics and to find the key definitions yourself within the text. If you think about textbooks in other disciplines, such as psychology or physical science, you may remember that sections of many texts have bold headings, bold terms, or boxed information that you can focus on when you are trying to get an idea of what may be most important. For most history textbooks, this is not the case. Because much of what happened in history is retold as stories, the information flows like stories. You need to read the text very attentively. You cannot scan the text in hopes of finding important information and ignoring the rest. The best thing to do is to summarize the information in your own words after you have read each section—this summary can become your own textbook of important information. **Use annotation (as described in Chapter 3) as you are reading history textbooks. Because these books read so much like stories, using a highlighter is not recommended. You are not going to find any answers in a single sentence; you must read the whole thing and get the main ideas. Consider transferring these summaries to index cards as a means of review. When you pick up an index card with a major event, person, or idea noted, talk about it aloud to expand on it—or see whether you can write a more in-depth answer on a piece of paper. Remember, that is what you will be doing on a test.**

Maps are often included to provide visual context for the story. Maps place the action in context. The maps help you to recall where the story took place and give you another way to remember the story. **These maps should be viewed in conjunction with the reading for the sections in which they appear.**

Pictures are also used to help you visualize the real people and places you are learning about. Yes, history textbooks are like good novels in that they are rich with interesting characters. They are unlike novels, however, in that many history texts provide color illustrations and photographs to enhance your understanding. You don't have to rely entirely on your imagination. **Study the pictures and use them to help bring life to the text. The visual images supplementing the written content will help you to remember better.**

Some history textbooks include a CD-ROM and information about accessing a related website. These CD-ROMs and websites often have practice chapter tests, primary source material, charts, maps, and graphs. Professors may use questions from those practice tests on the actual tests. Many students ignore the CD-ROM and website only to regret it when other students report that information provided there was on the test. **If your textbook has these study aids, use them!**

History textbooks lend themselves to essay tests. Many history professors give essay tests. This makes sense, in light of the type of course history is and the type of textbook you are reading. Administering essay tests enables instructors to test your ability to synthesize textbook facts and stories rather than just assessing your memorization skills. **To prepare for essay tests using your textbook, approach the guide questions and your annotated notes as possibilities for essay questions on the test. Then practice by preparing an outline for potential questions. Get together with some classmates and swap answers. Grade each other's essays and give feedback for improvement.**

Reading 1:   A Textbook Case

The following excerpt from a textbook chapter is included here because it is a clear example of how history tells a story. In this case, it is Gabriel's story. It also reflects the diversity in American history, including some stories that may have been overlooked in your high school textbooks. In coming to appreciate the diversity on your campus, it is important to understand the role of diverse Americans in our nation's beginnings. When you read this excerpt, keep in mind some of the strategies recommended above. Consider making your own timeline of the events, and annotate as you go along so that when you go back to review, you will have your own comprehension notes to help you. The timeline, in particular, will help you put Gabriel's Rebellion into its historical context, helping make the connection between it and the French Revolution.

BEFORE YOU READ

1. Brainstorm on everything you know about slavery in the United States. Make notes and keep a timeline.
2. Do you agree that reading history is like reading a story? Why or why not? Provide some examples from historical events you have learned about in the past, particularly events that you found especially memorable.
3. Have you ever wanted to defy someone in authority when you were convinced that something the authority believed was wrong? How did this desire make you feel? How

did you handle the situation? If you never have felt this way, what cause do you feel so strongly enough about that you would go against the wishes of someone in authority? Explain your feelings.

Black Republicanism: Gabriel's Rebellion

J. M. Murrin

Masters who talked of liberty and natural rights sometimes worried that slaves might imagine that such language could apply to themselves. The Age of Democratic Revolution took a huge step in that direction in 1789, when the French Revolution—fought in the name of "Liberty, Equality, and Fraternity"—went beyond American notions of restored English liberties and into the heady regions of universal natural rights. Among the first repercussions outside of France was a revolution on the Caribbean island of Hispaniola in the French colony of Saint-Domingue. That island's half-million slaves fought out a complicated political and military revolt that began with the events in Paris in 1789 and resulted—after the defeats of Spanish, English, and French armies—in the creation of the independent black republic of Haiti on the western one-third of the island. Slave societies throughout the hemisphere heard tales of terror from refugee French planters and stories of hope from the slaves they brought with them (12,000 of these entered South Carolina and Louisiana alone). In 1800, a conservative Virginia white complained that "Liberty and Equality has been infused into the minds of the negroes." A South Carolina Congressman agreed that "this new-fangled French philosophy of liberty and equality" was stirring up the slaves. Even Thomas Jefferson, who applauded the spread of French republicanism, conceded that "the West Indies appears to have given considerable impulse to the minds of the slaves ... in the United States."

Slaves from the 1790's onwards whispered of natural rights and imagined themselves as part of the Democratic Revolution. This covert republic of the slaves sometimes came into the open, most ominously in Richmond in 1800, where a slave blacksmith named Gabriel hatched a well-planned conspiracy to overthrow Virginia's slave regime. Gabriel had been hired out to Richmond employers for most of his adult life; he was shaped less by plantation slavery than by the democratic, loosely interracial underworld of urban artisans. In the late 1790's the repressive acts of the Federalist national government and the angry responses of the Jeffersonian opposition, along with the news from Saint-Domingue (present day Haiti), drove the democratic sensibilities of the world to new heights. Gabriel's plans took shape within that heated ideological environment.

Gabriel, working with his brother and other hired-out slave artisans, planned his revolt with military precision. Working at religious meetings, barbecues, and the grog shops of Richmond, they recruited soldiers among the slave artisans,

SOURCE: J. M. Murrin et al., "Black Republicanism: Gabriel's Rebellion." In *Liberty, Equality, Power: A History of the American People, Volume I: To 1877,* Concise Edition (with InfoTrac and American Journey Online), 3rd ed. (Fort Worth, TX: Harcourt, 2001), pp. 286–287. © 2004. Reprinted with permission of Wadsworth, a division of Thomson Learning: www.thomsonrights.com Fax 800 730-2215.

adding plantation slaves only at the last moment. Gabriel planned to march an army of 1,000 men on Richmond in three columns. The outside columns would set diversionary fires in the warehouse district and prevent the militia from entering the town. The center would seize Capitol Square, including the treasury, the arsenal, and Governor James Monroe.

Although his army would be made up of slaves, and although his victory would end slavery in Virginia, Gabriel hoped to make a republican revolution, not a slave revolt. His chosen enemies were the Richmond "merchants" who had controlled his labor. Later, a co-conspirator divulged the plan: The rebels would hold Governor Monroe hostage and split the state treasury among themselves, and "if the white people agreed to their freedom they would then hoist a white flag, and [Gabriel] would dine and drink with the merchants of the city on the day when it would be agreed to." Gabriel expected what he called "the poor white people" and "the most redoubtable republicans" to join him. He in fact had the shadowy support of two Frenchmen, and rumors indicated that other whites were involved—though never at levels that matched the delusions of the conspirators. Gabriel planned to kill anyone who opposed him, but he would spare Quakers, Methodists, and Frenchmen, for they were "friendly to liberty." Unlike those of earlier slave insurgents, Gabriel's dreams did not center on violent retribution or a return to reconstruction of West Africa. He was an American revolutionary, and he dreamed of a truly democratic republic for Virginia. His army would march into Richmond under the banner "Death or Liberty."

Gabriel and his co-conspirators recruited at least 150 soldiers who agreed to gather near Richmond on August 30, 1800. The leaders expected to be joined by 500 or 600 more rebels as they marched upon the town. On the appointed day, however, it rained heavily. Rebels could not reach the meeting point, and amid white terror and black betrayals, Gabriel and his henchmen were hunted down, tried, and sentenced to death. In all, the state hanged 27 supposed conspirators, while others were sold and transported out of Virginia. The condemned carried their radical republican dreams to their graves. A white Virginian marveled that the rebels on the gallows displayed a "sense of their [natural] rights, [and] contempt of danger." When asked to explain the revolt, one condemned man relied in terms that could only have disturbed the white republicans of Virginia: "I have nothing more to offer than what General Washington would have had to offer, had he been taken by the British and put to trial by them. I have adventured my life in endeavoring to obtain the liberty of my countrymen, and am a willing sacrifice in their cause."

Conclusion

Between 1790 and 1820, Americans had transformed their new republic—with paradoxical results. The United States more than doubled in both size and population during these years. American trade with Britain, continental Europe, and the Caribbean skyrocketed. Some Americans amassed fortunes; others made more modest gains; others saw their positions deteriorate. Nonwhite Americans experienced the expansion of the republic and the growth of commerce as unmixed catastrophes: Indians between the Appalachians and the Mississippi River lost everything;

their hunting grounds became American farmland, much of it worked by slaves who now knew that their masters would never voluntarily free them.

The transformation stemmed both from American independence and from the expansion of agriculture and increased exports of American farm products. When Americans traded plantation staples and surplus food for European (largely British) manufactured goods and financial services, however, they deepened their colonial dependence on the old centers of the world economy—even as they insisted on their independence with a bellicose republican nationalism. This formed the cluttered backdrop of social change, economic and geographic growth, and continuing vulnerability to the whims and needs of the Old World powers against which Federalists and Jeffersonian Republicans fought each other to determine the ultimate outcome of the American Revolution.

AFTER YOU READ

1. What connection was there between the French Revolution and attitudes toward slavery in America in 1800? What other impact did the French Revolution have on society?
2. How might history have been different had Gabriel's Rebellion succeeded? What does this show about the interconnectedness of historical events?
3. Why didn't Gabriel's plan work? If you had been him, would you have tried anything different? Why or why not?
4. Create a timeline of Gabriel's Rebellion. What should be included in the timeline?
5. Create a Venn diagram comparing Gabriel's Rebellion to a more recent event in the history of civil rights.
6. Reflect on the important aspects of this chapter excerpt, and formulate two essay questions that you think would elicit evidence of a student's understanding of the passage. Bring these two questions to class to share with your classmates. Take turns formulating answers to each other's questions.

Reading 2: Life After College

The end of the previous passage discusses how Native Americans in the Southeast lost their hunting grounds to European settlers who took over the land for farming—much of it performed by slaves. The next passage discusses how one Native American college student, a Cheyenne from Montana, plans to work as a curator in order to preserve some of his ancestors' culture that has been threatened over the years. When you have finished reading this passage, compare the determination of Two Moons to Gabriel's devotion to his cause.

BEFORE YOU READ

1. What kinds of things did you learn about Native-American history in grade school or high school? Make a concept web to illustrate what you know.
2. What do you see as the connection between wanting to be a museum curator and wanting to preserve your cultural heritage?
3. How does being a museum curator enable a person to be a part of the story of history? Be specific.

Two Moons Dreams of Being a Museum Curator

J. Davis

Morgan Wheeler Two Moons spent last summer in Providence, R.I., and now he is studying in Santa Fe, N.M., far from the open plains of Montana. Most likely, he won't stay away from his home on the Northern Cheyenne Reservation in southeastern Montana for long, however. Two Moons' rambling has been fueled by his dream—to become the curator of a museum on his reservation.

This is not a romantic impulse that sounds interesting, but rather his dream is grounded in an evolution of experiences that led Two Moons from coast to coast and ultimately to recognize his intense desire to work preserving the Cheyenne heritage. Born in Montana and raised on the reservation, Two Moons graduated from the Bureau of Indian Affairs school at Busby in 1987. He attempted college at nearby Dull Knife Memorial College but was going through a time of personal upheaval in his life. Starting out in the field of office skills, he soon knew this was not the future he wanted to pursue. He left school in 1991 and moved to Portland, Ore., for two years. Then Two Moons met a friend who suggested he visit New York City.

Ironically, this proved to be the move that started Morgan Wheeler Two Moons on his path back to Montana. In New York, the classes that Two Moons had taken at Dull Knife in office management opened the door to a position at the Metropolitan Museum of Art. Starting as a Visitor Service Assistant he began developing curricula for interpretative programs. Within months Two Moons was working in the resource department of the National Museum of the American Indian/ Smithsonian Institution. There he produced a charming booklet for teachers who bring their elementary students to the museum. His booklet highlights "my favorite objects in Creations Journey," combining personal information, a history

lesson, and questions to keep young children interested while learning about the exhibits.

"I loved seeing old objects like war shirts and buffalo robes that are in natural history museums," Two Moons said. "It instills a lot of pride, recognizing where you come from." Since he does beadwork and studied fashion design in New York, he took special interest in the objects. "This work can still be done. It has to be examined. I would like to build a cultural center program on my reservation and have museums loan stuff like that so anyone in the community could come and see it," he said.

After three years in New York, Two Moons returned to Dull Knife Memorial College where he focused on Cheyenne studies, laying the groundwork for his dream. Unlike most tribal members of his generation, Cheyenne was his first language. "For deep conversations, the majority of people I can speak to are 40 years old or more except for my brothers and sisters and some of my first cousins," he said.

Because of the tribal college's involvement in the Leadership Alliance through Montana State University, he was able to work last summer at the Heffenreffer Museum of Anthropology and at Brown University's anthropology department. "In anthropology, you have access to old, old material," he said. He worked on a traveling exhibit about Native American women, "Gifts of Pride," creating a worksheet for children to make cradleboards out of popsicle sticks and construction paper. There in Providence, his dream grew. "I would like to do costume design with Native film producers in my spare time," he said.

His mentors at Brown University encouraged Two Moons to return for graduate school in social anthropology and art history. In the meantime, he is studying at the Institute of American Indian Arts in Santa Fe, focusing upon museum studies

SOURCE: J. Davis, "Two Moons Dreams of Being a Museum Curator," *Tribal College 11,* 48–49.Reprinted with permission from Tribal College Journal of American Indian Higher Education, a quarterly magazine published at P.O. Box 720, Mancos, CO 81328. For information call (888)-899-6693, email info@tribalcollegejournal.org, or see the website at www.tribalcollegejournal.org.

and three-dimensional design and working in President Della Warrior's office. Asked about his journeys away from his home, Two Moons said, "It doesn't hurt to follow your dreams and go into the unknown. Believe me, I was so scared to go to New York and Santa Fe. I learned not to walk along with fear but to go against it."

Today Morgan Wheeler Two Moons can listen to the elders' stories in the Cheyenne language and can meet with the directors of museums and libraries. He exemplifies tribal college students who have been part of the city but choose to return home—for themselves and for what they can bring to their people.

AFTER YOU READ

1. Two Moons says that "the majority of the people I can speak [in Cheyenne] to are 40 years old or more." Why do you think this is? Can you compare this to any experience (language, customs, foods, or the like) that you have had in your own family/culture?
2. What can Two Moons' job experiences teach you about the winding nature of career paths? How did he overcome his failures?
3. Why is being a museum curator seemingly a perfect job for someone like Two Moons? What characteristics does he possess that seem to make him perfect for this line of work?
4. Compare the determination of Two Moons to the determination of Gabriel in reaching a dream. How do both of their "stories" reflect the story of their own ancestors?

Reading 3: Current Issues

In discussing health issues in this chapter, we covered numerous concerns for college students. One area of concern for public health officials is the constant threat of new viruses, such as HIV/AIDS, which was first identified in the 1980s. Recently, a new virus known as SARS (severe acute respiratory syndrome) appeared suddenly in Asia and spread rapidly around the globe. The following article discusses the identification of a "superspreader," one person who—unwittingly—served as an agent of the virus, spreading it to family members and the hospitals where she was treated.

BEFORE YOU READ

1. Identify at least two situations in which the perception of what happened did not accurately reflect the reality of what happened. Why do you think the perception and the reality were different, and how did that affect the people who were involved?
2. What knowledge do you have of viruses and how they are spread? Provide specific examples of viruses about which you have either first-hand knowledge (the common cold, for example) or background information from reading or watching the news. How much do you know about these viruses?

A "Superspreader" of SARS: How One Woman Touched Off Beijing Outbreak

Philip P. Pan

TAIYUAN, China—She had been running a 104-degree fever for nearly a week, and the city's best doctors were stumped. They suspected the 27-year-old businesswoman was suffering from a new flu rumored to have appeared in southern China, but [they] knew nothing about how to treat it. So the patient and her family decided to go to Beijing.

It was a simple decision, the woman recalled recently, because the nation's best hospitals were in Beijing, only 250 miles to the northeast. Her husband and a friend rode with her in the ambulance, while her mother and a doctor followed in a car. The trip took nine hours, including a delay caused by a flat tire.

At the time, in late February, the Chinese government was still trying to hide the outbreak of the disease now known as SARS. There was no way the woman, who asked to be identified only as Yu, could have known she was carrying the new virus or predicted that Chinese authorities would later say she was the first person to bring SARS to Beijing. Neither she nor her companions wore masks, gloves or other protective gear on the journey. And when she checked into the People's Liberation Army No. 301 Hospital after midnight on March 1, the staff seemed equally uninformed and unprepared. The hospital placed her in a general ward with other patients, she said, and the doctors and nurses took no special precautions while examining her.

Thus did the world's worst outbreak of severe acute respiratory syndrome begin. Yu passed the virus to her family and friends, to other patients and [to] doctors and nurses, who then spread the disease to countless others in Beijing, eventually undermining the government's cover-up and prompting a crisis that has shaken the ruling Communist Party. As of yesterday, SARS had infected 2,514 people in Beijing and killed 175 of them.

Other people brought SARS to Beijing, too. But authorities say this daughter of urban intellectuals in impoverished Shanxi province was the first "superspreader" to arrive in the Chinese capital. She and her family were treated in three hospitals, and all three emerged as early centers of the epidemic.

Now the outbreak appears to be slowing, and Beijing's Patient Zero is back home in Taiyuan, the provincial capital of Shanxi. A slender young woman with long, black hair, Yu appears to have made a full recovery, though her eyes are slightly puffy, perhaps from tears. The disease killed both her parents, and on the sleeve of her white blouse is a black button with a Chinese character, a traditional symbol of mourning.

"What we've been through is misery and misfortune that we never could have expected," said Yu, who asked that only her surname be used to protect her privacy and make it easier to speak freely.

She emphasized that she was not criticizing the government. But her story highlights much of what went wrong in the early stages of the SARS outbreak in Beijing, and she said she hoped people in China and elsewhere could learn from it. "I hope our miserable experience will not befall others. I hope our experience will serve as a warning to society," she said. "Sometimes, fixing things after a bad result can be a good thing." Yu still can't figure out how she was infected with SARS. But the details of her February business trip to southern Guangdong province are still fresh in her mind: the long flight from Taiyuan, the taxi rides in the bustling border city of Shenzhen, the clean, airconditioned hotels in Guangzhou.

Before making the trip, she had heard reports of an atypical pneumonia spreading through Guangdong. The government denied it was serious, and her mother, a Taiyuan journalist, called colleagues in the region and was told there was nothing to worry about. Still, Yu and her brother avoided crowds and stayed in clean places.

A few days into the visit, though, on February 22, she began to feel feverish during a bus ride from Shenzhen to Guangzhou. She said she considered going to a hospital, but her husband was worried and persuaded her to fly home the next day.

In Taiyuan, she told doctors at several hospitals that she might have been infected with the atypical pneumonia in Guangdong. But because the government was continuing to play down the outbreak, the doctors were skeptical.

"They thought it was a cold and gave her normal antibiotics," recalled Yu's husband, who asked to be identified only by his surname, Chen. "The health workers were very responsible, but it's a pity. They didn't have information about SARS."

Chen said he called one of Guangzhou's largest hospitals to ask about the new illness and was told it could be a form of chlamydia. Chinese officials promoted that theory for weeks, in part because such a disease would be less serious than one posed by a new virus. But Yu tested negative for chlamydia.

Meanwhile, her fever was getting worse, and she was getting weaker, unable even to eat. On February 27, the director of the respiratory department at the Shanxi Province People's Hospital concluded the situation was serious, moved Yu to a special ward and ordered staff to wear masks when treating her.

The next day, Chen decided to take his wife to Beijing, and the doctor agreed to accompany them. By then, according to state media, Yu had infected at least 11 people in Taiyuan. The city now has more cases of SARS than any other in China besides Beijing and Guangzhou.

The family arrived in Beijing in the middle of the night and went to the No. 301 Hospital, a well-known military facility that has a special ward for senior government officials but is also open to the public.

If a new virus was spreading through China, certainly the doctors at this hospital would know about it, Chen recalled thinking. But he was wrong. "The illness appeared in Guangdong last November. How could a national-level hospital not receive the necessary notice?" he said.

Yu said the hospital waited three days to transfer her from a room she shared with other patients to her own room in the respiratory ward. Chen credited a young doctor who searched for information about the new illness on the Internet. But the virus was moving quickly.

Both of Yu's parents came down with fevers. They tried to hide the fact, hoping not to upset their daughter. But on March 4, Yu's mother was admitted to the No. 301 Hospital. Her father flew to Beijing and checked in, too.

On March 5, Yu and her parents were moved to the People's Liberation Army No. 302 Hospital, because it specializes in infectious diseases. But Chen said the ambulance driver and medical staff took no safety precautions during the transfer.

Frustrated, he called a major state-run newspaper in southern China from his hotel room the next day, hoping to raise an alarm about the disease, he said. "We said, 'This disease is very dangerous and infectious. We hope the media will warn society,'" he recalled. "But the woman said, 'We've heard about this disease. We have it in Guangzhou. But we can't help you.'"

At the time, Chinese authorities had imposed a ban on reporting on the new illness. The National People's Congress, China's legislature, had just opened its annual session in Beijing. The meeting was of particular importance because it marked the beginning of a new government, with a new president and premier, and as a result negative news reports were forbidden.

Meanwhile, in a room in the No. 302 Hospital, Yu watched her father and mother, both in their early fifties, grow weaker. It became so difficult for her father to breathe, he was forced to sleep sitting upright to avoid violent fits of coughing. On March 6, a team of doctors performed a tracheotomy, but he died the next day.

Yu's husband came down with a fever next, as did friends who had accompanied the couple to Beijing. She also received bad news from home: Her year-old son, her brother and her brother's wife also had fevers. They all flew to Beijing and were admitted to the hospital.

At first, Yu said, the hospital put her son in her room. But she objected, saying the child might not have the infection, and persuaded the hospital to put him in a separate room. There were other clashes with hospital staff. Chen said some doctors and nurses avoided them, showing up only a few times a week to demand payment of their medical bills. But he said others risked their own health to help them.

Yu and her husband were in opposite rooms, and they communicated by speaking loudly from their beds and letting the sound carry across the hallway. They also watched television and saw Chinese officials continue to deny the epidemic. "We were all scared at the beginning, but when we were all lying down, there was nothing to be afraid of," Chen said. "Maybe we were just exhausted."

Yu said she never suffered serious pain or coughs, only a fever, aches and general weakness. After a few days, she and some of the others began to show signs of recovery, and doctors said they wanted to transfer them back to Taiyuan. The family resisted, arguing that they should be moved only if they had fully recovered. But the hospital wouldn't back down, saying the beds were needed for other patients.

By then, the virus was spreading among the hospital's staff, some of whom had tried to save Yu's father. On March 11, the chief of one of the respiratory wards collapsed, according to state media, and three doctors and two nurses also contracted the disease over the next three days.

It was snowing heavily on March 15, but doctors insisted on transferring Yu and her son to a hospital in Taiyuan. They departed at 4 p.m. but, because of the weather, did not arrive until 6 a.m. And while the ambulance made its way along the mountain roads, Yu's mother died in the No. 302 Hospital. That same day, the World Health Organization issued its first global warning about SARS.

It is unclear how many people Yu infected before leaving Beijing; epidemiological work in the city has been haphazard. One state-run newspaper reported at least 22 doctors and nurses infected with SARS in the No. 302 Hospital during that first month and "several" cases among the staff at the No. 301 Hospital, but [it] gave no information about cross-infection of patients.

State media also linked a major outbreak at the Youan Hospital in Beijing to Yu because her uncle was admitted there on March 12. At least 12 doctors and nurses at that hospital were infected, including a visiting doctor from Inner Mongolia who carried the virus back home, causing an outbreak that has infected as many as 100 people.

On April 9, Jiang Yanyong, 72, a retired surgeon at the No. 301 Hospital, accused the Chinese government of covering up the SARS outbreak, citing scores of cases at military hospitals and the death of Yu's parents. Days earlier, the Health Ministry had said there were only 12 cases of SARS in Beijing, and most of them were from Shanxi.

Chen was still at the No. 302 Hospital then, though his condition had improved. On April 11, he said, he asked when he would be discharged and was told he needed to wait seven days after his symptoms had disappeared. But the next day, the hospital suddenly released him. Two days later, state television announced that "more patients from Shanxi" had recovered and were being sent home.

On April 20, the Chinese government finally admitted a cover-up, fired the health minister and the mayor of Beijing, and launched a public campaign against SARS. For Yu, life is slowly returning to normal. Some people have posted messages on the Internet blaming her for the epidemic, but many more have sympathized with her. And while a few acquaintances and neighbors have been avoiding her, others are no longer afraid to see her.

Yu said she isn't convinced she was the first case of SARS in Beijing, but she tries not to dwell on it. "It doesn't matter," she said. "We're fine now."

AFTER YOU READ

1. Just as you did with "Gabriel's Rebellion," make a timeline of the events in this article. What do the events in this timeline tell you about the virus and its history?

2. According to the article, what events caused the spread to be so deadly? Who, according to the article, bears responsibility for the severity of the outbreak? What were some of the mistakes that were made, and what factors can you surmise were behind the mistakes?

3. How was perception (what health officials were telling people about the virus) different from reality (what was really happening) in this case?

4. Write an essay on how Yu, the 27-year-old woman in this article, must feel about the situation.
5. Investigate the spread of HIV/AIDS. Compare it to the spread of SARS. Prepare a visual aid that might be used to illustrate this comparison (Venn diagram, flow chart, or the like) that might be used to illustrate this comparison.

Compounding Your Interest: Further Readings

Armstrong, M. L., Owen, D. C, Roberts, A. E., & Koch, J. R. (October 2002). "College Tattoos: More Than Skin Deep." *Dermatology Nursing.*

Coley, B. (July/August 2002). "The Danger of Historical Amnesia." *Humanities.*

Grace, T. (September 2002). "The Meningococcal Vaccine Recommendation: What a Tangled Web We Weave." *Journal of American College Health.*

Johnston, A. (Winter 2003). "The Teaching of American History in a Time of Crisis." *Radical History Review.*

Pandina, R. (March 2002). "Drinking in College: One Professor's Personal History (Or Look Where You're Leaping)." *Journal of Studies on Alcohol.*

Ross, K. A. (March 1999). "Can Diversity and Community Exist in Higher Education?" *American Behavioral Scientist.*

Williams, D., & Clifton, D. (2001). *The 10 Lenses: Your Guide to Living and Working in a Multicultural World.* Washington, DC: Capital Books.

Worthington, J. (March/April, 2003). "Surviving the Everyday Stuff." *Careers and Colleges.*

References

Chronicle of Higher Education: Almanac Issue 2001–2002, Volume XLVII, Number 1, August 31, 2001.

Hingson, R. W, Heeren, T., Zakocs, R. C., Kopstein, A., & Wechsler H. "Magnitude of Alcohol-Related Mortality and Morbidity Among U.S. College Students Ages 18–24." *Journal of Studies on Alcohol 63*(2): 136–144, 2002.

National Institute on Drug Abuse. "Research Report Series: Nicotine Addiction." July 1998.

Wechsler, H., Lee, J. E., Kuo, M., Seibring, M., Nelson, T. F., & Lee, H. P. "Trends in College Binge Drinking During a Period of Increased Prevention Efforts: Findings from Four Harvard School of Public Health Study Surveys, 1993–2001." *Journal of American College Health 50*(5): 203–217, 2002.

Chapter 9

The Bottom Line: Managing Your Money in College

This chapter will cover the following topics:

Tuition. Books. Food. Rent. Entertainment. Car payments. Insurance. Clothes. As you know, these things don't come cheaply. College is expensive. You are aware of this already, even if you've only been in college for a little while. But effectively managing what little money you have now can make an enormous difference in your finances both today and for years to come. And understanding how to manage your money can be a very valuable learning experience in itself, an experience that is not as difficult as it may sound. The next few years in college can provide all the experiences you need to be ready to handle money when it really counts. Of course, as all the previous chapters in this text have shown, college isn't just about money—either having it or making it. But understanding money's role and managing it effectively will relieve you of a lot of pressure over the next few years. Thus, instead of seeing money management as a burden, see it as an opportunity.

First Things First

"A penny saved is a penny earned." Ben Franklin's words about savings may be difficult to grasp when you feel like you don't have much money to save. On the other hand, you also don't want to spend what you haven't already earned and simply trust that someday you will be able to pay the bills. Most college students take on some debt. In fact, according to a study cited in *Consumer Reports*, new college graduates leave school with an average debt of $17,000 in federal loans alone (2002), not to mention other loans and credit card debt, which we will discuss later. You need to know what you are getting into and how much debt is

---

Think About It

Answer the following questions in the space provided.

What are some ways in which you can save money as a college student (not to put money away as savings, but to spend less up front)? _____

_____

_____

_____

reasonable for you. You also need to decide whether earning some money now, instead of just borrowing, might be a worthwhile use of your time. The best thing to do now is to look ahead: Where do you want to be financially five years from now? How much money do you really need? Can you afford to work while you are in college? Can you afford *not* to work? What debt will you feel comfortable having when you leave school? What do you plan to do to pay back your debts? What can you do now to reduce debt? Invest in a simple financial plan now in order to prepare for your future. Remember, money is not an end in itself in college, but it is a means to an end. The end in college is opening yourself up to the world of new ideas and new experiences. Managing your own finances will be one of those new experiences. You just have to discover ways to do it responsibly and creatively. In the words of Ken Hakuta, "Lack of money is no obstacle. Lack of an idea is an obstacle."

Managing Your Finances

Learning to manage your finances is an important part of your education. This may well be the first time in your life that you have to manage your finances entirely on your own. If you learn how to handle your money, bills, and loans now, you will be better prepared to handle your money when you get your first job after college. But what does managing your finances mean? Just what should you be managing now? Consider the following:

► Any income (from part-time jobs, from savings, from parents or other relatives, from loans)
► Loans
► Bills (car payments, credit cards, rent, and the like)
► Expenditures
► Future planned expenditures

Consider the case of Melinda, a junior business major at a large urban university with a heavy course load, a busy social schedule, and a part-time job. Melinda

What Worked for Me

Larry, a marine biology major, was so concerned about money in college that he pushed himself to work as much as possible. "On paper," he said, "I thought it would be doable to work thirty hours a week in addition to taking fifteen credits." Those thirty hours, however, were on the overnight shift at a local warehouse. As the semester wore on, Larry found it increasingly difficult to make his 9:00 a.m. biology class. "I would get home at 7:00 a.m., take a shower, grab a bagel, and head right to class. After a while, though, I would flop onto the bed before taking a shower and fall asleep." Larry had to withdraw from the biology class and take it in the summer. "When I took biology again, I realized I was paying for something that I would have gotten out of the way the first time if I hadn't been working so many hours. I have cut my work schedule in half and have refocused on graduating on schedule. I learned that putting the time into my course work is more valuable in the long run. Otherwise, I would be spending many more years at the warehouse at minimum wage instead of working as a marine biologist at a decent salary."

always knew she wanted to own a restaurant someday. She wanted to be the one in charge—responsible for the décor, the theme, the menu, and the staff. She thought it made sense, then, to work in a restaurant while in college in order to learn the business from the inside out. Accordingly, in her sophomore year she started waitressing at an upscale restaurant about half an hour from campus. She began working just on the weekends, but soon she was working five nights a week and even assisting the manager on busy nights. Although the money was good, the rest of her life was not. She was carrying fifteen credits and also was involved in her sorority. She felt she was always on the run. When she got her mail, for instance, she just threw it in the back seat of her car on her way to work. The bills would sit in the back seat with the junk mail. She always cashed every paycheck and never got around to opening a savings account. With all that cash on hand, it was easy to spend it—money for take-out instead of cooking in her apartment, money to pay someone to type her papers because she never had any time. Soon, her car payments were late and she never seemed to have money when she needed to buy something, even though she worked all the time. She knew something needed to change. What needed to change was that Melinda needed to learn how to manage her finances.

Managing your finances is all about planning and organization. Think about what you learned about time management in Chapter 2. The same principles apply. Just as a lack of time management may result in lower grades, a lack of financial management may result in a lack of money, a poor credit rating, and a lot of stress.

Here are some very important things to consider in coming up with a sound plan to manage your finances:

Never spend money you do not have or money that you will need for something more important later. You should always know how much money you have in your wallet, in your savings account, and in your checking account. If you don't have money now, don't assume you will always be able to get it. It may feel great to take a spur-of-the-moment road trip or buy a new pair of sneakers when you go to the mall, but things happen. Cars break down and need repair. Projects require materials that need to be purchased. Books need to be bought for classes.

Be careful what you buy on credit. Always try to pay off your credit card balances each month. Too many students end up with very large credit card debts that are difficult to pay down or even pay at all. Sometimes students are unable to make credit card payments when the money is tight. This could damage your credit rating, which could seriously affect your long-term financial picture. Late payment of any bill is usually reported to a credit reporting bureau. If you still are able to get credit down the road, you may have to take out a loan with a higher interest rate than someone with an unblemished record of paying on time. (For example, someone with good credit may be able to get a loan at an interest rate of 4.25 percent, whereas someone with poor credit may have to pay 6.50 percent. Over time, the person with poor credit will end up spending more hard-earned money on interest.)

Sometimes it is better to wait to make a major purchase. Let's say that you see a new stereo system on sale that you have been hoping to buy. If you buy now on credit because you don't have the money up front, it may cost you more when all is said and done, because of the interest you have to pay, than if you had waited a couple of months and bought the stereo with cash.

Pay Down. Always pay down high-interest loans first; this results in a "virtual savings."

Open up a checking and savings account at a bank on or near campus. The danger of not having a checking or savings account is that any money you make may be too readily spent if you have cash lying around. A checking account is particularly convenient because you can put any money you earn into the account and then write checks to pay bills. At some banks you can use your checking account to do online banking, which is very convenient. You should learn how to manage a checking account while you have a smaller amount of money to deal with and fewer bills, in preparation for your first "real" paying job. Also, having a savings account will encourage you to put some money away on a regular basis to watch your balance grow. And if you run into an emergency or need to make a major purchase, you will have somewhere to go for money other than your credit card. Finally, if you have a checking account on or near campus, you will be able to cash or deposit checks instead of having to wait until you go home.

Learn to balance your checkbook. Before you think about balancing a checkbook, you of course need to open a checking account. When you decide to do this, look for a bank that offers free checking. When checking accounts are not free, you often need to maintain a certain minimum balance ($1000 or more). College students may have difficulty doing this. Once you start writing checks, you will receive a statement in the mail each month. You need to use this statement to balance your checkbook. Examine your statement to see that all your deposits went in, that your checks cleared for the proper amount (checks that you wrote recently may not have been cashed in time to appear on your statement), that ATM withdrawals are accounted for, and, most important, that you still have money in your account so you don't start bouncing checks (an expensive mistake). Watch for small fees that banks sometimes charge (for using another bank's ATM machine, for instance); you must be sure to deduct these from your balance as well.

Pare down expenses. When you pare an apple, you cut it down to the core. When you pare down expenses, you're essentially doing the same thing: cutting down to the core of what's most important. If you're running low on money, there are really two basic things you can do: Earn more money (which may not be feasible when you're in college) or spend less money. Cutting back on expenses is often the smartest decision because earning more money often means working longer hours, which can interfere with your course work. To cut back on expenses, first you have to know what you're spending your money on. Check out the Teamwork Activity later in this chapter to see how to get started on paring down your expenses.

Use Coupons. You might think of coupon clipping as a dull waste of time: more trouble than it's worth. But let's say you wanted to buy a Sunday paper that costs $1.50. You can make that paper pay for itself and then some if you clip out the coupons inside and use them to buy things you were going to need to buy anyway. If it takes you ten minutes to cut out coupons, and you've saved $10.00 by using them, that's like earning about $60 an hour. That's three to four times more than you're likely to make while you're working in college.

Consider renter's insurance. If you rent an apartment in college or after you graduate, consider purchasing renter's insurance. Many renters mistakenly assume that the insurance that the landlord has on the property also covers the renter's possessions. This can be a costly mistake in the event of a fire, flooding, or even a theft. Landlords are responsible for covering only the property itself; you are responsible for what you have in your apartment. This type of insurance is available at a very low cost and is well worth the investment.

DIY-Do-It-Yourself Activity

Make a budget covering your current financial situation. First, figure out what income you have right now (include money you earn from jobs as well as what you get from parents, relatives, scholarships, grants, and student loans). Then figure out what you are spending. Include only actual expenses (in other words, if your room is paid for by your parents, don't include that). When you add it all together, you will get a better sense of where you are spending your money, and it may also be clearer how you can save some money.

Keeping a Budget

Sometimes handling your money can be a problem. It could be a problem because you have very little money, or it could be a problem because you don't know how to spend what you have. Think back to Chapter 5 and what you learned about solving problems in the real world. A good critical thinker identifies a problem, examines possible solutions, and chooses the best solution. Keeping a budget can sometimes be a solution in itself to the problem of how to spend the money you have. It can also alert you to possible problems and possible solutions if you are spending the money in the wrong way. In any case, it is a good idea to learn how to keep a budget. It may seem like a lot of effort in the beginning, but the longer you do it, the more like second nature it will become. And your finances will be in much better shape! You will save time and money in the long run if you keep a budget. Here are some things to keep in mind:

Budgets rarely work out exactly. Estimate as best as you can, and then make adjustments as necessary.

Keep the budget simple to start. Don't worry about remembering every little thing. Be basic at first. Think major bills and monthly expenses. Keep a monthly budget and try to remember to record as much as you can throughout the month. At the end of each month, assess how you have done in terms of accuracy and the time spent on the budget.

Determine your monthly income. Determine how much money you will make or have each month. Here are some likely sources:

► Job earnings
► Money from home (parents, other relatives)
► Savings

Define major categories for your budget. Here are some of the possible major categories:

► Fixed expenses (rent, electric bill, magazines, phone bill, insurance)
► Short-term savings (new TV, video game, etc.)
► Long-term savings (new car, trip abroad, etc.)

Figure out the average cost per month for fixed expenses. The amount due each month for certain things, such as cell phone charges and electricity, vary from month to month. Car payments and rent do not. Do the best you can to determine what the average cost for each budget category will be. You may also have to base certain costs on what you *have* to spend. Certain bills you can make lower; you can reduce a cell phone bill or clothing bill by talking or spending less, for example. After the first month or two of keeping your budget, try to figure out whether you will have enough to pay the bills each month. Here are some examples:

► Rent: $400 a month ÷ 2 (if you have a roommate)
► Electric bill: $42 a month
► Phone bill: $38 a month

Determine short-term savings goals. A short-term savings goal may be to save enough to buy a new stereo system or an expensive item of clothing. If you know the cost, and you don't have the cash on hand, you need to adjust your spending elsewhere and save for the item. If you needed to save $480 in four months, you would need to figure out how you could put aside $120 each month.

Determine long-term savings goals. A spring break trip to Jamaica or a new car might be an example of a long-term savings goal. Even if you do not plan to make such major purchases during college, it is wise to set aside some long-term savings. If you do have such a specific goal in mind, you will have to figure out how much you will need, how long it will take you to save it, and where you can spend less or earn more. Make this saving plan a part of your monthly budget. A good rule of thumb for long-term savings is to put aside 10 percent of each paycheck.

Consider any money left over. Money left over can be used as "fun" money to spend for things you want instead of what you need to pay for each month. Examples include eating out, CD purchases, and going to the movies.

Keep track of what you actually spend on each item or category every month. Doing so will help you determine where your money is going. You may be surprised.

There can be some variation from month to month, but overall, the amount of money *going out* should not exceed the amount of money *coming in.*

Don't take on new fixed expenses (bills that you must pay each month). Doing so will require cutting back somewhere else (for example, on "fun" money), earning more money (which you may not have enough time to do), or borrowing more money (which is not a good idea at this time of your life).

Teamwork Activity

The object of this activity is to get some perspective on your personal budget. Spend two days keeping track of your own spending. Write down all of your expenses—small and large. If you spend 65 cents on a soda, write it down. If you buy the newspaper for 50 cents, make a note of it. Once you've completed the two-day period, bring your expense sheet to class. Also include the cost of cell phone plans, rent, car payments and insurance, and so on. You can divide the monthly cost by 15 to get your two-day expense. Gather in groups of three or four students to take a look at your budgets. Then, as a group, consider ways in which each of you could save money. If anybody in the group is trying to save to buy something big in the future (a new computer, for example), work together to develop a savings plan based on these new money-saving tips. You can use the following chart as a guide. List the item and its cost in the first two columns. Indicate whether the item is a necessity or a luxury that you can live without. When you gather again as a group, think of alternatives to both necessities and luxury items. For example, eating breakfast is a necessity, but you could purchase a store-brand cereal rather than a name brand in order to generate savings. Similarly, instead of stopping at the coffee shop as a luxury on the way to class, you could generate savings by making coffee in your room or at home and bringing a travel mug with you. Then calculate your total savings. This exercise will be good practice in formulating the personal budget plans that will be indispensable when you are out entirely on your own after you graduate.

Two-Day Expenditures/Savings Plan

Item	Cost	Necessity?	Luxury?	Alternative	Savings

Working versus Not Working

Getting a good job is a goal of most college students. After all, you are aspiring to careers open to those who hold a college degree. But what about working now, while you are in college? Is it a good idea? That is a good question. And one with different answers for different people. You have to take the time to discover what is best for you.

The types of jobs open to college students are as varied as the students themselves.

Some of the quickest and easiest jobs to find are **on-campus** jobs. Many on-campus jobs are earmarked for students who qualify financially for work-study programs. But not all jobs are. If you are not sure, ask. There are advantages to holding an on-campus job. For one thing, on-campus jobs are convenient because they are close by; you can work an hour here and there between classes and put in hours during the day when other students might be wasting time. On-campus employers are used to working with students (and they probably were also students themselves). They understand that you may need to study or write a paper one day instead of working. They also may let you change your hours if you have activities or projects with which you are involved. On-campus jobs are also a good way to get to know faculty, administrators, and staff who can share their expertise and also provide excellent references. On the other hand, on-campus jobs may be limited in the amount of money they pay. The compensation is typically fixed, and many work-study jobs pay minimum wage. The number of hours you are allowed to work in a week or semester may also be limited.

As an alternative, many students choose to pursue **off-campus** jobs. These opportunities may be more varied and often pay more money, but you must choose carefully. Many employers may not be sensitive to the time constraints of your student schedule. What starts out as a 10-hour-a-week job may turn into a 30-hour job very quickly. It is sometimes hard to say no to the money. But your school work may suffer as a result.

The question remains: Should you work and, if so, how much? One mistake a lot of students make is working so much that they fail a class. Depending on the tuition at their college or university, they may have spent more on the class than they earned at the job that caused them to fail it! This would hardly be a worthwhile investment. The bottom line is that classes come first. And you have to know how many hours you need for studying before you can determine what is left over for work.

Remember the time management formula you learned about in Chapter 2: you should expect to spend 2 hours studying outside of class for every hour you spend in class. If you are carrying 15 credits, you must reserve at least 30 hours to study in a week, in addition to the 15 hours you are in class. That equals 45 hours. If you want to get the recommended 8 hours of sleep a night, that is an additional 56 hours. You are now up to 101 hours out of a week that consists of 168 hours total. You are left with 67 hours to eat, relax, exercise, participate in campus activities, and, if you have time, work. That's less than 10 hours each day if you consider weekends.

A first-year student with a full-time course load should try to work no more than 10 hours a week. It is possible to work more hours a week if you are going to school only part-time. It's too difficult to try to do both. College is still too new, and there are a lot of adjustments you need to make. In addition, you don't want to be working so much that you miss out on other aspects of the total college experience. Remember the benefits of campus involvement that we discussed in Chapter 7. Those benefits are often worth much more than earning a few dollars.

If you are still wondering whether to work, it may be better not to, at least for a while. Many campus jobs can be obtained in the middle of a semester or during the spring semester, after you have seen what you are able to handle in the fall. If you are taking some difficult courses and may need extra help, working would not be the best option. Also, if you have heavy reading courses and are not a quick reader, or if you are enrolled in labs or studio courses that may demand extra hours of studying outside of class, you may want to hold off on working for that semester. Overall, it is better to start out small. Try a few hours a week to see whether you are still able to handle the work as well.

Then see how it goes financially. If you just need to put gas in the car or pay your way on the weekends to have a little fun, a few hours a week should suffice. If you need to work to pay for books or tuition, you may want to consider a reduced course load.

Time-Out Tip

If you have debts from more than one source, check your interest rates. You may want to consolidate high-interest debts into one lower-interest debt. This can save you a substantial amount of money each month. Finally, if you have a chance to pay off some of your debts, be sure to pay off the higher-interest debts first.

For more information on the advantages and disadvantages of working while in school, and whether to hold full-time or part-time employment in the summer, go to the website at http://studentsuccess.college.hmco.com/students.

Student Loan Debt

Taking out student loans is a way of life for most college students, and indeed, student loans are one of the most effective methods of paying for college. Many loans delay both payments and accrual of interest until after graduation, and they are typically at a low interest rate.

The good news about student loans is that they make paying for college a whole lot easier. Most people don't have the $10,000 or more that it costs each year to go to college. The bad news? Well, for starters, student loans are still loans—you must pay them back (or ruin your credit and face other consequences if you don't). Borrowing money is a good way to finance your education, but you need to borrow judiciously and always keep in mind the fact that you are going to have to pay loans back after you graduate. With this in mind, you want to "borrow smart" and avoid borrowing more than you need. As we have noted, the average college student graduates with over $17,000 of loan debt. That's just an average, which means that a substantial number of students are borrowing significantly more than that. Think about it. Even $17,000 is a lot of debt. And students who drop out of college with loan debt still have to pay it back, even though their career prospects are hampered by the lack of a college degree.

Just to give you an idea, a $20,000 student loan, spread out over 10 years, will cost you approximately $450 a month. Let's say you make $30,000 a year right out of college. That may be a little high or a little low, depending on what field you go into, but it will serve as our average, entry-level salary for a college graduate. That's $2500 a month. Take out $800 for taxes, retirement, and miscellaneous, and now you're down to $1700 a month. Rent: $600 (it could be a *lot* more, depending on where you live): Down to $1100. Do you want a car? $400 a month with principal and interest. You have $700 left. Now subtract the $450 for the student loan—$250. That's less than $10 a day for food and other miscellaneous expenses. Double the amount of your loan on that salary ($900 a month in payments), and you may have to live at home because you can't afford your own apartment. On the other hand, if you're careful about how much you borrow, you will reap the benefits when it comes time to repay. You will not have as high a monthly payment on top of new expenses that will arise later in your life. Also, be realistic about what you can expect to make in your field. A computer science major may make as much as $50,000 a year right out of college. A psychology major may expect to make about $25,000 a year. By all means, stay with the major you love, but try not to take on a debt load that is out of proportion to what you can expect to earn in the first few years after graduation.

Scholarships

One way to avoid too many student loans is to look into scholarships. You might think that you needed to get a scholarship before entering college, but that is not true. There are plenty of scholarships available to students already in college, and

Get Involved!

After taking a few accounting classes in his freshman year, Mitch decided he wanted to be a tax accountant. Although he was acquainted with a few people in the field, he didn't have any experience with tax accounting and knew he had to get some before he graduated. His friend Nolan convinced him to join the accounting club because he said the members actually get a chance to prepare tax returns. The faculty advisor had begun a program at the local senior citizen center, and they were always looking for students to help. In the spring of his sophomore year, Mitch and a few friends spent Saturdays at the center helping the seniors organize receipts and records and prepare their returns. Mitch's "clients" were very grateful, and Mitch received real-world experience in return. This experience helped Mitch get the internship he wanted the most—at a top accounting firm in New York.

many of them are right on your own campus. Check with the financial aid office. Don't hold back because you think only the class valedictorian gets a scholarship. There are literally thousands and thousands of scholarships out there, many of them in surprising places. Check out your parents' places of work: They might have a scholarship. Local civic groups, scholarships for paper deliverers, local businesses, churches—the list goes on and on. Some of these scholarships are not well advertised, either, and some have few (and sometimes no) applicants. Do your homework, and you can find that some or all of your student loan debt is replaced by scholarship. Even a $100 scholarship is $100 less that you don't have to pay back. And it looks good on your résumé. Your best source of scholarship information is your campus financial aid office. One warning: Beware of scholarship search services that charge you a fee. Some may be good, but often they are doing little more than supplying information that you can track down on your own—at no cost at all.

Credit Card Debt

The average college student now graduates with over $17,000 in student loans and over $2000 in credit card debt (Manning, 1999). Some students exceed that average by thousands (and even tens of thousands) of dollars. If you can beat the average by even a few thousand dollars, you can avoid delaying your ability to move to the next stages of your life: buying a car, getting married and having children, buying a house, and so on. The debt trap is as big a problem for college students as it has become for the rest of America.

As a college student, you will be inundated with credit card offers. You are a prime target for credit card issuers because they all want you to sign up for their card before you sign up for someone else's. Besides receiving flyers, you will probably see tables set up on campus enticing you with low interest rates and free

gifts. Just be aware that the low interest rates often expire after just a few months or may apply only to balances that you transfer from other cards. And you will pay for those "free gifts" over and over again if you carry a balance. As a college student, you are also less experienced financially than other credit card users and are therefore more likely to carry a balance rather than paying it off each month. Here are some tips for credit card use:

- ▶ If you think you need a credit card, get just one. That one should be a major credit card that can be used anywhere.
- ▶ Steer clear of smaller credit cards such as those offered by stores and catalogues.
- ▶ Look for the lowest interest rate and *no annual fees*. Be sure that interest rates are not temporary, introductory offers.
- ▶ Keep a low credit line. Resist offers to increase it.
- ▶ Use your card only for emergencies or for items you know you can pay off at the end of the month.
- ▶ Don't fall into the trap of paying only the minimum on your credit cards, because if you do this you will end up paying enormous amounts of interest. Pay off the entire balance each month. Consistently following this advice throughout your life will be one of the greatest money-saving moves you ever make. Incidentally, don't fall for the card issuer's occasional offers of a "payment holiday," meaning that there is no minimum payment that month.

This is an attempt to fool you into thinking it will cost you nothing to carry your whole balance that month. But because interest continues to be assessed, you wind up paying more—which of course was the company's goal in the first place. Don't be fooled. *Pay off the entire balance each month.* If you always do this—but *only* if you always do this and never make a late payment—you will be beating the credit card companies at their own game and borrowing money, for short periods of time, at no cost.

▶ Don't use your card for impulse purchases.

▶ Don't get in the habit of using it everyday or for minor purchases—you will lose track of how much you owe.

▶ Never allow friends to borrow money by putting a purchase on your credit card with a promise to repay you—if they can't afford it at the time of purchase, they may not be able to afford to pay you back before the bill is due, if at all.

▶ Be sure to avoid late payments. Most credit cards charge you a penalty fee when your payment is late. Also, take into account the amount of time your payment will take to get to the credit card company through the mail. Most will charge you a late fee even if you claim to have mailed it "in time." What matters is when it arrives. Send your check at least a week before the payment must reach its destination.

▶ Avoid taking out cash advances. Most credit card companies charge you a fee for this service, and interest begins accruing from the moment you take the money, whereas for regular purchases, you usually pay no interest until the bill is due.

▶ Keep track of where your credit card is—if it gets lost or is stolen, call the issuer immediately to cancel it.

The problem with credit card debt is that, because of the relatively high interest rates, you can pay the minimum without making much of a dent in the amount you owe. The following chart details exactly how the debt trap works. As you can see, this chart details the process of paying down a credit card debt over a 72-month period.

As you can see from this chart, getting out from under your debt on even a relatively low-interest credit card can take quite a lot of time, and you end up paying an extra $4018 in interest payments—money that you could have used for something else. Of course, if you have a higher-interest credit card at 17 percent or 18 percent, or even over 20 percent, you are going to be paying more and more interest and less and less principal. Also, this chart assumes that you haven't made any additional purchases, something that is hard to do once you have gotten into the habit of charging it and forgetting it.

The best way to handle credit cards is to keep in mind that they are not a source of free money. In fact, using credit cards without paying off the balance every month is one of the most expensive ways to borrow money. Although they can be convenient, credit cards can also become a burden if used improperly.

Assumptions: Graduated from college with $10,000 credit card debt.
  No new purchases are made on this credit card.
  Can afford to make a monthly payment of $200 after other living expenses.

Monthly Pmt: 200

Interest Rate: 12.74%   **Daily Periodic Rate:** 0.03490%
Note: Accrued interest is based upon 30 days/month.

MONTH	BALANCE	MINIMUM PMT	BALANCE AFTER PAYMENT	ACCRUED INTEREST	NEW BALANCE
1	10,000	200	9,800	103	9,903
2	9,903	200	9,703	102	9,804
3	9,804	200	9,604	101	9,705
4	9,705	200	9,505	100	9,604
5	9,604	200	9,404	98	9,503
6	9,503	200	9,303	97	9,400
7	9,400	200	9,200	96	9,297
8	9,297	200	9,097	95	9,192
9	9,192	200	8,992	94	9,086
10	9,086	200	8,886	93	8,979
11	8,979	200	8,779	92	8,871
12	8,871	200	8,671	91	8,762
13	8,762	200	8,562	90	8,651
14	8,651	200	8,451	88	8,540
15	8,540	200	8,340	87	8,427
16	8,427	200	8,227	86	8,313
17	8,313	200	8,113	85	8,198
18	8,198	200	7,998	84	8,082
19	8,082	200	7,882	83	7,965
20	7,965	200	7,765	81	7,846
21	7,846	200	7,646	80	7,726
22	7,726	200	7,526	79	7,605
23	7,605	200	7,405	78	7,482
24	7,482	200	7,282	76	7,359
25	7,359	200	7,159	75	7,234
26	7,234	200	7,034	74	7,107
27	7,107	200	6,907	72	6,979
28	6,979	200	6,779	71	6,850
29	6,850	200	6,650	70	6,720
30	6,720	200	6,520	68	6,588
31	6,588	200	6,388	67	6,455
32	6,455	200	6,255	66	6,321
33	6,321	200	6,121	64	6,185
34	6,185	200	5,985	63	6,048
35	6,048	200	5,848	61	5,909
36	5,909	200	5,709	60	5,769
37	5,769	200	5,569	58	5,627

38	5,627	200	5,427	57	5,484
39	5,484	200	5,284	55	5,339
40	5,339	200	5,139	54	5,193
41	5,193	200	4,993	52	5,045
42	5,045	200	4,845	51	4,896
43	4,896	200	4,696	49	4,745
44	4,745	200	4,545	48	4,593
45	4,593	200	4,393	46	4,439
46	4,439	200	4,239	44	4,283
47	4,283	200	4,083	43	4,126
48	4,126	200	3,926	41	3,967
49	3,967	200	3,767	39	3,806
50	3,806	200	3,606	38	3,644
51	3,644	200	3,444	36	3,480
52	3,480	200	3,280	34	3,314
53	3,314	200	3,114	33	3,147
54	3,147	200	2,947	31	2,978
55	2,978	200	2,778	29	2,807
56	2,807	200	2,607	27	2,634
57	2,634	200	2,434	25	2,460
58	2,460	200	2,260	24	2,283
59	2,283	200	2,083	22	2,105
60	2,105	200	1,905	20	1,925
61	1,925	200	1,725	18	1,743
62	1,743	200	1,543	16	1,559
63	1,559	200	1,359	14	1,374
64	1,374	200	1,174	12	1,186
65	1,186	200	986	10	996
66	996	200	796	8	805
67	805	200	605	6	611
68	611	200	411	4	415
69	415	200	215	2	218
70	218	200	18	0	18
71	18	18	0	0	0
72 (6 Years)	0	0	0	0	0
Total Paid		14,018	Interest Paid	4,018	

The Hard Way

"I can't believe that six months has changed my entire life!" Tanya, a former business major, moaned to her counselor as she tried to figure out a plan to get back into school. What Tanya was talking about was a bad relationship that lasted for six months and from which she has yet to recover. Tanya met Rick at a dance club in a town close to campus. He swept her off her feet, and she was engaged to him a month later, even though she was only a junior in college. What she didn't know when she met Rick, however, was that he was a manipulator. Tanya had been very lonely after the death of her mother and had never had a serious boyfriend. Rick seemed to be the answer to her problems. But in fact, he was the cause of many problems to come. In the beginning, Rick showered Tanya with the attention she craved, but what he lacked was a job. He kept asking Tanya for money, and she bought him presents to keep him around. He didn't have a car, so she always lent him hers. He had no money for rent. She bought him a keyboard and a computer on her credit cards. She even bought him a cell phone and he ran up the bill. She soon discovered he had no interest in getting married and that he was actually seeing someone else on the side. After six months of this, she was so depressed she stopped going to class. She flunked all her classes, lost her financial aid, and had to drop out of school— and she was up to $10,000 in debt on her credit cards. Tanya is now working full-time at a sports equipment shop and part-time as a waitress to pay off all her bills. She has learned a tough but valuable lesson. She has thrown away her credit cards and is working to return to school next year. "I wasted a lot of money and time on Rick. I only wish I had known then what I know now. No one else should go through what I went through."

Pitfalls to Avoid: Life Lessons from Those Who Have Been There

Even though your first year in college is full of new experiences, you don't have to learn everything for yourself. You can pick up a lot from the experiences of others who have already been where you are, and you may be able to avoid making the same mistakes that others have. Here are a few examples of students who experienced some common pitfalls and how they solved their problems.

Pitfall	Consequence	Solution
Joe became known as the pizza man on his floor because he always organized the late-night pizza orders. He would pay the delivery person up front to make it easier and then try to collect the	Joe ended up treating many of his friends to pizza. That's because some of them never got around to paying him back, or promised they would and never did, or gave him less money than they	The next semester, Joe made sure everyone put the money in a "pizza fund" before he placed the order. Only those who paid ate. Now Joe has more money of his own to spend on other things.

(Continued)

Lifeline

Are you having trouble paying for college? Are your monthly bills overwhelming you? You may not realize it, but your campus financial aid office is available for more than just filling out the FAFSA (Free Application for Federal Student Aid) and checking out your aid package. The financial aid office can also give you advice on alternative sources of funding and deferred-payment plans, and it can direct you to work-study positions on campus. If you feel you're drowning in bills, be sure to seek help at the financial aid office before things go too far. This office can also make sure that you have enough credits to continue receiving financial aid—generally 24 credits earned in a calendar year.

Pitfall	Consequence	Solution
money from everyone who ate the pizza.	should have. By the end of the semester, he was out of his spending money.	
Belinda the borrower always took out the maximum amount on her student loans. After her tuition, room and board, and books were paid for, she ended up with extra money. She thought this was great because she was able to go out at night and buy clothes when her friends were unable to do so.	By the time Belinda graduated from college, she was over $20,000 in debt and was concerned because she wanted to go to graduate school. She realized that she did not want to take out any more loans because the last time she did so, she spent extra money unwisely.	Belinda applied for and received a graduate assistantship that paid her tuition and gave her a small living stipend. She decided to force herself to live within her means and not take out any more loans. She cooked at home and purchased items only when she had the cash on hand and found a good sale.
Max the minimum payer ran up a huge credit card bill by the end of his freshman year in college. During the first week on campus, he was enticed to get a credit card when a company had a booth in the student center and offered free gifts. He used this card to buy purchases he would not have made if he had had only cash— CDs, clothes, concert tickets, and so on.	The problem was not only that Max ran up a huge credit card debt but also that he paid only the minimum balance each month, never getting ahead and paying way too much interest.	Max cut up his credit card and now has a part-time job to earn some extra spending money and pay off his credit card balance. He now pays as much as he can each month and will soon be free of credit card debt.

Increasing Your Yield:

Readings for Practical Application

This chapter has examined the financial aspects of being successful in college. You have learned about the merits (and the pitfalls) of working, student loans, and credit cards. You have learned how to manage your finances and keep a budget—and about some things to avoid.

Perhaps you are now convinced that managing your money in college and beyond can be as important an investment as preparing academically for your future career. The readings that follow are also a two-fold investment.

Because of the subject—money—this chapter has also been about numbers. Accordingly, the first reading, "A Textbook Case," comes from a math textbook. After examining the strategies recommended for reading a math text, you can apply them to the selection.

The "Life After College" reading in this chapter, "Working Your Degree: Applied Math Becomes More Popular Among Students," covers career options for math majors. You might be surprised at some of the possibilities.

Finally, in conjunction with the chapter's theme of finances, the "Current Issues" selection, "The Basics: Protect Yourself from Identity Theft," gives some important information about a risk everyone faces.

These readings will give you the opportunity to explore the unique and challenging discipline of mathematics while also building upon the financial theme of this chapter.

Reading and Study Tips: Math

Unique Features and Comprehension Strategies

Math textbooks require interactive learning. Think about it. You cannot simply read math. You also cannot just sit in class and listen or "tell" your professor an answer on a test. You must "do" math, and therefore, you must do the problems in your math textbook. Math textbooks are highly interactive. Even before the practice problems that may appear at the end of a chapter, the textbook author will engage you in problems that explain the concepts. Don't just read the words; work through the problems with the author. **For the most part, don't memorize. Although you do need to memorize some basic rules, math is not about memorization. Instead, you must understand the concepts in order to build upon them. Memorizing how to work through a problem will only get you through that problem. Change the numbers, and your whole strategy will backfire. Ask yourself why you are doing what you are doing in each problem. Even formulas need to be understood to be fully remembered. You must apply formulas. If you have simply memorized them as you would memorize a person's name or a date, you may not understand them and will probably forget them. Don't just "plug and chug"; in other words, don't just put numbers into formulas to get answers with no idea why. Understand the why, and you will be able to do any other problem of the same type.**

Math textbooks provide many examples. This type of textbook gives you examples and then follows them up with problems that you have to work through in order to understand the concept. **Do not skip any of the steps that were included in the example, and do them in the order shown. Speaking more generally, there are three simple steps to follow when reading a section of a math textbook:**

1. **Ask yourself, "Why is the author doing what he or she is doing?"**
2. **Cover up an author's example of a problem or concept (put a piece of paper over it), and try to reproduce the same one.**
3. **Try to come up with a similar example on your own to see whether you understand it.**

For each rule make up simple examples and pictures that are unique to you (such as a picture of a building on a flat piece of ground illustrating 90-degree angles). Personal examples are always more powerful than examples provided for you. Just the act of thinking them up helps you to work through a rule or concept and see whether you understand it thoroughly. Furthermore, you will remember better what you have written in your own words. In addition, make up flash cards of examples or homework problems. Mix the cards up to try to do the problems out of the context in which you originally learned them. This is excellent practice for tests.

Math textbooks are filled with numbers and formulas. This may sound obvious, but it is worth discussing because a textbook full of numbers and formulas can be daunting, especially for a student who has no intention of majoring in math or anything math-related. Don't be overwhelmed. Although you may not understand at first glance, the examples and problems will help you comprehend. The numbers and formulas are there to reinforce the concepts that you will come to understand through applying them. **Know the rules. Understand why the specific rules of math exist. Ask questions in class. Ask the professor to explain the "whys" when they don't make sense to you. Then apply the rules to what you read and work through in the textbook as well as on the tests.**

Math textbooks tend to be very graphic. Like textbooks in the visual and performing arts, math textbooks tend to be visual, but in a very different way. Photos and drawings may enliven the text or reinforce a concept, but will not be as crucial as they are in arts textbooks. Numbers and graphs are more important. You will see lots of material in boldface type, as well as many graphs and charts. Numbers and formulas are often displayed on lines by themselves so that they will stand out from the rest of the text. **Review all graphs and charts. Pay attention to what stands out in the text; this information may be very important. You may want to reproduce a graph or chart as a way to review information for a test.**

Math textbooks teach concepts that build upon one another. You need to stay on top of things. You can't afford to get behind in a math class. You have to keep up, because everything builds upon what came before. If you miss a few classes and then decide to catch up, you may not understand the new material because you have not learned the material on which it depends. The same is true of your math textbooks. You will see that the math chapters are related. **Review the basics. Math textbooks require you to apply concepts that you have learned earlier. Don't forget what you learned two chapters ago. It never hurts to go back and make sure you still know and understand what came before. Make it a point to keep up with the reading and to go to class. Get tutoring if you fall behind. Read slowly. You cannot read a math book very quickly. Slow down and get a thorough understanding of basic definitions. Take time to read definitions and rules more than once. Redo problems and examples given to you throughout the chapters. See why the problems work and how you might apply the rules to new problems.**

Reading 1: A Textbook Case

This reading is included here because almost every college student will take at least one math course in his or her college career. Math is a discipline that goes beyond the college classroom. Everyday life requires math, as you have seen in this chapter's discussions of managing money and debt. Keeping a budget definitely requires basic math skills. Many careers also require math—and not just those careers typically associated with math. Teachers, for instance, need basic math skills to compute students' grades. Artists need to use geometry in designing and executing their works. Psychologists use math in preparing and evaluating tests used in diagnosis and therapy. As a critical thinker, facility in math enables you to solve concrete problems and relate them to your own life. As you read this selection, apply the strategies you learned for reading math textbooks. When you are finished reading, think about how what you have learned is related to other areas of your life.

BEFORE YOU READ

1. How many great-grandchildren would you have if you had two children and each of their two children also had two children each? As a group, figure out how you can best solve this problem. Then try to solve it.
2. What has been your experience with math since you have been in school? Think back to when you started school. Do you find math enjoyable? Easy? Frustrating? Scary? Write about how you feel about math, including some specific experiences you have had that have shaped your attitude toward math.

Exponents and Scientific Notation

T. Pirnot

EXPONENTS AND SCIENTIFIC NOTATION

In this section, we will be able to answer the question that we posed at the very beginning of this chapter. If we were able to unravel all the atoms in your body, as though you were a great big ball of thread and then stretch out all those atoms in a straight line, how far would it reach? To be able to represent both the tiny size of an atom as well as the vastness of the size of the universe, we have to represent real numbers in a new way.

All exponent rules are based on the definition of exponents.

In order to write such very large and very small numbers efficiently, we will use exponential notation. Some examples of exponential notation are, $10^3 = 10 \cdot 10 \cdot 10 = 1,000$ and $2^5 = 2 \cdot 2 \cdot 2 \cdot 2 \cdot 2 = 32$. In general, we have the following definition.

> **DEFINITION**
>
> If a is any real number and n is a counting number, then
>
> $$a^n = \underbrace{a \cdot a \cdot a \cdot \ldots \cdot a}_{\substack{\text{product} \\ \text{of } n \text{ } a\text{s}}}$$
>
> The number a is called the **base**, and the number n is called the **exponent**.

This simple definition is the basis for all the rules for exponents that we will discuss in this section.

EXAMPLE 1   Evaluating Expressions with Exponents

Write each of the following expressions in another way using the definition of exponents then evaluate the expression.

a) $3 \cdot 3 \cdot 3 \cdot 3 \cdot 3$ b) 2^4 c) 0^6

d) $(-2)^4$ e) -2^4 f) 5^1

SOURCE: T. Pirnot, "Exponents and Scientific Notation." In *Mathematics All Around*, 2nd ed. (Boston: Pearson, 2004), pp. 292–295. Reprinted by permission of Pearson Education, Inc., publishing as Pearson Addison Wesley.

SOLUTION: a) $3 \cdot 3 \cdot 3 \cdot 3 \cdot 3 = 3^5 = 243$.

b) $2^4 = 2 \cdot 2 \cdot 2 \cdot 2 = 16$.

c) $0^6 = 0 \cdot 0 \cdot 0 \cdot 0 \cdot 0 \cdot 0 = 0$.

d) $(-2)^4 = (-2) \cdot (-2) \cdot (-2) \cdot (-2) = +16$.

e) This is not the same as d). Notice that here the exponent, 4, takes precedence over the negative sign. So first we multiply the four 2s and then insert the negative sign. Thus,

$$-2^4 = -2 \cdot 2 \cdot 2 \cdot 2 = -16$$

f) $5^1 = 5$.

Suppose in a physics class you encountered the expression $x^3 \cdot x^4$. If you did not know the rules for working with exponents that we are going to introduce, you could simplify this expression by using only the definition of exponents. You could reason as follows:

$$x^3 \cdot x^4 = (x \cdot x \cdot x) \cdot (x \cdot x \cdot x \cdot x) = x \cdot x \cdot x \cdot x \cdot x \cdot x \cdot x = x^7$$

$$\underbrace{\qquad}_{3 \ xs} \quad \underbrace{\qquad}_{4 \ xs} \qquad \underbrace{\qquad}_{7 \ xs}$$

Thus, $x^3 \cdot x^4 = x^7$.

By thinking of a simple example such as this, you can remember the following rule for rewriting certain products.

Product Rule for Exponents

If x is a real number and m and n are natural numbers, then

$$x^m x^n = x^{m+n}$$

Notice in this rule that all the bases are the same. This rule would not apply to an expression such as $x^3 y^5$ because the bases are different.

EXAMPLE 2   Applying the Product Rule for Exponents

Use the product rule for exponents to rewrite each of the following expressions, if possible.

a) $2^5 \cdot 2^9$ b) $3^2 \cdot 5^4$

SOLUTION: a) $2^5 \cdot 2^9 = 2^{5+9} = 2^{14}$

b) We cannot apply the product rule here. The product $3^2 \cdot 5^4$ contains two 3s and four 5s as factors and we cannot combine these six factors into a single expression. We could, however, rewrite this as $3 \cdot 3 \cdot 5 \cdot 5 \cdot 5 \cdot 5 = 5{,}625$.

Suppose that you wished to simplify the expression $(y^3)^4$ but did not recall the rule for doing so. Again you could use the definition of exponents and your common sense to do the simplification. Think of $(y^3)^4$ as (y^3) multiplied by itself 4 times. That is,

$$(y^3)^4 = (y^3)(y^3)(y^3)(y^3).$$

But now you can write each (y^3) as $y \cdot y \cdot y$. So we have

$$(y^3)^4 = (y \cdot y \cdot y)(y \cdot y \cdot y)(y \cdot y \cdot y)(y \cdot y \cdot y) = y^{12}.$$

We see that in this example, we multiplied the exponents to write the simplification. This leads us to the following rule for exponent expressions which are raised to powers.

Power Rule for Exponents

If x is a real number and m and n are natural numbers, then

$$(x^m)^n = x^{m \cdot n}$$

EXAMPLE 3   Applying the Power Rule for Exponents

Use the power rule for exponents to simplify each of the following.

a) $(2^3)^2$ b) $((-2)^3)^4$

SOLUTION: a) $(2^3)^2 = 2^{3 \cdot 2} = 2^6 = 64.$

b) $((-2)^3)^4 = (-2)^{3 \cdot 4} = (-2)^{12} = 4{,}096.$

PROBLEM SOLVING

The Three Way Principle in Section 1.1 suggests that a good way to remember what exponent rule to use in a particular situation is to think of simple examples. Then use the definition of exponents to recall how we derived the rule. For example, to remember whether you add or multiply exponents in simplifying the expression $(a^8)^7$, think what you would do with $(x^3)^2$. If you write this expression as $x^3 \cdot x^3 = x \cdot x \cdot x \cdot x \cdot x \cdot x = x^6$, then you recall that you are supposed to multiply exponents in this situation.

We often have to divide expressions containing exponents. For example, suppose that we wish to simplify the expression $\frac{x^7}{x^3}$. Using the definition of exponents, we can rewrite the numerator and denominator as follows:

$$\frac{x^7}{x^3} = \frac{x \cdot x \cdot x \cdot x \cdot \cancel{x} \cdot \cancel{x} \cdot \cancel{x}}{\cancel{x} \cdot \cancel{x} \cdot \cancel{x}} = \frac{x \cdot x \cdot x \cdot x}{1} = x \cdot x \cdot x \cdot x = x^4$$

This example leads us to the following quotient rule for exponents.

Quotient Rule for Exponents

If x is a nonzero real number and both m and n are natural numbers, then

This rule is fine provided m is greater than n. However, if $m = n$, then $m - n = 0$, and we have not defined what x^0 means. Also, if $m < n$, then we have $m - n < 0$, and we have not discussed what it means to raise x to a negative power. We will take care of these definitions before we give examples of the quotient rule.

DEFINITIONS

If $a \neq 0$, then $a^0 = 1$, and if n is a natural number, then $a^{-n} = \frac{1}{a^n}$.

These definitions tell us that $3^0 = 1$ and $4^{-2} = \frac{1}{4^2} = \frac{1}{16}$.

EXAMPLE 4   Applying the Quotient Rule for Exponents

Use the quotient rule to simplify the following expressions and write your answer as a single number.

a) $\dfrac{3^7}{3^5}$ b) $\dfrac{7^5}{7^8}$ c) $\dfrac{17^9}{17^9}$

SOLUTION: a) $\dfrac{3^7}{3^5} = 3^{7-5} = 3^2 = 9$

b) $\dfrac{7^5}{7^8} = 7^{5-8} = 7^{-3} = \dfrac{1}{7^3} = \dfrac{1}{343}$ c) $\dfrac{17^9}{17^9} = 17^0 = 1$

AFTER YOU READ

1. If you save three dollars on the first day of the week, save nine dollars on the second day, and continue to triple the money you save each day, how much will you have at the end of the week?

2. How many zeros are there in the numerical form of a million? In a billion? How would you write them using scientific notation? Do you enjoy figuring out this type of problem? What might this say about your interests if you do enjoy it?

3. How many memory bits does your computer have if the label on the computer states 100 megabytes? (Assume that each byte is composed of eight bits plus two more for error checking.)

Reading 2: Life After College

This reading is included to invite you to think about the many opportunities in the world of math. The article points out that few of those who major in math actually become mathematicians. There are many opportunities in business, education, computer science, and beyond. As a critical thinker, you are aware that math majors and those interested in math do not think about math in a vacuum. This article discusses applied mathematics: math for the real world. You may find that it gives you a whole new perspective on math!

BEFORE YOU READ

1. As a class, generate a list of jobs that math majors would probably be qualified to do. Then generate a list of jobs that math majors would be likely to enjoy.
2. Think about how math may help you in your current major and your anticipated future career. Are you comfortable now with the math background you have? What do you need to do in order to gain the math skills you will need in your major and career?

Working Your Degree: Applied Mathematics

S. K. Schwartz

There are those among us for whom math just makes *sense*.

They are the followers of Pythagoras. The ones who breezed through calculus. And more likely than not, the ones who can tell you how long it takes train A to catch train B—factoring in wind velocity, speed and freight loads.

They are the math majors of the world.

And despite their shrinking ranks, insiders say the undergraduate degree in mathematics remains a solid springboard for career advancement—especially when coupled with courses in computer science or economics.

"There are options out there," said Tom Rishel, associate director of programs and services at the Mathematical Association of America in Washington. "It's not just a question of being a teacher or actuary. There are all these other possibilities."

How They Fare

Mathematicians, as defined by the Bureau of Labor Statistics, use mathematical theory, computational techniques, algorithms and the latest computer technology to solve economic, engineering, physics and business problems.

They fall into one of two categories. The first, the BLS notes in its latest *Occupational Outlook* survey, is the theoretical mathematician, who develops new principles and recognizes previously unknown relationships between existing principles of math.

The second group is referred to as applied mathematicians, who use techniques such as mathematical modeling to solve practical problems in business, government and life. That can include helping companies streamline their manufacturing process or analyzing the efficacy of a new pharmaceutical product, the BLS notes.

For example, airlines frequently hire math majors, particularly those with a background in economics, to determine the amount of fuel required to fly their routes and project passenger demand and maintenance costs to produce flight schedules, *The College Majors Handbook*, published by JIST Works Inc., reports.

SOURCE: S. K. Schwartz, "Working Your Degree: Applied Math Becomes More Popular Among Students," *CNNMoney*, November 10, 2000. Retrieved on December 28, 2003, from http://money.cnn.com/2000/11/10/career/q_degree math/. Reprinted by permission of CNN ImageSource.

The number of students who major in general math is shrinking. Those who do often go on for a higher degree and eventually teach. Where such a program is offered, however, applied math is becoming the degree of choice for students looking to enter the corporate workforce.

"I would recommend an applied degree," said Carla Martin, a 1995 graduate of Virginia Polytechnic Institute and State University. "But either way I would recommend taking a few courses in computer science. When I was interviewing for jobs, the most common question I heard was, 'Do you know how to program?'"

She said companies aren't necessarily looking for a second major in compsci, or even a minor in it; they *are* looking for students who know the basics of programming.

Martin, who is back in school at Cornell University pursuing her Ph.D. to become a professor, had been working as a consultant for four years with PricewaterhouseCoopers, helping clients crunch their marketing numbers.

The Job Market

Few who major in math emerge from college to actually *become* mathematicians.

Job market data reveal [that] most these days specialize in computer science, engineering and economics, finding work in brokerage firms, investment banks, and software or consulting firms. Many ultimately, in fact, receive a double major in such concentrations, helping to enhance their marketability and earnings potential.

"Many of our students double major in economics or computer information systems, and if you talk to students across the country I think you'll find more and more the phenomenon of double majors," said Joseph Jerome, a math professor at Northwestern University. "With just an undergraduate degree in math, I'm afraid, the pickings are slim unless you get an advanced degree."

Just one-third of graduates from an applied mathematics, operations research or statistics program consider their job to be closely related to their major, the *Handbook* reveals. The majority

work as top- and mid-level managers, actuaries, computer systems analysts, computer programmers, [or] computer engineers, and in insurance, securities, real estate and business services.

About 8 percent of applied math majors end up in education, while 19 percent of general math majors teach.

"Bachelor's and master's degree holders with extensive training in mathematics and a related discipline, such as computer science, economics, engineering or operations research, should have good employment opportunities in related occupations," the BLS wrote in its latest report.

For math majors, whether they specialized in general or applied math, the Bureau notes some of the most common positions they land are:

▶ Statisticians, who analyze and interpret numerical data, including "sampling," where they obtain information about a population or group of people by surveying a small cross-section of them.

▶ Actuaries, who are used by insurance companies, pension funds and other organizations to determine risk levels in a transaction, make price decisions and formulate investment strategies. . . .

▶ Operations research analysts, who work with an organization's management team to define a performance or inventory problem. The analyst then breaks the problem down into its basic parts and analyzes each part to determine how best to increase efficiency and lower costs. Some of the larger employers of operations research analysts include telecommunications firms, air carriers, computer and data processing firms, financial institutions and the federal government.

Consulting Grows

Mathematicians held about 14,000 jobs in 1998; [in addition, there were] another 20,000 . . . faculty positions at colleges and universities, the American Mathematical Society reports.

According to Rishel of the MAA, consulting work for companies like PricewaterhouseCoopers and William M. Mercer also has become an increasingly popular career path for math majors with a bachelor's degree. Such firms seek out math-minded recruits, he said, to gather and analyze statistical data that help clients decide where to market their products, and how to do it cost effectively.

He also notes [that] the federal government, specifically the National Security Agency, hires large numbers of math grads for cryptography work, which involves encoding and decoding data. Telemetry work also is in demand, which essentially just means you pick signals out of the airwaves and translate them to determine who is using which part of the airwaves and for what.

"The NSA is one of the largest employers of math majors in the United States, but they don't talk about what they do," Rishel notes. "They just take them, and that's the last we ever hear about it."

The job market for all three leading occupations for math majors—actuaries, statisticians and operations research analysts—is expected to grow less than 10 percent through 2008, the BLS reports.

But jobs that involve computer programming are projected to grow 21 to 35 percent over the next eight years.

Paycheck Check-up
Salaries in the field can be quite high.

The *Handbook* reports that annual average salaries of general math majors with a bachelor's degree is $56,500, 17 percent higher than the average for all college grads. The average for applied mathematics graduates is closer to $53,900, which is 12 percent higher than the overall average.

More specifically, the BLS reports that operational research analysts earned roughly $49,000 in 1998, the most recent year for which data are available. The top 10 percent earned roughly $88,000 and the lowest 10 percent earned just under $30,000.

Median annual earnings of actuaries that same year were $66,000, with the top 10 percent earning $124,000 and the bottom 10 percent earning $36,000.

Lastly, the BLS reports statisticians brought in roughly $49,000, with the top 10 percent earning $87,000 and the lower 10 percent earning $28,000.

But it's not just about the money.

"Math majors do fairly well [on income], but it's a lot of hard work and you have to be willing to work hard," said Stephen Chase, associate chairman and director of undergraduate studies at Cornell University. "They should be able to handle abstractions and substantial doses of theory."

He notes, too, that there's no single personality type best suited for such a degree.

"The standard assumption is that math majors have a shy, retiring personality, and there are certainly a share of those, but we have many types of personalities and many people with a wide variety of interests outside of math."

AFTER YOU READ

1. What is the difference between a theoretical mathematician and an applied mathematician? How do you think they might differ in personality?
2. This article emphasizes the fact that math majors should also take computer science courses in college. Why?
3. What are the most common jobs for math majors, according to this article? Are you surprised by any of them? Why or why not?
4. Does this article refute the stereotype of the shy, retiring mathematician? Do you agree or disagree with that stereotype? What type of people do you feel would do best in the field of mathematics?
5. What types of activities can students participate in now to improve their math skills and explore possible math careers?

Reading 3: Current Issues

The following article is included here because of the important discussion in this chapter on students' use of credit cards and management of credit card debt. Excessive credit card debt is not the only thing to worry about when you use credit cards. Another major concern right now is identity theft. You are just beginning to develop a good credit history, and you certainly want to take all steps possible to protect your own name and credit. Just as you should be aware of the pitfalls of taking on too much debt and of mismanaging your money, so should you be aware of this important issue. Identity theft can happen to anyone. While you are reading this article, think about what you can do to protect yourself. Also, think about what careers would involve discovering identity theft and fraud and protecting people from it. Do you find this interesting?

BEFORE YOU READ

1. What do you think of when you hear the words *identity theft*? What is involved?
2. How many credit cards and forms of identification do you have? How often are they accessible to someone else? What are you doing (or not doing!) to protect your credit cards?

Protect Yourself from Identity Theft

S. Okula

Although it's well over a billion-dollar-a-year racket, most people don't lose any sleep over credit card fraud.

If bogus charges show up on your bill, or if your card is lost or stolen, you simply call the credit card issuer. Getting things straightened out takes a little time, but usually it doesn't cost you anything. Visa or MasterCard or American Express eats the losses—not you, the customer.

Of course, we all ultimately pay for credit card fraud—it's part of the reason for those sky-high interest rates. But as long as you check your statements, you're not going to be personally hurt by a credit thief. Right?

Wrong.

Two types of credit fraud can hit individuals very hard. The first is debit-card theft, which takes a direct hit on your bank account, and not on the hefty coffers of Visa or MasterCard.

The second, and [more] serious, is outright identity theft. A swindler assumes your credit identity and embarks on a spree that can last for years, even decades.

Living Large on Your Good Name

Last August, Marvin Young Jr. of Oakland, California, received a letter from Sears, Roebuck & Co., denying his credit application. The only trouble was that Young had not applied for a Sears card. Sensing trouble, Young obtained a copy of his credit report and found that more than 30 new credit cards had been issued in his name in the previous 90 days. "I almost had a heart attack," says Young, who hadn't asked for any of those accounts.

He had a pretty good idea of who did open those accounts, however. In 1990, a former roommate had obtained Young's Social Security number

SOURCE: S. Okula, "The Basics: Protect Yourself from Identity Theft," *MSN Money*. Retrieved on December 28, 2003 from http://moneycentral.msn.com/articles/banking/credit/1342.asp Reprinted with permission from the Microsoft Corporation and MSN Money, www.MoneyCentral.com.

and birth date and subsequently opened a checking account, a business and at least one credit account in Young's name.

Apparently, the warning Young placed on his credit report seven years ago expired. Now he is busy supplying stores such as Bloomingdale's and J.C. Penney with notarized affidavits to prove he is not responsible for the thousands of dollars in bills charged by the impostor.

What's most infuriating is that Young, like all identity theft victims, has to notify every single credit issuer of the fraud. That one mistake by the credit bureau can take years to untangle. "It's not easy when someone takes over your life like this," Young says, a common lament of victims of identity theft.

No agency keeps statistics on identity theft, but law enforcement agencies agree the problem is growing, with thousands of new cases being reported each month. MasterCard reported that credit card losses from identity theft in 1996 were four times greater than in 1995; Visa doesn't keep such statistics. However, the Federal Reserve Board reported to Congress in March 1997 that, overall, identity theft losses to the U.S. financial system are comparatively small. Of course the Fed, like most of America, has a major stake in easy credit. But if Fed Chairman Alan Greenspan is ever victimized, we wonder what the official reaction would be.

Names in the Trash

Make no mistake: An identity thief can ruin your life. Thieves, who may work individually or as part of large international crime rings, obtain identifying information about their victims in many ways, says Beth Givens, director of the Privacy Rights Clearinghouse, a nonprofit consumer information and advocacy program in San Diego.

They may be roommates, relatives, friends, estranged spouses or household workers with ready access to their victims' personal papers. Or they get the information by stealing a wallet or a purse, going through your trash and picking out financial statements or credit card slips, or taking your mail. Sometimes they even switch the addresses of victims to their own post office boxes and wait for the

credit applications and card renewals to come to them.

They also get essential information—including the quality of prospective victims' credit—by illegally accessing the huge databases of the three credit reporting bureaus. All have thousands of computer terminals in places like car dealerships or real estate agencies. They can shop for victims at will.

They can also get information through your employer. "We learned of a case where a member of a Nigerian crime ring was employed temporarily at a very large corporation," Givens says. "He downloaded the employee list containing Social Security numbers and then one by one the employees' identities were used for fraudulent purchases."

Identity thieves can even photocopy your vital credit information legally at the local courthouse, says Joseph Seanor, a private investigator in Alexandria, Virginia. If you've been divorced, the transcripts of your case, including the financial and credit account information you divulged as part of the proceedings, as well as your Social Security number, are part of the public record. "Why go dumpster diving?" asks Seanor.

Finding Victims Through the Internet

The Internet provides another opportunity for identity thieves to glean personal information, Seanor says. Thieves can design very official-looking e-mail messages that imply they are from a major company, and successfully obtain personal information from trusting individuals.

Once the crooks have some of your personal information, they can start applying for credit cards in your name, often giving an address that is different from yours. Sloppy credit-granting procedures give thieves plenty of opportunities. "A lot of credit granters are not checking records," Givens says. "They are more interested in new applicants than in verifying the authenticity of the applicants."

Identity thieves may buy a car or rent an apartment in your name. Some may even commit crimes in your name. Givens relates one case where the impostor was a major drug dealer using the identity of a highly ranked corporate executive. When traveling overseas, the executive has to carry an official letter that explains he is not the drug dealer. Still, cops recently broke into the man's house and into his bedroom with guns drawn.

While this is an extreme case, many identity theft victims have been denied student loans, mortgages, credit accounts and even jobs. Some wrongly have had their telephone service disconnected and their driver's licenses suspended or [have] been harassed by collection agencies.

The sad part is [that] it is next to impossible to stop a determined identity thief. Who is going to apprehend him? Occasionally law enforcement agencies, including the Secret Service, bust up identity theft crime rings that involve many victims and millions of dollars. But they don't chase down single crooks who commit "victimless" crimes.

While victims may not be liable for the credit bills an identity thief runs up, they still are compelled to spend time, effort and money to clear up the mess. "They spend hours and hours filing expensive legal affidavits and writing letters and making telephone calls to clear their good names," says Ed Mierzwinski, consumer program director for PIRG.

Looking Out for Yourself

Mierzwinski believes that both the credit-granting institutions and the credit bureaus need to improve verification systems to help prevent identity theft. But there's little chance of anything meaningful being done to make it harder for anyone to get credit. You have to look out for yourself.

"The most important thing that consumers can do is to order their credit reports once a year so they are not caught by surprise," Givens says. You can order a copy of your report online from Equifax (in most states), Experian and Trans Union. Cost: $8 in most states, unless you have recently been denied credit. Then the reports are free.

Givens and other experts also suggest the following:

▶ Don't carry unneeded credit cards, your Social Security card, your birth certificate or other personal documents in your purse or wallet.

▶ Keep track of all your ATM, credit card, debit card and other receipts. Either store them in a safe place or destroy them before putting them in the trash.

▶ Cancel all your unused credit card accounts.

▶ Keep a list of your credit card account numbers and the companies' telephone numbers in a safe place so you can cancel them quickly and easily [if ever] they are stolen or lost. A handy way of doing this is to use a copying machine. Just be careful where you leave the hard copy.

▶ Protect your Social Security number as much as you can. Do not give it out to any person or company unless you are familiar with them and you have initiated your communication with them.

If you become an identity fraud victim, PIRG suggests that you take three steps immediately:

▶ Report the identity theft to local law enforcement authorities, including the police, postal inspectors and Secret Service.

▶ Contact all banks and others where your name has been used fraudulently, sending a copy of a police report or other documentation to show that you are a fraud victim.

▶ Call the fraud departments of the three major credit bureaus to get copies of your credit report and to have fraud flags and statements added to your report saying that all potential creditors should contact you to verify credit applications.

If the first three steps fail to resolve the problem, we would add a fourth: Call a lawyer. Credit issuers and reporting agencies are sometimes slow in responding to complaints from consumers. The threat of lawsuits can provide some incentive.

For a more complete discussion of the precautions, as well as the steps to take if you become a victim of identity theft, visit the Privacy Rights Clearinghouse and PIRG Web sites.

"You ultimately cannot prevent identity theft from happening to yourself," Givens says, "but you can reduce the odds."

AFTER YOU READ

1. What are some of the different types of credit card theft? What two types can hit the hardest? Why?
2. What are some ways in which thieves can steal your identity?
3. How might college students be particularly at risk?
4. Beth Givens, director of the Privacy Rights Clearinghouse, notes, "You ultimately cannot prevent identity theft from happening to yourself, but you can reduce the odds." How can you do this?

Compounding Your Interest: Further Readings

Downing, D. (1995). *Dictionary of Mathematics Terms*, 2nd ed. Hauppauge, NY: Barrons.

Paulos, J. A. (1998). *Once Upon a Number: The Hidden Mathematical Logic of Stories.* New York: Perseus.

References

Manning, R. D. *Credit Cards on Campus: Costs and Consequences of Student Debt.* Washington, DC: Consumer Federation of America, 1999.

"Graduated Payments: There Are Ways to Get Out from Under Those Big College Loans." *Consumer Reports*, July 2002, 54–55.

Chapter 10

The Payoff: Your Career and Your Future

This chapter will cover the following topics:

Now that you are nearing the end of this textbook, you have come a long way in learning how to be a college student. Yet you may be wondering why you have to think about your career already? Or your future? It probably still seems too far away in the face of more pressing issues such as final exams and housing lotteries. But if you imagine yourself in a certain job, city, or graduate school, now is the time to start making those dreams a reality. And even if you are not sure what you want to do, it is still helpful to look ahead—in fact, it may be even more important to do so, because you have a lot of decisions to make. Now may be the time to take another look at your major or possible major, especially if you have taken a course or two as an introduction. It is also a good time to remember that it is wise not to change your major too hastily but, rather, to see what other doors may open for you in a particular major.

Thinking about possible careers now may also help you make other decisions while in college, including what activities to participate in and what courses to take. College may be one of the few periods in your life when you are exposed to so many different opportunities and ideas in one place. You don't have to commit yourself to a future path; you can just try out many different things.

If you wish to head to graduate school, or if you even think you might want to, now is the time not only to research where you might want to go but also to be sure you are getting the grades you need and to prepare for the necessary standardized tests (such as the LSAT, MCAT, or GRE). Of course, interviews are a part of this process—for graduate school as well as for that first job out of school. Preparing now for the interview process (which includes offering a stand-out résumé and cover letter) will make it less nerve-wracking when it really counts. You may be dreaming now of landing a certain job, or you may be

---

Think About It

Answer the following questions in the space provided.

Picture your ideal career. Now imagine waking up on a typical day once you are established in this career. What specific things do you picture yourself doing on this typical day? Also, describe what skills you envision needing to complete the tasks you have listed. Be as detailed as possible. _____

_____

_____

thinking about how great it will be to live in a certain city. These plans need to be backed up with hard work and research to ensure their transition from starry-eyed possibility to concrete reality.

Looking ahead can also serve as a powerful motivator. Students who have even a vague sense of direction tend to do better than those who really don't know why they are in college, no matter whether they are earning a two-year or a four-year degree.

First Things First

The French philosopher Simone Weil noted, "The future is made of the same stuff as the present." What does this mean for you? It means that the future you will have will be defined by what you do now—in your first year of college and all through your college years. That may seem like a lot of pressure, but it's really no different from what you've been doing all your life. Your performance in high school affected your placement in college, whether you thought much about it or not. Now, however, you will give yourself an advantage if you think consciously about preparing for what lies ahead. There are lots of questions to think about: What kind of job do I want? Will I need to go to graduate school? What kinds of courses should I be taking? What major should I have? What kinds of grades will I need? How do I get a good internship? You don't need to have the answers to all of these questions right now, but you want to begin thinking about them in order to be aware of all the issues involved.

Thinking Ahead: What You Should Be Doing Now

First of all, what you are already doing now—going to class, being involved in clubs or athletics, attending campus events, socializing—is very important for the present. You want to have as rich and diverse an undergraduate experience as possible. In other words, don't put all of your stock in the future—you want to enjoy the moment. But you should also make sure that the things you are doing and enjoying now are leading toward something positive. In addition to jobs, internships, campus activities, and the various other opportunities discussed in previous chapters, it is a good idea to connect the goals you have for your future and your career to resources on and around your campus that you can take advantage of now. Here are some possibilities:

▶ Spend some time in the career center on your campus. Many career centers have libraries through which you can browse for very interesting information about career possibilities, trends, salaries, and graduate schools.

▶ Talk with a few professionals in your chosen or possible career field. Ask them to talk about the day-to-day aspects of their jobs. Visit them on the job if possible.

▶ Talk with professors about your plans for graduate school. Find out where they went—especially if they are in the field you hope to enter. It is important to find out what graduate schools may be best for you and which are known for excellence in your particular field.

▶ Even though you would not be ready to take the MCAT or the LSAT (see Chapter 4 for more information on these and other tests) now, it would be a good idea to get information about what is on the test or tests you may need to take for graduate school. Planning now can help direct you to courses that will help prepare you for the test as well as for the graduate programs themselves.

What Worked for Me

"I always thought I would be the next Steven Spielberg," Andy said. "But life sometimes takes you in directions you least expect to go." As a film major in an East Coast college, Andy directed and produced a number of student films that drew rave reviews on his campus—he even won some national student awards. After graduation, he took the standard "direct to Hollywood" route, waiting on tables and looking for his "big break." He did manage to find a job as a production assistant on a couple of direct-to-video movies, but soon he realized that he could take a different direction. "I had learned a lot about production by the time I heard about an opportunity working at a major pharmaceutical company in their own video production department. After two years there, I realized I really liked the corporate environment." The following year, Andy came back to the East Coast and is now the head of production at a national chemical company. "Sometimes life leads you to far-away places, but it can also bring you home again." Andy learned that interesting and unusual opportunities sometimes exist right in front of you if you are ready to take advantage of them.

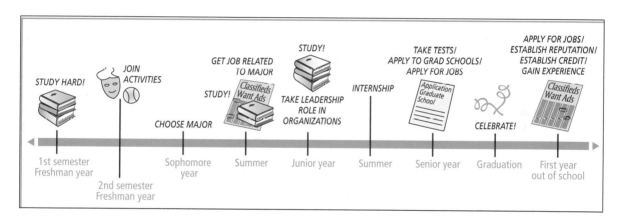

▶ If you find a graduate program you are interested in, see what courses you will need as an undergraduate so that you will be prepared when you apply.

There are so many things you can do now. If you feel overwhelmed, though, it may be easier not to do anything, so it is far better to pick one thing and devote even an hour a week to it in order to get started.

Keeping Up with Current Events

Part of the expectation most people would have of college students is that they not only know their major but also are well-rounded, educated people. They are aware of the world around them. So you'd better be aware of what's going on around you. Have you ever heard of "shooting the breeze"? In an interview for a summer job or an internship, there will be a formal part of the interview with questions you can more or less predict: "Why are you interested in this job?" "What are your qualifications?" And so on. But what about the time before the formal interview begins? The interviewer might just "shoot the breeze" by bringing up current events. When you're on the job, the stereotypical "water cooler" conversations include people's ruminations on the day's news. You want to be able to contribute intelligently. Let's say you're an art history major looking to get an internship at a major art museum in your hometown. You land an interview, during which they ask you what you think was the most important exhibition to tour the country last year. If you haven't been following the news at all, you're not going to have much of an answer, and you're probably not going to get that internship.

How, then, do you go about keeping up with current events? In the age of the Internet, it's really not that difficult. You can just click your way right to a news website. Of course there is always the newspaper for more in-depth reports, and television news provides the visuals. With any news story, you want to apply your critical thinking skills in assessing the objectivity or possible bias of a report. And you want to keep an open mind so that you can appreciate all perspectives when you are discussing current issues with people in the work world.

The career path you want to follow can also help determine which medium you use to access current events. If you are a journalism or English major, you should be reading at least one or two major newspapers each day—not just for the news but also to get a sense of style and format. Business majors are often required to get a subscription to *BusinessWeek* or the *Wall Street Journal*. Communications majors should watch the news on TV, being sure to check out the styles and points of view of several different channels, which will also yield a sense of who the major players are and why. If you make this a habit, then during a conversation with someone in the field, you'll be prepared to speak intelligently not just about the news itself but also about the people covering the news. A science or pre-med major should follow the news to keep up on how scientific advancements are being covered in the popular press. He or she would also be well-advised to get a subscription to a major scientific or medical journal. This is a relatively simple way to better prepare yourself, and in the process, you are turning into the well-rounded person you enrolled in college to become. Taking this extra step shows others how committed you are to your chosen field. And if you find you're not particularly interested in following current events in your chosen field, this may be a sign that you should consider whether a different field related to your major might be a better choice.

How Your Major Defines Your Career Choice, and How It Doesn't

By now, you may realize that more opportunities for you exist than you may have thought. Although your choice of major is important, and it does help define what kinds of opportunities you will have, it does not prevent you from seeking other opportunities not obviously defined by the major. Let's clarify. If Nate is an English major, for example, who does not take more than a science course or two as an undergraduate, Nate will not be prepared for medical school because med schools would expect him to have a solid science background. If Celine majored in studio arts, she should not expect to be offered a job as a high school math teacher, and she would have to go back to school to take quite a few math and education courses before getting her certification and applying for such a job. On the other hand, there are many jobs and graduate programs that are not as interested in your particular major as in the fact that you have a college degree. For example, many companies have training programs for people with any type of college degree—for management, sales, and account executives and many other types of positions. A graduate with a psychology degree would be a fine candidate for a sales training program at an insurance company. A graduate with a degree in education would be a possible choice for a training program at an educational software company. As you can see, the career choices you may be familiar with now in connection with your chosen major may be just a few of many other possibilities that will open up to you through good planning and research.

What do you do when you are having trouble narrowing your choice of major down to one? Now, when you are taking general electives, explore the many possibilities you have available to you while you are selecting a major. Let's say you are still attracted by two different majors. You could always just pick one, but there is another possibility: Get creative. At many colleges, you can be creative in your choice of major. You might be able to do a **double major** (biology and criminal justice, for example) or to pick a **minor** that complements your major in a unique way (a photography major with a minor in marketing). At some colleges, you can

The Hard Way

Mark and Shawn had been roommates since freshman year. As seniors, they decided to rent an apartment off campus, and they found that they enjoyed having friends over for small parties and to watch football. They shared an off-the-wall sense of humor and enjoyed playing pranks on each other and their friends. As business majors, they both began preparing for their careers in the spring of senior year. They had both had good internships and summer jobs and knew they were in good shape for permanent positions, Mark with an accounting firm and Shawn in an electronics corporation as a marketing trainee. They had sent out many résumés and were taking advantage of on-campus interviews. After a particularly good on-campus interview, Shawn was looking forward to being called back for an onsite interview at the company's West Coast office. The call never came. Instead, he received a rejection letter two weeks later. Crestfallen, Shawn tried to figure out what had happened. He called the person who had done the onsite interview. "Shawn," she said, "I really thought you did a great job in the interview. We made the calls for the onsite interview in the boardroom on the speaker phone, and when my manager heard your answering machine message, he just said, 'Next!' I'm very sorry." Shawn felt really embarrassed as he played his message back, realizing that he and Mark had never changed it to reflect their status as would-be employees. The message started with a blaring teen-pop song that they thought was funny, followed by Mark saying, "Leave a message. If we feel like it, maybe we'll get back to you." Shawn, who did change his message and find a different job eventually, shakes his head ruefully when he thinks back on it now: "We thought it was a joke at the time, but the joke was on us."

even **create your own major** by working with a professor or a committee to develop a unique program that draws on several existing programs in such a way as to meet your individual needs.

Let's go back to Nate, the English major who wants to go to medical school. Because he waited until after he graduated to make this decision, he is facing a year or more of science courses before he can even take the entrance exams. If, instead, he had double-majored in English and biochemistry, he would have been able to pursue his interest in literature and prepare himself for medical school at the same time. Celine, if she really wanted to be a math teacher, could have pursued her teaching degree while minoring in studio arts, thus making herself even more marketable as a job applicant because she could do more for the school. Even though your choice of major will play a role in shaping the opportunities you will have upon graduating, this doesn't mean you will have to do one thing for the rest of your life just because you majored in it. And if you do have diverse interests, use a little bit of creativity, and you will find that you can study what you really like *and* better prepare yourself for opportunities after college.

Professional Organizations

Ever heard of HOSA? How about AIAS? If you haven't, you might want to find out about some professional organizations related to your field. HOSA is the Health Occupation Students of America (*www.hosa.org*), and AIAS is the American Institute

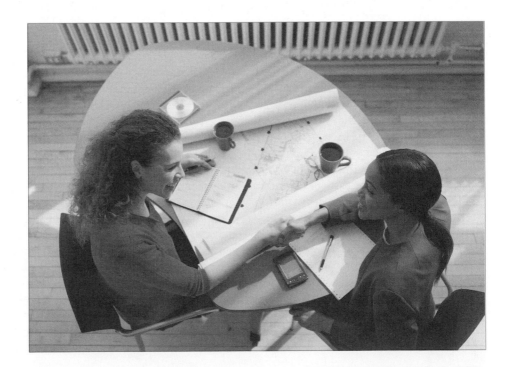

Get Involved!

Ever since he was a kid, Marty had always liked working on computer hardware, taking computers apart, and putting them back together again. His friends and family always knew he could help them if something went wrong with their computers or if they had a question about how to set something up. When he went to college, he decided to study computer science to become a software engineer. During his sophomore year, one of his professors recommended him for a job in the IT department as a troubleshooter who went around campus helping people solve computer problems. In the process of doing this, he gained a lot of valuable knowledge about both software and hardware, which helped him in his coursework. It opened a lot of doors for him, and when he went for interviews he was well-prepared. Before graduating, he landed a job as a printed circuit board designer for a major computer manufacturer.

of Architecture Students (*www.aiasnatl.org*). Most such organizations encourage student membership, and these memberships not only look good on a résumé but can also provide you with some great experience and connections. In addition, such organizations are a good source of information about the field, which can help you decide whether that profession is really what you want. For more information about organizations related to your major or future career, see the website.

Why do you think provision is made for students to be affiliated with professional organizations? You are the future of your profession. Your early involvement benefits you and the profession. Being associated with a professional organization will set you apart from the rest of the pack. And who knows? The local chapter president may end up being a future employer!

Internships

An internship is frequently designed for the student to get specific training, whereas in a "job," the employee is just doing the work that needs to be done. Internships sometimes pay, and sometimes they don't. An intern will often be assigned to a mentor, will do some job shadowing (observing a person while he or she is working), and will be involved in various activities and projects that are meant to benefit the intern as much as the company or organization. For example, if you had a regular summer job at Disney World, you might find yourself shepherding visitors through the lines at Space Mountain. If you were an intern at Disney World, you could find yourself participating in staff meetings, working on public relations efforts or designs for traffic flow, or helping plan the parade down Main Street. Also, you can frequently get credits toward your graduation for internships. You can earn three or more credits for an internship in your chosen field. Some college degree programs even require internships. If yours doesn't, you still may be able to arrange one. Talk to your advisor or department chair to find out more, or see the website.

Thinking About Graduate School?

It may seem too early in your undergraduate career to be thinking about graduate school, and in a way, it is. There are a lot of things you need to do and focus on right now. As you think about your future after college, however, you may begin to wonder whether graduate school may be a necessity in your chosen field or a personal goal you wish to achieve. Graduate school is indeed a goal for many students, but it is one that demands planning and hard work in undergraduate school.

Many students come to college unaware that the field they hope to break into may require an advanced degree. Some students even end up changing their chosen major when they later find out they would need to attend graduate school to pursue a particular career. Some students look forward to spending many years as a student, whereas others wonder whether they will make it through the first four. In any case, there is no need to worry at this point about whether to extend your academic career beyond undergraduate work. You will have plenty of time to explore majors and to ponder whether or not graduate school is for you.

Obviously, most students know that if you want to become a doctor or a lawyer, you must continue going to school after you graduate from college. Many students are not aware, however, that there are many other fields that generally require an advanced degree. What is an advanced degree? It is any degree beyond your bachelor's degree. Some of the most widely known are

- ▶ M.A. (Master of Arts—a master's degree in the liberal arts, such as history, English, modern languages, and philosophy)
- ▶ M.S. (Master of Science—a master's degree in the physical and social sciences, such as biology, physics, psychology, sociology, computer science and math)
- ▶ M.Ed. (Master of Education—a professional degree for teachers in both elementary and secondary schools and in specific content areas, such as English, social studies, special education, bilingual education, and reading)
- ▶ M.S.W. (Master of Social Work—a degree for practicing social workers that often includes state licensure)
- ▶ M.B.A. (Master of Business Administration—an advanced degree for professionals in the field of business that often includes specialization in areas such as accounting, finance, and marketing)
- ▶ M.F.A. (Master of Fine Arts—a degree for artists working in areas such as painting, sculpture, creative writing, theater, and photography)
- ▶ J.D. (Juris Doctor—a degree held by practicing attorneys)
- ▶ Ph.D. (Doctor of Philosophy—a degree in a wide variety of fields covering everything from engineering and computer science to anthropology and speech communications)
- ▶ Ed.D. (Doctor of Education—a professional degree for educators in elementary and secondary education, including those who become qualified to hold administrative positions, such as principals and school superintendents)
- ▶ M.D. (Doctor of Medicine—a degree held by practicing physicians with specialties that involve training even beyond school, such as pediatrics, dermatology, neurology, cardiology, and orthopedics. Some doctors have a D.O.— Doctor of Osteopathy—instead of an M.D.

▶ D.M.D. (Doctor of Dental Medicine—a degree held by dentists)
▶ D.V.M. (Doctor of Veterinary Medicine—a degree held by a practicing veterinarian)

There are as many degrees as there are possibilities for your career field. Research is one of the best ways to learn about what you need and why, and you should try to begin this process as early as possible. A nodding acquaintance with the above degrees, however, will help. How do you know which degree, if any, you might need beyond undergraduate school? Let's begin with those types of careers for which you may need no advanced degree at all, at least to get started in the field. For example, if you are majoring in business, you will be able to begin your career right out of college. Many large companies hire great numbers of recent college graduates to fill their training programs. Students with degrees in the liberal arts and in science may find jobs this way. Students majoring in such areas as graphic design can also expect to be hired right out of college, provided, of course, that they have the portfolio to get the job. On the other hand, a student majoring in psychology who wants to be a practicing psychologist cannot expect to do so without an advanced degree. In some fields, such as teaching, you can get a job with just a bachelor's degree, but you may need to get a master's degree or take many additional credits to continue to work in the field and receive permanent certification. In some majors, whether you will need an advanced degree depends on the type of job you actually want. For example, a person graduating with a degree in English can be hired right out of college as an editorial assistant, staff writer, or public relations trainee. If he or she wants to teach English at the college level, however, a master's is a prerequisite to obtaining even a temporary job, and a doctorate is generally required for a permanent position at a college or university.

As you continue in your undergraduate career, you will have many opportunities to think about these options and to affirm or change your major or career focus. It is important to keep in mind that you should not be afraid of graduate school or worry about the money to pay for it. The biggest difference between undergraduate and graduate courses is that in the latter, you are focusing completely on one subject and becoming an expert on it. By the time you get to graduate school, you will already know a lot about your chosen field. Also, your classes will tend to be a lot smaller and more interactive. You will be responsible for directing your program in terms of what you want to focus on and which courses you want to take. And you will undoubtedly have opportunities to work in the field while you are in school. Many students are able to apply for and receive graduate assistantships in their programs and departments. These assistantships generally require the student to teach introductory courses or help professors with research. In return, the student is paid a small living stipend and receives free tuition. As you can see, the benefits are many: priceless experience, an opportunity to work professionally with experts in your field, and a chance to go to school without cost, while making enough money for rent and other living expenses and remaining debt-free.

Looking at the other side of this issue, it is also important to know when not to go to graduate school—at least not right away. If, for instance, you want to be a first-grade teacher, you may be better off getting a job and some experience before going to school for your master's. After all, your school district may also pay for your degree, and you can take classes at night and in the summer. If you graduate with a business degree, it may also be important to get some experience first to bring to the courses that often demand it. Another reason not to go to graduate school right away is uncertainty about whether you want to take this step. If you only think you *might* want to be a lawyer, for instance, it may be better to wait until you know for sure than to spend two years and a lot of money on law school only to drop out before entering your third year.

Even though it is still a few years off, and you may not really know whether you want or need to go to graduate school, there are still a few things you can do at this time. First, watch your GPA One of the primary entrance criteria is how good your grades in undergraduate school are. You should aim for at least a 3.0, but at competitive schools you may need an even higher GPA, as well as high scores on the required standardized tests (see Chapter 4). And finally, if you are a senior and still are not sure graduate school is for you, remember that many people end

Teamwork Activity

 This activity will give you the chance to research the job of your dreams. Organize yourselves into groups of four. This is the group you will return to when your research is finished. After introducing yourselves to each other, go around the group and list the career each member would like to research—software engineer, staff reporter for a newspaper, speech pathologist, clinical psychologist—wherever your interests lie. Now, in the library, at the career services office on campus, or on the web, research the career you listed and fill in the information about that job asked for in the table that follows.

	1.	2.	3.	4.
Minimum Degree Needed				
Highest Degree for That Field				
Any Certifications Which Are Necessary or Desirable				
Starting Salary				
Possible "Pay Your Dues" Starting Position (for example, holding cue cards for local weatherman as starting job for on-air news anchor)				

Reassemble into your original groups and share what you have learned. Each person in your group will have information on each job listed in the table. Allow time for everyone to ask questions, and fill in the table. You may be surprised by what you have discovered about your chosen career and about those of others.

up entering graduate school years after leaving college. Opportunities will be there for you at many different points in your career.

What People Really Do on the Job Every Day

Does being a forensic scientist sound like a really cool job to you? How about being an attorney? Or maybe you've always wanted to be an accountant—or a sports agent. Everybody has a different dream job. The idea of a forensic scientist may appeal to one student, whereas another may find the idea of doing crime scene investigations stomach-turning. Being an accountant and dealing with numbers all day might strike some students as dull, others as a gratifying challenge. A student's impression of what her or his dream job might be are shaped in part by what the student *thinks* those jobs are all about. Sometimes it's based on pretty good second-hand information ("My mother's been an accountant for twenty years"), sometimes on what the student has seen in movies or on TV ("I like that guy on that one show—that job looks like it'd be fun").

Chances are, though, that most students don't know what an accountant or a forensic scientist or a sports agent does in a typical day on the job. How could they? Well, there are a couple of things you can do now to find out. Earlier in this chapter, we've talked about internships. They are a great way to find out exactly what goes on in a particular workplace. After experiencing an internship, many students feel confident that they've chosen the right profession; others, however, decide that a particular field isn't for them. Because of the internship, they can

	Campbell	Krissy	Lorenzo	Michele	Frank
	Financial Analyst for a Major Retailer	Marketing Manager for an Athletic Equipment Maker	Physical Therapist	Attorney Specializing in Contract Law	Corporate Trainer for an Investment Firm
College degree:	B.S. in International Business; Minor in History	B.A. in Journalism	B.S. in Biology; M.S. in Physical Therapy	B.S. in Finance; J.D.	B.A. in English
Describes job as:	"Fun and interesting—I get to work with both the design aspect and the financials."	"Always something different. I work on everything from the product design to the sales."	"Physically demanding—but it keeps me in shape. I also have to do a lot of planning."	"Challenging but it can be stressful—one mistake with a comma could cause major problems. The days can be very long—but the pay is excellent."	"It's a very fast-paced environment. I often do several training sessions for different groups in one day. It's very demanding, but I thrive on the energy of the place."
7:00–8:00	Home in bed; getting ready for work	Getting ready for work	Meets with first patient; reviews chart and teaches patient exercises for sprained ankle	Arrives in office; reviews materials and begins work on contracts	Planning for first session; breakfast at desk
8:00–9:00	Commute time; bagel at coffee shop	Battles traffic into city	Meets with second patient for the first time; conducts interview	Works on contracts: proofreading, editing, writing new sections, researching applicable case law	Meeting with support staff to go over the training plan
9:00–10:00	Arrives in office; checks messages; looks at previous day's financial reports	Has a conference call with ad agency to go over a new ad concept	Staff meeting; discussion of new office procedures	Works on contracts	First training for new computer software for 200 investment analysts
10:00–11:00	Meeting with designers to discuss new product for next year's lines	Writes copy for a hang tag that will go on a new piece of equipment	Meets with third client	Meets with client to discuss contracts	Training session continues until 10:30; analyzes feedback
11:00–12:00	Meets with designers to discuss new product for next year's lines	Meets with colleagues to get feedback on copy; reviews layout sent by ad agency	Meets with fourth client	Works on contracts	Prepares for post-lunch session

Time					
12:00–1:00	Lunch with friends	Lunch with co-workers	1/2-hour lunch followed by paperwork	Works on contracts; lunch in office	Lunch meeting with senior managers
1:00–2:00	Reviews designers' proposals; begins crunching numbers	Visits local dealers in company equipment to check out displays and talk to managers	Meets with fifth client	Works on contracts	Leads a train-the-trainers session for his staff on a new support network
2:00–3:00	Continues crunching numbers	Visits local dealers of their equipment to check out displays and talk to managers	Meets with sixth client	Works on contracts	Interviews employees for an open position on her staff
3:00–4:00	Continues crunching numbers; meets with senior analyst to discuss projections	Visits local dealers in company equipment to check out displays and talk to managers	Writes up reports for daily activities; leaves at 3:30	Works on contracts	Interviews continue; discusses candidates with other staff and managers
4:00–5:00	Finishes weekly report	Begins a research project on examining the equipment being sold by competitors	Jogs in the park near the office	Works on contracts	Meets with his supervisor
5:00–6:00	Leaves office and goes to the gym for spinning class	Continues research project on examining the equipment being sold by competitors	Home	Works on contracts; has dinner in the office	Has dinner at desk; prepares materials for new training sessions
6:00–7:00	Meets friends for sushi	Meets friends after work		Works on contracts	Prepares materials for new training sessions
7:00–8:00	Meets friends for sushi	Leaves for home		Works on contracts	Prepares materials for new training sessions
8:00–9:00	Home	Home		Works on contracts; arrives home by 10:00	Leaves for home

change their major or explore other courses or options before they go any further. If you're planning to become a teacher, it is nearly certain that student teaching will be part of the curriculum. But before you even get to that point, you will probably have done numerous classroom observations. Another thing you can do to learn more about a particular workplace is to spend a day in the office. If you know someone in the field, you might be able to "shadow" him or her at work for a day. If you don't know anyone in the field in which you are most interested, talk to your career center about setting something up for you.

In the meantime, see whether any of these "typical day" scenarios appeal to you, surprise you, or affirm what you already believe.

Thinking Out of the Box When Preparing for Your Career

Ultimately, breaking into the career you want isn't necessarily limited to following one straight path from point A to point B: taking the right classes, earning a 4.0, completing the prized internship, and getting the right degree. Sure, these things can help, but sometimes taking a side road can lead you to an unexpected but very pleasant destination. For example, Josie was a special education major who had been a cheerleader in high school. During college, she auditioned for and was given the chance to perform as the college's mascot at games and social functions. This led to a summer job as a mascot for a local radio station, which gave her more experience in a larger public forum. She loved the job so much that after graduating, she auditioned to be the mascot for an NBA team and applied to work in their marketing department. She worked as the mascot for five years and loved being in front of the crowd while also learning the ropes of sports marketing. She is now the team's marketing director, a job in which she was able to create a new team mascot and hire the people for the mascot job. Even though her degree was in special education, she did not confine herself to one type of opportunity. The experience she had working with children in her major has certainly helped her in her current job. Her "detour" into jobs as various mascots led her to her main career. How can *you* think outside of the box? It would help to start by remembering the following sage advice:

> "Chance favors the prepared mind."—Cicero

What does that mean? It means that you have to be prepared for unexpected opportunities and not be afraid to take chances. Josie did not start out by saying she wanted to portray the mascot for an NBA team. She just took a chance when she auditioned for the part at her college. One thing led to another. Right now, you may have a major or a particular interest in a major. Starting today, don't let that major define or limit the path you take.

Résumés and Cover Letters

Résumés and cover letters are often your potential employer's first opportunity to form an impression of you. Employers are likely to decide whether or not to meet you on the basis of how you come across in these two important documents.

Therefore, investing time preparing effective cover letters and résumés will pay off in your being invited to more interviews, and that, of course, will make it more likely that you will receive offers of employment or an acceptance to graduate school.

Before you even start to write your résumé, think about the skills you have gained through courses, sports, extracurricular activities, internships, summer jobs, and so on. Employers are looking for people with skills that can be used on the job, so it is important that you make your skills known. Many students overlook the significance of their learning how to work on a team while playing basketball in college or of their managing a budget as treasurer of a student organization. You may have gained valuable skills in meeting deadlines as a member of the newspaper staff or stage crew of a campus production. You may have learned creative teaching strategies for preschool children by being an arts and crafts counselor at a summer camp. Even volunteer experience, which you may have gained because you simply love helping people, may be acutely relevant to a particular job. What about delivering meals to the elderly? Or working with disabled children? What about the skills you have gained through hobbies? You may have taught yourself how to design your own web page or how to edit digital photos. All these skills can be used on the job. Let employers know what you can do for them already.

Your Résumé

You should begin drafting your résumé now, in your first year of college. Think of your résumé as a work in progress, just as your college experience is a work in progress. As you experience new things, take on additional responsibilities, and learn new skills in jobs during the school year or the summer, you should add them to your résumé. Then, in your senior year, you will just have to fine-tune your résumé instead of trying to remember everything you want to add to it from the last four years or more. Remember also that you will add to and subtract from your résumé as your career goals change or come into a clearer focus.

There are basically three types of résumés:

1. *Chronological:* This type of résumé traces the individual's work history by listing his or her jobs in order, *with the most recent first.*
2. *Functional:* This type of résumé highlights areas that are the most pertinent to the job you are seeking.
3. *Combination:* This type of résumé uses elements of both the chronological and the functional résumé.

The type of résumé you are most likely to develop in college is the **chronological résumé,** with your education coming before your work experience. Right out of college, the most important qualification you will be able to offer is that college degree. The rule of thumb is that if you are a recent graduate or have less than five years of work experience, *your education should come first.* Also, if you are in the academic or scientific professions, your education should come first.

Your **GPA** is another important addition to your résumé if you are a recent graduate. Keep in mind, however, that you generally want to list it only if it is 3.0

or higher. Employers will assume that your GPA is on a 4.0 scale, so if your school does not use this scale, be sure to explain clearly the scale your school does use (for example, a 4.5 or 5.0 scale)

Of course, if you have a high GPA, you may also have earned some **honors** during your years in school. These should be noted on your résumé. For example, if you graduate cum laude, magna cum laude, or summa cum laude, you should note that next to your degree. If you were inducted into any honor societies or won any scholarships or awards during your college career, you should note those as well. Examples include Dean's List, Phi Beta Kappa, and the Senior Science Research Awards.

As a new college graduate, you will want to highlight your **college experiences** on your résumé This is another good reason to be involved on your campus and in your major. For example, you will want to highlight activities such as senior projects, internships, related course work, and offices held in student organizations.

Here are some specific tips for creating an effective résumé:

▶ **Be concise.** Your résumé should be a snapshot of your strengths and qualifications. Your résumé is not your life story. The ideal length, for a new college graduate, is one page. If you have to go onto a second page, do so, but your résumé should never be over two pages long at this stage of your career.

▶ **Be honest.** This really goes without saying. You should never, ever lie about job experiences you don't have or grades you didn't get. Lies will come back to haunt you, even years down the road.

▶ **Be neat.** The appearance of your résumé should be as professional as your own appearance when you go to the interview.

▶ **Be careful.** Proofread. Make sure you have no typos or spelling errors. Make sure your dates and numbers are correct.

▶ **Be professional.** The physical appearance of your résumé should "say" professional. Use high-quality paper in conservative colors such as white, tan, or grey. The envelope should also match your cover letter and résumé paper. Include an e-mail address on your résumé; however, if your address is something like "hotchick99" or "beerman2020," get another e-mail address—and be sure to check that it is active and accessible.

▶ **Use action phrases and power verbs.** The words you choose will convey the best message if they are clear and powerful. Be specific about what you have done. For example, words such as "managed," "developed," "designed," "analyzed," "wrote," and "coordinated" create a clear picture in the reader's mind of what you *did*.

▶ **Emphasize.** You should emphasize any special accomplishments. Also, you want to emphasize skills you have that will transfer to the job you want, as you read about at the beginning of this section. These may include strong writing, math, or computer skills.

▶ **Don't include personal information.** Employers do not need to know your age, your health history, or what you look like at this point.

▶ **Have others review it.** After staring at your résumé many times, you may find it hard to really see it anymore, and mistakes may get past you. Always bring in a fresh pair of eyes—not just to catch any mistakes but also to give advice in terms of how you could make your résumé better.

Objective: An entry-level management position that will utilize leadership skills and my computer experience. This is an objective you might see on a typical résumé of a new college graduate. Some career professionals advocate the use of objectives, but others don't. If you use an objective, be sure to keep it simple and to the point, just like the example.

Sean Liu
2057 Lighthouse Dr.
Oakhaven, OH 12345
(456) 555-1212
SLiu57@email.com

OBJECTIVE	An entry-level management position that will utilize my leadership skills and computer experience.
EDUCATION	Bachelor of Science, Business Management, (Magna Cum Laude), Oakhaven College of Eastern Ohio, May 2006. Minor: Computer Science. GPA: 3.8.
	Related Coursework: Management, Accounting, Finance, Marketing, Leadership for Business Professionals, Organizational Psychology, Structured Programming, Computer Systems Architecture, Visual Basic, C++.
SPECIAL SKILLS	Bilingual (English/Cantonese), Familiar with Microsoft Windows Operating Systems, PC Hardware, and Microsoft Word. Programming skills in C++ and Visual Basic. Proven organizational and leadership skills.
HONORS	Dean's List, Senior Leadership Award, Outstanding Senior Thesis Award.
EXPERIENCE	*May 2002–August 2002* **Intern** **Computer Systems International, Cleveland, Ohio** Performed system integration testing on second generation information system product for dental office management. Authored Engineering Verification Test (EVT) documents; recorded test results and met with software developer to review findings.
	August 2001–May 2002 **Student Manager of Computer Help Desk** **Oakhaven College of Eastern Ohio, Oakhaven, Ohio** Handled incoming requests. Assigned duties to team of five student employees. Generated monthly reports.
ACTIVITIES/ INTERESTS	Computer Club President, Residence Hall Assistant, Freelance website designer.
REFERENCES	References available upon request.

Also, make sure that your objective is precise and shows what you have to offer the company. Since you may be sending out many résumés at one time, be sure to alter your objectives for different positions. For example, the objective cited here would not be suitable for a sales position. Many people place an objective at the top of their résumé, where it becomes the first thing a potential employer sees. If it is too general, it really is a waste of time. As you are crafting your résumé, seek advice from your career center staff about whether including an objective will enhance or detract from it.

On the previous page you will find a sample résumé for a new college graduate (you can visit our website for other examples).

Your Cover Letter

You need to develop an effective résumé before you write a cover letter because the cover letter is just what the term implies: a "cover" for your résumé. The cover letter introduces your résumé, and you yourself, to a potential employer. If it is well written, the letter will encourage a potential employer to read more about you.

There are two types of cover letters:

1. A letter of application. This type of letter is used to apply for a specific position that has been advertised. Thus it is a direct response to the employer's account of the qualifications needed for the position. The letter of application shows that your qualifications and experiences match those that the potential employer is looking for in a person to fill that position.
2. A letter of inquiry. This type of letter expresses your interest in working for the company, even though the company is not presently advertising for applicants and, indeed, no specific job opening may exist.

Let's focus on the first type of letter, because this is the type you will write more often and the type that more often gets results.

There are some important things to keep in mind when you write a cover letter:

- ▶ **Sell yourself.** You need to grab the reader's attention right from the beginning.
- ▶ **Be assertive.** Tell the reader what you want (an interview, an application, the job) and why you think you should get it.
- ▶ **Meet the employer's needs.** Address the job requirements and show how you meet them.
- ▶ **Spell correctly and watch your grammar.** This may be obvious but is worth repeating. Many applicants miss errors, but employers don't.
- ▶ **Keep it to one page.** Employers don't have the time to read a book! Get to the point.
- ▶ **Use the person's title.** Find the right person to send the letter to, even if you have to call the company. Make sure you address the letter to that individual and that you use her or his proper title.
- ▶ **Don't overuse the word "I."** Vary your sentence structure.

Lifeline

Need help writing your résumé? The staff at your campus career services office can help. But don't wait until the spring semester of your senior year. Start now! As you get involved in campus activities and gain experience in on-campus or summer jobs, get them on your "working résumé" right now. You will be surprised at how easily you can forget details later. Furthermore, the job of writing your résumé will not be as overwhelming—you will just add to it as you go along and then clean it up in your senior year. Remember that offices such as career services are inundated with seniors who wait until the last minute. You won't get the kind of help you really need then. Be smart and write your résumé a little at a time. You also never know when you will need a résumé for a summer job or internship.

▶ **Use positive words.** Show your strengths, not your weaknesses. Also, remember that you don't want to come across as a complainer.

▶ **Review your work.** Proofread! Have someone else read your cover letter as well.

Here is a suggested format for an effective cover letter:

Sample Cover Letter Format

Date

Reader's Name
Title
Company/Organization
Street
City, State Zip

Dear Mr./Ms./Dr.,

Paragraph One: This should tell what you are writing the letter about and why. Be as specific as possible. For example, "With this letter, I am applying for the position of Management Trainee at Computer Systems International, as advertised in *The Oakhaven Press*." You should also be very specific about why you are applying and who you are: "I am a recent graduate from Oakhaven College of Eastern Ohio with a degree in Business Management and experience in computer programming."

Paragraph Two: This paragraph is the body of your letter. This is where you can really sell yourself. Focus on the skills and experiences you have gained that will directly apply to the position. Don't give too many details—your objective is simply to get the recipient interested enough to read your resume.

Paragraph Three: This is the closing paragraph. Offer to send recommendations and any additional information the employer might need. End with the words, "Thank you."

Sincerely,

Your Signature

Your Name
Street Address
City, State, Zip
Telephone Number
E-mail Address

Visit the website for more samples of effective cover letters: http://studentsuccess.college.hmco.com/students

The Interview Process

An effective résumé may get you an interview, but a successful interview is what will get you the job—or will make a big difference if you're applying for graduate school. You need to get ready for this part of the process to ensure that what a potential employer or graduate admissions counselor sees on paper will actually be highlighted and enhanced when he or she meets you in person.

Why an Interview?

You may dread the thought of an interview, but interviews are very important and can actually help you if you learn how to succeed at them. The purpose of an interview is to collect as much information as possible about a candidate. An organization, through an interview, will be able to assess whether you are a "good fit" not only for the position but also for the organization as a whole. An interview can also help you assess a potential employer to see whether you think the organization is what you are seeking. You may be so concerned about getting a job that you are tempted to accept any job that is offered. But you also need to be selective. You don't want to have to start the job search all over again in a few months. That will not help you or the employer. Here are some things to consider when deciding whether a job is right for you.

▶ Will the job require frequent relocation? (This of course is not a problem if you are not choosy about where you live or are not trying to stay close to home.)

- ▶ Are there opportunities to grow within the company, or do you think you might be in the same position too long?
- ▶ Do you like the hours? Or does the job entail working nights and weekends when you really don't want to? What may sound fine at first may become a real drag later on.
- ▶ Is there a lot of travel involved? Will you be flying across country frequently? Decide whether or not this appeals to you.
- ▶ Is the pay adequate? Remember to consider where you will be living. You will need a higher salary in some parts of the country than in others. Will you need to find a roommate or to live at home for a while? (Remember that the pay for many jobs starts low, but your salary may increase quickly as you gain experience and prove yourself.)
- ▶ How are the benefits? A lower salary may be acceptable if it is supplemented by excellent benefits, including health insurance, tuition reimbursement, and vacation time.
- ▶ How do you think you will get along with the employees you meet during the interview?
- ▶ How is the working environment? This is important. You will be spending many hours at work.
- ▶ If you're going to graduate school, you want to consider what kinds of jobs you might have as a graduate assistant. Will you teach courses? Will you conduct research? Will you have time to do your own work? What is the pay? Are there any benefits?

Remember that interviews serve a purpose for both the employer and the potential employee. Thinking about interviews this way will help you to see them as a more positive experience. Keep in mind, however, that you also have to be realistic about your employment prospects. There are a couple of variables that will affect how choosy you can be. First, the overall job market is a major factor. In a hot market, employers need to hire people to keep up with the demand for the company's goods and services. They may be much more flexible in what they'll do—offer bonuses, relocation allowances, and the like—to people they want to hire. In a slow market, however, the employer has the upper hand. In either case, there's not much you can do to control that situation. What you *can* control is the image you present in making yourself a desirable prospect. The interview is a factor, as are your grades, the types of courses you take, and the types of experiences you accumulate. Even in a slow market, employers are going to want to find the best new people to hire.

What Is Involved in an Interview and How Do You Survive It?

First of all, interviewing is a skill, and skills can be practiced. The more you interview, the better at it you will become. An interview consists of five major steps:

1. **Preparation.** Find out as much as you can about the organization or graduate school. Consult websites, corporate literature, graduate catalogues, and

(if possible) people you know who have a connection to the organization. Learn about its products and services, organizational philosophy, and company goals. If possible, learn something about the interviewer. This will help you to break the ice and may give you some idea of what to expect. Find out what you should wear from someone in the field. A professor or career counselor can also help with this. Generally, dress conservatively. Make sure you know what time your interview is, where you need to be, and how to get there. If you're driving, be sure you know where to park. Always—*always*—give yourself extra time so that after you arrive, you can calm down, catch your breath, and focus on the interview itself. Do a practice interview with a friend or with a career counselor—or even with someone in the field. Know your résumé inside and out.

2.   **Starting off on the right foot.** As the old cliché has it, first impressions last. Be confident. Offer a firm handshake and make eye contact. Listen for the interviewer's name and title so that you can refer to him or her properly. Establish a good rapport with the interviewer by making appropriately casual conversation.

3.   **Q & A.** This is the heart of the interview. You will be asked questions and will be expected to provide the best answer possible. Make sure you understand the question and think about your answer before speaking. If any question is unclear to you, don't be afraid to ask for clarification. Interviewers use different techniques—don't be thrown off balance. For example, although many interviewers adopt a friendly, conversational style, others are very formal. They may not respond to your answers at all and, instead, may simply go on to the next question. Their responses may not give you any indication of whether they are impressed with you or not. Also, remember to avoid slang and any bad habits such as throwing "like" and "you know" into your sentences. It is important to keep your answers fairly short and to the point. If your interviewer wants more information, he or she will ask you. Or you can ask, "Would you like me to expand on that?" Make sure that what you say is actually an answer to the question. You will generally also be expected to ask questions. Be prepared with some questions in advance. When asked if you have any questions, you never want to say, "No, not really." The questions you ask will show your interest in the position and the employer.

4.   **Wrap-up.** At this point, you should thank the interviewer for his or her time. Interviewers should have no objection to your asking when you can expect to hear from them. You might also invite the interviewer to contact you for more information. Get a business card from the interviewer and re-emphasize your interest in the position. Be sure, within two days, to send a thank you note that re-emphasizes your strengths and interests.

5.   **Self-evaluation.** At home, shortly after the interview, take some time to review and reflect on your performance. After all, even if it didn't go well (or didn't seem to go well), you can still learn something from it. Remember, you may be doing this more than once.

How Do You Handle Special Interview Situations?

Not all interviews will be face-to-face with one person. You may find yourself in a unique interview situation. If you prepare for these possibilities, you can make the most of them.

> ▶ **The telephone interview.** Phone interviews are not uncommon, particularly if you are a candidate for a job that is geographically distant. They may also be conducted as the first stage of an interview process. Many organizations use phone interviews to whittle down their list of candidates and decide whom to bring onsite. Try to think positively about a phone interview. Think of it as an open-book test. You can have all of your notes in front of you. If a group is interviewing you, write down their names as they introduce themselves. Then address them by name again throughout the interview. Take notes as the interviewers talk to you so that you can refer to the notes as you answer questions. Try to speak slowly and clearly and to be as upbeat as possible. Consider getting a speaker phone or a hands-free attachment so that you can write and page through your notes more easily. Remember that the phone interview may be the deciding factor in whether you get the opportunity to interview in person. Therefore, prepare for a phone interview as seriously as you would a face-to-face interview.

> ▶ **Group interview.** There are two types of group interviews. *In the first and most common, a group of people from the company or graduate school gather together to interview you.* Sometimes you may have a group interview right after you interview with the person who initially contacted you. You may feel intimidated at first because it may seem that you are "on stage" in front of an audience, but the questions will be no different than they would be if each person interviewed you separately. Many companies and schools hold group interviews for the sake of time saving and convenience. Keep in mind that even though one person at a time will ask you a question, when you answer you should make eye contact with the whole group. *In the second and less common type of group interview, more than one candidate is interviewed at the same time.* In this setting, interviewers are often observing how candidates interact with each other as well as how they answer the questions. The type of job you are interviewing for may determine what kind of person the company is seeking. For example, if you are interviewing for a sales position, the company may want to find the candidate who is the friendliest or the most outgoing of the group. In such interviews, then, you want to interact not just with the interviewers, but with the other candidates as well. You want to make sure you stand out without appearing too domineering.

> ▶ **Lunch or dinner interview.** A lunch or dinner interview brings with it the added pressure of having to worry about table etiquette! You may have a lunch or dinner interview for two reasons: This type of interview may be more convenient for the interviewer, who can do two things at once, or the interviewer may want to see how you perform in a less traditional setting. Perhaps the job you are applying for will require you to attend many lunch and dinner meetings, so this interview will be an indicator of how well you might do at

such a job. This type of interview has many potential pitfalls. Apart from knowing your table etiquette (see below), there are a few things you should do, and a few you should not do, to navigate this experience successfully. First, do not order alcohol, even if the interviewer does. Doing so merely adds an unnecessary element of risk. Second, do not send your food back, even if you are not happy with it. This occasion is not about the food. You do not want to appear to be a complainer, and you want to stay focused on the conversation. Also, don't order any messy food (such as pasta with sauce, which you may end up slurping or dripping on your clothes) or food that you need to eat with your fingers (such as hot wings or a burger with the works, which could make you preoccupied with using your napkin after every bite). It is best to stick with clean, easy-to-eat foods such as broiled chicken or fish (without bones— you don't want your interviewer to have to perform the Heimlich maneuver!).

Your interview experience may also end up being a combination of many types of interviews. Your journey with one company may begin with a phone interview, progress to a group interview on site, and conclude with a lunch or dinner meeting. Also, in a given day, you may meet with one person individually and then go on to a small group meeting. You need to be prepared.

How Do You Prepare for Interview Questions?

First, prepare by practicing responses to common interview questions. Give responses that show your strengths such as how you solve problems, make decisions, set priorities and goals, work with others, and plan and organize.

Prepare answers to the specific types of questions you will be asked. First, you will nearly always get at least one *introductory question*: "Can you tell me about yourself?" "How did you choose your college or major?" "How did you become interested in this field?" "Why are you interested in this position?" "What are your strengths and weaknesses?" "Where do you see yourself in five to ten years?" Prepare answers for these ahead of time, no matter what the job. Practice giving these answers until they are second nature. Be ready for *behavioral questions* such as "When did you feel you best were able to solve a problem and how did you do it?" and "When did you need to be in a leadership position and how did you handle it?" Prepare these questions by reviewing the positive and negative experiences you have had so that you can easily recall them during the interview. Finally, be prepared for aggressive follow-up questions such as "We have several candidates applying for this position; what can you offer that they can't?" or "Why should we hire you?" Again, review your strengths before you interview. Ask those who know you what your strengths are.

Be prepared for possible "off-the-wall" questions. Occasionally, interviewers will throw you something completely unexpected. For example, an interviewer might ask, "How many golf balls would it take to fill this room?" When you hear this, you don't want to say, "Huh?" Yet clearly, there's no way you could know the answer to that question. So what do you do? First, you need to understand why the interviewer is asking you this question. The interviewer doesn't really expect you to know, and he or she doesn't care what the answer is. What the interviewer is

Time Out Tip

Many colleges and universities hold "mock" interviews to help seniors (but you don't have to wait until your senior year) get ready for the actual interviews they will experience. Take advantage of these— they are often set up by the career services office on campus. During these mock interviews, a staff member or graduate student will ask you questions that you would typically be asked in a professional interview. Usually, these interviews are videotaped so that you can critique your performance. The interviewer will also give you comments and suggestions. You may be surprised to learn you have a bad habit, such as saying "like" or "you know" or pulling on your hair or constantly shifting your weight in the chair. It may be a humbling experience, but it is far better to improve your interview skills now so that the job you really want doesn't slip away! By the way, if your campus does not hold mock interviews, set them up yourself with some friends.

trying to find out is whether you can think on your feet and what process you would use to answer the question. You might answer by saying, "Here's what I would do to find out." And then explain your plan.

Overall, the interview process can be very rewarding if you prepare for all possibilities and learn from each and every experience you have. By the time you get to an interview, you want to show a potential employer what you can offer. Interviews are your chance to sell yourself. Make the most of them!

Social Skills of the Successful Person

Why a section on social skills? Because developing good social skills is a critical element in achieving your goals, and because, in the process of focusing on getting good grades, taking the right classes, and choosing a major, many students overlook the importance of developing good social skills. Having a great GPA and a long list of honors and awards may attract the attention of employers and graduate schools, but in order to get very far, you have to have the social skills that will complement all of your other talents. Here are some general tips on how you can improve your social skills to give yourself an edge.

Be a "two-way talker." What is a "two-way talker"? Well, let's start by looking at what a one-way talker is. Perhaps you've met one (sometimes, it's even a

relative). Let's take Carl from down the hall, who jumps right into a conversation with you and talks primarily about himself. He might first tell you everything he did that day and then go on to complain about the work he has to do for class and his various physical ailments (strained knee, mono, you name it). You know that when he's finished, he'll say something like "I'm going to let you go now," without ever having asked you a single question about yourself or having drawn you into the conversation at all. Is this an interesting experience for you? Probably not. But you may unwittingly become a Carl yourself if you are not careful. Sometimes people talk only about themselves because they're nervous (as in an interview situation) or because they really haven't learned how to be two-way talkers. Or maybe they really do care only about themselves, which generally isn't that impressive to others.

A successful person—both professionally and personally—is more likely to be a two-way talker. A two-way talker is someone who both talks to you and lets you talk to him or her with honest interest. When someone asks you how you're doing, answer this polite question—but don't forget to ask it right back. It's surprising how many people don't. If you are meeting people for the first time in a potential new employment situation, it's important to show that you are interested in getting to know them, too. Ask how they came to work there, where they're from, or where they went to school. After they answer, the two-way talker should then show interest in what they have said by either commenting or asking additional questions. For example, if you asked a new acquaintance where he grew up, and he said, "Cleveland," you might ask him what it's like there or mention some personal connection to it if you have one. You will be surprised at the power of two-way talking. If you don't have the ability to carry on a good conversation, all of your academic preparation, hard work, and good grades will not get you as far as they otherwise could.

Remember your table etiquette. Even if you weren't born with a silver spoon in your mouth (or anywhere else near you), you need to know which spoon to use for your soup and which one is for dessert. True, in the campus cafeteria, you probably aren't sitting down at a table set with a dozen pieces of silverware (chances are, rather, that you're grabbing your spoon out of a plastic bucket on a stainless steel serving cart). And even if you're living at home, you are unlikely to be sitting down to a formal meal every night. Nevertheless, when the occasion presents itself, you must be prepared. When will the occasion present itself? Some types of job interviews will involve a lunch or dinner with a potential boss. You may be invited to a formal graduation dinner or awards banquet. Even though society has become more informal over time, you still need to know how to handle yourself so that you will feel much more comfortable in situations—such as a job interview—in which you are under a lot of pressure already. The last thing you need is anxiety about your table manners. How do you make sure you know everything you need to know? One of the best ways is to attend an "Etiquette Dinner," if one is offered at your college. These events feature an actual dinner at which the rules are explained at every stage of the meal. It's a great way to learn, and it's fun. You can also read about etiquette in books on the subject. Or you can just pay careful attention to someone who seems to have good etiquette.

Don't forget the other stuff. Etiquette extends beyond table manners. It also includes knowing how to greet someone, sending appropriate thank you notes (especially after interviews) and RSVPs, and even just answering the phone. When you meet someone for the first time, especially in a formal situation such as an interview, you should look him or her in the eye and shake hands. Sounds simple—but even this can take some practice. Have you ever shaken hands with someone whose handshake made you wince with pain? Or with someone who had such a weak grip that it felt like a dead fish? If you're not sure about your handshake, practice with a friend. Remember the name of the person you meet. One way to do this is to say it out loud: "Hi, Dr. Ryan, nice to meet you." After someone has met with you for any reason—such as giving you information about an internship or summer job send a handwritten thank you note. This is a powerful tool that many, many people overlook. And it takes hardly any time to do it. Make sure you don't have an annoying or offensive message on your answering machine. It may be funny to you and your friends, but a potential employer or professor might not agree. Make it short and simple, and save the jokes for other situations. How you answer the phone also matters. Even if you're sleepy, make an effort to sound awake. Clear your throat *before* you answer the phone. At least feign enthusiasm (even though you may have a splitting headache) for calls from people outside your peer group (professors, college staff, potential employers).

Dress the part. Every work environment has its own standard of dress, even if it is just an unspoken one. Dress plays an important role in how people perceive you, and your manner of dress is an integral part of the way you present yourself in a work or social setting. At a hip clothing manufacturer, for instance, even the CEO may come to work in tattered jeans, whereas at a Capitol Hill lobbying firm, even the people in the mail room might wear ties. Even now, as you begin college, you have the opportunity to learn when to be casual and when to wear something a little more formal. Just because you are in college doesn't mean you can or should always wear jeans and t-shirts. Let's say you are being inducted into an honor society in your major. You are invited to the ceremony and a dinner to follow. If professors and a guest speaker—and maybe even the college president—will be among you, what do you think you should wear? If you are not sure, ask. It may not be the best idea to ask another student who is also going for the first time. Ask the honor society advisor. Chances are, you will be told to wear business casual (for men, khakis and a sports coat, and for women, a skirt or nice pants and a matching top). If you are going to a barbecue for your department, then shorts and a t-shirt will do. The environment and the occasion dictate the fashion. If you don't have something appropriate to wear with you at college, try to borrow or wear the best item of clothing you can. Keep in mind that dressing the part is not the same as selling out. You tend to feel more comfortable if you don't stand out from the majority of the other people around. Also, you don't want what you are wearing to be the focus of attention and detract from other qualities you want people to see in you. Of course, when it comes time to interview—for a summer job, an internship, or an actual position when you graduate—you need to find out what people wear who hold a similar position at that company. Then wear the same type of

DIY-Do-It-Yourself Activity

If you are interested in practicing your own table etiquette, but your college doesn't schedule dinners for this purpose or you would rather do it in a smaller, private setting, host your own. Get the rules from an etiquette book (which you may find in the library or at your career services office). Then invite a few close friends and, to hold down the cost, ask each of them to bring something to include in the meal. Set the table to mimic an up-scale restaurant (even if you have to use paper plates and plastic forks and knives). You may even want to videotape this practice session to view later and critique yourselves. What better way to have fun *and* help each other feel more comfortable later, when it really counts!

outfit—and maybe even a bit more formal. In situations related to business, it is better to be a little more formal than a little too casual.

To make etiquette rules even more confusing (at least at first), they vary greatly depending on where you are. If you work on a skateboard manufacturer's marketing team, the rules of etiquette that apply at the office are going to be quite different from those of a Wall Street law firm. But ultimately, understanding etiquette—and being able to play by the rules of the game when necessary—can help you achieve your own goals.

Increasing Your Yield:

Readings for Practical Application

As the closing chapter of the textbook, this chapter focused on the future: your future. It explored how what you do this year, your first year, can help you when you graduate from college. To that end, this chapter helped you reflect on what you should be doing now, on how your major may or may not define your career choice, and on how you can learn about careers and graduate schools. Of course, choosing a major and a possible career is much more difficult if you do not have enough information about what you will really be doing in the job you choose. That is why this chapter helped you to look at what people do in certain jobs. Finally, once you feel confident in the direction you want to go with your career, you need to learn the most effective way to present yourself in résumés, cover letters, and interviews, as well as to hone your social skills to make the most of new situations.

All of this information can be related to the world of technology. Why, you ask? Technology is always changing and adapting to the needs of people in business and education, as well as in many other aspects of modern life. Just as technology adapts, so do you need to adapt to the ever-changing field in which you hope to build a career. You need to keep up with developments in your field—even now, as a first-year student. As the field changes, so will your opportunities as well as your responsibilities. One of the responsibilities that every student has, regardless of what career he or she wishes to pursue, is to stay current with technology.

In the first reading, "A Textbook Case," we take a look at the programming language known as C++. This selection examines some of the basics of programming, and if you are not familiar with C++, it really will seem like a foreign language. Yet, if you work your way through the very linear explanation of the basics, you will begin to gain at least a rudimentary understanding of the processes behind computer languages.

The second reading, in the "Life After College" section, looks at XML, a computer language that focuses on Internet data. Students interested in the computer field may find themselves programming in XML some day. For others, it may be interesting to learn how material gets programmed for the Internet.

The third reading, the "Current Issues" selection, makes readers aware of a serious concern: computer viruses. The author focuses specifically on how vulnerable college students are and on what steps they can and should take to prevent being victimized.

Reading and Study Tips: Technology

Unique Features and Comprehension Strategies

Technology and computer science textbooks tend to be very math-oriented. If you do not have a solid math background, you will have difficulty comprehending the material. You should have completed at least one college-level math course before taking a computer science course. Many times, computer science courses have prerequisite courses—courses that must be completed prior to enrollment in the computer science course. When any such requirement exists, it is noted in the student class listings. **Read a computer science textbook like a math textbook. Read slowly and make sure you do the problems and understand the logic** behind the solutions. You may also need to review material from previous computer science classes, such as programming languages and math classes, in order to understand the material. Have that material at hand before you start reading.

Computer science textbooks contain lots of algorithms. Algorithms are step-by-step approaches to solving problems; they are much like the recipes in a cookbook. Understanding the steps necessary to solve a problem is paramount in writing a good software program and one that solves the problem at hand. **Think of algorithms as the "tried and true" way to achieve a goal. Once you understand "how" to do something, actually doing it becomes much simpler. Work through the algorithms in your textbook step by step.**

You will see lots of sample code. Because software development ultimately results in the creation of software programs, lengthy sections of computer science textbooks are dedicated to sample code. Oftentimes it is easy to skim the sample code contained in the textbook and understand how it works, but this is not always the best approach. You will better understand the concept or technique being taught if you work through the sample code yourself. **Try typing the program into the computer and compiling the code. You'll be surprised how many mistakes you will make during this simple process. The exercise of understanding what errors the compiler generates and working through your mistakes is often well worth the effort.**

These texts are very abstract. Many people go into the field of computer science because they like the hands-on aspect of computers. When they get to college, however, they are learning concepts in addition to just working on computers, which causes them to struggle until they get used to dealing with abstract texts. You may read about how electrons flow through a computer chip, although you can't really imagine that in concrete images. **You may want to draw a picture to help you understand what you have read and remember it better. The text may also contain a lot of diagrams that convey important information; use them to reinforce what you have read.**

Computer science texts tend to use one computer language to teach the material. You must be able to apply that instruction to the language that you yourself are programming in—depending on the course, some focus on hardware concepts, some on software concepts. Either way, introductory textbooks build from a basic knowledge and work toward a firm understanding of advanced concepts. For example, software textbooks that teach a new language, say $C++$, will begin with the basic operators $(+, -, /, *)$, followed by the language constructs (for loops, while loops). This often leads to programming samples that employ the basic concepts. Textbooks that focus on hardware are similar in that they teach the basic building blocks, such as logic gates, and work toward more complex topics, such as advanced circuitry. **Either way, it is important that you understand the basics thoroughly if you are to understand the advanced concepts later. If your instructor does not review these basics, you may need to do that on your own.**

You may see some coding examples that are incorrect. The purpose of their inclusion is to give you experience in correcting mistakes. As mentioned above, it is just as important to understand and recognize when something is wrong as to know when something is right. The old slogan "learn from your mistakes" can certainly be applied when it comes to software development. **You will need to work through the code, find the mistakes, and then fix them.**

Reading 1:   A Textbook Case

The following excerpt from an introductory computer science textbook was selected to give you an idea how such a textbook reads. You'll discover that there is a lot of math in the passage. Many students come out of high school with an interest in computer science because they are experts at finding their way around the Internet or are interested in creating video games. What some of them don't realize is that getting a computer science degree, particularly one with a focus on programming, will require considerable skill in math. When reading the passage below, follow the suggestion of reading it like a math book: Read slowly and work your way through the problems deliberately, with understanding.

BEFORE YOU READ

1. File sharing has been a major issue on college campuses in recent years. Do you think sharing of copyrighted materials (music, videos, and the like) should be illegal? Why or why not?

2. Computers have had a major impact on everyday life in the last 25 years. Make a list of all the ways that you have used computers (or computer technology) in the past week. Referring to this list, reflect on how you would have done—or *could* have done—those things if you had not had access to computer technology.

Arithmetic Operators and Operator Precedence
D. S. Malik

One of the most important uses of the computer is its ability to calculate. You can use standard arithmetic operators to manipulate integral and floating-point data types. There are five arithmetic operators:

1. + addition
2. − subtraction
3. * multiplication
4. / division
5. % remainder (modulus operator)

You can use the operators +, −, *, and / with both integral and floating-point data types. You use % with only the integral data type to find the remainder in ordinary division. When you use / with the integral data type, it gives the quotient in ordinary division. That is, integral division truncates any fractional part; there is no rounding.

Since high school, you have been accustomed to working with arithmetic expressions such as the following:

```
3 + 4
2 + 3 * 5
5.6 + 6.2 * 3
x + 2 * 5 + 6 / y
```

In these expressions, x and y are some unknown numbers. Formally, an **arithmetic expression** is constructed by using arithmetic operators and numbers. The numbers appearing in the expression are called **operands.** Moreover, the numbers that are used to evaluate an operator are called the operands for that operator.

In the expression 3 + 4, 3 and 4 are the operands for the operator +. Therefore, when + is evaluated, the result of the expression 3 + 4 is 7. Note that in the expression 3 + 4, the operator + has two operands. Operators that have two operands are called **binary operators.**

Operators that have only one operand are called **unary operators.** In the expression

```
−5
```

− has only one operand, which is 5, so − acts as a unary operator. Recall that it is not necessary to put + in front of a positive number. Thus, in the expression

```
+27
```

+ is a unary operator.

Unary operator: An operator that has only one operand.
Binary operator: An operator that has two operands.

In the expressions

```
3 + 4
23 − 45
```

Both + and − are binary operators. Thus, − and + are both unary and binary arithmetic operators. However, as arithmetic operators, *, /, and % are binary and so must have two operands.

The following examples show how arithmetic operators—especially / and %—work with integral data types. As you can see from these examples, the operator / represents the quotient in ordinary division when used with integral data types.

Example 2–4

Arithmetic Expression	Result	Description
2 + 5	7	
13 + 89	102	
34 − 20	14	
45 − 90	−45	
2 * 7	14	
5/2	2	In the division 5/2, the quotient is 2 and the remainder is 1. Therefore, 5/2 with the integral operands evaluates to the quotient, which is 2.
14/7	2	
34 % 5	4	In the division 34/5, the quotient is 6 and the remainder is 4. Therefore, 34% 5 evaluates to the remainder, which is 4.
−34 % 5	−4	In the division −34/5, the quotient is −6 and the remainder is −4. Therefore, −34 % 5 evaluates to the remainder, which is −4.
34 % −5	4	In the division 34/−5, the quotient is −6 and the remainder is 4. Therefore, 34% −5 evaluates to the remainder, which is 4.
−34 % −5	−4	In the division −34/−5, the quotient is 6 and the remainder is −4. Therefore, −34 % −5 evaluates to the remainder, which is −4.
4 % 6	4	In the division 4/6, the quotient is 0 and the remainder is 4. Therefore, 4% 6 evaluates to the remainder, which is 4.

Note that in the divisions 34/5 and −34/−5, the quotients, which are 6, are the same, but the remainders are different. In the division 34/5, the remainder is 4; in the division −34/−5, the remainder is −4.

The following expressions show how arithmetic operators work with floating-point numbers.

Example 2–5

Expression	Result
5.0 + 3.5	8.5
3.0 + 9.4	12.4
16.3 − 5.2	11.1
4.2 * 2.5	10.50
5.0/2.0	2.5

Order of Precedence

When more than one arithmetic operator is used in an expression, C++ uses operator precedence rules to evaluate the expression. According to the order of precedence rules for arithmetic operators,

$*, /, \%$

are at a higher level of precedence than

$+, -$

Note that the operators $*$, $/$, and $\%$ have the same level of precedence. Similarly, the operators $+$ and $-$ have the same level of precedence.

When operators have the same level of precedence, the operations are performed from left to right. To avoid confusion, you can use parentheses to group arithmetic expressions. For example, using the order of precedence rules,

$3 * 7 - 6 + 2 * 5/4 + 6$

means the following:

$(3 * 7) - 6 + ((2 * 5)/4) + 6$
$= 21 - 6 + (10/4) + 6$ (Evaluate $*$)
$= 21 - 6 + 2.5 + 6$ (Evaluate /)
$= 15 + 2.5 + 6$ (Evaluate $-$)
$= 17.5 + 6$ (Evaluate first $+$)
$= 23.5$ (Evaluate $+$)

Note that the use of parentheses in the second example clarifies the order of precedence. You can also use parentheses to override the order of precedence rules (see, for instance, Example 2–6).

Example 2–6

In the expression

$3 + 4 * 5$

$*$ is evaluated before $+$. Therefore, the result of this expression is 23. On the other hand, in the expression

$(3 + 4) * 5$

$+$ is evaluated before $*$ and the result of this expression is 35.

Because arithmetic operators are evaluated from left to right, unless parentheses are present, the **associativity** of arithmetic operators is said to be from left to right.

NOTE **(Character Arithmetic)** Since the **char** data type is also an integral data type, C++ allows you to perform arithmetic operations on **char** data. You should use this ability carefully. There is a difference between the character '8' and the integer 8. The integer value of 8 is 8. The integer value of '8' is 56, which is the ASCII collating sequence of the character '8'.

When evaluating arithmetic expressions, $8 + 7 = 15$, '8' + '7' = $56 + 55$ yields 111, and '8' + 7 = $56 + 7$ yields 63. Furthermore, because '8' * '7' = $56 * 55 = 3080$ and the ASCII character set has only 128 values, '8' * '7' is undefined in the ASCII character data set.

These examples illustrate that many things can go wrong when you are performing character arithmetic. If you must employ them, use arithmetic operations on the **char** type data with caution.

AFTER YOU READ

1. If you have a strong computer science background, the previous passage may have made a lot of sense. On the other hand, the passage may have seemed very confusing if you are new to the material. What does this tell you about the importance of background knowledge in reading? In this case, how could you increase your background knowledge?

2. How did reading this passage compare to reading the history passage in Chapter 8? How did reading it compare to reading the passage from the speech communications textbook in Chapter 5? Did you read it more slowly or more rapidly? What caused the difference?

Reading 2: Life After College

In the passage above, you read about programming in the computer language C++. As an extension of this theme, the following passage discusses XML, a language focused on Internet data. The difference between the two passages will quickly become apparent: Whereas the former is a technical explanation of how to program in a language, the latter is focused on describing the language to a more general audience. As you read, think about how the two purposes differ.

BEFORE YOU READ

1. Even if you don't know what XML is, what do you think it means that some are comparing XML to a Swiss Army knife?

2. Technology has affected our lives in many ways. Cite some ways in which technology has affected your life. Has it been for better or for worse?

3. If you could improve the Internet, what would you make better?

Creating a Brave New World Wide Web
D. Page

XML is not the next junk sport league. It's actually the next generation of HTML, the language currently used to create World Wide Web pages.

Extensible Markup Language (XML) simplifies and streamlines the process, allowing Web developers to create customized tags that organize and deliver content more efficiently—essentially taking the training wheels off computer communication.

XML reaches beyond the Web. According to the XML specification, XML is not just for Web pages. It can be used to store any kind of structured information and to enclose or encapsulate information in order to pass it between different computing systems that would otherwise be unable to communicate.

Historically, computer systems have generated output and consumed input in radically diverse formats. A supplier's system to generate and print invoices, for example, would normally create an invoice that is incapable of being automatically posted to a customer's accounting system without someone first physically keying in the invoice information. XML, an open standard whose Release 1.0 was introduced in 1998, solves this problem by introducing an intermediary format that encapsulates the output of one system in such a way that any other system can understand and process it without human intervention.

"HTML made the Web the world's library. Now its sibling, XML, is making the Web the world's commercial and financial hub," said Charles Goldfarb in a white paper posted on *XML.org*. It was Goldfarb who coined the term "markup language" in 1970 and who invented SGML (Standard Generalized Markup Language), the mother tongue of both HTML and XML.

With the development of XML, the Web is becoming much more than a static library. Increasingly, users are accessing the Web for "Web pages" that aren't actually on the shelves. Instead, the pages are generated dynamically from information available to the Web server. That information can come from databases on the Web server, from the site owner's enterprise databases, or even from other Web sites, Goldfarb said.

All that dynamic information needn't be served up raw. It can be analyzed, extracted, sorted, styled, and customized to create a personalized Web experience for the end user. "For this kind of power and flexibility, XML is the markup language of choice," Goldfarb said.

Inside XML

While both XML and HTML are based on SGML, the differences are readily apparent.

In HTML

```
<p>P266 Laptop
<br>Friendly Computer Shop
<br>$1438
```

In XML

```
<product>
<model>P266 Laptop
<dealer>Friendly Computer Shop
<price>$1438
</product>
```

Both of these may look the same in a browser, but according to Goldfarb the XML data is "smart data." HTML tells how the data should look, but XML tells you what it means," he said.

With XML, your browser knows there is a product, and it knows the model, dealer, and price. From a group of these it can show you the cheapest product or closest dealer without going back to the server.

Unlike HTML, with XML you create your own tags (code within a data structure that gives instructions for formatting or other actions) so that

---

SOURCE: D. Page, "XML: Creating a Brave New World Wide Web." Retrieved February 16, 2003 from hightechcareers.com and reprinted by permission of High Tech Careers.

they describe exactly what you need to know. As a result, your client-side applications can access data sources anywhere on the Web, in any format. New "middle-tier" servers sit between the data sources and the client, translating everything into your own task-specific XML, Goldfarb said.

But XML data isn't just smart data; it's also a smart document. This means that when you display the information, the model name can be a different font from the dealer name, and the lowest price can be highlighted in green. Unlike HTML, where text is just text to be rendered in a uniform way, with XML text is smart, so it can control the rendition.

"Plus, you don't have to decide whether your information is data or documents; in XML, it is always both at once. You can do data processing or document processing or both at the same time," Goldfarb said.

Organizations can use Document Type Definitions (DTDs) to define their own "vocabulary" of XML tags, specifying their names, order, and frequency. As a result, once two or more organizations agree to standardize on a DTD, they can exchange data with each other seamlessly, since the data will be in the same XML format.

"DTDs will eventually be succeeded by Schemas," said Steve Heckler, president of West-Lake Internet Training. "Schemas offer all the features of DTDs, plus data typing [i.e., the ability to specify that a field should specifically contain an integer or a floating point number or a string], range restrictions [e.g., specifying that the field should contain a value between 0 and 100], and easier syntax."

From Commerce to Chemistry

The opportunities are endless and far from limited to business transactions. Architectural drawings and chemical structures can be exchanged between disparate databases. Weather information can be posted to navigation systems. Complex mathematical formulas from an electronic version of a textbook published on the Web can immediately start drawing curves in a math simulation application on the desktop.

"With that kind of flexibility, it's no wonder that we're starting to see a brave new Web of smart, structured information," Goldfarb said. "Your broker sends your account data to Quicken using XML. Your channel subscriptions are in XML. Everything from math to multimedia, chemistry to commerce, is using XML or is preparing to start."

Some of the more glamorous applications include Microsoft's .NET, which uses XML as the backbone for all of its cross-application communications—thus essentially dumping its previously much ballyhooed DCOM protocol. (DCOM, or Distributed Component Object Model, was developed by Microsoft for Windows Operating Systems to support sharing binary objects across networks.)

Another company, WebMethods, a Fairfax, Virginia, seller of software that helps link computer systems within or between companies, has attracted a number of customers with a suite of solutions that, in essence, create XML out of the output of the most popular systems, such as SAP. (SAP is the world's leading provider of e-business software solutions.) On the opposite side, the software lets the most popular systems consume XML, thus allowing for such conventions as, say, automatic invoice sharing between large companies, many of which now demand XML interfaces from all of their new internal developments and external vendors.

Other interesting applications of XML include Covisint, an effort to tie auto makers and their suppliers together; Commerce One, which ties buyers and suppliers together across multiple industries; and SurePay, which provides an XML-based service that enables companies to handle electronic funds transfer and credit card transactions online.

There are five principal forces driving XML, according to Ron Schmelzer, founder and senior analyst of ZapThink, a Waltham, Massachusetts, firm focused on XML and XML standards.

1. The increased need to integrate and share data outside the walls of a corporation
2. The desire to conduct e-business, thus reducing the cost of transactions and increasing the number of trading partners

3. The desire to archive, store, and accurately retrieve information that is overwhelming in volume

4. The presence of the Internet, which has increased organizations' desire to interact and integrate with each other, even though their control over each other's internal processes is minimal

5. People's growing familiarity with the Internet's protocols and standards, of which XML is a cousin

"XML and e-business and e-commerce go hand in hand," Schmelzer said. "Its primary point of influence is the fact that users have no control over another trading partner's systems. Therefore, without XML and standards, there is no way to reliably conduct electronic business on a large scale. XML enables an easier and hopefully seamless exchange of business information, which is not possible without a structured language such as XML."

High-Tech Hype?

While most industry experts applaud the impact, benefit, and beauty of XML, not all of them are standing.

"XML provides a great way to transfer text but has no support for transferring binary data such as Word documents or video clips," Heckler said. "It would be great to see an extension that supported this."

Some see the potential of XML eclipsed only by its hype. "As promising as XML is, it's been much over-hyped by the industry, as is always the case in high tech," said Alex Karpovsky, president and founder of Kanda Software, a Concord, Massachusetts, portal builder.

"XML itself is nothing but a standard for defining 'dialects,' sets of tags that concisely and precisely define the information they delimit," he said. "It is the first (and easier) step toward enabling diverse computer systems and applications to communicate between themselves with little or no human involvement. The second (and harder) step of defining the actual universally understood industry or domain-specific dialects is just beginning to shape up and will take years to complete."

Karpovsky also said it would be nice if XML were able to translate between different XML dialects. The big danger here is that if too many incompatible dialects are developed, then there will still be an inordinate amount of effort spent every time one computer needs to talk to another.

"If one dialect has a tag NAME and another LAST_NAME, they immediately become incompatible," he said. Resolution requires human involvement. Someone would have to write a "filter" between, say, the Invoice XML and the Accounting System's XML—thus defeating the whole purpose of XML.

Karpovsky also questioned the maturity of XML's debugging tools, especially XSL (a companion language that transforms XML into HTML or other formats). "Due to XML's popularity, there are a lot of rather sophisticated applications being developed with it, but the development environments are still rather primitive," he said.

Eventually, mere knowledge of XML will soon be insufficient as a differentiation in the job market, according to Karpovsky. "More precise skills, such as XML/database interactions, specific dialects, XSL coding, or system architecture based on .NET, will be required," he said. "There will be specialists in each area of XML deployment, but just about everybody in IT organizations will be running into XML on a daily basis."

AFTER YOU READ

1. Why is XML considered a more powerful successor to HTML?
2. On the basis of this reading, list three ways in which XML, if it lives up to its promise, could affect you.
3. In this chapter, you read about a typical day on the job for several different employees. What do you think a typical day would be like for someone whose main job responsibility requires him or her to use XML?

4. Technology clearly has an impact on our daily lives. Think of how your daily life would have been different as a college student twenty years ago. What do you think will be different for college students twenty years from now in terms of technology?

Reading 3: Current Issues

Until recently, worms and viruses meant more in a biology course than anywhere else on campus. But with the increase in computer use among college students, those words have to have taken on a new meaning: trouble. If you use a computer but haven't installed any protective software, you could find yourself a victim of a worm or virus. The following article discusses the issue of computer security and college students, and the author makes some suggestions on how to protect yourself.

BEFORE YOU READ

1. Are you aware of any recent computer viruses? What have you heard about them?
2. Has your computer been affected by viruses? If so, what problems did they create? How did you resolve those problems?
3. Who do you think on your campus would protect computers from such viruses?

The Virus of Youthful Irresponsibility
A. Salkever

College kids just don't pay enough attention to computer security. Thank goodness adults on campus are prepared to force the issue. Hey, college students, it's time for a pop quiz: If an attachment arrives in your inbox with a suffix of .exe, do you (A) click on it? (B) click on it only if it promises you free stuff? or (C) always click on it if it appears to be from your best friend?

Not enough of America's best and brightest know that the answer is none of the above. As waves of students arrive on campuses across the country, university network administrators have found that significant numbers of computers owned by America's young scholars are riddled with nasty worms and viruses.

Fighting Back
Joe and Jane College may be able to wax [eloquent] about Nietzsche and Voltaire or define a Golgi apparatus, but far too many of them can't distinguish antivirus software from KaZaA. And not enough of them understand that computer-security software is part of the price of entrance to the broadband Internet. Some campuses report that up to 25% of students' PCs on their networks are infected with malicious code.

Worse, a significant percentage of students [haven't] installed antivirus software, even after the latest attacks of SoBig and the Blaster worm. So network administrators have resorted to extreme defense tactics. At Georgia State University, students recently were required to wait in long lines while tech-support staffers scanned their machines. At Temple University, network administrators insisted that students install antivirus software before they be allowed on the campus broadband grid. And at Indiana University, network-security administrators required students to submit their computers to an online scan before they could log on.

For the life of me, I don't understand why so many college kids are flunking basic computer security. After all, they've grown up with computers and are far more likely than the general population to surf the Internet and understand information technology. They intuitively understand e-mail.

Not Rocket Science

Two common excuses are offered for the failing grade. One is that computer security remains too difficult and complex, even for America's sharpest young minds. The other is that most people, regardless of their age and intelligence, don't consider computer security a real concern, even if they understand information technology.

Hogwash to the contention that computer security is too difficult. I've personally installed antivirus software on more than a dozen computers. This isn't rocket science. For the most part, you put the CD in the machine, click buttons, and install the security software as you would any other. Then, you can walk through a series of easy interfaces that allow you to set your system to scan the entire hard drive as often as you like—automatically.

Several prominent antivirus companies offer diagnostic tools that can be downloaded . . . free and will scan computers for vulnerabilities. To run these scans you have to click two or three times, at most. They're painless to use. They're harmless. And they're easy to find.

Basic Training

Even some more sophisticated desktop firewalls are becoming easy to install (Norton Internet Security from Symantec (SYMC), for example). Sure,

some users will have problems with compatibility. But people have the same issues with almost every other piece of mass-market software. My wife runs ZoneAlarmPro, a fairly sophisticated firewall, on her computer. She's no security guru. She had never even heard of a firewall before we were married. But she picked it up quickly. Now she understands: Never leave your machine running if you're plugged into a broadband connection and you don't have a firewall and antivirus software installed.

At college, the ability to make this simple leap of logic should be regarded as Computer 101, a basic approach to security that can save the hassle of pulling all-nighters talking with the tech administrators in an attempt to fix crashed networks.

O.K., so I'm picking a little bit on college students. There's plenty of blame to go around. Companies that make bug-ridden software deserve lots of it—yes, that means Microsoft (MSFT). And security software outfits could help more with the education process. When my wife's firewall asks her if it's O.K. for filemask45.dll to access the Internet, she has no idea if that's a valid part of Windows or a Trojan on her desktop. Nor do I, for that matter. A better tutorial explanation of what filemask45.dll is would be immensely helpful.

No Excuses

At the root of all this is the more serious issue: the common misconception that running a computer should require no more knowledge than turning on the TV. Wrong. Yes, some rough edges still must be ironed out in computer security. But students, listen to those university system administrators. You have no excuse for failing to heed the seriousness of what they say.

I know I sound like your father. But let me use a car analogy to emphasize my point. If the engine of your car seizes on the freeway because you haven't bothered to check the oil in seven years and people are subsequently injured in a crash, you can bet that someone is going to blame you for not understanding the basics of driving and caring for a car.

Like a car, a computer requires constant care and a general knowledge of its workings to run properly. Plug that PC into a broadband connection, and you assume certain responsibilities. So when college network administrators make you wait in line to check your hard drive for worms and stop you from accessing the Web via the campus network until you've cleaned your computer of viruses, be patient. Friends don't send friends .exe files.

AFTER YOU READ

1. How would you describe the author's tone? Do you think it's effective in reaching the intended audience?
2. Why do you think people create computer viruses? What punishments, if any, do you think are appropriate when such people are caught?
3. Can you find out the job titles of employees who are responsible for protecting computers from viruses? What degree would a person need to get such a job? In what kind of environment would such a person work?
4. Judging on the basis of the information in this reading, what are some practical steps you can take to protect your computer from viruses?

Compounding Your Interest: Further Readings

Bolles, R. N. (2002). *What Color Is Your Parachute?* Berkeley, CA: Ten Speed Press.

Gallo, M. A., & Hancock, W. M. (1999). *Networking Explained.* Boston: Digital Press.

Petzold, C. (1999). *Code: The Hidden Language of Computer Hardware and Software.* Redmond, WA: Microsoft Press.

Rosenthal, M. (2002). *Build Your Own PC,* 2nd ed. New York: McGraw-Hill.

Index